SOURCES OF EUROPEAN ECONOMIC AND BUSINESS INFORMATION

FIFTH EDITION

SOURCES OF EUROPEAN ECONOMIC AND BUSINESS INFORMATION

FIFTH EDITION

Edited by
THE UNIVERSITY OF WARWICK BUSINESS INFORMATION SERVICE

Gower

Published by
Gower Publishing Company Limited
Gower House, Croft Road, Aldershot, Hampshire GU11 3HR, England

Gower Publishing Company, Old Post Road, Brookfield, Vermont 05036, USA

British Library Cataloguing in Publication Data

Sources of European economic and business information - 5th ed.
1. Western Europe, Economic conditions. Information sources
I. University of Warwick, Business Information Service
330.94'0558

ISBN 0-566-02658-9

The editors and publishers have used their best efforts in collecting and preparing material for inclusion in *Sources of European Economic and Business Information: Fifth Edition.* They do not assume, and hereby disclaim, any liability to any party for any loss or damage caused by errors or omissions in *Sources of European Economic and Business Information: Fifth Edition* whether such errors or omissions result from negligence, accident or any other cause.

Typeset by Lazerset, Aldershot, Hants
Printed in Great Britain by BPCC Wheatons Ltd, Exeter

CONTENTS

INTRODUCTION

The fifth edition of Sources of European Economic Information has been radically revised since the fourth edition published in 1983.

The aim of the directory is to provide a listing of the major sources of economic and statistical information by country, covering both Eastern and Western Europe. The definition of 'economic' is a generous one and the publications listed cover a wide range of areas such as economic conditions, socio-economic data, public finance, industry, business and commerce. However, since the emphasis is on publications giving economic data, areas such as economic theory and thought are not covered by the directory. The publishers identified and listed represent a wide range of bodies – international organisations, national statistical offices, government departments, specialist publishing bodies, banks and financial institutions and professional and trade associations.

The emphasis is on economic publications which appear on a regular basis. For this reason some of the material included in previous editions has been excluded, in particular one-off monographs and trade directories/buyers' guides.

Questionnaires were sent to all the publishers of items appearing in the previous edition (apart from those excluded as above). Their responses have been incorporated in this edition; where no response has been received from a publishers, the items have included with an asterisk to show that the information has not been checked.

Besides updating existing entries, the coverage has also been extended by listing a large number of publications and publishing bodies not included in earlier editions.

The main body of the directory, Part One, consists of a listing of sources, arranged by country and then alphabetically by title. The divisions by country refer to the country with which the source deals, not that where the publisher is located. Each source has been given a unique entry number.

Sample entry

	Entry	
	01051 **DEVELOPMENT COOPERATION**	title
Publishing body	**Organisation for Economic Cooperation and Development (OECD)**	
country or region covered	International – English annual 1962	language of publication; frequency; date of first issue
	300pp	approximate number of pages
cost	£12/DM76/US$34/FrF170	
ISBN/ISSN	ISSN 0629 4823	
subject coverage	Reviews including statistics on current trends and policy issues on official development assistance and occasionally on particular aspects of development cooperation. Also a valuable statistical annex reflecting various aspects of international cooperation.	

Part Two lists the names and full address of the publishing bodies, and where possible their telephone, fax and telex numbers. These are arranged alphabetically and are followed by the entry numbers.

The book concludes with two indexes – one by title and the other by subject. Index 2 is subdivided – one sequence is organized by subject and then country, the other sequence by country and then subject. In each case, the item numbers or relevant publications are given.

This edition has been compiled by staff of the University of Warwick Business Information Service, with the assistance of Kay Smith, Sian Price, Margaret Liposits and Pamela Maguire.

The University of Warwick Business Information Service

The University of Warwick Business Information Service is a commercial information service based in the university library. It was established over ten years ago and provides statistical, market and business information to companies and other organisations. The service is based on a comprehensive international collection of statistical and market research data.

In addition to the enquiry service, the Business Information Service organizes a regular programme of seminars and is involved in a series of research projects. It has published a number of reviews and directories, the latest of which is *Sources of Unofficial UK Statistics*, first published by Gower in 1986 (second edition 1990).

Staff of the service are:

Margaret Brittin
David Sykes
Alison Kent
Christine Warburton
Christine Crabtree
Herjit Sandhu

Currency key

£	Pound sterling
AS	Austrian schilling
BF	Belgian franc
C£	Cypriot pound
DF	Dutch florin
DKr	Danish kroner
DM	Deutschmark
Dr	Drachma (Greece)
ECU	European currency unit
Esc	Escudo (Portugal)
Fmk	Markka (Finland)
FrF	French franc
Ft	Forint (Hungary)
I£	Irish Pound
IKr	Icelandic kroner
Kcs	Koruna (Czechoslovakia)
L	Lira (Italy)
Lek	Lek (Albania)
Leu	Leu (Romania)
Leva	Leva (Bulgaria)
LF	Luxembourg franc
Lm	Maltese lira
Mils	Mils (Cyprus)
NKr	Norwegian kroner
PTA	Spanish pesetas
Rs	Rupee (India)
Rub	Roubles (USSR)
SF	Swiss franc
SKr	Swedish kroner
TL	Turkish Lira
US$	US dollar
YD	Dinar (Yugoslavia)
Yen	Japanese yen
Zl	Polich Zloty

Part One
SOURCE PUBLICATIONS

INTERNATIONAL

01001 **ACTUALIDAD AGRARIA – AGRICULTURE TODAY**
Confederacion Nacional de Camaras Agrarias

International – Spanish weekly 1978
PTA2968 (inc. VAT)

Agricultural economics and policies both national and international, with many subjects relating to the EEC.

01002 **AGRA EUROPE**
Agra Europe (London) Ltd

International – English weekly £466 UK, £504 Europe, £516 World

European and world developments affecting the production and marketing of food and agricultural commodities.

01003 **ANNUAL BULLETIN OF EXPORTS OF CHEMICAL PRODUCTS**
United Nations

International – English/French/Russian annual US$24.00

01004 **ANNUAL BULLETIN OF STATISTICS FOR TEA**
International Tea Committee Ltd

International – English annual 143pp
£110.00

Tea acreage, production, exports, imports, consumption, auction prices, absorption, UK stocks, re-exports, instant tea, duties and a directory of the tea trade.

01005 **ANNUAL BULLETIN OF TRADE IN CHEMICAL PRODUCTS**
UN Economic Commission for Europe

International – English annual 1974 US$30

Data on import/export of chemical products for 22 countries worldwide and about 67 commodities a year.

01006 **ANNUAL OIL AND GAS STATISTICS**
International Energy Agency

International – English/French annual £20/ DM89/US$40/FrF200

Comprehensive statistics on oil and natural gas based on annual submissions by member states covering supply and consumption by end use sector and trade.

01007 **ANNUAL OIL MARKET REPORT**
International Energy Agency

International – English annual 1984 60pp
£7/DM31/US$14/FrF70

Draws together the principal results of the IEA analyses published in monthly oil market report and presents them as a performance of the oil industry and oil refining.

01008 **ANNUAL REPORT – ECONOMIC COMMISSION FOR EUROPE**
UN Economic Commission for Europe

International – English/French/Russian annual
2 volumes

01009 **BOLETIN DE INFORMACION EXTRANJERA – BULLETIN OF FOREIGN INFORMATION**
Ministerio de Agricultura, Pesca & Alimentacion

International – Spanish bimonthly 1960
PTA1600
ISSN No. 0534-3313

Information on the agricultural fisheries and food sectors of Spain and the EEC and on international organizations and their bilateral and multilateral relations.

01010 **BULLETIN FOR INTERNATIONAL FISCAL DOCUMENTATION**
International Bureau of Fiscal Documentation

International – English monthly 1946
DF250

Contributed articles on tax laws around the world; bibliography conference agenda; IKA news.

01011 **ANNUAL REPORT – INTERNATIONAL TIN COUNCIL**
International Tin Council

International – English/French annual
£6.00

Summary of the main operations of the Tin Agreement including meetings of the council, export control, the buffer stock, prices in the agreement, the statistical position, disposals from the USA strategic stockpile. Statistics on the world position in tin metal production and consumption, prices, exports of tin during control periods and disposals from the USA stockpile.

01012 **ANNUAL REPORT**
International Cocoa Organisation

International – English/French/Spanish/ Russian annual 1973/4 30pp free

Report on work of ICCO and world cocoa economy.

01013 **ANNUAL REPORT – INTERNATIONAL ASSOCIATION OF HORTICULTURAL PRODUCERS**
International Association of Horticultural Producers

International – English annual free

01014 **ANNUAL REVIEW OF THE CHEMICAL INDUSTRY**
UN Economic Commission for Europe

International – English annual 1971 US$30

Data on production, import/export of chemical products and employment in the industry in European countries, Japan, Canada and the USA.

01015 **ANNUAL SUMMARY OF MERCHANT SHIPS COMPLETED IN THE WORLD**
Lloyd's Register of Shipping

International – English annual 15pp free
ISSN No 0261 2720

Statistical summary of world completions and launchings for all ships of 100 gross tonnage and above.

01016 **L'APRES DOLLAR – ANALYSE ET SIMULATION DU SYSTEME MULTI-DEVISES**
La Documentation Francaise

International – French irregular 184pp
FrF98
ISBN 2 7178 1099 4

Analysis of international monetary system.

01017 **L'AUTOMOBILE DANS LE MONDE**
Fabrimetal

International – French/Dutch annual
c140pp

Data on motor vehicles including numbers, new registrations, production, imports/ exports. Figures analysed by make, country of origin, type and size.

01018 L'AVENIR DE L'INDUSTRIE AUTOMOBILE MONDIALE: QUELLES STRATEGIES?
La Documentation Francaise

International – French FrF48

The world motor industry with details of production and trade.

01019 B1/COL: WORLDWIDE SURVEY OF EXECUTIVE LIVING COSTS
Business International

International – English Twice a year SF710

Cost of living data for 102 key cities worldwide.

01020 BP STATISTICAL REVIEW OF WORLD ENERGY
The British Petroleum Company Ltd, UK

International – English annual 36pp single copies free

Annual statistics on world oil production, reserves, refining, transportation, trade and consumption. Also data on total primary energy, natural gas, coal and hydro/nuclear power consumption.

01021 BALANCE OF PAYMENTS STATISTICS
International Monetary Fund

International – English monthly and year book US$38.00

Monthly issues and a two-part yearbook containing balance of payments statistics for about 140 countries. The monthly issues contain aggregated presentations covering annual data and where available monthly, quarterly or semiannual data. Part 1 of the yearbook contains aggregated as well as detailed presentations of annual data and explanatory notes. Part 2 provides 70 tables of data featuring area and world totals of balance of payment components and aggregates.

01022 BALANCES OF PAYMENTS OF OECD COUNTRIES
Organisation for Economic Cooperation and Development (OECD)

International – English Occasional £12/ DM53/US$24/FrF120

Brings together the main series of individual OECD countries' balances of payments for the last 20 years with totals for the OECD area. Details on current invisibles transactions and capital movement.

01023 BANK PROFITABILITY: STATISTICAL SUPPLEMENT, FINANCIAL STATEMENT OF BANKS
Organisation for Economic Cooperation and Development (OECD)

International – English/French annual 100pp

01024 BARCLAYS REVIEW
Barclays Bank Ltd., UK

International – English quarterly c25pp free

Economic review.

01025 BENN'S MEDIA DIRECTORY
Benn Business Information Services Ltd, UK

International – English annual 2 vols

Directory to all forms of media, newspapers, periodicals and electronic publishing. Vol.1 covers the UK and Vol.2 the rest of the world.

01026 BASIC INTERNATIONAL CHEMICAL INDUSTRY STATISTICS
Chemical Industries Association Ltd

International – English annual 1987 40pp (tables also available on floppy disc) book £60/floppy disc £100

A selection of annual national chemical industry data e.g. sales, production, employment trade.

01027 BULLETIN OF THE INTERNATIONAL STATISTICAL INSTITUTE
International Statistical Institute, Netherlands

International – English bi-ennially 4vols DF150

Proceedings of the biennial session of the Institute.

01028 BULLETIN OF STATISTICS ON WORLD TRADE IN ENGINEERING PRODUCTS
UN Economic Commission for Europe

International – English annual 1963pp US$35

Statistics on flow of machinery, transport, scientific, medical, optical and measuring equipment, watches and clocks in 36 countries.

01029 BULLETIN TRIMESTRIEL (QUARTERLY BULLETIN)
Institut Monetaire Luxembourgeois

International – French quarterly 1977 40-80pp
150LF per issue

Domestic and international financial and statistical analysis.

01030 BUSINESS INTERNATIONAL FORECASTING SERVICES
Business International

International – English quarterly SF750

Covers 40 countries and includes an annual basic forecast and quarterly forecast update. Regular features include executive summary fact sheets, in-depth analysis and quantitative forecasts.

01031 BUSINESS INTERNATIONAL MONEY REPORT
Business International

International – English weekly SF1750

Analyses latest developments in the world's financial and currency markets with interest and exchange rate updates and forecasts as well as hedged borrowing costs.

01032 CIRFS –INFORMATION ON MAN-MADE FIBRES
Comité International de la Rayonne et des Fibres Synthetiques

International – English/French/German annual 130pp

Production, consumption, employment, end-uses and foreign trade in man-made fibres.

01033 CTC REPORTER
(UNCTC) United Nations Centre on Transnational Corporations

International – English bi-annually 1976 US$20 subscription

The study of transnational corporations and research related to international business.

01034 CARRIER NEWSLETTER
Universal Federation of Travel Agents' Associations

International – English monthly 30pp

Activities of the UFTAA as a whole and development within individual national members.

01035 CHANGING LEAD MARKET
Metal Bulletin Books Ltd, UK

International – English 1979 £30/ US$69.00/DM150

This in-depth market analysis examines the many factors affecting present trends in supply, production and demand, including world reserves, mine production, inventory, scrap and pricing. A quality detailed report.

01036 CHEMICAL INDUSTRY DIRECTORY
Benn Business Information Services Ltd

International – English annual

Directory of chemical firms throughout the world giving addresses, leading personnel and details of products.

01037 COAL INFORMATION
OECD/IEA

International – English annual £40/DM145/ US$80/FrF400

Information on coal reserves, production, trade, demand, prices, transport infrastructure, coal-fired power stations, emission standards for coal-fired boilers and on technology and the environment. Historical statistics series and forecasts.

01038 **COMMODITY REVIEW & OUTLOOK**
Food and Agriculture Organisation

International – English annual 132pp £20.00

Part 1 reviews the general commodity market situation and international action; part 2 gives a review and outlook by commodity.

01039 **COMMODITY SURVEY 1986**
UNCTAD

International – English 1986

Information and analysis on major factors and developments including certain structural aspects affecting international commodity trade in recent years.

01040 **COMMODITY TRADE AND PRICE TRENDS**
World Bank

International – English/French/Spanish annual 138pp US$25

Factual historical information on the export trade of developing countries and 84 market price quotations of 55 commodities which figure importantly in international trade. Actual current dollar prices and constant dollar prices are shown in tabular and graphic form to indicate commodity price movements relative to the international price level. Time series for most commodities date from 1950.

01041 **COMMODITY TRADE STATISTICS**
United Nations

International – English US$100

Detailed import-export data for 150 countries arranged by SKC code.

01042 **COMMODITY TRADE STATISTICS MARITIME TRANSPORT STUDY**
UN

International – French irregular 1950 US$38

Data on international sea trade statistics arranged so as to give aggregates which enable a pattern of goods flowing in worldwide sea lanes to be established.

01043 **COMMODITY TRADE STATISTICS**
UN

International – English 28 issues per year 1950 Subscription US$100, single issue US$8

Analyses more than 150 groups of commodities exported or imported by the world's principal trading nations.

01044 **COMPETITION POLICY IN OECD COUNTRIES**
Organisation for Economic Cooperation and Development (OECD)

International – English annual 1972 £6/DM27/US$12/FrF60

Previously 'Annual Reports on Competition Policy in OECD Member Countries'.

01045 **CONSTRUCTION STATISTICS YEARBOOK**
UN

International – English annual 1974 US$30

Statistics on dwelling construction with data for each country over a ten-year period.

01046 **CONSUMER POLICY IN OECD COUNTRIES**
Organisation for Economic Cooperation and Development (OECD)

International – English annual 1972 £7.50/DM33/US$115/FrF75

Until 1984 issued as 'Annual Reports on Consumer Policy in OECD countries'.

01047 **COUNTRIES OF THE WORLD AND THEIR LEADERS YEARBOOK**
Gale Research Co. Frank Bair

International – English annual (with semi-annual supplement) 1974 1606pp US$120.00 US$58.00 supplement

Reviews for each country the following: population, people, history, government, political conditions, economy, relations with the United States, government officials, and selected bibliography.

01048 **COUNTRY REVIEW SERVICE**
Eurofinance, France

International – English report on each country annually FrF10,200

Forecasts of economic and financial trends for 12/18 months in the following countries: West Germany, UK, Italy, Belgium, Netherlands, Spain, Sweden and Switzerland. Topics covered: political outlook, financial markets, GNP growth, energy, production exchange rates, unemployment.

01049 **COUNTRY STATEMENTS**
International Textile Manufacturers Federation

International – English annual 1977 SF70.00

A review of the current state of the textile industry in each member country with data relating to the general economic situation, textile manufacturing capacity, activity levels and trade in textiles. Both short-staple sector and pan textile data are shown in tabular form accompanied by a commentary.

01050 **DEVELOPMENT BUSINESS**
United Nations Development Programme

International – English bi-monthly 16 pages US$295 annually in US, US$250 developing countries

Issued by the United Nations Division for Economic and Social Information to announce business opportunities (technical sub-contracts and equipment of the European Communities; Inter-American development bank; African, Asian and Caribbean development banks; and various governments).

01051 **DEVELOPMENT COOPERATION**
Organisation for Economic Cooperation and Development (OECD)

International – English annual 1962 300pp £12/DM76/US$34/FrF170

Reviews including statistics on current trends and policy issues on official development assistance and occasionally on particular aspects of development cooperation. Also a valuable statistical annex reflecting various aspects of international cooperation.

01052 **DEMOGRAPHIC YEARBOOK**
UN

International – English annual 1949 1100pp US$80

A comprehensive collection of international demographic statistics covering 220 countries or areas. Tables give world summaries and country data on population, natality, infant mortality, nuptuality and divorce.

01053 **DIRECTION OF TRADE STATISTICS**
International Monetary Fund

International – English monthly 143pp US$4 per copy

Data on the distribution by partner countries and by areas of countries, exports and imports. Covers data for recent periods for 135 countries and for industrial countries reported as an area reported by themselves or by their partners.

01054 **DIRECTION OF TRADE STATISTICS – YEARBOOK**
International Monetary Fund

International – English annual 430pp US$10.00

Covers 161 countries giving 7 years' data for individual countries and 2 sets of world and area summaries, world and area trade as seen by the reporting countries and as seen by the partner countries to those transactions.

01055 **EBU REVIEW**
European Broadcasting Union

International – English and French bi-monthly January 1958 64pp SF45 6 issues ISBN/ISSN No. 0012-7493

Developments in programme, administrative and legal aspects of radio and television broadcasting worldwide.

01056 **EEC DAIRY FACTS AND FIGURES**
Milk Marketing Board

International – English annual £6.50

Dairying and the dairy industry in Europe with summary data on production and trade in the rest of the world.

01057 **EFTA**
European Free Trade Association (EFTA)

International – English annual leaflet free

A pocket leaflet with statistics on EFTA.

01058 **EFTA ANNUAL REPORT**
European Free Trade Association (EFTA)

International – English/French/German annual 1967 free

The work of EFTA for the preceding year.

01059 **EFTA WHAT IT IS, WHAT IT DOES**
European Free Trade Association (EFTA)

International – English/French/German/ Norwegian/Swedish irregular leaflet free

Brief folder leaflet with general information about the history and purposes of EFTA.

01060 **EFTA BUILDS FREE TRADE**
European Free Trade Association (EFTA)

International – English/French/German irregular free

A12-page booklet outlining the history and working of EFTA with a section on the free trade agreements with the European Communities.

01061 **ECONOMIC AND SOCIAL BULLETIN**
International Confederation of Free Trade Unions

International – English bi-monthly BF250.00

01062 **ECONOMIC BULLETIN**
Gower Publishing Company Ltd, UK for DIW, Berlin

International – English monthly £90.00

01063 **ECONOMIE PROSPECTIVE INTERNATIONALE**
Centre d'Etudes Prospectives et d'Informations Internationales (CEPII)
Documentation Francaise

International – French quarterly January 1980 130pp FrF280

International economics, commerce and finance. Economic models and prospects.

01064 **ECONOMIC QUARTERLY**
Dresdner Bank AG

International – English quarterly 1984 8pp free to bank customers

Economic conditions, business, regional and foreign trade.

01065 **ECONOMICS BULLETIN**
Chemical Industries Association Ltd

International – English quarterly 5-6pp £30 (£50 abroad)

Chemical industry: production, sales, trade, profits and investments.

01066 **ECONOMICS WORKING PAPERS**
Trans Media/The Oceana Group & University of Warwick Library, John Fletcher

International – English semi-annual 1973 250pp and 10 reels of microfilm US$825.00 combined microfilm and bibliography service: US$125.00 bibliography only

Working papers with the results of current research being undertaken by the institutions throughout the world.

01067 **ENERGY BALANCES OF OECD COUNTRIES**
Organisation for Economic Cooperation and Development (OECD)

International – French/English annual £10/ DM44/US$20/FrF100

01068 **ENERGY POLICIES AND PROGRAMMES OF IEA COUNTRIES**
OECD/IEA

International – English annual 1978 £28/ DM124/US$56/FrF280

Evaluation of national energy policies of IEA member countries.

01069 **ENERGY PRICES & TAXES**
Organisation for Economic Cooperation and Development (OECD)

International – French/English quarterly 315pp £40/DM178/US$80/FrF400

Compilation of energy prices at all market levels: import prices, industry prices and consumer prices. The statistics cover main petroleum products, gas, coal and electricity, giving for imported products an average price both for importing country and country of origin.

01070 **ENERGY STATISTICS**
OECD/IEA

International – French/English annual 1961 £10/DM44/US$20/FrF100

Detailed statistics on production, trade and consumption for each energy source in all OECD countries. Vol. 1 gives statistical data on Australia to Iceland and the regions OECD, IEA, N. America, Pacific, Europe and EEC. Vol.2 includes data from Ireland to Yugoslavia and data on member countries' maximum electricity generating capacity for the last 5 years.

01071 **ENERGY STATISTICS YEARBOOK**
UN

International – English annual 1952 440pp US$45

A global framework of comparable data on trends and developments in the supply of all forms of energy, covering each type of fuel aggregate data for the total mix of commercial fuels.

01072 **ENTWICKUNG UND ZUSAMMENARBEIT**
Nomos Verlagsgesellschaft

International – German/English/French/ Spanish monthly (German), 6 times per year (English, French, Spanish) DM33 (German), DM19 (English /French/ Spanish)

A journal covering cooperation and development.

01073 **ETUDES (Studies)**
Institut Monetaire Luxembourgeois

International – French irregular July 1987 LF150 per issue

Monetary, economic and legal studies concerning Luxembourg and the job of the IML.

01074 **EUROPE ENERGY**
EUROPE ENERGIE
European Information Service, Belgium

International – English/French semi-monthly c30pp BF10,400

Report on the activities of governments and international organizations, especially EEC and the International Energy Agency in relation to energy.

01075 **EUROPA YEARBOOK**
Europa Publications

International – English 3,351pp £130.00

A basic source of detailed information on every country, listing approximately 1,500 international organizations. It includes directories and surveys for each country.

01076 **EUROPEAN CAR INDUSTRY REVIEW**
Eurofinance, France

International – English annual c45pp

Five-year forecasts of demand and production per country.

01077 **EUROPEAN TIMBER TRENDS AND PROSPECTS TO THE YEAR 2000 AND BEYOND**
Food and Agriculture Organisation

Europe – English occasional 2 vols, 600pp US$120

01078 **EXTERNAL DEBT STATISTICS**
OECD

International – English annual 30pp

Statistics on the volume and composition of the external debt of all 150 countries including estimates of the amortization payments each country is due to make in the following year.

01079 **F.A.O. FERTILISER YEARBOOK**
Food and Agriculture Organisation

International – English/French/Spanish annual 124pp £10.00

Review of world production, trade, consumption and prices of fertilizers.

01080 **F.A.O. PRODUCTION YEARBOOK**
Food and Agriculture Organisation

International – English/Spanish/French annual 330pp £14.25

Production data by crop and by country including land usage, population, farm machinery, pesticides and prices.

01081 **F.A.O. TRADE YEARBOOK**
Food and Agriculture Organisation

International – English/Spanish/French annual 372pp £17.50

Data in value and volume for imports and exports of agricultural products by country.

01082 **FISHERY STATISTICS—COMMODITIES**
Food and Agriculture Organisation

International – English/Spanish/French annual 305pp £22.75

Annual statistics on a worldwide basis for a varying series of recent years, in the production and international trade of fishery commodities. Also food balance sheets for fish and fishery products.

01083 **FERTILIZER INDUSTRY SERIES**
UNIDO

International – English irregular 1968 US$2.50

Various guides and directories on the fertilizer industry.

01084 **FEUILLE D'INFORMATION DU COI (INFORMATION SHEET)**
International Olive Oil Council

40 countries–French/Spanish fortnightly 1962 30pp annual/Europe US$54

Data and statistics on olive oil, olive-pomace oil and table olives and on other edible vegetable oils, legislative information.

01085 **FINANCIAL MARKET TRENDS**
Organisation for Economic Cooperation and Development (OECD)

International – English/French 3 times a year 1977 £13/DM58/US$26/FrF130 per year

An assessment of trends and prospects in the international and major domestic financial markets of the OECD. Each issue contains a comprehensive commentary, statistics and charts on current developments in internationally syndicated medium-term euro credits, other international bank lending, euro banks and traditional foreign bond issues. This will be supplemented by special features dealing with financial matters of topical interest.

01086 **FINANCIAL STATISTICS OF OECD PART 1: MONTHLY FINANCIAL STATISTICS**
OECD

International – English/French 24 issues a year 60pp £50/DM220/US$100/FrF500 subscription to 3 parts

Published in 2 sections. Section 1 contains figures on the preceding months' operations in the international financial markets, medium- and long-term international and foreign bank loans. Section 2 deals with domestic financial markets and interest rates in international and domestic markets.

01087 **FINANCIAL STATISTICS OF OECD PART 2: FINANCIAL ACCOUNTS**
OECD

International – English/French biannual cost see part 1

Flow-of-funds accounts and balance sheet accounts of 20 countries by institutional sectors and financial investments.

01088 **FINANCIAL STATISTICS OF OECD PART 3: NON-FINANCIAL ENTERPRISES FINANCIAL STATEMENTS**
OECD

International – English/French annual 100pp cost see part 1

Balance sheets and statements of income, as well as details on sources and uses of funds of a representative sample of enterprises in 12 countries.

01089 **FINANCING AND EXTERNAL DEBT OF DEVELOPING COUNTRIES**
OECD

English annual £9.50/DM42/US$19/FrF95

Information on financial resources flows to developing countries and their external indebtness. Statistical tables include aggregate resource flows and debt by main income groups and selected continents as well as of total debt and debt service of each developing country.

01090 **FINANCING FOREIGN OPERATIONS**
Business International

International – English each country updated annually SF2300

A reference service for international finance covering domestic financial environments in 33 countries detailing the financial, regulatory and economic conditions operating in each.

01091 **FIVE YEAR ROLL-OVER FORECASTS***
Eurofinance, France

International – English, semi-annually 35pp FrF18.00

Five-year span giving forecasts year by year for major economic and financial variables for the following countries: France, Germany, Italy, UK, USA and Japan.

01092 **FOOD CONSUMPTION STATISTICS**
OECD

International – French/English occasional £23/DM102/US$56/FrF230

01093 **FORECASTS OF EXCHANGE RATE MOVEMENTS***
Henley Centre for Forecasting, UK

International – English monthly c40pp £330.00

Forecasts for sterling rate against 17 other currencies for three months, twelve months and five years ahead.

01094 **FOREIGN ECONOMICS STATISTICS QUARTERLY**
The Bank of Japan

International – Japanese quarterly 75pp 2800Yen annually

Data on key statistics by principal country; statistics by country; statistics by international institution; names of various foreign currencies; foreign exchange quotations.

01095 **FOREIGN EXCHANGE**
World Reports (UK) Ltd.

International – English monthly £150.00 UK–US$395.00 overseas

Newsletter providing a commentary on world currencies, money markets and financial and economic developments.

01096 **FOREIGN TRADE BY COMMODITIES (SERIES C)**
OECD

International – English/French annual £15/DM74/US$30/FrF150

Matrix tables showing trade between OECD countries and partner countries for commodity groups at the 1 and 2 digit SITC level. Separate volumes are issued for exports and imports.

01097 **FRAMEWORK FORECASTS FOR THE EEC ECONOMIES***
Henley Centre for Forecasting, UK

International – English quarterly c40pp £260.00

Forecasts of key economic variables with commentaries on present and prospective developments for the entire region and individual countries.

01098 **FREE LABOUR WORLD**
International Confederation of Free Trade Unions (ICFTU)

International – English/French/German/Spanish fortnightly January 1984 4 pages BF750

Trade union, social, economic and human rights issues.

01099 **THE FREE TRADE AGREEMENTS OF THE EFTA COUNTRIES WITH THE EUROPEAN COMMUNITIES**
EFTA

International – English/French/German

01100 **FRUIT AND TROPICAL PRODUCTS**
Commonwealth Secretariat, UK

International – English semi-annually c120pp £40.00

Review of the trading situation for fruit, coffee, cocoa, spices, oilseeds and vegetable oils. Covers production, consumption,stocks and international trade.

01101 **GAS DIRECTORY**
Benn Business Information Services Ltd, UK

International – English annual

Directory to the world's gas industries including detailed guide to British Gas.

01102 **GENERAL BUSINESS GUIDE**
United Nations Development Programme

International – English/French annual 90-100pp free

Practical data on requirements and procedures for securing contracts and equipment orders for UNDP-assisted projects worldwide. Describes the IAPSU, a business information centre for potential suppliers and UN agencies.

01103 **GENERAL CONDITIONS APPLICABLE TO LOAN AND GUARANTEE AGREEMENTS– INTERNATIONAL BANK FOR RECONSTRUCTION AND DEVELOPMENT**
World Bank

International – English/French/Spanish 1985 16pp free

Sets forth certain terms and conditions generally applicable to loans made by the World Bank regarding interest and other charges, repayment, currencies, withdrawal of proceeds, maturity, and other provisions.

01104 **GEOGRAPHICAL DISTRIBUTION OF FINANCIAL FLOWS TO DEVELOPING COUNTRIES**
Organisation for Economic Cooperation and Development (OECD)

International – English/French annual 300pp £16/DM70/US$32/FrF160

The volume and sources of the external financial resources provided to individual developing countries and territories. Data on the geographical distribution of net and gross disbursements, commitments and terms with background economic data to provide perspective in interpreting the resource flow information for each country.

01105 **GLUCKAUF MINING REPORTER**
Verlag Gluckauf GmbH

International – English quarterly free

New developments in mining equipment.

01106 **GOLD AND SILVER SURVEY***
World Reports (UK) Ltd

International – English monthly £215.00-UK, US$525.00-overseas

Changes in the value of gold and silver investments in the following countries: UK, USA, France, Switzerland, West Germany, South Africa, Belgium, Netherlands, Italy, Australia, Canada, Singapore and Hong Kong.

01107 **GOVERNMENT FINANCE STATISTICS YEARBOOK**
International Monetary Fund

International – English annual 1017pp US$20.00

Detailed data on revenue, grants, expenditure, lending, financing and debt of central governments and amounts represented by social security funds and extrabudgetary operations. Also data for state and local governments, information on the institutional units of government and the accounts through which they operate and lists of sources of information, non-financial public enterprises and public financial institutions.

01108 **GRAPHIQUES CONJONCTURELS BENELUX BENELUX CONJUNCTUUR-GRAFIEKEN***
Union Economique Benelux

International – French/Dutch annual BF200.00 DF14.00

Figures for current economic trends in Benelux countries.

01109 **GROSS RATES CURRENCY ADVISORY SERVICE**
Business International

International – English monthly SFr2400

Forecasts for 22 currencies over short, medium and long term.

01110 **GUIDE TO DOCUMENTARY CREDITS**
International Chamber of Commerce

International – English/French 1985

Guide to the use of documentary credits in international trade, based on the ICC letter of credit rules, UCP400.

01111 **GUIDES TO EUROPEAN TAXATION: SUPPLEMENTARY SERVICE**
International Bureau of Fiscal Documentation

International – English monthly DF1800/ updating service DF730

Includes tax tables (corporate and individual) full texts (in English) of double taxation treaties: European Communities directives on taxation; OECD Mode Conventions; worldwide bibliography of new documents and publications.

01112 **GUIDES TO EUROPEAN TAXATION: THE TAXATION OF PRIVATE INVESTMENT INCOME**
International Bureau of Fiscal Documentation

International – English updated 3 times per year DF620/Updating service DF310

Analyses of effective tax burden on dividends and interest received by individuals in West European countries.

01113 **GUIDES TO EUROPEAN TAXATION:TAXATION IN EUROPEAN SOCIALIST COUNTRIES**
International Bureau of Fiscal Documentation

International – English updated annually DF600/updating service DF30

01114 **HRD – INFORMATION BULLETIN**
Diamond High Council

International – English/French/Dutch quarterly 1983 50pp BF500/year

Articles of general interest to the diamond sector (trade and industry), statistics and diamond index.

01115 **HANDBOOK OF INTERNATIONAL TRADE & DEVELOPMENT STATISTICS**
UNCTAD (United Nations Conference on Trade and Development)

International – English irregular 1969 US$50

A complete basic collection of statistical data relevant to the analysis of world trade and development.

01116 **HANDBOOK OF THE NATIONS**
Gale Research Co. Compiled by US Central Intelligence Agency

International – English annual 292pp US$78.00

A brief guide to the economy, government, land, demographics, communications and national defence establishments of 206 nations and other political entities.

01117 **HANDBUCH DER WIRTSCHAFTSDATENBANKEN**
Verlag Hoppenstedt & Co.

International – German annual 624pp DM260

Information on 700 economic databanks and their providers.

01118 **HANDBUCH FUR INTERNATIONALE ZUSAMMENARBEIT**
Nomos Verlagsgesellschaft

International – German looseleaf DM180

A handbook of international co-operation.

01119 **HIDES AND SKINS**
Commonwealth Secretariat, UK

International – English semi-annually c70pp £25.00

Review of out-put and markets with statistics on production, consumption, trade and markets.

01120 **HISTORICAL STATISTICS OF FOREIGN TRADE, SERIES A**
OECD

International – English/French occasional £5.50/DM28/US$11/FrF55

01121 **HOPPENSTEDT CHARTS–AUSLANDSWERTE**
Verlag Hoppenstedt & Co.

International – German weekly DM 94 per month

280 securities and the corresponding overall indices of the stock exchange in Belgium, France, Great Britain, Italy, The Netherlands, Austria, Switzerland, Spain, Canada, Japan, Hong Kong and Singapore.

01122 **HOPPENSTEDT CHARTS–DEVISEN**
Verlag Hoppenstedt & Co.

International – German fortnightly DM54 per month

Currency and financial data, currency rates in Frankfurt, Zurich, London, New York.

01123 **ICFTU CONGRESS REPORT**
International Confederation of Free Trade Unions

International – English frequent BF450.00

01124 **IFAP NEWS***
International Federation of Agricultural Producers, France

International – English monthly c25pp

General articles on agricultural developments.

01125 **IFPI NEWSLETTER**
IFPI Dave Laing

International – English every 2 months 8pp
ISSN No. 0264 617X

World sound and video recording industry copyright reform; piracy; private copying.

01126 **IFPI REVIEW**
IFPI

International – English annual 1983 70pp £5.00
ISSN No. 0265 5438/0 9508655 2 4

World sound and video recording industry; copyright reform; piracy; private copying.

01127 **IMS MONITOR REPORTS (VOL I)**
Imsworld Publications Ltd.

International – English quarterly Full set of 12 reports – US$510. Set of 4 regional reports – US$210. Individual reports – US$85.

A quarterly magazine covering world trends and developments in pharmaceuticals with a regular focus on topics of marketing interest in each regional area. The 4 regions are Europe, America, Middle East and Africa, Far East and Australasia.

01128 **IMS MONITOR REPORTS (VOL II)**
Imsworld Publications Ltd.

International–English quarterly Full set of 12 reports – US$510. Set of 4 regional reports – US$210. Individual reports –US$85.

A quarterly magazine covering world trends and developments with a regular spotlight focus on topics of marketing interest in each regional area. The 4 regions are Europe, the Americas, Middle East and Africa, Far East and Australasia.

01129 **IMS PHARMACEUTICAL NEWSLETTER (VOL I)**
Imsworld Publications Ltd.

International – English weekly US$240 50 issues

A comprehensive weekly report on financial and trade developments in the international pharmaceutical and health care industry.

01130 **IMS PHARMACEUTICAL NEWSLETTER (VOL II)**
Imsworld Publications Ltd

International – English weekly US$240 50 issues

A comprehensive weekly report on financial and trade developments in the international pharmaceutical and health care industries.

01131 **INDICATORS OF INDUSTRIAL ACTIVITY**
Organisation for Economic Cooperation and Development (OECD)

International – English/French quarterly £16/DM70/US$32/FrF160

An overall view of short-term economic developments in different industries for all OECD member countries with indices of output, new orders, unfilled orders, prices and employment. The statistics are classified by SITC.

01132 **INDUSTRIAL DEVELOPMENT SURVEY**
UNIDO

International – English biennial cost varies per issue

Reviews current trends in industry that have a particular relevance to global developments and analyses aspects of future industrial development.

01133 **INDUSTRIAL MINERALS**
Metal Bulletin Books Ltd., UK

International – English monthly £79 US$173.01 DM395 annually

Regular features include: articles on the winning, processing and application of industrial minerals, surveys of trends and developments in the industry, detailed price quotations, statistics, world-wide news digests, freight reports, company and personnel news, notes on publications, exhibitions, etc. Coverage embraces all minerals except metallic ores and fuels.

01134 **INDUSTRIAL MINERALS DIRECTORY**
Metal Bulletin Books Ltd., UK

International – English 1986 £60 US$144 DM300

Detailed coverage on a country basis, of non-metallic mineral producers plus a buyers' guide listing, under mineral headings, suppliers of a given mineral with country of origin. Over 1700 entries.

01135 **L'INDUSTRIE PETROLIERE EN 1986: DIRECTION DES HYDORCARBURES**
La Documentation Francaise

International– French irregular 1985 136pp FrF95
ISBN/ISSN No. 2 11 001800 3

The worldwide market for oil.

01136 **INDUSTRIAL STATISTICALS YEARBOOK**
UN

International – English annual 1950 1450pp US$50

Statistics on industrial establishments, employers/employees, wages, output in various sectors, investments, commodity production data of individual products and other areas.

01137 **INDUSTRIAL STRUCTURE STATISTICS**
OECD

International – English annual 1982 £8.50/DM38/US$17/FrF85

In 2 parts. Part 1 contains the data derived directly from the industrial statistics surveys and the foreign trade data. Part 2 presents the estimates provided by the national accounts disaggregated by industry. All data is classified to ISIC.

01138 **INDUSTRY & DEVELOPMENT**
UNIDO

International – English bi-annually 1978 cost varies per issue

Focuses on applied economics and tries to link practitioners and theorists working on related aspects of industrialization.

01139 INFORMATIONEN INTERNATIONALE PREISE
Bundesanstalt fur Agrarwirtschaft

International – German weekly 1976 20pp AS280

International agricultural prices.

01140 L'INFORMATION DU NORD AU SUD: UN COMPLEXE INDUSTRIEL TRANSNATIONALISE – NOTES ET ETUDES DOCUMENTAIRES No. 4809–1986
La Documentation Francaise

International – French 144pp FrF48

An analysis of the world information technology industry and the companies involved in it.

01141 INTEREST RATE SERVICE
World Reports (UK) Ltd

International – English 20 issues annually £250.00-UK, US$650.00-overseas

Loose-leaf reports on interest rates in 20 countries, giving commentaries and charts with summaries of important monetary authority initiatives.

01142 INTERNATIONAL BUSINESS MONITOR
Eurofinance, France

International – English bi-monthly c40pp FrF1,800

Statistical data which analyses economic developments in an international framework. Topics covered: GNP, industrial production, private consumption, investment indicators, foreign trade, money supply and foreign exchange.

01143 INTERNATIONAL BUSINESS OPPORTUNITIES SERVICE
World Bank

International – English US$225.00

A subscription service designed to improve public awareness of procurement opportunities in upcoming bank-financed projects, regular mailings to clients include contract awards, procurement notices, data sheets and notebooks.

01144 INTERNATIONAL COTTON INDUSTRY STATISTICS
International Textile Manufacturers Association

International – English annual 1958 SF70.00

Data on the production capacity (ring spindles o-e rotors, shuttle and shuttle-less looms), machinery utilization and raw material consumption in the short-staple sector of the textile industry in virtually all countries of the world.

01145 INTERNATIONAL COTTON SYSTEM FIBRE CONSUMPTION STATISTICS
International Textile Manufacturers Association

International – English annual Qtr3, 1974 SF20.00

Provides information on consumption and stocks of fibres (cotton and man-made) in the short-staple sector of the textile industries.

01146 INTERNATIONAL CURRENCY ISSUE
Maxwell Stamp Associates, UK

International – English semi-monthly £220.00-UK annually £260.00 overseas

Forecasts of the values of 42 currencies one year ahead, against both the £ and the US$. Short reports are published on four to six countries with each issue.

01147 INTERNATIONAL CURRENCY REVIEW
World Reports (UK) Ltd

International – English bi-monthly £70.00-UK, US$185.00-overseas

World economic and financial affairs euromarket developments, interest rate trends and other matters of interest to the financial community. Detailed reviews of specific currencies.

01148 INTERNATIONAL ECONOMIC DATA SERVICE
World Reports (UK) Ltd

International – English 10 issues annually £250.00-UK US$650.00

Essential data covering 20 leading economies on currency rates, monetary indicators, inflation, public and domestic economic information.

01149 INTERNATIONAL ECONOMIC REVIEW
International Economic Review

International – English quarterly 250pp per issue US$70
ISSN 0020 6598

Specialized articles on a variety of topics of international economic interest, particularly in the field of quantitative economics.

01150 INTERNATIONAL FAIR MAGAZINE/ MESSEMAGAZINE INTERNATIONAL
AGPOL–Polexportpress

International – Polish/German annual 1976 92pp DM2

Perspectives for trade between East and West.

01151 INTERNATIONAL FINANCE CORPORATION (IFC) ANNUAL REPORT
World Bank

International – English/French/Spanish annual 64pp free

Reports on the fiscal years investment, financing, and technical assistance activities, and assesses the world investment and trade climate. Includes IFC's financial statements, a statement of its loan and equity investments, and a statement of voting power and subscriptions of member countries.

01152 INTERNATIONAL FINANCIAL STATISTICS
International Monetary Fund

International – English/French/Spanish monthly 590 US$100 surface mail 12 issues and yearbook

Shows for most countries current data needed in the analysis of problems of international payment and of inflation and deflation; i.e. data on exchange rates, international liquidity, money and banking, international transaction prices, production, government finance, interest rates etc. Information is presented in country tables for 137 countries and in tables of area and world aggregates.

01153 INTERNATIONAL FINANCIAL STATISTICAL–YEARBOOK
International Monetary Fund

International – English/French/Spanish annual 744pp US$100 surface mail

Shows for most countries of the world current data needed in the analysis of problems of international payments and of inflation and deflation, i.e. on exchange rates, international liquidity, money and banking, international transactions, prices, production, government finance, interest rates and other items and activities. Information is presented in country tables for 137 countries. A chart section presents trends for the past 30 years for certain key time series.

01154 INTERNATIONAL MARKETING DATA AND STATISTICS
Euromonitor

International – English annual 384pp

Data encompasses all key indicators of business, marketing, social and economic activity. Topics include demographics, population trends and forecasts., standard of living indicators, retail market size estimates, consumption of food, imports and exports, cultural facilities, health, housing and education data.

01155 THE INTERNATIONAL MARKETS FOR MEAT 1986/87
General Agreement on Tariffs and Trade
GATT Secretariat

International – English/French/Spanish annual 1985 96pp SF12
ISSN No. 0259 8183

The meat market situation during the year under review based on information and documentation furnished by the participants to the Arrangement Regarding the Bovine meat in force since 1980.

01156 INTERNATIONAL RUBBER DIGEST
International Rubber Study Group

International – English monthly £25.50/ US$51.00 UK/surface, £32.00/US$64.00 airmail

Summary of current trends in the rubber

industry under the following classifications: natural rubber, synthetic rubber, consumption, trade and prices, general and shipping.

01157 **INTERNATIONAL STATISTICAL REVIEW**
International Statistical Institute, Netherlands

International – English 3 times a year £20.00 US$36.00

01158 **INTERNATIONAL STEEL STATISTICS**
UK Iron & Steel Statistics Bureau

International – English annual 1970 41pp £25.00 (£28.00 airmail)
ISSN No. (applied for)

Country Books – 24 annual books for separate countries or groups of countries showing production, materials consumed, apparent consumption and detailed imports and exports of 130 iron and steel products by quality and market.

01159 **INTERNATIONAL TEXTILE MACHINERY SHIPMENT STATISTICS**
International Textile Manufacturers Federation

International – English annual SF100.00

Shipments by country of destination, of ring spindles, o-e rotors, shuttle and shuttle-less looms. In presenting separate data for different types of machinery, the survey provides a complete picture of machinery capacity installed in virtually all countries of the world.

01160 **INTERNATIONAL TRADE FINANCE**
Financial Times Business Information

International – English monthly £297 UK, £330 overseas

Reports on problem countries with payment delays and publishes forfeiting rates for all key trading nations; weighs the pros and cons of project finance packages and reviews policy schemes in export credit finance.

01161 **INTERNATIONAL TRADE STATISTICS YEARBOOK**
UN

International – English annual 1950 US$80

Issued in 2 volumes it gives international coverage of foreign trade statistics through summary tables showing overall trade by regions and countries, world exports by origin and area of destination as well as by product.

01162 **INVESTING, LICENSING AND TRADING CONDITIONS ABROAD**
Business International

International – English each country updated annually looseleaf SF1600

A looseleaf reference service covering 56 countries with details on regulations governing establishment of new industrial enterprises, local financing, taxation, labour conditions, import controls etc.

01163 **IRON ORE DATABOOK**
Metal Bulletin Books Ltd
Henry Cooke, John Bailey

International – English irregular 1987 156pp £40.00
ISBN No. 0-947671-04-8

Information on international iron ore, mines, traders and representatives with extensive price movements, production statistics, analysis.

01164 **IRON ORE: RECENT DEVELOPMENTS IN THE WORLD MARKET AND THE SHORT-TERM OUTLOOK**
United Nations Conference on Trade and Development (UNCTAD)

International – English/French/Spanish 1984

Indicates briefly the recent salient developments in the world market for iron ore and major market trends.

01165 **IRON & STEEL INDUSTRY**
OECD

International – English/French annual 1955 £5/DM25/US$10/FrF50

01166 **IRON AND STEEL WORKS OF THE WORLD**
Metal Bulletin Books Ltd, UK

International – English 1983 £60 US$144 DM306

Each entry includes, wherever possible: name of company and location of plant, telephone and telex numbers, cable address, directors and executive staff, number of employees, capital details of plant and processes, list of products, brand names, capacity and output, expansion plans, head office, sales offices, agents, ownership and subsidiaries. Over 1900 entries.

01167 **JAHRBUCH FUR BERGBAU, ENERGIE, MINERALOL UND CHEMIE***
Verlag Gluckhauf, Essen

International – German annual c1300pp DM58.00

Directory giving information on the European energy and mineral industries. Over 5,000 organizations are covered in the following sectors: coal mining in Germany and Europe; metal and minerals in Germany; petroleum and natural gas in Germany and the North Sea; electricity and power in Germany and the European Economic Community; gas in Germany and the EEC; the petroleum industry including refineries and pipe-lines in the EEC. There is also information on European organizations, policies and technical developments in these fields.

01168 **JOINT PRODUCTION OF LEAD AND ZINC**
International Lead & Zinc Study Group

International – English annual £30.00

01169 **JOURNAL OF DEVELOPMENT PLANNING**
UN/DIESA (Department of International Economic Social Affairs)

International – English irregular 1972 US$19

Focuses upon the development problems in the North/South agenda.

01170 **KNOW MORE ABOUT OIL: WORLD STATISTICS**
Institute of Petroleum Information Service

International – English occasional 8pp free

Petroleum statistics, production and trade.

01171 **KONJUNKTURINDIKATOREN**
IFO – Institut Für Wirtschaftsforschung

International – German monthly 1p DM58
ISSN No. 0722-0227

Looseleaf sheet on key economic indicators.

01172 **KONJUNKTUR TENDENSER I UDVALGATE LANDE**
Danmarks Statistik

International – Danish every 2 months DKr315.57
ISBN/ISSN No. 0109 1272

Economic trends in selected countries.

01173 **KONZERNE IN SCHAUBILDERN**
Verlag Hoppenstedt & Co.

International – German continuously updated Basic work DM1800 updates DM2.45 each

Intercompany relations.

01174 **LABOUR FORCE STATISTICS**
OECD

International – English/French annual 1968 £19.50/DM86/US$39/FrF195

Historical time series of the evolution, population and labour force of the OECD. Part 1 contains general tables, part 2 figures by country and part 3 participation rates and unemployment rates by age and sex.

01175 **LABOUR RELATIONS IN 16 COUNTRIES**
Svenska Arbetsgivareföreningen/ C. Bratt

International – English 1986 140pp SKr60

Relations between employer and employees and the structure of the labour market in Belgium, Denmark, Finland, France, Italy, Japan, Yugoslavia, The Netherlands, Norway, Switzerland, USSR, UK, USA, West Germany, Austria, Canada, Sweden and Spain.

01176 **LANDERANAYSEN**
Girozentrale Vienna

International – German annual 30pp
AS3000/year

Economic surveys covering 25 individual countries with data on consumption, prices, labour market, finance.

01177 **LANDERBERICHT EG–STAATEN**
Federal Statistical Office of Germany

European Communities German irregular
DM7.90

Statistical survey of the EC including demography, geography, education, employment, agriculture, production, overseas trade, transport, tourism, finance, wages and prices and national accounts.

01178 **LLOYD'S REGISTER OF SHIPPING ANNUAL REPORT**
Lloyd's Register of Shipping, UK

International – English annual c50pp

Annual report including a brief survey of developments in the shipping sector.

01179 **LLOYD'S REGISTER OF SHIPPING–STATISTICAL TABLES**
Lloyd's Register of Shipping, UK

International – English annual c80pp

Details of the world's merchant fleets, ships built and lost. Fleets are analysed by type, size, age and tonnage .

01180 **LONDON CURRENCY REPORT**
World Reports (UK) Ltd

International – English 18 issues annually
£250.00-UK, US$650.00-overseas

Loose-leaf reports on all major currencies.

01181 **MACKINTOSH YEARBOOK OF WEST EUROPEAN ELECTRONIC DATA***
Mackintosh Publications Ltd, UK

International – English annual c140pp
£90.00

Survey of the West European electronics industry covering forecasts and situation for each country and providing data on production and consumption of specific products.

01182 **MAIN ECONOMIC INDICATORS**
Organistion for Economic Cooperation and Development

International – English/French monthly
£36.00 DM160 US$72.00 FrF360 annually

This monthly publication based on the most up-to-date techniques of tabular and graphical presentation, is designed to provide at a glance a picture of the most recent changes in the economy of the OECD countries, and a collection of international statistics on the economic developments affecting the OECD area in the past few years. The indicators selected cover national accounts, industrial production, deliveries, stocks and orders, construction, retail sales, labour, wages, prices, domestic and foreign finance, interest rates, trade and payments.

01183 **MAIN ECONOMIC INDICATORS–HISTORICAL STATISTICS**
OECD

International – French/English annual
650pp £17.50/DM78/US$35/FrF175

Historical economic indicators statistics for the world and OECD countries in particular.

01184 **MAITRISE DE L'ENERGIE ET RECHERCHE: QUEL BILAN? QUEL AVENIR?**
La Documentation Francaise

International – French 62pp FrF190
ISBN No. 211 001652 3

Energy use in industry, agriculture, transport and the home.

01185 **MANAGEMENT AND ACCOUNTING WORKING PAPERS BIBLIOGRAPHY**
Trans Media/The Oceana Group & University of Warwick Library
Geoffrey E.Cleave

International – English semi-annual 1982
100pp US$100.00

Bibliography of working papers produced by leading academics from all over the world in the field of management and accounting.

01186 **MANUFACTURING CHEMIST**
Morgan-Grampian (Process Press)
Neil Eisberg

International – English monthly 1930 100pp
£48 p.a.
ISSN No. 0262 4230

Chemical industry with particular interest in specialities, fine chemicals, research, production, packaging, marketing.

01187 **MARITIME TRANSPORT**
OECD

International – English annual 1954 £8/
DM35/US$16/FrF80

Report contains a statistical annexe which brings together the principal elements of international seaborne trade and bulk commodities, the world fleet and the various freight markets.

01188 **MARKET REPORT**
International Wheat Council

International – English/French/Russian/
Spanish 8 or 9 per year £40 UK, £45
Europe/US £75 overseas

Comprehensive facts and figures covering current and prospective developments in grain production, trade, stocks, prices, ocean freight rates and national products, together with background notes of topical interests.

01189 **MARKET SITUATION FOR LEAD**
International Lead and Zinc Study Group

International – English every 2 years
£65.00

01190 **THE MARKET SITUATION FOR ZINC**
International Lead and Zinc Study Groiup

International – English every 2 years
£65.00

01191 **MEAT BALANCES IN OECD COUNTRIES**
OECD

International – English/French annual [illegible]
180pp £7.50/DM33/US$15/FrF75

The volume is in 2 parts. The first consists of general tables each dealing with a specific subject such as livestock numbers, consumption and foreign trade for specific types of meat. Part 2 consists of country tables each series consisting of 10 tables dealing with specific meat categories.

01192 **MEAT AND DAIRY PRODUCTS**
Commonwealth Secretariat, UK

International – English semi-annually
c80pp £25.00

Review of supply and markets with statistics on production, trade and consumption.

01193 **MERCHANT SHIPBUILDING RETURNS**
Lloyd's Register of Shipping

International – English quarterly 20pp free
ISSN No. 0261 1848

Quarterly statistical summaries of world shipbuilding for all self-propelled ships of 100 gross tonnage and above, which are under construction or on order.

01194 **METAL BULLETIN**
Metal Bulletin Books Ltd, UK

International – English semi-weekly
£175.00 US$416.10 DM950.00 annually

Has current price quotations, market reports, the trade and industry concerning metal, in over 100 countries.

01195 **METAL BULLETIN PRICES & DATA**
Metal Bulletin Books Ltd, UK

International – English annual £20
US$48.00 DM100

Covers ores, non-ferrous metals including ferro-alloys, rare and precious metals, iron and steel and scrap, and provides in meticulous detail, figures on imports, exports, production, consumption, and stocks, together with an equally intensive coverage of prices.
Also includes a memoranda section with specifications for ferrous and non-ferrous metals, tariffs of the major countries, foreign state trading organizations, internal trade associations, world iron ore loading and discharging ports, chemical

compositions of steel and non-ferrous alloys, metrication preferred sizes, physical constants of metals, trade abbreviations.

01196 **METAL BULLETIN MONTHLY**
Metal Bulletin Books Ltd, UK

International – English monthly £101 US$119.27 annually

A subscription to Metal Bulletin includes the monthly edition, which complements the twice-weekly news coverage. Originally conceived as a source of background material, it has over a number of years developed an identity of its own, with reviews and original surveys which develop and interpret information published in Metal Bulletin. It contains articles contributed by specialists from the industry. Regular topics include surveys of countries, markets and products, reports on new processes, international conference reports; plants, personalities, and publications; works and equipment; mines; regular market roundups; and a diary of coming events. Metal Bulletin Monthly frequently contains special features which group together a number of articles on a single theme. Every year the March issue includes a review of major events in the previous year. Metal Bulletin Monthly is also available on separate subscription.

01197 **METAL TRADERS OF THE WORLD**
Metal Bulletin Books Ltd, UK

International – English 1986 £45 US$108 DM225

A new worldwide directly of non-ferrous metal merchants, traders and producers' agents who trade either nationally or internationally. In the first section traders are listed alphabetically under their respective countries. The second section is a classified guide listing non-ferrous ores, metals and products, with detailed information on those companies involved in their trade, providing a quick reference to sources of supply. Each entry includes where possible: name, head office, telephone, telex and cable addresses, management, trading personnel, year established, capital, ownership, subsidiary and associated companies, branches, history, nature of activities, specialization and geographical areas favoured, products handled, companies represented, associations and memberships.

01198 **MICROTABLES–ANNUAL FOREIGN TRADE STATISTICS BY COUNTRIES (SERIES B)**
OECD

International/OECD – English/French annual 150 microfiche £150/DM675/ US$300/FrF1500

The microfiches give the origins of imports and the destinations of exports for each OECD member country and Yugoslavia. Data shown are value and quantity for the 2650 commodities and commodity categories of the SITC. Data are also available for a single country, an aggregate imports only or exports only – prices on demand.

01199 **MICROTABLES–ANNUAL FOREIGN TRADE STATISTICS BY COMMODITIES (SERIES C)**
OECD

International/OECD – English/French annual 110 microfiches £80/DM360/ US$160/FrF800

The origins and destinations of the 2,650 products and groups of products of the SITC are shown in value. Quantity data for imports and exports are given at the 3, 4 and 5 digit levels of the classification.

01200 **MILK AND MILK PRODUCTS BALANCES IN OECD COUNTRIES**
OECD

International – French/English annual 1974 180pp £9.50/DM42/US$19/FrF95

The volume is divided into 2 parts. Part 1 gives general consumption and foreign trade, data for each OECD member country and totals by groups of countries. Part 2 consists of country tables giving detailed balances of milk and milk products.

01201 **MONTHLY BULLETIN LEAD AND ZINC STATISTICS**
International Lead and Zinc Study Group

International – English monthly £85 surface mail, £100 airmail

01202 **MONTHLY BULLETIN OF STATISTICS**
Food and Agriculture Organisation

International – English/French/Spanish monthly 72pp US$20 annual

Contains data by crop and country on production, trade and price.

01203 **MONTHLY BULLETIN OF STATISTICS**
UN

International – English/French monthly 1947 US$150 subscription, 1 issue US$16

Provides monthly statistics on 74 subjects from over 200 countries and territories, including special tables which portray important economic developments. Quarterly data for significant world and regional data are also issued.

01204 **MONTHLY COMMODITY PRICE BULLETIN (TD/B/CI/CPB/L57-67)**
United Nations Conference on Trade and Development (UNCTAD)

International – English/French/Spanish monthly

Contains price indices and series of monthly average prices of 20 primary commodities exported by developing countries.

01205 **MONTHLY COMMODITY PRICE BULLETIN**
UN

International – English/French/Spanish monthly 1969 Subscription US$36 , 1 issue US$4

Contains tables and graphs with monthly and average annual prices for all types of commodities.

01206 **MONTHLY NEWSLETTER**
International Silk Association

International – English/French monthly November 1975 12 issues included in subscription

Economic and technical data on all aspects of the silk industry including detailed statistical tables.

01207 **MONTHLY OPERATIONAL SUMMARY**
World Bank

International – English monthly 72pp US$75.00

Reports on the status of every project under consideration for financing by the bank from the point a project is identified to the time it is approved.

01208 **MONTHLY STATISTICAL BULLETIN**
International Tin Council

International – English monthly 64pp £48.00 annually

Contains over 100 tables on tin mine production, tin smelter production (primary and secondary), consumption (primary and secondary) and consumption by main uses for leading consuming countries, trade in tin-in-concentrates and tin metal, production and trade in tinplate, and tin prices. Indexed in English and French.

01209 **MONTHLY STATISTICAL SUMMARY**
International Tea Committee Ltd

International – English monthly 12pp £70.00

Tea acreage, production, exports, imports, consumption, auction prices, absorption, UK Stocks re-exports, instant tea, duties and a directory of the tea trade.

01210 **MONTHLY STATISTICS OF FOREIGN TRADE (SERIES A)**
OECD

International – French/English monthly 110pp £35/DM150/US$68/FrF340

Contains a detailed regional analysis of trade of the main country groupings in the OECD area. Series are shown non-adjusted and seasonally adjusted. Total trade in US$ for OECD member countries and groupings of member countries is shown with individual partner countries.

01211 **MULTINATIONAL SERVICE***
European Information Service, Belgium

International – English semi-monthly c25pp BF17,600

Report on major activities in multinational businesses.

01212 NATO FACTS AND FIGURES
NATO Information Service

International – English/French/Italian/German/Spanish 1981 free

Detailed account of the history, structure and operation of NATO.

01213 NATIONAL ACCOUNTS OF OECD COUNTRIES
OECD

International – English/French annual 1966 2 volumes £103.10/DM455/US$206/FrF1031

Published in 2 volumes. Volume 1, Main Aggregates, is issued in 2 parts. Volume 2, Detailed Tables, is issued in 3 parts.

01214 NATIONAL ACCOUNTS STATISTICS
UN

International – English annual 1957 US$165, 3 volumes

Provides international coverage of statistical data on national accounts, giving specific data on GDP, national income and capital transactions, government and consumer expenditures, social security, household funds and the like.

01215 NATIONAL LEGISLATION AND REGULATIONS RELATING TO TRANSNATIONAL CORPORATIONS
UNCTC

International – English irregular 1978 US$23

Information by country about legislation relating to ownership, foreign exchange, investment guarantees and other significant aspects of carrying out international business in each country.

01216 NEWSLETTER
Federation Belge des Entreprises de Distribution FEDIS

International – French/Dutch weekly 1980 4pp BF1325

Review of current developments in distribution in Belgium, EEC countries and the USA.

01217 NON FERROUS METAL WORKS OF THE WORLD
Metal Bulletin Books Ltd, UK

International – English irregular 1967 647pp £60.00
ISBN No. 0-900542 95 0

Guide to the world's non-ferrous metal smelters, refiners, semi-fabricators and secondary ingot makers with over 1800 entries.

01218 NORDIC CO-OPERATION*
Nordic Council

International – English quarterly c6pp free

Newsletter giving brief accounts of current trends and developments in Nordic co-operation.

01219 NORDIC COUNTRIES BUSINESS OUTLOOK*
Copenhagen Handelsbank Den Norske Credit Bank Kansallis-Osake-Paukki, Helsinki Svenska Handelsbanken available from Nordic Bank, UK

International – English monthly c24pp

Brief review of current trends in the economies of the four Nordic countries.

01220 THE NORDIC ECONOMIC OUTLOOK
Sveriges Industriförbund available from Naringslivets Forlag

International – English bi-annual approx 60pp SKr30.00

English language summary of the economic situation in the Nordic countries.

01221 NOTES ON TIN
International Tin Council

International – English monthly £18.00 annually

General information on tin, tinplate and canning.

01222 OECD ECONOMIC OUTLOOK
OECD

International – English/French bi-annual 100pp £13.00

Twice a year it surveys the latest economic developments in the OECD area. Includes up-to-date statistical information on the growth of real GNP and GDP, development of domestic demand, manufacturing capacity, unemployment rates, productivity, foreign trade etc.

01223 OECD ECONOMIC STUDIES
OECD

International – English/French bi-annual 1983 200pp £14/DM62/US$28/FrF140

Focuses upon the area of applied macroeconomic and statistical analysis, generally with an international or cross-country dimension.

01224 OECD ECONOMIC OUTLOOK–HISTORICAL STATISTICS
OECD

International – English/French annual £8.50/DM27/US$17/FrF85

This publication shows how OECD economies have evolved. Figures are expressed in terms of rates of change or percentage share and provide an historical background to the OECD Economic Outlook current analysis and forecast.

01225 OECD EMPLOYMENT OUTLOOK
OECD

International – English annual 1983 £11/DM49/US$24/FrF110

Provides an annual assessment of labour market developments and prospects in Member countries. Each issue contains an overall analysis of the latest labour market trends and short-term forecasts, and examines key labour market developments. Reference statistics are included.

01226 OECD OBSERVER
Organisation for Economic Co-operation and Development (OECD)

International – English bi-monthly 38pp £5.50 US$11.00 FrF50 DM25 annually

Coverage of most important OECD issues including facts and recommended solutions in such areas as economic growth, employment and unemployment, energy, multinational enterprises, finance markets, environment, science and technology, aid to and trade with developing countries. Regular features include highlights of OECD countries: Europe, North America, Japan, Australia and New Zealand.

01227 OECD SCIENCE & TECHNOLOGY INDICATORS
OECD

International – English occasional 1984 cost varies

01228 OIL DATA SHEETS
Institute of Petroleum

International – English free

A series of 20 data sheets giving concise facts and figures on various aspects of the world oil industry.

01229 OIL NEWSLETTER*
Wood, Mackenzie and Co., UK

International – English quarterly c23pp

Summary of current situation in international oil industry.

01230 OIL WORLD ANNUAL
Ista Mielke GmbH, FRG

International – English annual 400pp DM87

World statistics for oilseeds, oils and fats with textual analysis of the prospects for the new season.

01231 OIL WORLD WEEKLY
Ista Mielke GmbH, FRG

International – English weekly c20pp DM65.00

Survey of the prospects for oilseeds, oils and fats including regular statistical reports.

01232 OLIVAE
International Olive Oil Council

International – English/French/Spanish/Italian 5 times a year April 1984 48pp annual/Europe US$20
ISSN No. English 0255 9994
ISSN No. French 0255 9978

General information, economic, scientific and technical articles, press review.

01233 **OPERATING EXPERIENCE WITH NUCLEAR POWER STATIONS IN MEMBER STATES**
International Atomic Energy Agency (IAEA)

International – English annual AS1320

Gives annual performance data and outage information and historical summary of production and outages during the lifetime of individual plants.

01234 **OPERATION AND EFFECTS OF THE GENERALIZED SYSTEM OF PREFERENCES**
UNCTAD

International – English irregular 1973 cost varies per issue

Evaluates the effects of preferential tariff treatment granted to imports from developing countries by developed countries.

01235 **PAPER AND PACKAGING BULLETIN ***
The Economist Intelligence Unit

International – English quarterly £110.00 annually

Comprehensive review of the world paper industry. Each issue contains a report on the world situation, a report on the recent performance of one of the major producing areas, in-depth reports on the demand for these products, and relevant data and statistics.

01236 **PAPER REVIEW OF THE YEAR**
Benn Business Information Services Ltd, UK

International–English annual

Reports from leading paper-manufacturing countries covering technical developments, marketing, and export and import statistics.

01237 **PHILLIP'S PAPER TRADE DIRECTORY**
Benn Business Information Services Ltd, UK

International – English annual

Comprehensive directory to international pulp, paper and paper board mills which are listed alphabetically by country and company giving information about products, equipment and personnel.

01238 **POPULATION BULLETIN OF THE UNITED NATIONS**
UN

International–English irregular 1952 US$11

Presents brief articles on population which are aimed at research institutions and individuals engaged in social and economic research.

01239 **POPULATION AND VITAL STATISTICS REPORT**
United Nations

International – English quarterly US$10.00 annually, US$3.00 per copy

Analysis of the latest census returns, giving statistics of births, deaths and infant mortality for all countries.

01240 **POPULATION AND VITAL STATISTICS**
UN

International – English quarterly 1949 Subscription US$18, 1 issue US$6

Provides latest census data, plus worldwide demographic statistics on birth and mortality.

01241 **PRESERVED MILK**
Agra Europe (London) Ltd, UK

International – English monthly £154-UK, £165-Europe, £170-world

Report on the market for milk and milk products with statistical data on European and world production, stocks, exports, imports and prices.

01242 **PRICES OF AGRICULTURAL PRODUCTS AND SELECTED INPUTS IN EUROPE AND NORTH AMERICA**
UNECE

International – English annual 1950 US$19

Includes an annual ECC/FAO price review of products.

01243 **PRICES AND PRICE INDICES IN FOREIGN COUNTRIES (2171100)**
W. Kohlhammer, GmbH

International–English/German 1977 DM4.50

This is a statistical publication.

01244 **PRINCIPAL USES OF LEAD AND ZINC**
International Lead and Zinc Study Group

International – English every 4 years with annual update £50.00

01245 **POTATO MARKETS**
Agra Europe (London) Ltd, UK

International – English weekly £466-UK-£490—Europe, £500-world

Information on the European potato market with comparative price data from North America.

01246 **LES PRIVATISATIONS A L'ETRANGER. ROYAUME-UNI, RFA, ITALIE, ESPAGNE, JAPAN**
La Documentation Francaise

International–French 1986 ISSN No. 0029-4004

Covers privatization in UK, Germany, Italy, Spain and Japan.

01247 **PROBLEMS POLITIQUES ET SOCIAUX**
La Documentation Francaise

International – French fortnightly 1970 40pp FrF16 per issue

Covers international political and social problems.

01248 **PROJECT CYCLE**
World Bank/W.Baum

International – English/French/Spanish 1982 25pp free

Explains the World Bank's lending operations which are concentrated on sound, productive projects that contribute to the development of the borrowing country's economy and ensure its capacity to repay the loan. Describes in detail the Bank's procedures for selecting, preparing, appraising and supervising projects, and evaluating the results upon completion. Also briefly reviews how the Bank's lending and development strategy has evolved over the years.

01249 **PUBLISHED OFFICIAL SOURCES OF FINANCIAL STATISTICS**
OECD

International – English/French 1980 £4.90/DM28/US$11/FrF44

01250 **PULP AND PAPER INDUSTRY**
OECD

International – English/French annual 1960 £7.50/DM33/US$15/FrF75

01251 **QUARTERLY BULLETIN OF COCOA STATISTICS**
International Cocoa Organisation

International – English/French/Spanish/Russian quarterly December 1974 45pp £15 UK/Europe, £25 outside Europe

Statistical data on the world cocoa economy – includes cocoa production, grindings, exports, imports, prices.

01252 **QUARTERLY COPPER STATISTICS**
World Bureau of Metal Statistics WBMS

International – English one off 100pp £925/US$1950

World copper production and consumption statistics.

01253 **QUARTERLY LABOUR FORCE STATISTICS**
OECD

International – English/French quarterly 87pp £12/DM53/US$24/FrF120

This quarterly bulletin provides data for the short-term evaluation of the major labour force components and employment by sector. The graphs show the evolution for the last 10 years and the statistical tables present the most recent available quarterly data for the last 6-year period.

01254 QUARTERLY NATIONAL ACCOUNTS
OECD

International – English/French quarterly 165pp £16/DM70/US$32/FrF160

Presents in the form of standardized tables, data on production, consumption, expenditure, capital formation, income and outlay and capital transactions of the main institutional sectors.

01255 QUARTERLY OIL AND GAS STATISTICS
OECD

International – English/French quarterly 293pp £48/DM210/US$95/FrF480

Provides detailed data in time series from Q1 1975 on production of crude oil, natural gas, liquids and refinery feedstocks, refinery intake and output, final consumption, stock levels. Supply and demand balances for 9 product groups are given and trade data by 48 origins and 31 export destinations.

01256 QUARTERLY REVIEW OF INTERNATIONAL STATISTICS
Federal Statistical Office, Belgrade

International – Serbo-Croat biannual YD100.00

Basic statistical data on economic matters, covering the whole world but with the emphasis on Europe.

01257 RADIO COMMUNICATION STATISTICS*
International Telecommunication Union

International – English/French/Spanish 1977 SF42.00

Annual statistics for radiocommunications available for the past three years.

01258 RECENT DEVELOPMENTS AND SHORT–TERM OUTLOOK IN THE TUNGSTEN MARKET
United Nations Conference on Trade and Development (UNCTAD)

International – English annual

An analytical review of the recent developments in the tungsten market.

01259 REFLEXIONS SUR LE PRIX DU PETROLE DANS LE LONG TERM DIRECTION DES HYDROCARBURES
La Documentation Francaise

International – French irregular 1987 64pp FrF45
ISBN No. 2 11 001772 4

Statistics on the supply, demand and prices of oil.

01260 REPORT FOR THE CROP YEAR
International Wheat Council

International – English/French/Russian/Spanish annual £10

A detailed review of the activities of the International Wheat Council and its committees and a summary of major grain developments in the crop year.

01261 RESTRICTIONS ON TRADE AND STRUCTURAL ADJUSTMENT
United Nations Conference on Trade and Development (UNCTAD)

International – English annual

Provides information on developments in trade actions and legislation and gives an assessment on trade measures in developed and developing countries. It discusses imperatives and prospects for trade liberalization.

01262 RESTRICTIVE BUSINESS PRACTICES INFORMATION
United Nations Conference on Trade and Development (UNCTAD)

International – English quarterly

Short notes containing information concerning major developments in the area of restrictive business practices.

01263 REUTER COCOA REPORT
Reuters Ltd, UK

International – English daily £2280

Marketing and price figures, including weekly crop purchases from Ghana delivered to subscribers by teleprinter.

01264 REUTER COFFEE REPORT
Reuters Ltd, UK

International–English £1680

Market reports, production and consumption figures and prices delivered to subscribers by teleprinter.

01265 REUTER GRAIN AND OILSEED REPORT
Reuters Ltd, UK

International – English daily £2280

Production, consumption and stock figures particularly from the EEC and USA delivered on a regular basis to subscribers.

01266 REUTER INTERNATIONAL COMMODITY REPORT
Reuters Ltd, UK

International – English regular

News, prices and market reports of major commodities delivered to subscribers throughout the day by a teleprinter service.

01267 REUTER METAL REPORT
Reuters Ltd, UK

International – English daily £1680

Prices and market reports particularly of copper, tin, lead, zinc and silver delivered to subscribers regularly by teleprinter.

01268 REUTER RUBBER REPORT
Reuters Ltd, UK

International – English daily £1680

Prices and market news from Singapore, Kuala Lumpur, London, New York, Paris, Bangkok and Colombo delivered to subscribers on a regular basis.

01269 REUTER SHIPPING REPORT
Reuters Ltd, UK

International – English daily £1380

International news relevant to world trade: reports from foreign exchange markets and current news from the Baltic Freight market delivered regularly to subscribers.

01270 REUTER SUGAR REPORT
Reuters Ltd, UK

International – English daily £2280

News of price fluctuations and regular market reports from London, Hong Kong, New York and Paris delivered to subscribers by teleprinter.

01271 REUTER WOOL REPORT
Reuters Ltd, UK

International – English daily £1380

News from the future markets in Nagoya, Sydney, Roubaix, London and New York provided regularly to subscribers.

01272 REVENUE STATISTICS OF OECD MEMBER COUNTRIES
OECD

International – French/English annual £11/DM49/US$22/FrF110

Contains information on tax levels and structures in OECD member countries.

01273 REVIEW OF FISHERIES IN OECD MEMBER COUNTRIES
OECD

International – English annually 1968 340pp £10/DM44/US$20/FrF100

The review describes major developments affecting the commercial fisheries of OECD countries, particularly in areas such as government action, production, processing and marketing and international trade.

01274 REVIEW OF MARITIME TRANSPORT (TD/B/C.4/178)
United Nations Conference on Trade and Development (UNCTAD)

International – English/French/Spanish 1985 US$14

Review of current and long-term aspects of maritime transport which includes, among others, chapters on international seaborne trade; the world merchant fleet, world ship prices and the fleets of developing countries, and trends in shipbuilding and freight markets, as well as a chapter on port development.

01275 **REVIEW OF THE WORLD ECONOMIC SITUATION**
International Confederation of Free Trade Unions

International – English/French/German/ Spanish annual

01276 **REVUE BENELUX***
Union Economique Benelux

International – French/Dutch quarterly BF250.00

General economic review with a supplement of statistical tables.

01277 **RUBBER STATISTICAL BULLETIN**
International Rubber Study Group, UK

International–English monthly c50pp £62.00/US$124.00 UK/Surface £72.00/US$144.00 airmail

Statistics on output, production, stocks, trade, consumption and prices in the world rubber industry.

01278 **SCENARIO PROGRAM***
Eurofinance, France

International–English 4 reports annually FrF4,200

Alternative economic forecasts for the next five years covering France, Germany, Italy, UK, USA and Japan.

01279 **SCIENCE, TECHNOLOGY, INDUSTRY REVIEW**
OECD

International – English bi-annual £15/ DM66/US$30/FrF150

01280 **SERVICE DE CONJONCTURE**
Institute de Recherches Economiques

International – French/English monthly/ quarterly 1937 60pp BF119 per year

Survey of international and national recent economic developments and macroeconomic short- to medium-term forecasts.

01281 **SHIPMENTS OF WHEAT AND WHEAT FLOUR**
International Wheat Council

International – English/French/Russian/ Spanish annual £15

Commercial and non-commercial shipments of wheat and flour by origin and destinations, includes separate tables for Durum.

01282 **SHIPYARD ORDERS WEEKLY REPORT**
Lloyd's Register of Shipping

International – English weekly £360 p.a.

A list of confirmed orders reported during the week, showing selected data. Lists of reported cancellations and completions are also included.

01283 **LA SITUATION ECONOMIQUE A L'ETRANGER**
Banque de France

International – French 3 times a year

Looks at the economic and financial situation in Germany, USA, Italy, Japan and UK.

01284 **SPOTLIGHT ON THE WORLD ECONOMY**
T. C. Coombs & Co.

International – English monthly 27pp

Statistical survey and commentary on the world economy plus forecasts, data of main economic indicators for USA, Japan, France, Germany, Italy and UK.

01285 **STAINLESS STEEL INTERNATIONAL SURVEY AND DIRECTORY**
Metal Bulletin Books Ltd, UK

International – English 1985 £25/US$60/ DM125

Features articles on the industry, world list of stainless steel refining plants and international directory of stainless steel producers, product buyers' guide – 220 entries approx.

01286 **STATEMENT OF LOANS, STATEMENT OF DEVELOPMENT CREDITS**
World Bank

International – English quarterly US$100.00

Provides cumulative financial transaction history of all approved IBRD loans and IDA credits.

01287 **STATISTICAL BULLETIN**
International Tin Council

International – English monthly 1949 64pp £60 p.a.

Mine and smelter production of tin, tin metal consumption by main uses, stocks and trade in tin-in-concentrates and tin metal production, consumption and trade in tinplate, tin prices.

01288 **STATISTICAL BULLETIN/ BULLETIN STATISTIQUE**
International Office of Cocoa, Chocolate and Sugar Confectioners. Herman Pohlmann, chairman of the joint International Statistics Committee

International – English/French annual 95+pp BF1000/US$25

International comparison of consumption of the products of the chocolate, sugar confectionery and biscuit industry.

01289 **STATISTICAL BULLETIN**
International Sugar Organization

International – English monthly £30.00

Data on production, consumption, supply and foreign trade.

01290 **STATISTICAL YEARBOOK**
United Nations

International – English/French annual US$70

A yearbook of statistics covering all countries of the world, with a wide range of economic and social data. Topics include: population, agriculture, manufacturing, construction, transport, trade, balance of payments, national income, education and culture. The coverage of the yearbook has been improved to widen the territorial scope of many of the tables and to provide more comprehensive and accurate world and continental aggregates.

01291 **STATISTICS ON IRON ORE (TD/B/ IPC/IRON ORE/AC 1/3)**
United Nations Conference on Trade and Development (UNCTAD)

International – English/French/Spanish annual

Statistical information on production of iron ore, agglomerates, pig iron and steel as well as consumption, trade and stocks of iron ore.

01292 **STATISTICS OF WORLD TRADE IN STEEL**
UNECE

International – English annual 1961 US$8.50

Provides basic data on exports of semi-finished and finished steel products from European and other steel-exporting countries in the world.

01293 **THE STEEL MARKET**
UNECE

International – English annual 1953 150pp US$16.50

This review analyses international developments, provides statistical information submitted by governments and reports on steel market trends and their outlook on a country-by-country basis including Japan, the US and other industrialized countries.

01294 **THE STEEL MARKET IN 19XX AND OUTLOOK FOR 19XX**
OECD

International – English annual £12/DM53/ US$24/FrF120

Gives data on consumption by area, steel trade balance by area, steel market by area and manpower.

01295 **STEEL TRADERS OF THE WORLD**
Metal Bulletin Books Ltd, UK

International – English 1986 £45 US$108 DM225

01316 **UNDP COMPENDIUM OF APPROVED PROJECTS**
United Nations Development Programme

International – English annual 500pp US$15.00

Annual listing of UNDP-assisted projects, identified by country and region. Includes breakdown of projects by sector, cost to UNDP and recipient country, dates and duration of projects, and their executing agencies.

01317 **UNCTAD BULLETIN**
United Nations Conference on Trade and Development (UNCTAD)

International – English monthly

A succinct review of UNCTAD activities.

01318 **UNCTAD COMMODITY YEARBOOK**
United Nations Conference on Trade and Development (UNCTAD)

International – English annual

Provides statistical series at the regional and country levels for trade in selected agricultural primary commodities and minerals, ores and metals.

01319 **UNESCO STATISTICAL DIGEST**
United Nations Educational Scientific and Cultural Organisation (UNESCO)

International – English/French/Spanish annual 335pp

01320 **UNESCO STATISTICAL YEARBOOK**
United Nations Educational Scientific and Cultural Organisation (UNESCO)

International – English/French/Spanish annual 1200pp

Contains data on population, education, science, technology, culture and communications in more than 200 countries and territories. Statistical data is also given on libraries and museums.

01321 **THE URBAN EDGE**
World Bank

International – English 10 issues a year US$28.00

Provides coverage of urban development in developing countries.

01322 **VADEMECUM DER INVESTMENTFONDS**
Verlag Hoppenstedt & Co.

International – German every 2 years 810pp DM155

Investment funds.

01323 **VIERTELJAHRESHEFTE ZUR AUSLANDSSTATISTIK (5100000)**
W. Kohlhammer GmbH

International – English/German quarterly DM15.90

A statistical publication.

01324 **WAGES AND TOTAL LABOUR COSTS**
Svenska Arbetsgivareforeningen
Sw. Employer's Confederation

International – English/Swedish/French/German annual 74pp SKr90
ISSN No. 0280-4743

An international survey covering Belgium, Denmark, Finland, France, Ireland, Italy, Japan, Canada, The Netherlands, Norway, Switzerland, Great Britain, Sweden, United States, West Germany and Austria. Latest issues covers 1974-1984.

01325 **DIE WELTWIRTSCHAFT**
Institut fur Weltwirtschaft

International – German semi-annual 180-220pp and statistical appendix DM40.00
ISBN/ISSN No. 0043-2652

Reports on the business situation in West Germany and in the major industrialized countries and structural analyses.

01326 **WELTWIRTSCHAFTLICHES ARCHIV (REVIEW OF WORLD ECONOMICS)**
Institut fur Weltwirtschaft

International – English quarterly 200pp per issue/800 per year DM36.00
ISBN/ISSN No. 0043-2636

Journal for the study of international economics.

01327 **WHO OWNS WHAT IN WORLD BANKING**
Financial Times Business Information

International – English annual 218pp £48 UK, overseas £52, US$78
ISBN No. 0 902101 81

Details of subsidiary and affiliated banking interests of over 250 of the world's largest banks including multinational and consortium banks.

01328 **WOOL QUARTERLY**
Commonwealth Secretariat, UK

International – English quarterly 90pp £70.00

Reviews current situation and outlook in both raw wool and wool textile manufacturing countries: contains quarterly statistics on production, disposals, utilization, and trade in both raw wool and intermediate products.

01329 **WOOL STATISTICS**
Commonwealth Secretariat, UK

International – English annual 60pp £20.00

Provides an analysis of all aspects of the wool industry and outlook. It covers on a worldwide basis sheep numbers, wool production, prices, utilization of materials and production and stocks of processed wool and intermediate products by the wool textile industry, employment, machine capacity and international trade in raw wool and intermediates.

01330 **WORLD BANK**
World Bank

International – English bi-annual free

Describes current economic research within the World Bank and developments in areas of special relevance to development policy.

01331 **WORLD BANK**
World Bank

International – English/French/Spanishj/German/Arabic 1981 12pp free

Leaflet summarizing the operations of the World Bank and IDA provision of technical assistance aid co-ordination, ownership and control.

01332 **WORLD BANK ANNUAL REPORT**
World Bank

International – English/Spanish/Japanese/Arabic annual 290pp free

Presents summary and background of the activities of the World Bank and the International Development Association (IDA), highlighting questions of trade, agriculture and rural development, mineral and fuel development, and non-farm employment and rural activities, and examines external public debt and capital flows to developing countries. Separate chapters give details of lending operations by region and a summary of projects assisted during the fiscal year. Also reviews technical assistance and aid co-ordination activities, interagency co-operation, borrowings and finance, and major policy decisions. Includes a statistical annex on the debt situation of 96 developing countries and on foreign and international bond issues, the financial statements of the World Bank and IDA, with statements of voting power and subscriptions of member countries, and appendices giving cumulative totals of lending by major purpose and region, and by country. Includes statistical annex and 24 appendices.

01333 **WORLD BANK: A FINANCIAL APPRAISAL**
World Bank/Eugene Rothberg

International – English/French 1981 35pp free

Summarizes informal remarks made in seminars and information meetings on the World Bank's lending policies, including the evaluation of borrower's creditworthiness, project appraisal and supervision, costs and benefits; its capital structure and borrowing programme, borrowing costs, and debt structure; and its liquidity policy. Briefly describes IDA's role and, in the annex, gives selected financial data.

01334 **WORLD BANK ATLAS**
World Bank

International – English/French/Spanish annual 28pp US$5.00

Contains data on population, gross national product (GNP) and GNP per capita for 184 countries. In addition to the standard data on population, such as life expectancy, data are presented on total fertility rate and total school enrolment, both primary and secondary.

01335 WORLD BANK COUNTRY STUDIES
World Bank

International – English c.15 studies published yearly US$3.50-20.00

Provides comprehensive information on the economies of developing countries.

01336 WORLD BANK ECONOMIC REVIEW
World Bank

International – English 3 issues a year free

A professional journal for the dissemination of World Bank sponsored research. Emphasises policy relevance and operational aspects of economics, rather than theoretical and methodological issues.

01337 WORLD BANK RESEARCH PROGRAM: ABSTRACTS OF CURRENT STUDIES
World Bank

International – English annual 218pp free

A compilation of abstracts of current projects funded by the World Bank's Central Research Program. The projects are grouped into eight functional categories that deal with general issues of development policy as well as specific sectoral problems of concern to the Bank's operations in developing countries (developing policy and planning, international finance and trade, agriculture and rural development, industry, transportation, public utilities, urbanization and regional development, and population and human resources).

01338 WORLD COPPER DATABOOK
Metal Bulletin Books Ltd, UK

International – English 1986 £60 US$144 DM300

Information on international copper, mines, traders and representatives with detailed lists of stockholders, warehouses, assayers and samplers, copper contract specifications and associations.

01339 WORLD DAIRY STATISTICS DIGEST*
International Federation of Agricultural Producers, France

International – English/French quarterly c20pp

International statistics for all types of dairy products.

01340 WORLD DEBT TABLES
World Bank

International – English annual with 3 supplements 538pp US$125

Provides data on the external debt of 109 developing countries. Presents statistical tables by country reporting or estimating data for public and publicly guaranteed long-term debt, private non-guaranteed long term debt (where available), short-term debt, and the use of International Monetary Fund credit. Gives aggregate position of all countries, major borrowers, and seventeen highly indebted borrowers. Outlines characteristics of the debt situation. Includes for each reporting country a set of four charts depicting debt stocks and associated indicators, as well as flows of debt service and associated debt-service ratios.

01341 WORLD DEVELOPMENT REPORT
World Bank

International – English/French/German/Spanish/Portuguese/Japanese/Arabic annual 266pp US$12.95

The 1987 edition examines the effects of foreign trade on the pace and scale of industrialization. It includes a statistical appendix and numerous maps, graphics, and case studies to supplement the text. The final portion, 'World Development Indicators', contains 33 statistical tables giving economic and social profiles of 128 countries.

01342 WORLD ECONOMIC SURVEY
UN

International – English annual 1948 US$15

An authoritative assessment of the world economy including an overview of salient developments for the previous year and an outlook for the future. It focuses on studying the growth in the world economy, current policy stances, international trade and payments and international capital flows to developing countries.

01343 WORLD ENERGY YEARBOOK
United Nations

International – English annual

Contains annual data on the production, imports, exports and consumption of solid fuels, petroleum and its principal refined products, gases and electricity (thermal, hydro, geothermal and nuclear). The origin and destination of world trade in solid fuels, crude petroleum and natural gases is also shown.

01344 WORLD HEALTH STATISTICS ANNUAL
World Health Organisation

International–English/French 700pp SF90.00

01345 WORLD IMPORT DUTIES AND TAXES
IFPI (International Federation of Phonogram and Videogram Producers)

International – English 1984 120

Books, films, records, matrices, compact discs, audio tapes, video discs and video recorders.

01346 THE WORLD MARKETS FOR DAIRY PRODUCTS–1986
General Agreement on Tariffs and Trade
GATT Secretariat

International – English/French/Spanish annual 1985 75 SF12
ISBN/ISSN No. 0259 8213

The report, issued under the International Dairy Arrangement, analyses the main trends and developments of the dairy market during the year under review.

01347 WORLD POPULATION PROJECTIONS 1985: SHORT AND LONG TERM ESTIMATES BY AGE AND SEX WITH RELATED DEMOGRAPHIC STATISTICS
World Bank

International – English 480 US$50

01348 WORLD RUBBER STATISTICS HANDBOOK
VOL 3 1960-1985
International Rubber Study Group

International – English every 5 years Vol. 1, 1974 (1946-70); Vol.2, 1984 (1965-1980) 48pp £45 by airmail

Providing national statistics of synthetic and natural rubber production, consumption, imports, exports, stocks and prices for up to 58 countries and includes statistics on vehicle production and vehicles in use as well as tyre production figures for 27 countries.

01349 WORLD STAINLESS STEEL STATISTICS
World Bureau of Metal Statistics WBMS

International – English annual 100 £150, US$350

01350 WORLD STATISTICS
Institute of Petroleum, UK

International – English annual c8pp free in the UK

Summarized statistics on the world oil industries covering demand, production and capacity.

01351 WORLD STATISTICS IN BRIEF
UN

International – English annual 1976 US$5

A statistical pocketbook providing data on the last decade's indicators in demography and labour force, national accounts, agriculture and industry, trade, finance and tourism, transport and communications, education, health and nutrition. Data are given for 156 countries, by regions and for the world as a whole.

01352 WORLD STAINLESS STEEL STATISTICS
Metal Bulletin Books Ltd, UK

International–English 1983 £140 US$336 DM700

Provides data for the non-communist countries of the world ranging, in many cases, over five or more years, covering: production by countries of ingots, production for selected countries of castings, imports by shapes and sources, exports by shapes and destinations, plus an overall survey of production trends during the year preceding publication. Published annually (Autumn).

01353 WORLD STEEL TRADE DEVELOPMENTS: A STATISTICAL ANALYSIS
OECD

International – English £4.50/DM23/US$9/FrF45

Provides an insight into the longer-term developments in international trade in steel. It contains and analyses data by country and by area on production, consumption and trade including market share.

01354 WORLD TABLES 1984
Johns Hopkins University Press Ltd

International – English 1984 2 vols. hardcover US$65, paperback US$32.50

This publication presents from the data files of the World Bank, basic economic data as continuous time series for individual countries, derived economic indicators for selected years or periods suitable for making comparisons among countries and country groups, and demographic and social data. Also available on tape, updated annually.

01355 WORLD TIN MINING: OPERATIONS, EXPLORATION AND DEVELOPMENTS

International – English irregular 1982 122pp £20.00

Directory of over 360 tin-mining operations in 40 countries setting out the nature of their mining operations, the latest production details and, where applicable, planned development.

01356 WORLD TOURISM
World Tourism Organization

International – English/Spanish/French annual 1981 330pp US$25.00

Tourism trends in the 6 WTO regions (Africa, Americas, Europe, Middle East, East Asia and the Pacific, South Asia), international and domestic tourism demand, development of tourism and tourism administration policies.

01357 WORLD TRADE IN LEAD AND ZINC
International Lead and Zinc Study Group

International – English every 4 years £50.00

01358 WORLD TRADE–STAINLESS, HIGH SPEED & OTHER ALLOY STEEL–1987
UK Iron & Steel Statistics Bureau

International – English quarterly 1979 61pp £125.00 (£140.00 airmail)
ISSN No. (applied for).

A quarterly cumulative book detailing the export trade of major steel-producing countries in selected alloy products. A companion volume covering value of trade is published annually and is included in the price.

01359 WORLD TRADE STEEL–1987
UK Iron & Steel Statistics Bureau

International – English quarterly 1970 61pp £125.00 (140.00 airmail)

A quarterly cumulative book detailing the export trade of 16 major steel-producing countries collectively accounting for over 80 per cent of world exports. The book covers 28 product groups and 100 export markets. Available about five months after the quarter end. A companion volume covering value of trade is published annually and is included in the price.

01360 WORLD WHEAT STATISTICS
International Wheat Council

International – English/French/Russian/Spanish annual £35 UK

Long-term data series on wheat and flour production, consumption, trade, prices, ocean freight rates, national support prices and bread prices.

01361 WORLD WROUGHT COPPER STATISTICS
World Bureau of Metal Statistics WBMS

International – English annual 100pp £150/US$350

01362 YEARBOOK OF FOREST PRODUCTS
Food and Agriculture Organisation

International – English/French/Spanish/Italian annual 348 £22.00

Contains data on the production and trade in forest products for the current year and a time series. The tables are in 3 parts. The first contains tables dealing with the volume of production, the volume and value of trade. The second part deals with the direction of trade and the third with unit value in trade of some commodities.

01363 YEARBOOK OF INTERNATIONAL COMMODITY STATISTICS
United Nations Conference on Trade and Development (UNCTAD)

International – English annual 1984 US$52

Provides statistical data at the regional and country levels for trade in selected agricultural primary commodities, minerals, ores and metals.

01364 YEARBOOK OF INTERNATIONAL TRADE STATISTICS
United Nations

International – English annual

Volume 1–trade by country; Vol,. 2–trade by commodity, commodity matrix tables.

01365 YEARBOOK OF NATIONAL ACCOUNTS STATISTICS
United Nations

International – English 3 vols per year

Detailed estimates of national income and related economic measures for many countries and areas. Among the many subjects covered are: gross domestic product, composition of private consumption expenditure, government and revenue expenditure and external transactions.

01366 YEARBOOK OF TOURISM STATISTICS
World Tourism Organization

International – English/French/Spanish annual 1947 870pp US$33 for 2 volumes

Tourism statistical data for the analysis of tourism development at the world, regional and national levels.

01367 WORLD METAL STATISTICS YEARBOOK
World Bureau of Metal Statistics

International – English annual 1984 125pp £50, US$100

Statistics on worldwide production, consumption, trade, prices and stock of major non-ferrous metals.

01368 YEARBOOK OF MINING, OIL AND GAS, ELECTRICITY, CHEMICAL INDUSTRY
Verlag Gluckauf GmbH

International – English annual 1893 1300pp DM98

A reference book on the energy and mineral raw materials economy of Europe, containing information on 10,000 people and 6,000 undertakings, organizations and authorities.

01369 YEARBOOK OF NORDIC STATISTICS
Nordic Council

International–Swedish/English annual c370pp

Statistical data on the five Nordic countries with selected data for Greenland and the Faroe Islands.

01370 ZAHLEUSPIEGEL BUNDESREPUBLIK DEUTSCHLAND/DEUTSCHE DEMOKRATISCHE REPUBLIK EUI VERGLEICH
Bundesminister fur Innerdeutsche Beziehungen

Germany, East and Germany, West German annual 144pp

Comparative statistics on the FGR and DDR.

ALBANIA

02001 **ABECOR COUNTRY REPORT–ALBANIA**
Abecor

Albania – English 1985 2pp free

Brief economic report.

02002 **ALBANIA–A COUNTRY PROFILE**
Department of Trade and Industry

Albania – English occasional 14pp

Surveys the political, geographical and economic climate (including special sections on metallurgy, energy and engineering, agriculture, foreign trade). Contains a statistical annexe of Albanian overseas trade and a list of Albanian foreign trade enterprises.

02003 **ALBANIAN FOREIGN TRADE**
Chamber of Commerce of the PSR of Albania

Albania – English/French bimonthly 22pp

Brief reports on Albanian industry with news items of relevance to Albanian trade.

02004 **L'ALBANIE, EVOLUTION POLITIQUE, ECONOMIQUE ET SOCIALE NOTES ET ETUDES DOCUMENTAIRES N.4482**
La Documentation Francaise

Albania – French 1978 FrF50

Account of the politics, economics and social organizations of Albania.

02005 **BUJQUESI SOCIALISTE (AGRICULTURE)**
Collets Holdings Ltd

Albania – Albanian monthly

Agriculture.

02006 **COUNTRY PROFILES**
Economist Publications Ltd

Romania, Bulgaria, Albania – English annual 40pp £25 UK, subscription varies in the rest of the world

Resumé of politics, economy and industry including statistical summaries.

02007 **COUNTRY REPORTS**
Economist Publications Ltd

Romania, Bulgaria, Albania–English quarterly 25pp £58 UK, subscription varies in rest of world

Economic policies and development plans, trends in production and demand, monetary and fiscal conditions, wages and prices, merchandise trade, invisibles, capital flows, exchange rates and foreign debt plus a forecast of the economic prospects.

02008 **ECONOMIC PROBLEMS**
Instituti i Studimeve Ekonomike, Institute of Economic Studies

Albania – Albanian Table of contents and summaries of articles in French 4 p.a. 1952 130-140pp Lek5

Articles on a variety of economic problems, such as the development of the productive forces in industry, agriculture and other fields of the economy, the perfecting of the socialist relations in production, the effectiveness of social production, problems of the world economy etc.

02009 **LANDERBERICHT ALBANIEN**
Federal Statistical Office of Germany

Albania – German irregular DM7.90

Statistical survey of Albania including such areas as demography, geography, education, employment, agriculture, production, overseas trade, transport, tourism, finance, wages and prices and national accounts.

02010 **NDERTUESI (THE BUILDER)**
Collets Holdings Ltd

Albania – Albanian 6 per year

02011 **PERMBLEDHJE (INDUSTRY AND MINES)**
Collets Holdings Ltd

Albania – Albanian 3 per year

02012 **PUNA (TRADE UNIONS)**
Collets Holdings Ltd

Albania – Albanian twice a week

02013 **TEKNIKA**
Collets Holdings Ltd

Albania – Albanian quarterly

02014 **35 YEARS OF SOCIALIST ALBANIA**
The '8 Netori' Publishing House

Albania – English 1981 140pp Lek13

A statistical survey on the development of Albanian economy, culture and society. Covers such areas as population, employment, industry, agriculture, transport, trade, education and health services.

AUSTRIA

03001 ABECOR COUNTRY REPORT – AUSTRIA
Abecor

Austria – English 1987 2pp free

Brief economic report.

03002 AKTUELLER WIRTSCHAFTSDIENST
Osterreichische Länderbank

Austria – German monthly 20pp free

Business, exchange and foreign trade information, statistical information.

03003 DIE ARBEITSKOSTEN IN DER INDUSTRIE OSTERREICHS
Bundeskammer der Gewerblichen Wirtschaft

Austria – German every 3 years

Statistics on labour costs in Austrian industry including forecasts.

03004 DER AUSSENHANDEL OSTERREICHS SERIE 1A
Osterreichisches Statistisches Zentralamt

Austria – German quarterly 1340pp AS1120 annually

Statistics on imports and exports giving volume and value classified by commodity and country.

03005 DER AUSSENHANDEL OSTERREICHS SERIE 1B
Osterreichische Statistische Zentralamt

Austria – German semi-annually 575pp AS420 annually

Statistics on foreign trade listing commodities according to country of origin or destination.

03006 DER AUSSENHANDEL OSTERREICHS SERIE 2
Osterreichische Statistische Zentralamt

Austria – German semi-annually 290pp AS350 annually

Analysis of foreign trade according to the international SITC classification.

03007 AUSTRIA
National Westminster Bank

Austria – English irregular 4pp free

Brief economic report.

03008 THE AUSTRIAN ALTERNATIVE: A GUIDE FOR FOREIGN INVESTORS
Girozentrale Vienna

Austria – German/English annual or every two years 50pp free

Tax and foreign exchange regulations.

03009 AUSTRIAN BANKING INDUSTRY
Girozentrale Vienna

Austria – German/English 1986

03010 AUSTRIA'S MONETARY SITUATION SURVEY*
Osterreichische Nationalbank

Austria – English monthly free

Abridged version of the regular monthly report of the Austrian national bank on the current monetary situation.

03011 BAUSTATISTIK
Osterreichische Statistische Zentralamt

Austria – German annual 2 vols AS480 AS450

Building statistics. Vol. 1 gives details of output, employment, wages, energy consumption and hours of work for each sector of the industry. Vol. 2 is an analysis of the financial organization of the construction industry.

03012 BEREICHSZAHLUNGEN
Osterreichische Statistische Zentralamt

Austria – German every 5-7 years

A general trade survey in 12 parts covering industry, production, transport, tourism, energy etc.

03013 BERICHT DER WIENER BORSEKAMMER UBER DAS GESCHAFTSJAHR
Wiener Borsekammer

Austria – German annual 90pp free

Annual report of the Vienna Stock Exchange.

03014 BESTANDSSTATISTIK DER KRAFTFAHRZEUGE IN OSTERREICH IM JAHRE
Osterreichische Statistische Zentralamt

Austria – German annual 110pp AS630

Statistics on motor vehicles including capacity, registrations, type and model.

03015 BETEILIGUNGSREPORT
Girozentrale Vienna

Austria – German annual 100pp free

Annual report for investors in the savings bank.

03016 BODENNUTZUNGSERHEBUNG
Osterreichische Statistische Zentralamt

Austria – German every 3-4 years 80pp AS230

Survey of land use.

03017 DIE BORSE
Girozentrale Vienna

Austria – German annual

Annual survey of the Austrian capital market.

03018 BORSENBERICHTE*
Creditanstalt Bankverein

Austria – German monthly free

Monthly report on the stock exchange.

03019 BORSENDIENST
Girozentrale Vienna

Austria – German weekly

Weekly service containing current information on the stock exchange including news of securities and a Eurobond bulletin.

03020 BUNDESVORANSCHLAG
Bundesministerium fur Finanzen

Austria – German annual 1967 free

A statistical overview of the budget.

A reference work providing detailed information on companies engaged in any aspect of international trading in iron and steel products, including international merchants, trading companies, agencies for foreign steel producers and distributors and companies importing iron and steel products for distribution to third parties.

Each entry shows, wherever possible: name, head office, telephone, telex and cable address, executive staff, trading personnel, year established, capital, ownership, subsidiary and associated companies, branches, activities, products handled, association memberships.

Also included is a guide to agents, comprising an alphabetical listing of steel producers with information on the names, territories and product coverage of agents and representatives, and export organizations.

01296 SUGAR YEARBOOK
International Sugar Organization, UK

International – English annual c370pp £12.50

Statistics on production, consumption, imports and exports and prices in industrial countries.

01297 SUMMARY SURVEYS OF FOREIGN TRADE (2070100)
W. Kohlhammer GmbH

International – English/German monthly DM9.50

01298 SUPPLEMENTARY REPORT 1: IMPORTS BY COUNTRIES OF PRODUCTION AND OF SALE BY COMMODITY GROUPS (2070310)
W. Kohlhammer GmbH

International – English/German annual DM19.50

01299 SUPPLEMENTARY REPORT 2: EXPORTS BY COUNTRIES OF CONSUMPTION AND OF PURCHASE AND BY COMMODITY GROUPS (2070320)
W. Kohlhammer GmbH

International – English/German annual DM22.50

01300 TAX HAVENS ENCYCLOPAEDIA
Butterworth and Co. (Publishers) Ltd, UK/
B Spitz ed

International – English 1975 with frequent updatings

Loose-leaf work covering advantages and disadvantages of all available tax havens covering regulations, taxation, exchange control.

01301 TAX NEWS SERVICE
International Bureau of Fiscal Documentation

International – English fortnightly DF260

Concise newsletter reporting the latest tax developments around the world.

01302 THE TAX TREATMENT OF TRANSFER PRICING
International Bureau of Fiscal Documentation

International – English biannual DF1100

An in-depth publication on the transfer pricing law and practice in countries where multinational enterprises have their major activities.

01303 TECHNICAL CO-OPERATION ACTIVITIES OF UNCTAD
United Nations Conference on Trade and Development (UNCTAD)

International–English annual

Describes in detail UNCTAD's technical co-operation activities by geographical region and fields of activity.

01304 TIMBER BULLETIN
UN

International – English/French quarterly 1948 Subscription US$80, 1 issue US$10

Contains statistics by country on exports, imports and production of wood, woodpulp and paper.

01305 TIN STATISTICS
International Tin Council

International – English/French annual 1963 64pp £20.00

Tin mine production, trade and stocks of tin-in-concentrates; production, consumption, trade and stocks of tin metal (primary and secondary); production, apparent consumption and trade in tinplate, tin prices, price ranges in the Tin Agreement and price indices of non-ferrous metals.

01306 TOBACCO QUARTERLY
Commonwealth Secretariat, UK

International – English quarterly c70pp £70.00

Data on production, trade and consumption analysed by area.

01307 LE TOURISM: UN PHENOMENE ECONOMIQUE–NOTES ET ETUDES DOCUMENTAIRES No.4811
La Documentation Francaise

International – French 1949 144pp FrF48

Looks at social, demographic and cultural aspects of tourism.

01308 TOURISM POLICY AND INTERNATIONAL TOURISM IN OECD MEMBER COUNTRIES
OECD

International – English annual 1955 £9.80/ DM44/US$19/FrF98

Describes tourism trends and relevant government policy developments. It covers aspects of policy such as organization and planning, supply and demand, forecasting objectives, and technical cooperation.

01309 TRADE AND DEVELOPMENT REPORT (UNCTAD/TDR/6)
United Nations Conference on Trade and Development (UNCTAD)

International–English annual

A comprehensive review of the world's economic development with a focus on the dynamics of the deflationary process, the transmission of growth and the prolonged crisis of debt and development.

01310 TRADING IN METALS
Metal Bulletin Books Ltd, UK

International – English 1983 £25 US$60 DM125

A textbook setting out a complete analysis of the means and methods used in the metal trade and unravelling the complexities of dealing in metals.

01311 TRENDS IN CONSUMPTION OF LEAD AND ZINC
International Lead and Zinc Study Group

International–English £30.00

01312 TRENDS AND POLICIES IN TRADE AND ECONOMIC COOPERATION AMONG COUNTRIES HAVING DIFFERENT ECONOMIC AND SOCIAL SYSTEMS
United Nations Conference on Trade and Development (UNCTAD)

International – English annual

Contains a review of recent developments in world trade and economic co-operation.

01313 TRENDS IN PRODUCTION OF LEAD AND ZINC
International Lead and Zinc Study Group

International – English every 4 years £30.00

01314 TRENDS IN PRODUCTION AND TRADE IN ALL SECTORS AND THEIR UNDERLYING FACTORS
United Nations Conference on Trade and Development (UNCTAD)

International – English annual

Contains an overview of recent trends and shifts in patterns of output, employment and trade in the sectors of manufacturers, agriculture and services.

01315 TUNGSTEN STATISTICS
United Nations Conference on Trade and Development (UNCTAD)

International – English quarterly

Provides statistical data on tungsten ores and concentrates and tungsten products including prices, production, consumption, trade and stocks.

03021 **CA QUARTERLY: FACTS & FIGURES ON AUSTRIA'S ECONOMY**
Creditanstalt Bankverein

Austria – English quarterly 30pp

Articles on Austria's economy and selected economic indicators.

03022 **CHART-SERVICE**
Girozentrale Vienna

Austria – German/English fortnightly 1986 60pp 2580-AS/year

Data on companies' performance on the Vienna Stock Exchange.

03023 **COUNTRY PROFILES**
Economist Publications Ltd

Austria – English annual 40pp £25 UK, subscription varies in rest of world

Resumé of politics, economy and industry including statistical summaries.

03024 **COUNTRY REPORTS**
Economist Publications Ltd

Austria – English quarterly 25pp £58 UK, subscription varies in rest of world

Economic policies and development plans, trends in production and demand, monetary and fiscal conditions, wages and prices, merchandise, trade, invisibles, capital flows, exchange rates and foreign debt plus a forecast of the economic prospects.

03025 **DEMOGRAPHISCHES JAHRBUCH OSTERREICHS**
Osterreichische Statistische Zentralamt

Austria – German annual AS290.00

Annual demographic data on births, deaths, marriages, divorces and internal migration. Also contains three alternative population projections.

03026 **EINKOMMENSTEURSTATISTIK**
Osterreichische Statistische Zentralamt

Austria – German annual 130pp AS260.00

Statistics on income tax.

03027 **EMPIRICA**
Nationalokonomische Gesellschaft

Austria – English/German twice yearly 250pp AS200.000-300.000
ISSN No. 0340/8744

Austrian economic papers.

03028 **ENERGIEVERBRAUCH DER HAUSHALTE IM JAHRE**
Osterreichische Statistische Zentralamt

Austria – German biennial 180pp AS160

Data on energy consumption of households.

03029 **ENERGIEVERSORGUNG OSTERREICHS**
Osterreichische Statistische Zentralamt

Austria – German monthly 175pp AS570.00

Statistics on energy.

03030 **ERGEBNISSE DER LANDWIRTSCHAFTLICHEN STATISTIK IM JAHR ...**
Osterreichische Statistische Zentralamt

Austria – German annual 128pp AS230.00

Annual statistics on agriculture giving details of land under cultivation, crop yields, size of herds and machinery used. The data is analysed by province.

03031 **FINANZ ZEITUNG**
Girozentrale Vienna

Austria – German monthly

Financial news designed for the non-specialist.

03032 **FOREIGN TRADE: A GUIDE FOR AUSTRIAN EXPORTERS AND IMPORTERS**
Girozentrale Vienna

Austria – German/English 90pp free

Gives information on finance for foreign trade, foreign exchange etc.

03033 **DER FREMDENVERKEHR IN OSTERREICH IM JAHRE...**
Osterreichische Statistische Zentralamt

Austria – German annual 300pp AS380.00

Detailed information on foreign visitors to Austria giving figures for the month, half-year and year.

03034 **GEBARUNGSUBERSICHTEN**
Osterreichische Statistische Zentralamt

Austria – German annual 300pp AS530

Data on public expenditure and administration.

03035 **GELD UND KREDITWESEN, PRIVATVERSICHERUNG 1983**
Osterreichische Statistische Zentralamt

Austria – German every 5-7 years 406pp AS560.00

Statistics on money, credit and insurance derived from the 1983 census.

03036 **GEWERBESTATISTIK**
Osterreichische Statistische Zentralamt

Austria – German annual 2 vols 350pp AS520

Industrial statistics covering volume and value of output of industries with data for the preceding year. Vol. 1 covers major industries. Vol. 2 gives figures for establishments with less than 20 employees.

03037 **GEWERBESTEUERSTATISTIK**
Osterreichische Statistische Zentralamt

Austria – German annual 150pp AS230

Statistics on the taxation of industry.

03038 **GROSS-UND EINZELHANDELSSTATISTIK**
Osterreichische Statistische Zentralamt

Austria – German annual 120pp AS170

Statistics on wholesale and retail businesses analysed by product and district.

03039 **GROSSZAHLUNG 1981: AUSGEWAHLTE MASSZAHLEN NACH GEMEINDEN**
Osterreichische Statistische Zentralamt

Austria – German AS200

Selected statistical parameters of the 1981 Census by community, giving data on population, employment, housing etc.

03040 **GRUNDERWERG**
Osterreichische Statistiche Zentralamt

Austria – German annual AS50

Data on land and property prices.

03041 **HANDBUCH FUR INVESTORENINFORMATION**
Bundesministerium fur Wirtschaftliche Angelegenheiten

Austria – German 1985 AS500

Handbook for potential investors in Austria giving details of legal requirements, infrastructure, subsidies.

03042 **HANDELS REGISTER OSTERREICH**
Jupiter-Verlag

Austria – German

Directory of Austrian businesses giving addresses, chief executives, major products or services.

03043 **HINTS TO EXPORTERS**
Department of Trade and Industry

Austria – English annual

Practical guide for businessmen giving general information, useful addresses, methods of doing business and relevant regulations.

03044 **INDEX DER GROSSHANDELSPREISE REVISION 1986**
Osterreichische Statistische Zentralamt

Austria – German AS70

Index of wholesale prices.

03045 **INDEX DER VERBRAUCHERPREISE REVISION 1986**
Osterreichische Statistische Zentralamt

Austria – German AS70

Index of consumer prices.

03046 **INDUSTRIE UND GEWERBESTATISTIK**
Osterreichische Statistische Zentralamt

Austria – German annual 300pp AS310

Industrial and manufacturing statistics.

03047 **INDUSTRIESTATISTIK**
Osterreichische Statistische Zentralamt

Austria – German annual 600pp AS580

Industrial statistics.

03048 **INFORMATIONSDIENST WAHRUNG WIRTSCHAFT INTERNATIONAL***
Creditanstalt Bankverein

Austria – German weekly free

Newsletter giving information on the currency and economy of Austria.

03049 **DER INTENSIVOBSTBAU IN OSTERREICH**
Osterreichische Statistische Zentralamt

Austria – German every 3 years AS250

Statistics on the fruit farming industry.

03050 **INVESTING AND FINANCING IN AUSTRIA**
Girozentrale Vienna

Austria – German /English 1986

03051 **JAHRESBERICHT**
Fachverband der Erdolindustrie Osterreichs

Austria – German annual

A review of the Austrian petroleum industry including statistics.

03052 **JAHRESBERICHT DES LANDESFREMDENVERKEHRSAMTES: TEIL II: STATISTIK**
Ober Osterreich Verkaufsforderund Landes-Fremdenverkehrsverband

Austria – German annual 36pp

Statistics on tourism in Upper Austria.

03053 **JAHRBUCH DER WIENER BORSE***
Creditanstalt Bankverein

Austria – German annual

Yearbook of the Viennese stock exchange.

03054 **KONSUMERHEBUNG 1984 HAUPTERGEBNISSE**
Osterreichische Statistische Zentralamt

Austria – German every 10 years 113pp AS120

Survey of household consumption.

03055 **KRAFTFAHRZEUGZULASSEN NACH ZULASSUNGSBEHORDEN**
Osterreichische Statistische Zentralamt

Austria – German monthly

Data on motor vehicle registrations according to registration authority.

03056 **LANDERBERICHT OSTERREICH**
Federal Statistical Office of Germany

Austria – German irregular DM7.90

Statistical survey of Austria including such areas as demography, geography, education, employment, agriculture, production, overseas trade, transport, tourism, finance, wages and prices and national accounts.

03057 **LAND-UND FORSTWIRTSCHAFTLICHE ARBEITSKRAFTE**
Osterreichische Statistiche Zentralamt

Austria – German every 3-4 years AS370

Statistical data on land and forest under cultivation.

03058 **LANDWIRTSCHAFTLICHE MASCHINENZAHLUNG**
Osterreichische Statistische Zentralamt

Austria – German every 5 years 126pp AS190

Results of a survey of agricultural machinery and equipment. There is also comparative international data.

03059 **LOHNSTEUERSTATISTIK**
Osterreichische Statistische Zentralamt

Austria – German annual 200pp AS350

Statistics on wages, taxes and national insurance.

03060 **MADE IN AUSTRIA**
Jupiter-Verlag

Austria – German/English/French

Directory of Austrian exports designed to inform foreign businessmen interested in Austrian products. It gives information on financial services, methods of transport and carriage and details of exports classified by product group. There is also a register of firms engaged in foreign trade.

03061 **MARKET INDICATORS**
Girozentrale Vienna

Austria – German/English quarterly c10pp free

Brief survey of the Austrian economy.

03062 **MIKROZENSUS– JAHRESERGEBNISSE**
Osterreichische Statistische Zentralamt

Austria – German annual 190pp AS250

Data on population, industry, living conditions, demographic and socio-economic characteristics derived from the partial census.

03063 **MONATLICHE KRAFTFAHRZEUG-ZULASSUNGSSTATISTIK**
Osterreichische Statistische Zentralamt

Austria – German monthly AS3000 annual

Monthly statistics on vehicle registrations.

03064 **MONATSBERICHTE DES OSTERREICHISCHEN INSTITUTS FUR WIRTSCHAFTSFORSCHUNG**
Osterreichische Institut fur Wirtschaftsforschung

Austria – German monthly 1927 125pp AS1650 yearly

Monthly report on the development of the Austrian economy including a statistical survey.

03065 **MONATSBERICHTE UBER DIE OSTERREICHISCHE LANDWIRTSCHAFT**
Bundesanstalt fur Agrarwirtschaft

Austria – German monthly 1952 100pp AS870

Monthly review of Austrian agriculture including production, market and price.

03066 **NUTZENERGIEANALYSE**
Osterreichische Statistische Zentralamt

Austria – German every 5 years 80pp AS100

Data on energy usage and energy issues.

03067 **NUTZTIERHALTUNG IN OSTERREICH**
Osterreichische Statistische Zentralamt

Austria – German biennial 230pp AS330

A census of working animals.

03068 **OECD ECONOMIC SURVEYS–AUSTRIA**
OECD

Austria–English annual 70pp £2.40/DM12/US$5/FrF24

Provides a detailed analysis of recent developments in demand, production, employment, prices and wages, conditions in the money and capital markets and developments in the balance of payments. It includes short-term forecasts as well as analyses of medium-term problems of specific relevance to the elaboration of the country's economic policies.

03069 **OSTERREICH, TATSACHEN UND ZAHLEN**
Bundespressedienst

Austria – German/English/French/Russian/Italian/Spanish/Portuguese/Arabic/Dutch/Serbo-Croat, summaries in Japanese, Hungarian and Indonesian

Facts and figures on Austria.

03070 **OSTERREICH IN ZAHLEN**
Bundespressedienst

Austria – German/English/French/Spanish/Italian/Portuguese annual

Statistics on all aspects of life in Austria.

03071 **OSTERREICHES VOLKSEINKOMMEN**
Osterreichistische Statistische Zentralamt

Austria – German annual 280pp AS240

Data on national income.

03072 **OSTERREICHS WIRTSCHAFT IN ZAHLEN**
Creditanstalt Bankverein

Austria – German/English/French annual free

The Austrian economy in figures.

03073 **DIE OSTERREICHISCHE TEXTILINDUSTRIE IM JAHRE**
Fachverband der Textilindustrie Osterreichs

Austria – German annual 60pp

Annual report for the Austrian textile industry giving statistics on production, foreign trade and investment.

03074 **PERSONEN–UND HAUSHALTSEINKOMMEN VON UNSELBSTANDIG BESCHAFTIGTEN UND PENSIONISTEN, ERGEBNISSE DES MIKROZENSUS SEPTEMBER 1985**
Osterreichische Statistische Zentralamt

Austria – German every 3 years AS110

Data on employees' income for individuals and households.

03075 **PFERDE–UND RINDERRASSENERBEBUNG IM JAHRE ...**
Osterreichische Statistische Zentralamt

Austria – German every 8-10 years 45pp AS160.00

Statistics on stocks of horses and cattle.

03076 **REISEGEWOHNHEITEN DER OSTERREICHER IN DEN JAHREN ...(HAUPTURLAUBE, KURZURLAUBE, DIENST UND GESCHAFTSREINEN, KURAUFENTHALTE)**
Osterreichische Statistische Zentralamt

Austria – German AS240

Details of journeys including reasons, duration, frequency and type of traffic employed. Both inland and external journeys are covered.

03077 **REPORT ON THE AUSTRIAN ECONOMY**
Osterreichische Landerbank

Austria – English quarterly 8pp free

Business, exchange and foreign trade information, statistical information.

03078 **SCHRIFTTUM DER AGRARWIRTSCHAFT FUR AGRARWIRTSCHAFT**
Bundesanstalt fur Agrarwirtschaft

Austria – German twice monthly 1961 90pp AS710

Literature in agricultural economics including regional planning, agricultural science and agrarian politics.

03079 **SOZIALSTATISTICHE AUSWERTUNGEN AUS DER KONSUMERHEBUNG 1984**
Osterreichische Statistische Zentralamt

Austria – German every 10 years AS100

Data on household structure and expenditure.

03080 **STATISTIK DER AKTIENGESELLSCHAFTEN IN OSTERREICH IM JAHRE ...**
Osterreichische Statistische Zentralamt

Austria – German annual 135pp AS250

Statistics on Austrian joint stock companies.

03081 **STATISTISCHE DATEN OSTERREICH**
Osterreichische Landerbank

Austria – German/English annual 16pp free

Statistical data about Austria.

03082 **STATISTISCHE NACHRICHTEN**
Osterreichische Statistische Zentralamt

Austria – German monthly AS1,060 annually

Monthly statistical newsletter which contains in addition to statistical data on all aspects of the population and economy, a textual commentary and background information.

03083 **STATISTISCHER BERICHT**
Fachverband der Textilindustrie Osterreichs

Austria – German quarterly 15pp

Statistics on the Austrian textile industry including production and overseas trade.

03084 **STATISTISCHES HANDBUCH FUR DIE REPUBLIK OSTERREICH**
Osterreichische Statistische Zentralamt

Austria – German (English subtitles) annual 666pp AS570

Annual statistical handbook containing tables on: population, agriculture, industry, energy, tourism, finance, foreign trade, transport, employment, education, social welfare, education and culture. There are also comparative international statistics.

03085 **STRASSENVERKEHR-SICHERHEIT IM JAHRE...**
Osterreichische Statistische Zentralamt

Austria – German annual 231pp AS310

Details of road traffic including numbers of accidents and damage caused to both people and property. Also gives details of driving licences issued.

03086 **SURVEY OF THE AUSTRIAN ECONOMY**
ORAC Publishing House (Austrian Museum for Economic and Social Affairs)

Austria – German/English annual 70pp
ISBN No. 385368789X–German edition
ISBN No. 3853687903–English edition

Presents in popularized form a picture of Austria's economy and its international position.

03087 **UMSATZSTEUERSTATISTIK**
Osterreichische Statistische Zentralamt

Austria – German annual 120pp

Statistics on value added tax.

03088 **UMWELTBEDINGUNGEN DES WOHNENS**
Osterreichische Statistische Zentralamt

Austria – German every 3 years 93pp AS110

Data collected during the partial census on damage caused to houses by external factors and including the characteristics of dwelling places such as facilities in general.

03089 VERMOGENSTEUERSTATISTIK
Osterreichische Statistische Zentralamt

Austria – German every 3 years 280pp AS520

Statistics on property tax.

03090 VIENNA STOCK EXCHANGE... THE MOST IMPORTANT FACTS
Wiener Borsekammer

Austria – English annual 10pp free

A brief survey of the Vienna stock exchange including a list of other publications.

03091 VOLKSZAHLUNG 1981
Osterreichische Statistische Zentralamt

Austria – German every 10 years

Results of the 1981 population census:
Final results classified by parish -AS40.00
Burgenland-AS90
Karnten-AS90
Niederosterreich-AS150
Oberosterreich AS140
Salzburg-AS90
Steiermark-AS150
Tirol-AS100
Vorarlberg-AS70
Wien-AS90
Osterreich-AS90
Householders and families-AS110
Inland migration-AS100
Schools and students-AS220
Employees by employment and commuting-AS220
Educational qualitifications-AS220

03092 DER WEINBAU IN OSTERREICH
Osterreichische Statistische Zentralamt

Austria – German biennial 120pp AS230

Statistics on Austrian viniculture.

03093 WIRTSCHAFTSBERICHT
Bundesministerium fur Finanzen

Austria – German annual 1972 free

A review of the economy of Austria.

03094 WIRTSCHAFTSBERICHTE*
Creditanstalt Bankverein

Austria – German quarterly c50pp free

Specialist articles on all aspects of the Austrian economy.

03095 WIRTSCHAFTSSTATISTIK DER ELEKTRIZTATSVERSORG-UNGUNTERNEHMEN
Osterreichische Statistische Zentralamt

Austria – German annual 55pp AS80

Information on structure and performance of the electricity industry.

03096 WOHNUNGSDATEN
Osterreichische Statistische Zentralamt

Austria – German annual 256pp 2 vols AS420

This publication collates two collections of statistics – house building statistics and the results of the partial census which gives details of the types of house and their facilities. Both volumes give details for the whole country and also for the larger districts.

03097 ZIVILLUFTFAHRT IN OSTERREICH
Osterreichische Statistische Zentralamt

Austria – English/German annual 147pp AS170

Statistics on the development and structure of air traffic in Austria, including the respective shares of both Austrian airlines and foreign airlines.

BELGIUM

04001 **ANNALES DES MINES DE BELGIQUE***
Ministere des Affaires Economiques, Administration des Mines

Belgium – French/Dutch monthly

Statistics relevant to the mining industry.

04002 **ANNUAIRE STATISTIQUE**
Federation Professionelle des Producteurs et Distributeurs d'Electricite de Belgique

Belgium – French annual 75pp

Statistical data on equipment, production and consumption of electricity.

04003 **ANNUAIRE STATISTIQUE DE LA BELGIQUE**
Institut National de Statistique

Belgium – French/Dutch annual BF1235

General statistics on all aspects of economic and social conditions.

04004 **ANNUAIRE STATISTIQUE/ STATISTISCH JAARBOEK–FIGAZ**
FIGAZ–Federation de l'Industrie du Gaz

Belgium – French/Dutch 50pp

Statistical Yearbook of the Belgian Gas Industry Federation.

04006 **ANNUAIRE STATISTIQUE DE POCHE**
Institut National de Statistique

Belgium – French/Dutch annual BF190

Statistical pocket book giving abridged figures from the 'Annuaire Statistique de la Belgique'.

04007 **ANNUAIRE DES STATISTIQUES REGIONALES**
Institut National de Statistique

Belgium – French/Dutch annual BF560

Regional statistics on population, housing, public health, agriculture, industry and finance, education, energy, transport and services, social issues.

04008 **ANNUAL REPORT–BANQUE NATIONALE DE BELGIQUE**
Banque Nationale de Belgique

Belgium – French/Dutch/English annual c150pp

Annual report including survey of the economy of the country.

04009 **ANNUAL REPORT–FEDERATION BELGE DES ENTREPRISES DE DISTRIBUTION**
Federation Belge des Entreprises de Distribution

Belgium – French/Dutch annual 1977 70pp BF150/BF250 overseas

Information on distribution in Belgium.

04010 **ANNUAL REPORT–FEDERATION DE L'INDUSTRIE CIMENTIERE**
Federation de l'Industrie Cimentiere

Belgium – French/Dutch annual

Annual report of the Federation of the Cement Industry.

04011 **ANNUAL REPORT–FETRA**
FETRA–Federation des Industries Transformatrices de Papier et Carton

Belgium – French/Dutch annual

Annual report of the Belgian Federation of Paper and Cardboard Processors in two parts: general report, statistical yearbook.

04012 **ANNUAL REPORT–FIGAZ**
FIGAZ–Federation de l'Industrie du Gaz

Belgium – French/Dutch annual

Annual report of the Belgian Gas Industry Federation.

04013 **APERCU ECONOMIQUE TRIMESTRIAL**
Ministry of Economic Affairs

Belgium – French/Dutch quarterly 1984 150pp BF850

Economic analysis covering Belgium and its seven most important trading partners. Includes tables and charts.

04014 **L'ASSURANCE EN BELGIQUE DE VERZEKERING IN BELGIE**
UPEA–Union Professionnelle des Entreprises d'Assurances Belges et Etrangeres operant en Belgique

Belgium – French/Dutch annual

Annual report of the official federation of insurance companies.

04015 **AUTOMOBILE REVIEW**
Fabrimetal

Belgium – French/Dutch annual 114pp BF530

Review of the car industry.

04016 **BLEU–EXCHANGE REGULATIONS**
Kredietbank NV

Belgium – Dutch/French

04017 **BLEU–EXCHANGE REGULATIONS IN RESPECT OF FOREIGN AND DOMESTIC ACCOUNTS**
Kredietbank NV

Belgium – Dutch/French 15pp

04018 **BELGIAN EXPORTS**
Verlag Hoppenstedt & Co.

Belgium – English/French/German/Spanish annual

2 volumes covering exported products and export trade in industrial products and services, consumer goods, non-food and food, commercial gardening and farming.

04019 **BELGIUM/LUXEMBOURG**
UK Iron & Steel Statistics Bureau

Belgium and Luxembourg – English 1986 with annual statistical summary £25.00

Report on the steel industry showing production, consumption and details of imports and exports.

04020 **BELGISCH ABC**
Verlag Hoppenstedt & Co.
Belgisch ABC

Belgium and Luxembourg – Dutch/French annual 1900pp DM162.50

Information on 18,000 manufacturers, importers and products.

04021 **BETON**
FEBE – Federation de l'Industrie du Beton

Belgium – French/Dutch bi-monthly

General review of the concrete industry.

04022 **BULLETIN**
Kamer voor Handel en Nijverheid van Het Arrondissement Leuven

Belgium – Dutch monthly 10pp BF100

Monthly bulletin of the Louvain Chamber of Commerce, covering local economic projects, small business projects and promotion of regional industry.

04023 **BULLETIN DES ASSURANCES DE VERZEKERING**
UPEA–Union Professionnelle des Entreprises d'Assurances Belges et Etrangeres operant en Belgique

Belgium – French/Dutch 4 times yearly

Bulletin giving information on legal and other scientific aspects of insurance.

04024 **BULLETIN DE LA BANQUE NATIONALE DE BELGIQUE**
Banque Nationale de Belgique

Belgium – French/Dutch monthly BF650.00 annual

Economic bulletin.

04025 **BULLETIN FEBELGRA TIJDSCHRIFT FEBELGRA**
FEBELGRA–Federation Belge des Industries Graphiques

Belgium – French/Dutch bi-monthly

Official bulletin of the federation of graphic industries.

04026 **BULLETIN DE LA FEDERATION DES ENTREPRISES DE BELGIQUE***
Federation des Entreprises de Belgique

Belgium – French/Dutch every ten days BF1,480 annually

General review of the economy.

04027 **BULLETIN FINANCIER***
Banque Bruxelles Lambert

Belgium – French bi-monthly 8pp free

Review of the world monetary situation with reference to the implications for the Belgian economy.

04028 **BULLETIN MENSUEL DE L'ENERGIE ELECTRIQUE**
Administratie voor Energie

Belgium – French monthly c40pp

Statistical data on electricity.

04029 **BULLETIN DE STATISTIQUE**
Institut National de Statistique

Belgium – French/Dutch monthly BF2035

Monthly statistical bulletin.

04030 **CAUSES DE DECES**
Institut National de Statistique

Belgium – Dutch/French annual BF530

Figures for causes of death.

04031 **COMMUNIQUE HEBDOMADAIRE**
Institut National de Statistique

Belgium – French/Dutch weekly BF1,425

Weekly statistical bulletin.

04032 **LES COMPTES NATIONAUX DE LA BELGIQUE**
Institut National de Statistique

Belgium – French annual 80pp
ISSN No. 0069 8075

A detailed breakdown of the national accounts, giving 10 years' figures.

04033 **LA CONSTRUCTION/HET BOUWBEDRIFF**
Confederation Nationale de la Construction

Belgium – French/Dutch weekly 36pp BF5,000

Information on the building industry.

04034 **CONVERSION COMPANIES**
Kredietbank NV

Belgium – Dutch/French/English 1987 10pp

04035 **COURRIER HEBDOMADAIRE***
Centre de Recherche et d'Information Socio-Politique–CRISP

Belgium – French weekly c40pp BF7,500

Journal presenting the result of research projects carried out by the centre, on themes of politics and social life throughout Europe but with particular emphasis on Belgium.

04036 **COUNTRY PROFILES**
Economist Publications Ltd

Belgium and Luxembourg – English annual 40pp £25 UK, subscription varies in rest of world

Resumé of politics, economy and industry including statistical summaries.

04037 **COUNTRY REPORTS**
Economist Publications Ltd

Belgium and Luxembourg – English quarterly 25pp £58 UK subscription varies in rest of world

Economic policies and development plans, trends in production and demand, monetary and fiscal conditions, wages and prices, merchandise trade, invisibles, capital flows, exchange rates and foreign debt plus a forecast of the economic prospects.

04038 **CRITERES DE RENTABILITE EN AGRICULTURE: NOTIONS ET RESULTATS**
Institut Economique Agricole
R. Debergh

Belgium – French 1986 58pp

A study of profitability in Belgian agriculture.

04039 **L'ECONOMIE BELGE**
Ministere des Affaires Economiques

Belgium – French annual 2 vols BF500.00 pt 1 BF800.00 pt 2

Economic survey.

04040 **ENTERPRISE ZONES IN FLANDERS: RECOMMENDED LOCATIONS FOR THE REALIZATION OF YOUR PLANS**
Kredietbank NV

Belgium – Dutch/French/English 1987 10pp

04041 **ENTREPRENDRE***
Chambre de Commerce de Bruxelles

Belgium – French monthly c100pp

Official journal of the chamber of commerce with current news on all aspects of business and finance.

04042 **ESTIMATION DU REVENUE AGRICOLE EN1986**
Institut Economique Agricole
A. Mottoulle

Belgium – French 1987 11pp

Estimation of agricultural revenues in Belgium.

04043 **EVOLUTION COMPAREE DES STRUCTURES DE L'AGRICULTURE WALLONNE ET FLAMANDE AU COURS DE LA PERIODE 1970-1985**
Institut Economique Agricole
J.M. Van Haeperen

Belgium – French 1987 36pp

A comparison of Walloon and Flemish agriculture.

04044 **HINTS TO EXPORTERS**
Department of Trade and Industry

Belgium – English annual

Practical guide for businessmen giving general information, useful addresses, methods of doing business and relevant regulations.

04045 INNOVATION COMPANIES
Kredietbank NV

Belgium – Dutch/French/English 1987 10pp

04046 INVESTMENT INCENTIVES IN BELGIUM
Kredietbank NV

Belgium – Dutch/French/English 1987 120pp

04047 THE JOURNAL
Belgo-Luxembourg Chamber of Commerce in Great Britain

Belgium – English 9 issues per year 25pp £5.00

Articles on economic, business and trade subjects. Also full reports on the activities of the Chamber.

04048 KOMPASS REGISTER
Kompass Publishers, UK

Belgium – English/French/German/Spanish/Italian annual £120.00

Comprehensive business directory giving information on over 15,000 companies listed geographically and cross-referenced to a directory of products and services.

04049 LETTRE DE CONJONCTURE
Ministere des Affaires Economiques

Belgium – French monthly 5pp BF350
ISSN No. 0772 0831

'Statistics on industrial production, employment, prices, consumption and public finance.

04050 MARKETING CONSUMER GOODS–BELGIUM, 1986
Department of Trade and Industry

Belgium – English irregular 36pp

Gives information on the market for consumer goods, distribution and buyers as well as general business information.

04051 MONTHLY REVIEW AND MONTHLY NEWSLETTER
Kamer voor Handel en Nijverheid van Het Gewest Gent

Belgium – Dutch monthly

Review of the Gent Chamber of Commerce and newsletter with trade purposes.

04052 MOUVEMENT DE LA POPULATION DES COMMUNES BELGES
Institut National de Statistique

Belgium – Dutch/French BF85 annually

Population figures.

04053 NEWSLETTER–FIGAZ
FIGAZ–Federation de l'Industrie du Gaz

Belgium–French/Dutch monthly

Newsletter of the Federation of Gas Industries.

04054 NOMBRE DE DETENTEURS D'APPAREILS DE RADIO ET DE TELEVISION
Institut National de Statistique

Belgium – Dutch/French annual BF315

Figures on radio and television owners.

04055 NOTES MENSUELLES SUR LA SITUATION ECONOMIQUE
Conseil Central de l'Economie

Belgium – French monthly 26pp

Gives data on economic activity, consumption, prices, public finance and employment.

04056 OECD ECONOMIC SURVEYS–BELGIUM-LUXEMBOURG
OECD

Belgium and Luxembourg – English annual 70pp £2.40/DM12/US$5/FrF24

Provides a detailed analysis of recent developments in demand production, employment, prices and wages, conditions in the money and capital markets and developments in the balance of payments. It includes short-term forecasts as well as analyses of medium-term problems of specific relevance to the elaboration of the countries' economic policies.

04057 PARC DES VEHICULES A MOTEUR
Institut National de Statistique

Belgium – Dutch/French annually BF390

Statistics on car parking and numbers of vehicles.

04058 PERSPECTIVES DE POPULATION–LE ROYAUME 1981-2025
Institut National de Statistique

Belgium – Dutch/French BF350
Part 1: Methodology and principal results
Part 2: Belgium and the regions
Part 3: the Provinces

Population perspectives to 2025.

04059 POPULATION DES COMMUNES FUSIONNEES
Institut National de Statistique

Belgium – French/Dutch BF70

Population figures for districts.

04060 PROJECTION DE L'AGRICULTURE JUSQ'EN L'AN 2000: NOMBRE ET DIMENSION DES EXPLOITATIONS
Institut Economique Agricole
G. Pevenage and H. Everaet

Belgium – French 1986 20pp

Forecasts on the number and size of agricultural concerns in Belgium to the year 2000.

04061 RAPPORT DU GOUVERNEMENT–EVOLUTION DE L'ECONOMIE AGRICOLE ET HORTICOLE
Institut Economique Agricole

Belgium – French annual 180pp

Government report on the Belgian agricultural and horticultural industries.

04062 RECENSEMENT AGRICOLE ET HORTICOLE
Institut National de Statistique

Belgium – Dutch/French annual BF200

Agricultural and horticultural census.

04063 RECENSEMENT DE LA CIRCULATION ROUTIERE
Institut National de Statistique

Belgium – Dutch/French every 5 years BF200

Census of road traffic.

04064 RECENSEMENT DE LA POPULATION ET DES LOGEMENTS AU 1 MARS 1981
Institut National de Statistique

Belgium – French every 10 years BF200-400 per part

In various volumes, some giving general results, some on specific subjects such as housing, nationality and educational level.

04065 RECUEIL STATISTIQUE/STATISTISCHE GEGEVENS
Federation des Entreprises de Metaux Non Ferreux

Belgium – French/Dutch annual 70pp

Statistics on production, import and export for the non-ferrous metals industry.

04066 LA RENTABILITE DE L'EXPLOITATION AGRICOLE EN 1985-1986
Institut Economique Agricole

Belgium – French 1987 71pp

Data on the profitability of Belgian agriculture.

04067 REVENUS IMPOSABLES DES PERSONNES PHYSIQUES
Institut National de Statistique

Belgium – Dutch/French annual BF275

Figures for personal taxation giving also regional distribution according to the level of revenue.

04068 **REVIEW OF FABRIMETAL**
Fabrimetal

Belgium – French/Dutch/German/English biennial 600pp BF2,120

Review of metal manufacturing industry, mechanical engineering, electrotechnical engineering and electronics, transportation materials, and plastic conversion.

04069 **REVUE DU TRAVAIL***
Ministere de l'Emploi et du Travail

Belgium – French/Dutch monthly BF300.00 annual

Official journal of the Ministry of Labour.

04070 **SERVICE DE CONJONCTURE/ BUSINESS TRENDS SURVEY**
Institut de Recherches Economiques

Belgium – French/English monthly/ quarterly 1937 60pp BF119,000 (1987) per year

Survey of international and national recent economic developments and macroeconomic short- to medium-term forecasts.

04071 **LA SIDERURGIE**
Groupement de la Siderurgie

Belgium – French annual 50pp

Report on iron and steel industry including data on the market, prices, production, investments and employment.

04072 **STATISTICAL REVIEW**
Fabrimetal

Belgium – French/Dutch every 5 years 100pp free

Statistical review of metal manufacturing industry, mechanical engineering, electrotechnical engineering and electronics, transportation materials and plastic conversion.

04073 **STATISTICAL YEARBOOK**
FIGAZ–Federation de l'Industrie du Gaz

Belgium – French/Dutch annual

Statistical yearbook of the Belgian Federation of Gas Industries.

04074 **STATISTIQUE ANNUELLE***
Ministere des Affaires Economiques, Administration des Mines

Belgium – French/Dutch annual c60pp free

Annual statistics for the consumption and production of coal, coke, iron and steel, and quarried minerals. Includes employment figures.

04075 **STATISTIQUE MENSUELLE***
Ministere des Affaires Economiques, Administration des Mines

Belgium – French/Dutch monthly free

Statistics on coal, coke, iron and steel and quarrying covering both production and consumption.

04076 **STATISTIQUES**
Federation de l'Industrie du Verre

Belgium – French/Dutch annual July/ August 1980 15pp free

Official statistics about the glass industry in Belgium.

04077 **STATISTIQUES AGRICOLES**
Institut National de Statistique

Belgium – Dutch/French quarterly BF1600/ year

Agricultural statistics.

04078 **STATISTIQUE ANNUELLE DE LA PRODUCTION**
Institut National de Statistique

Belgium – Dutch/French annual BF390

Production statistics for industry.

04079 **STATISTIQUES ANNUELLE DU TRAFFIC INTERNATIONAL DES PORTS**
Institut National de Statistique

Belgium – Dutch/French annual 2 vols BF300 per volume

Statistics on international traffic in ports.

04080 **STATISTIQUES DU COMMERCE EXTERIEUR DE L'UNION ECONOMIQUE BELGO-LUXEMBOURGEOISE**
Institut National de Statistique

Belgium and Luxembourg – French annual BF660

Foreign trade.

04081 **STATISTIQUES DU COMMERCE EXTERIEUR DE L'UNION ECONOMIQUE BELGO-LUXEMBOURGEOISE**
Institut National de Statistique

Belgium and Luxembourg – French/Dutch monthly BF6170

Monthly statistical bulletin on foreign trade in the Belgo-Luxembourg economic union.

04082 **STATISTIQUES DU COMMERCE INTERIEUR ET DU TRANSPORT**
Institut National de Statistique

Belgium – Dutch/French monthly BF2000

Trade statistics covering retail and wholesale trade, tourism and transport.

04083 **STATISTIQUES DE LA CONSTRUCTION ET DU LOGEMENT**
Institut National de Statistique

Belgium–Dutch/French 1986 BF425 annual

Statistics on building and housing.

04084 **STATISTIQUES DEMOGRAPHIQUES**
Institut National de Statistique

Belgium – Dutch/French irregular + 3 issues per year BF590

04085 **STATISTIQUES FINANCIERES**
Institut National de Statistique

Belgium – French/Dutch irregular BF730/ year

Statistics on finance covering all aspects of taxation of individuals and sales of real estate.

04086 **STATISTIQUES INDUSTRIELLES**
Institut National de Statistique

Belgium – Dutch/French monthly BF1800

Industrial production statistics.

04087 **STATISTIQUES SOCIALES**
Institut National de Statistique

Belgium – Dutch/French irregular BF590 per year

Social statistics including prices, salaries, accidents at work, and strikes.

04088 **TAX AND INVESTMENT PROFILE**
Touche Ross International, USA

Belgium – English free

Survey covering investment, trade, labour, business practices, financial system. Frequently updated.

04089 **TRADE ENQUIRIES**
Belgo Luxembourg Chamber of Commerce in Great Britain

Belgium – English semi-monthly 2pp free

Contains trade enquiries and business opportunities between the 3 countries.

04090 **LES TRANSPORTS EN BELGIQUE**
Ministere des Communications

Belgium – French annual 200pp

Detailed statistics on road, rail, air and waterborne transport.

04091 **VADEMECUM DES ENTREPRISES**
Ministere des Affaires Economiques

Belgium – French/Dutch 1988

Regulations relevant to industry and commercial enterprises including details of assistance to industrial projects.

04092 VEHICULES A MOTEUR NEUFS MIS EN CIRCULATION
Institut National de Statistique

Belgium – Dutch/French annual BF390

Statistics on numbers of new cars in circulation.

04093 YEARBOOK
Belgo-Luxembourg Chamber of Commerce in Great Britain

Belgium – English annual 1987 90pp £8.00

Contains commercial and economic news, latest national statistics, useful addresses and a classified list of companies.

BULGARIA

05001 **ABECOR COUNTRY REPORT – BULGARIA**
Abecor

Bulgaria – English 1986 2pp free

Brief economic report.

05002 **BULGARIA–ECONOMIC DEVELOPMENT**
Bulgarian Chamber of Commerce and Industry

Bulgaria – English/French/German/Spanish/Russian annual 1980 40pp free

An annual review of the country's economic development and foreign trade performance.

05003 **BULGARIA – FOREIGN ECONOMIC RELATIONS**
Bulgarian Chamber of Commerce and Industry

Bulgaria – English/French/German every 2-3 years 1984 70pp free

A practical analysis of Bulgaria's trade and economic relations with foreign countries.

05004 **BULGARIA–TECHNO-SCIENTIFIC AND SOCIO-ECONOMIC DEVELOPMENT 1986-1990**
Bulgarian Chamber of Commerce and Industry

Bulgaria – English/French/German/Spanish/Russian 1987 23pp free

Guidelines of the country's development during the period 1986-1990.

05005 **BULGARIA IN FIGURES**
Bulgarian Chamber of Commerce and Industry

Bulgaria – English/French/German/Spanish/Russian every 2-3 years 1983 15-20pp free

Statistical data by main indicators of the socio-economic development of Bulgaria.

05006 **BULGARIAN FOREIGN TRADE**
Bulgarian Chamber of Commerce and Industry

Bulgaria – English/Russian/French/German six issues per year 1951 48pp US$48
ISSN No. 0204 8892

News of Bulgarian trade, new products and business opportunities.

05007 **BULGARIAN FOREIGN TRADE ORGANIZATIONS**
Bulgarian Chamber of Commerce and Industry

Bulgaria – English/French/German/Spanish annual 1953 70pp free

Address and short description of activity of the foreign trade organizations.

05008 **BULGARIAN TRADE UNIONS**
Collets Holdings Ltd

Bulgaria – English bi-monthly £11.80

05009 **BULGARIA'S ECONOMIC RELATIONS WITH THE DEVELOPING COUNTRIES**
Bulgarian Chamber of Commerce and Industry

Bulgaria – English/French/Spanish/Arabic every 2-3 years 1983 40pp free

Development and structure of trade, forms and fields of cooperation.

05010 **BULGARSKA TYUTYUNI**
Collets Holdings Ltd

Bulgaria – Bulgarian bi-monthly £22.40

05011 **BULGARSKI PROFSAYUZI**
Collets Holdings Ltd

Bulgaria – Bulgarian monthly £16.00

05012 **COUNTRY PROFILES–ROMANIA, BULGARIA, ALBANIA**
Economist Publications Ltd

Bulgaria – English annual 40pp £25 UK, subscription varies in rest of world

Resumé of politics, economy and industry including statistical summaries.

05013 **COUNTRY REPORTS–ROMANIA, BULGARIA, ALBANIA**
Economist Publications Ltd

Bulgaria – English quarterly 25pp £58 UK, subscription varies in rest of world

Economic policies and development plans, trends in production and demand, monetary and fiscal conditions, wages and prices, merchandise trade, invisibles, capital flows, exchange rates and foreign debt plus a forecast of economic prospects.

05014 **DOING BUSINESS IN BULGARIA**
Price Waterhouse

Bulgaria – English irregular 100pp

A guide aimed at foreigners wishing to do business in Bulgaria. It gives an overview of Bulgaria and its economy before covering in detail such areas as tourism, the trade system, the banking system and exchange controls, industrial and commercial standards, supplier credit and counter trade, trade licences, legislative background, joint ventures, the Bulgarian investment board and information for foreigners in Bulgaria.

05015 **ECONOMIC NEWS OF BULGARIA**
Bulgarian Chamber of Commerce and Industry

Bulgaria – English/Russian/French/German Spanish monthly 1960 8pp US$24
ISSN No. 0205-1400

Newsletter including news of the Bulgarian economy, new products, business opportunities.

05016 **ECONOMIC MECHANISM IN BULGARIAN FOREIGN TRADE**
Bulgarian Chamber of Commerce and Industry

Bulgaria – English

A survey of the economics and management of Bulgarian foreign trade.

05017 **ENERGETIKA**
Collets Holdings Ltd

Bulgaria–Bulgarian bi-monthly £19.20

05018 **EXPORT AND IMPORT**
Central Statistical Office to the Council of Ministers

Bulgaria – English quarterly 15pp 0.25leva per issue

Broad summary of Bulgarian overseas trade including import/export breakdown by groups of countries, by individual countries, by commodity groups and by commodity.

05019 **EXTERNAL TRADE**
Central Statistical Office

Bulgaria – Bulgarian annual 300pp

Detailed statistical breakdown of Bulgarian overseas trade by products and country for the current and previous 2 years.

05020 **GORSKO STOPANSTVO I GORSKA PROMISHLENOST**
Collets Holdings Ltd

Bulgaria – Bulgarian monthly £33.60

05021 **HINTS TO EXPORTERS**
Department of Trade and Industry

Bulgaria – English annual

Practical guide for businessmen giving general information, useful addresses, methods of doing business and relevant regulations.

05022 **HRANITELNA PROMISHLENOST (FOOD INDUSTRY)**
Collets Holdings Ltd

Bulgaria – Bulgarian bi-monthly £12.80

05023 **IKONOMICHESKI ZHIVOT (ECONOMIC LIFE)**
Collets Holdings Ltd

Bulgaria – Bulgarian weekly £22.40

05024 **IKONOMIKA NA SELSKOTO STOPANSTUO (ECONOMY AND AGRICULTURE)**

Bulgaria – Bulgarian 8 times a year £22.40

05025 **INFORMATION BULGARIA**
Pergamon Books Ltd
Bulgarian Academy of Science

Bulgarian – English 1985 1016pp £90
ISBN No. 0 08 0318533

Comprehensive reference work on People's Republic of Bulgaria. Covers engineering, manufacturing, food, tourism, publishing, press, culture, history, foreign policy.

05026 **JOINT VENTURES IN BULGARIA**
Bulgarian Chamber of Commerce and Industry

Bulgaria – English/French/German 1986 30-70pp free

Practical comments on the normative acts regulating the setting up and activity of joint ventures with foreign participation in Bulgaria.

05027 **LANDERBERICHT BULGARIEN**
Federal Statistical Office of Germany

Bulgaria – German irregular DM7.90

Statistical survey of Bulgaria including such areas as demography, geography, education, employment, agriculture, production, overseas trade, transport, tourism, finance, wages and prices and national accounts.

05028 **LOZARSTUO I VINARSTVO (VINE GROWING AND WINE PRODUCTION)**
Collets Holdings Ltd

Bulgaria – Bulgarian bi-monthly £22.50

05029 **MACHINOSTROENE (MACHINE BUILDING)**
Collets Holdings Ltd

Bulgaria – Bulgarian monthly £37.60

05030 **MECHANIZATSIA NA SELSKOTO STEPANSTUO (MECHANIZATION OF AGRICULTURE)**
Collets Holdings Ltd

Bulgaria – Bulgarian bi-monthly £12.00

05031 **NEWS FROM BULGARIA***
Sofia Press

Bulgarian – English monthly c20pp

Current economic and political news.

05032 **NORMATIVE ACTS ON THE FOREIGN ECONOMIC RELATIONS OF THE PR OF BULGARIA**
Bulgarian Chamber of Commerce and Industry

Bulgaria – English/French/German 390pp free

Translation of basic normative acts in the field of foreign economic relations of Bulgaria.

05033 **OUOSKTARSTVO, GRADINATSTVO I KONSERUNA PROMISHLENOST (FRUIT GROWING, GARDENING AND CANNING)**
Collets Holdings Ltd

Bulgaria – Bulgarian bi-monthly £10.40

05034 **RADIO, TV, ELEKTRONICA (RADIO, TV, ELECTRONICS)**
Collets Holdings Ltd

Bulgaria – Bulgarian monthly £22.40

05035 **RUDNICHAR**
Collets Holdings Ltd

Bulgaria – Bulgarian weekly £16.00

05036 **SOCIALIST TRADE**
Collets Holdings Ltd

Bulgaria – Bulgarian weekly £14.40

05037 **STATISTICAL HANDBOOK**
Central Statistical Office

Bulgaria – Bulgarian annual 300pp

See Statistical Reference Book.

05038 **STATISTICHESKI IZUESTIYA**
Collets Holdings Ltd

Bulgaria – Bulgarian quarterly £14.40

05039 **STATISTICAL REFERENCE BOOK PR OF BULGARIA**
Central Statistical Office

Bulgaria – English annual 120pp

Pocket Statistical Yearbook covering the following topics: geography, economy, science and technology, industry, construction, agriculture, transport, communications, foreign trade, demography, social welfare, income and expenditure, culture and environment.

05040 **TOURISM**
Central Statistical Office to the Council of Ministers

Bulgaria – English/Bulgarian annual

Compares all basic statistical data on the development of tourism for previous years to date. Data is included on international tourism, domestic tourism and accommodation, regional data is also included on domestic tourism and accommodation.

05041 **TRANSPORTEN GLAS (TRANSPORT VOICE)**
Collets Holdings Ltd

Bulgaria – Bulgarian weekly £11.20

CYPRUS

06001 **AGRICULTURAL STATISTICS**
Department of Statistics and Research

Cyprus – English annual 1969 145pp
C£2.00
ISSN No. 0379-0924

Summarized economic accounts of the broad agricultural sector. Detailed data in quantity and value terms, on crop and livestock production, forestry and fishing, intermediate inputs, employment, investments, indices and land utilization.

06002 **AGROECONOMIC ANALYSIS OF FARMS IN THE MOUNTAIN REGION OF CYPRUS**
Agricultural Research Institute

Cyprus – English 1982 26pp

06003 **ANNUAL REPORT–CENTRAL BANK OF CYPRUS***
Central Bank of Cyprus

Cyprus – English annual c80pp

Annual report including review of the economy.

06004 **ANNUAL REPORT–CYPRUS EMPLOYERS & INDUSTRIALISTS FEDERATION**
Cyprus Employers & Industrialists Federation

Cyprus – Greek annual 70pp

Economic conditions in Cyprus, employment issues, developments in industry, activities of the federation.

06005 **ANNUAL REPORT–CYPRUS PORTS AUTHORITY**
Cyprus Ports Authority

Cyprus – English annual 60pp free

Annual Report including statistics.

06006 **ANNUAL REPORT OF THE DEPARTMENT OF CIVIL AVIATION**
Ministry of Communications & Works

Cyprus – English annual 70pp

The first part is a survey of the civil aviation industry including labour force, air traffic services, aeronautical services, flight safety, revenue and expenditure, air services from major airports. The second part is a series of statistical appendices in support of the first part.

06007 **ANNUAL REPORT OF THE CUSTOMS & EXCISE DEPARTMENT**
Department of Customs and Excise

Cyprus – English annual 34pp

Import/export data by broad product groups and type of entry, excise duty and its origin, and a list of high excise yielding products and the value of the excise raised from them.

06008 **ANNUAL REPORT OF THE DEPARTMENT OF ELECTRICAL SERVICE**
Ministry of Communications & Works

Cyprus – Greek annual 115pp

06009 **ANNUAL REPORT OF THE DEPARTMENT OF FISHERIES AND THE CYPRUS FISHERIES**
Agricultural Research Institute

Cyprus – English annual 120pp

Part 1 covers the activities of the department in the year whilst part 2 covers the fishing industry as a whole. A series of tables gives detailed statistical data for the industry.

06010 **ANNUAL REPORT OF THE MINES SERVICE**
Mines Service

Cyprus – English annual 30pp

Survey of mining in Cyprus including detailed statistical tables.

06011 **BANK OF CYPRUS BULLETIN**
Bank of Cyprus Ltd

Cyprus – English quarterly 1973 30pp free

Economic developments.

06012 **BULLETIN–CENTRAL BANK OF CYPRUS**
Central Bank of Cyprus

Cyprus – English quarterly 90pp

The first part contains articles on monetary developments. The second part is a statistical compendium covering such areas as money and banking, interest rates and yields, public finance, balance of payments, exchange rates, foreign trade, prices, national accounts.

06013 **BUSINESS PROFILE SERIES–REPUBLIC OF CYPRUS**
Hong Kong & Shanghai Banking Corporation

Cyprus – English annual 50pp free

A general economic survey including information for visiting businessmen and tourists.

06014 **CENSUS OF AGRICULTURE 1985**
Department of Statistics and Research

Cyprus–English irregular 1979 500pp
C£8.00
ISBN No. 9963-34-318-X

Information on the structure of agricultural holdings in 1985.

06015 **CENSUS OF COTTAGE INDUSTRY 1982**
Department of Statistics and Research

Cyprus – English irregular 1983 75pp
C£2.00

Data on establishments, employment, output, investments structure and regional distribution of cottage industry.

06016 **CENSUS OF HOUSING 1982 - VOL.1-ALL DISTRICTS**
Department of Statistics and Research

Cyprus – English irregular 1984 400pp
C£8.00
ISBN No. 9963-34-303-1

Analytical data on the supply and characteristics of housing facilities and demographic data on all Cyprus.

06017 **CENSUS OF HOUSING 1982 - VOL.II-NICOSIA DISTRICT**
Department of Statistics and Research

Cyprus – English irregular 1984 330pp
C£2.50
ISBN No. 9963-34-305-08

Analytical data on the supply and characteristics of housing facilities and demographic data on Nicosia District.

06018 **CENSUS OF HOUSING 1982 - VOL.III-LIMASSOL DISTRICT**
Department of Statistics and Research

Cyprus – English irregular 1985 330pp C£3.00
ISBN No. 9963-34-306-6

Analytical data on the supply and characteristics of housing facilities and demographic data on Limassol District.

06019 **CENSUS OF HOUSING 1982 - VOL.IV-LARNACA AND FAMAGUSTA DISTRICTS**
Department of Statistics and Research

Cyprus – English irregular 1985 400pp C£3.00
ISBN No. 9963-34-307-4

Analytical data on the supply and characteristics of housing facilities and demographic data on Larnaca and Famagusta Districts.

06020 **CENSUS OF HOUSING 1982 - VOL.V-PAPHOS DISTRICT**
Department of Statistics and Research

Cyprus – English irregular 1985 330pp C£3.00
ISBN No. 9963-34-308-2

Analytical data on the supply and characteristics of housing facilities and demographic data on Paphos District.

06021 **CENSUS OF INDUSTRIAL PRODUCTION 1981**
Department of Statistics and Research

Cyprus – English usually every five years 1983 300pp C£3.00

Detailed data on the number of enterprises, employment, labour costs and other expenses, output, sales, stocks, fixed assets and capacity. It pertains to mining and quarrying, manufacturing, electricity, gas and water.

06022 **CENSUS OF POULTRY, 1982**
Department of Statistics and Research

Cyprus – English irregular 1982 50pp C£0.75

Number of holders, structure and size of poultry units and number of poultry. Types of poultry covered: chicken, pigeons, rabbits and quails.

06023 **CENSUS OF WHOLESALE AND RETAIL TRADE 1981**
Department of Statistics and Research

Cyprus – English irregular 1983 270pp C£2.00

A complete enumeration of trade establishments, giving data on the number of establishments by size of employment, persons engaged, sales, costs, stocks, gross margins, value added and capital expenditure, turnover and turnover by commodity source and destination.

06024 **CONSTRUCTION AND HOUSING STATISTICS**
Department of Statistics and Research

Cyprus – English annual 1966 120pp C£3.00
ISSN No. 0253-8725

Statistical data on construction industry and housing. Analysis of sectoral distribution of construction output, capital formation, value added, inputs analysis, price indices of labour costs and materials, dwellings completed, dwelling stock and the contribution of these sectors to GDP.

06025 **COUNTRY PROFILES**
Economist Publications Ltd

Cyprus – English annual 40pp £25 UK, subscription varies in rest of world

Resumé of politics, economy and industry including statistical summaries.

06026 **COUNTRY REPORTS**
Economist Publications Ltd

Cyprus – English quarterly 25pp £58 UK, subscription varies in rest of world

Economic policies and development plans, trends in production and demand, monetary and fiscal conditions, wages and prices, merchandise trade, invisibles, capital flows, exchange rates and foreign debt plus a forecast of the economic prospects.

06027 **THE CYPRIOT EXPORTER**
Cyprus Chamber of Commerce & Industry

Cyprus – English quarterly November 1986 20pp free

Cypriot exports.

06028 **CYPRUS**
National Westminster Bank

Cyprus – English irregular 4pp free

Brief economic report.

06029 **CYPRUS ECONOMY IN FIGURES**
Bank of Cyprus Ltd

Cyprus – English annual 1983 5pp free
ISSN No. 0256-8284

Economic statistical information.

06030 **CYPRUS PORTS–AN OBVIOUS CHOICE**
Cyprus Ports Authority

Cyprus – English April 1987 35pp free

Information on Cyprus ports and related areas.

06031 **DEMAND AND PRICE ANALYSIS OF LIVESTOCK PRODUCTS IN CYPRUS**
Agricultural Research Institute

Cyprus – English 1983 21pp

06032 **DEMOGRAPHIC REPORT**
Department of Statistics and Research

Cyprus – Greek/English annual 1963 185pp C£3.00
ISSN No. 0590-4846

Population estimates by month, mid-year estimates by five-year age-groups, births and fertility statistics, deaths and mortality statistics, life tables, marriages, divorces and migration.

06033 **ECONOMIC NEWS**
Bank of Cyprus Ltd

Cyprus – Greek quarterly 1982 8pp free
ISSN No. 0256-839X

Economic developments.

06034 **ECONOMIC REPORT**
Department of Statistics and Research

Cyprus – English annual 1954 200pp C£3.00
ISSN No. 0070-2412

Comprehensive information on the Cyprus economy.

06035 **THE ECONOMICS OF DRYLAND MIXED FARMING IN CYPRUS**
Agricultural Research Institute

Cyprus – English 1975

06036 **ELECTRICITY AUTHORITY OF CYPRUS ANNUAL REPORT**
Electricity Authority of Cyprus

Cyprus – English/Greek annual 87pp

Surveys the work of the authority in the previous year, its technical, commercial and domestic services and its finances. Each section is supported with statistical data.

06037 **EMPOROVIOMICHANIKI-MERCHANTINDUSTRIALIST**
Cyprus Chamber of Commerce and Industry

Cyprus – Greek monthly 1983 16pp free

Economic, industrial, financial and commercial matters.

06038 **FARM TYPES IN CYPRUS**
Agricultural Research Institute

Cyprus – English 1982 10pp

06039 **FOREIGN ECONOMIC TRENDS AND THEIR IMPLICATION FOR THE UNITED STATES–CYPRUS**
US Department of Commerce

Cyprus – English irregular 12pp US$1.00

Includes data on key economic indicators, followed by a survey of the economy including a forecast for the long-term economic outlook with particular reference to prospects for US-Cypriot trade.

06040 FOURTH EMERGENCY ECONOMIC ACTION PLAN 1982-1986
Planning Bureau

Cyprus – English every 5 years 1982 133pp

Summary of the objectives, targets and measures of the economic plan for Cyprus.

06041 HEALTH AND HOSPITAL STATISTICS
Department of Statistics and Research

Cyprus – English annual 1984 180pp C£3.00
ISSN No. 0258-7955

Statistics on out-patients, in-patients, surgical operations, bed-occupancy and on medical nursing and paramedical manpower. It incorporates the data previously published in the reports 'Health Statistics' (annual), 'Health Statistics' (quarterly) and 'Hospital Statistics'.

06042 HINTS TO EXPORTERS
Department of Trade and Industry

Cyprus – English annual

Practical guide for businessmen giving general information, useful addresses, methods of doing business and relevant regulations.

06043 HOUSEHOLD INCOME AND EXPENDITURE SURVEY 1984/85
Department of Statistics and Research

Cyprus–English irregular 1986 620pp C£6.00
ISBN No. 9963-34-314-7

Covers both urban and rural households residing in the Government Controlled Area and collects for the first time detailed information on the level and sources of income.

06044 IMPORTS AND EXPORTS STATISTICS
Department of Statistics and Research

Cyprus – English monthly December 1950 250pp C£2.00
ISSN No. 0253-858X

Detailed statistics of imports and exports by commodity.

06045 INDUSTRIAL STATISTICS
Department of Statistics and Research

Cyprus – English annual 1985 260pp C£5.00
ISSN No. 1010-1160

Broad account of industrial statistics by incorporating the data previously published in the reports 'Industrial Production Survey', 'Sales of Vine Products, 'Price Index for the Manufacturing Sector', 'Employment, Output and Capital Formation in the Industrial Sector', which have been discontinued.

06046 INTERREGIONAL VARIATION IN PRODUCTION–PRODUCTIVITY OF WINE GRAPES IN CYPRUS
Agricultural Research Institute

Cyprus – English 1980 18pp

06047 LABOUR STATISTICS REPORT
Department of Statistics and Research

Cyprus – English annual 1982 185pp C£4.00
ISSN No. 0255-8386

Annual statistics on employment, unemployment, vacancies, government labour force etc. It also incorporates the data previously published in the reports 'Vacancies Notified and Filled', 'Registered Unemployed', 'Manpower Survey', 'Employment Survey' and 'Statistics of Wages, Salaries and Hours of Work'.

06048 LANDERBERICHT ZYPERN
Federal Statistical Office of Germany

Cyprus – German irregular DM7.90

Statistical survey of Cyprus including such areas as demography, geography, education, employment, agriculture, production, overseas trade, transport, tourism, finance, wages and prices and national accounts.

06049 LIMASSOL AND LARNACA PORTS
Cyprus Ports Authority

Cyprus – English October 1986 10pp free

Outlining facilities and conditions prevailing at Larnaca and Limassol Ports.

06050 MONTHLY ECONOMIC INDICATORS
Department of Statistics and Research

Cyprus – English monthly January 1978 105pp C£2.00
ISSN No. 0253-8555

It brings together selected economic indicators so as to provide a comprehensive picture of significant short-term developments in the Cyprus economy.

06051 NORM INPUT-OUTPUT DATA OF THE MAIN CROPS OF CYPRUS
Agricultural Research Institute

Cyprus – English 1976 260pp

Detailed input-output data derived from agricultural surveys.

06052 PRODUCTION ECONOMICS OF OLIVES
Agricultural Research Institute

Cyprus – English 1985 5pp

06053 REGISTRATION OF ESTABLISHMENTS
Department of Statistics and Research

Cyprus – English every five years 1967 775pp C£6.00
ISBN No. 9963-34-316-3

Number of establishments by size (persons engaged), employment by sex, occupation and working status, economic activity, legal entity and geographical location.

06054 STATISTICAL ABSTRACT
Department of Statistics and Research

Cyprus – English annual 1955 400pp C£6.00
ISSN No. 0253-875X

Summarized statistics concerning the economic and social conditions in Cyprus on a time series basis.

06055 TOURISM, MIGRATION AND TRAVEL STATISTICS
Department of Statistics and Research

Cyprus – English annual 1973 145pp C£3.00
ISSN No. 0253-8790

Movements of travellers, departures and returns of permanent residents, emigrants and immigrants, hotels, hotel-capacity and guest-nights.

06056 TRANSPORT STATISTICS
Department of Statistics and Research

Cyprus – English annual 1986 140pp C£3.00
ISSN No. 1010-1209

Data on the broad transport, storage and communications sector, incorporating the reports 'Motor Vehicles and Road Accidents', 'Shipping Statistics', 'Registration of Motor Vehicles' (quarterly) and 'Transport, Storage and Communications Survey'.

CZECHOSLOVAKIA

07001 **ABECOR COUNTRY REPORT – CZECHOSLOVAKIA**
Abecor

Czechoslovakia – English 1987 2pp free

Brief economic report.

07002 **CHEMICAL REVIEW***
Incheba Foreign Trade Corporation

Czechoslovakia–Slovak/English/German/Russian bi-monthly c40pp

Official journal of the chemical industry.

07003 **CHEMICKY PRUMYSL**
Collets Holdings Ltd

Czechoslovakia – Czech monthly £40.50

07004 **COUNTRY PROFILES**
Economist Publications Ltd

Czechoslovakia – English annual 40pp £25 UK, subscription varies in rest of world

Resumé of politics, economy and industry including statistical summaries.

07005 **COUNTRY REPORTS**
Economist Publications Ltd

Czechoslovakia – English quarterly 25pp £58 UK, subscription varies in rest of world

Economic policies and development plans, trends in production and demand, monetary and fiscal conditions, wages and prices, merchandise trade, invisibles, capital flows, exchange rates and foreign debt plus a forecast of the economic prospects.

07006 **CS ARCHITEKT (CZECHOSLOVAK ARCHITECTS)**
Collets Holdings Ltd

Czechoslovakia– Czech fortnightly £21.80

07007 **CS RYBARSTUI (FISHERIES)**
Collets Holdings Ltd

Czechoslovakia – Czech monthly

07008 **CZECHOSLOVAK ECONOMIC DIGEST**
Orbis Press Agency

Czechoslovakia – English bi-monthly 80pp

Commentaries, essays and academic articles on economic developments in Czechoslovakia including new legislation.

07009 **CZECHOSLOVAK ECONOMIC PAPERS***
Academia

Czechoslovakia – English annual c210pp 65.00Kcs

Academic articles on a variety of economic subjects.

07010 **CZECHOSLOVAK FOREIGN TRADE**
Rapid Czechoslovak Advertising Agency

Czechoslovakia – English/French/German/Russian/Spanish monthly US$37.30 inc. postage

Official journal of the Czechoslovak Chamber of Commerce containing basic information on foreign trade.

07011 **CZECHOSLOVAK HEAVY INDUSTRY**
Rapid Czechoslovak Advertising Agency

Czechoslovakia – English/French/German/Spanish/Russian monthly 32pp US$40.50 inc. postage

Information on the Czechoslovak metallurgy and heavy engineering industries.

07012 **CZECHOSLOVAK MOTOR REVIEW**
Collets Holdings Ltd

Czechoslovakia – German/English/French/Russian monthly £18.20

07013 **CZECHOSLOVAK TRADE UNIONS**
International Confederation of Free Trade Unions

Czechoslovakia – English BF20.00

07014 **ECONOMIC DIGEST***
Czechoslovak Chamber of Commerce and Industry

Czechoslovakia – English monthly c30pp

Brief news on economic developments.

07015 **ECONOMIC SUPPLEMENT**
British Embassy, Prague

Czechoslovakia – English frequent

Translation of extracts from Czechoslovakian press on current economic developments.

07016 **EKONOMIKA POLNOTOSPODARSTVA/ ECONOMICS OF AGRICULTURE**
Collets Holdings Ltd

Czechoslovakia – Czech monthly £33.00

07017 **EKONOMIKA STAVEBNICTVA/ ECONOMICS OF THE BUILDING TRADE**
Collets Holdings Ltd

Czechoslovakia – Czech monthly £42.00

07018 **FACTS ON CZECHOSLOVAK FOREIGN TRADE**
Czechoslovak Chamber of Commerce and Industry

Czechoslovakia – English annual 218pp

Analysis and detailed statistics of foreign trade. The figures appear in the SITC nomenclature revision 2.

07019 **FOR YOU FROM CZECHOSLOVAKIA**
Rapid Czechoslovak Advertising Agency

Czechoslovakia – English/French/Spanish/German/Russian quarterly c96pp US$13.90

Information on the Czechoslovak consumer goods industry.

07020 **FOREIGN ECONOMIC TRENDS AND THEIR IMPLICATIONS FOR THE UNITED STATES-CZECHOSLOVAKIA**
US Department of Commerce

Czechoslovakia – English irregular 10pp US$1.00

Includes data on key economic indicators followed by a survey of the economy including a forecast for the long-term economic outlook with particular reference to prospects for US-Czechoslovak trade.

07021 **GLASS REVIEW***
Rapid Czechoslovak Advertising Agency

Czechoslovakia – English/French/German monthly Russian semi-annually c32pp US$23.10

General information on the Czechoslovak glass and ceramics industry.

07022 **HINTS TO EXPORTERS**
Department of Trade and Industry

Czechoslovakia – English annual

Practical guide for businessmen giving general information, useful addresses, methods of doing business and relevant regulations.

07023 **HOSPODAR SKE NOVINY (ECONOMIC NEWS)**
Collets Holdings Ltd

Czechoslovakia – Czech weekly £55.40

07024 **INVESTA***
Rapid Czechoslovak Advertising Agency

Czechoslovakia – English/French/Spanish/German/Russian bi-monthly c32pp US$22.30

Information on the Czechoslovak textile, shoe and leather machinery industries.

07025 **KOVOEXPORT**
Rapid Czechoslovak Advertising Agency

Czechoslovakia – English/French/Spanish/German/Russian bi-monthly c32pp US$22.30

Information on Czechoslovak precision engineering producers including nuclear equipment, office equipment, laboratory instruments and telecommunications equipment.

07026 **KOZARSTVI/LEATHER INDUSTRY**
Collets Holdings Ltd

Czechoslovakia – Czech monthly £28.00

07027 **KUASNY PRUMYSL**
Collets Holdings Ltd

Czechoslovakia – Czech monthly £32.80

07028 **LANDERBERICHT TSCHECHOSLOWAKEI**
Federal Statistical Office of Germany

Czechoslovakia – German irregular DM7.90

Statistical survey of Czechoslovakia including such areas as demography, geography, education, employment, agriculture, production, overseas trade, transport, tourism, finance, wages and prices and national accounts.

07029 **LISHY CUKROVARNICKE/SUGAR INDUSTRY**
Collets Holdings Ltd

Czechoslovakia – Czech monthly £33.60

07030 **MANIPULACE, SKLADOVANI, BALERI/MATERIAL HANDLING STORAGE AND PACKING**
Collets Holdings Ltd

Czechoslovakia – Czech monthly £34.80

07031 **MISTRI HOSPEDARSTVI (LOCAL ECONOMY)**
Collets Holdings Ltd

Czechoslovakia – Czech monthly £9.50

07032 **OBCHOD, PRUMYSL, HOSPODARSTVI (COMMERCE, INDUSTRY, ECONOMY)**
Collets Holdings Ltd

Czechoslovakia – Czech quarterly

07033 **PRUMYSL POTRAVIN (FOOD INDUSTRY)**
Collets Holdings Ltd

Czechoslovakia – Czech monthly £42.30

07034 **RAPID COMPUTER NEWS***
Rapid Czechoslovak Advertising Agency

Czechoslovakia – Czech 2 times weekly

07035 **REVUE OBCHODU, PRUMYSLU, HOSPODARSTVI***
Rapid Czechoslovak Advertising Agency

Czechoslovakia – Czech monthly Russian quarterly c64pp

Review of trade, industry and economy produced by the Czechoslovak Chamber of Commerce. It contains articles on external economic relations, technological developments, and news of companies.

07036 **SKODA REVIEW***
Rapid Czechoslovak Advertising Agency

Czechoslovakia – English/Spanish/German/Russian quarterly c64pp

Review of products of the Skoda works in Plzen .

07037 **SLEVARENSKVI (FOUNDRY INDUSTRY)**
Collets Holdings Ltd

Czechoslovakia – Czech monthly £37.70

07038 **SOCIALISTICKY OBACHAD (SOCIALIST TRADE)**
Collets Holdings Ltd

Czechoslovakia – Czech monthly £38.70

07039 **STATISTICAL SURVEYS**
Federalni Statisticky Urad (Federal Statistical Office of Czechoslovakia)

Czechoslovakia – Czech/Russian/English monthly 1967 30pp 6Kcs

Basic statistical date in time series.

07040 **STATISTICAL YEARBOOK**
Federalni Statisticky Urad (Federal Statistical Office of Czechoslovakia)

Czechoslovakia – Czech (translation of the contents in English/Russian available on request) annual 1956 700pp 78Kcs

Data on population, social product and national income, state budget and financial economy, employment rate, capital construction, scientific and technical development, price development and development of individual branches of national economy.

07041 **STATISTICKA ROCENKA CESKOSLOVENSKE SOCIALISTICKE REPUBLIKY**
Federalni Statisticky Urad

Czechoslovakia – Czech annual 700pp

A statistical survey of all aspects of Czechoslovak life and economy.

07042 **STATISTICKE PREHLEDY**
Federalni Statisticky Urad

Czechoslovakia – Czech monthly 160pp Kcs6- per issue

Monthly bulletin of social and economic statistics.

07043 **TRACTOR REVIEW***
Rapid Czechoslovak Advertising Agency

Czechoslovakia – English/French/Spanish/German semi-annually c48pp

Review of the agricultural machinery industry.

07044 **TRADING WITH CZECHOSLOVAKIA**
Department of Trade and Industry

Czechoslovakia – English irregular 15pp free

Information on how to do business in Czechoslovakia including sections on the economic system, foreign trade, UK trade with Czechoslovakia, organization of foreign trade, joint ventures, countertrade, import/export regulations, how to approach the market and a list of useful addresses. Also includes a statistical annex on the top 10 UK exports to and from Czechoslovakia and statistics on its Western trading partners.

07045 **VELETRYNI (BRNO TRADE FAIR NEWS)**
Collets Holdings Ltd

Czechoslovakia – Czech monthly

07046 **ZAHRANICNI OBCHOD***
Rapid Czechoslovak Advertising Agency

Czechoslovakia – Czech monthly c32pp

Theoretical and practical issues of foreign trade.

07047 **ZEMEDELSKA EKONOMIKA (AGRICULTURAL ECONOMICS)**
Collets Holdings Ltd

Czechoslovakia – Czech monthly £46.40

DENMARK

08001 **ABECOR COUNTRY REPORT – DENMARK**
Abecor

Denmark – English 1986 2pp free

Brief economic report.

08002 **ANNUAL REPORT AND ACCOUNTS – COPENHAGEN HANDELSBANK**
Copenhagen Handelsbank

Denmark – Danish/German/English annual c32pp free

08003 **ARBEDSMARKED: STATISTISKE EFTERRETNINGER**
Danmarks Statistik

Denmark – Danish monthly 8pp
DKr125,000
ISSN No 0108 5514

08004 **ARBEJDSMARKEDSSTATISTIK**
Danmarks Statistik

Denmark – Danish quarterly DKr131.15

Statistics on the labour market.

08005 **BEFOLKNING OG VALG: STATISTISKE EFTERRETNINGER**
Danmarks Statistik

Denmark – Danish monthly 30pp
DKr103,00
ISSN No 0108 5530

08006 **BEFOLKNINGEN I KOMMUNERNE**
Danmarks Statistik

Denmark – Danish annual 168pp DKr73.77

Detailed statistical tables covering the population in municipalities.

08007 **BEFOLKNINGENS BEVAEGELSER**
Danmarks Statistik

Denmark – Danish annual 260pp DKr57.38

Report on vital statistics.

08008 **BIANNUAL REPORT**
Kobenhavns Fondsbors

Denmark – Danish/English biannual 20pp free

Covers trade in bonds and shares that year. It also covers indices, interest rates etc.

08009 **BORDER ANALYSIS**
Danmarks Turistrad

Denmark – English annual 1983 8pp

Tourism including duration of stay, size of travel group, tourists' daily consumption, numbers of advance bookings etc.

08010 **BØRSEN***
Forlaget Børsen A/S

Denmark – Danish daily c35pp DKr880.00

Newspaper giving financial and business news including information on the stock market.

08011 **BYGGE–OG ANLAEGSVIRKSOMHED: STATISTISKE EFTERRETNINGER**
Danmarks Statistik

Denmark – Danish monthly 8pp DKr91,00
ISSN No 0108 5549

08012 **CLIENT MEMORANDUM**
Price Waterhouse

Denmark – English frequent c8pp free

Up-to-date service giving information on legislation affecting the economy.

08013 **COUNTRY PROFILES**
Economist Publications Ltd

Denmark, Iceland – English annual 40pp
£25 UK Subscription varies in rest of world

Resumé of politics, economy and industry including statistical summaries.

08014 **COUNTRY REPORTS**
Economist Publications Ltd

Denmark, Iceland – English quarterly 25pp
£58 UK Subscription varies in rest of world

Economic policies and development plans, trends in production and demand, monetary and fiscal conditions, wages and prices, merchandise trade, invisibles, capital flows, exchange rates and foreign debt plus a forecast of the economic prospects.

08015 **THE DANISH INSURANCE INDUSTRY**
Insurance Information Services

Denmark – English annual 32pp free

The Danish insurance industry and its relation to the Danish and international communities, in text, figures and illustrations.

08016 **THE DANISH TRADE UNION MOVEMENT**
Danish Federation of Trade Unions

Denmark – English 1988 29pp

Brief review of the trade union movement.

08017 **DANMARKS SKIBE OG SKIBSFART**
Danmarks Statistik

Denmark – Danish annual 121pp DKr40.98

Statistical report on shipping.

08018 **DANMARKS VAREINFØRSEL OG–UDFØRSEL**
Danmarks Statistik

Denmark – Danish annual
vol.1 312pp DKr98.36
vol.2 310pp DKr98.36

Detailed statistical tables and text on external trade: Vol.1, general outline and trade classified by commodities and countries. (SITC)
Vol.2 trade classified by commodities. (CCCN)

08019 **DANISH ECONOMIC REVIEW***
Privatbanken

Denmark – English quarterly c20pp free

Brief review of the Danish economy.

08020 **DENMARK & GREECE**
UK Iron and Steel Statistics Bureau

Denmark – English 1986 £25.00

Report on the steel industry showing production, consumption and details of imports and exports.

08021 **DENMARK – BASIC FIGURES**
Den Danske Bank

Denmark – English annual 20pp free

Summary of basic statistical data including comparative figures for the preceding five years.

08022 DENMARK – QUARTERLY REVIEW
Copenhagen Handelsbank

Denmark – English/German quarterly c16pp free

Brief survey of the economy and Danish politics.

08023 DENMARK REVIEW
Royal Danish Ministry of Foreign Affairs

Denmark – English quarterly c25pp free

General commercial and business news.

08024 DETAILPRISER
Danmarks Statistik

Denmark – Danish quarterly DKr45.08

Statistics on retail prices.

08025 ECONOMIC SITUATION*
Den Danske Bank

Denmark – English monthly c4pp free

Brief account of the economy.

08026 ELECTRICITY SUPPLY IN DENMARK 1985
Electricity Council

Denmark – English irregular 20pp

Covers the structure of the industry, generation, production, consumption, transmission and distribution.

08027 FAERDSELSUHELD
Danmarks Statistik

Denmark – Danish annual 140pp DKr40.98

Statistical report on road traffic accidents.

08028 GROWTH POLICIES IN A NORDIC PERSPECTIVE 1987
Institute of Industrial Economics

Norway, Sweden, Finland, Denmark – English 1984
ISBN No. 91 7204 276 - 1

Economic policies and outlook.

08029 HINTS TO EXPORTERS
Department of Trade and Industry

Denmark – English annual

Practical guide for businessmen giving general information, useful addresses, methods of doing business and relevant regulations.

08030 INDKOMST, FORBRUG OG PRISER: STATISTISKE EFTERRETNINGER
Danmarks Statistik

Denmark – Danish monthly 12pp
DKr150,00
ISSN No 0108 5565

08031 INDKOMSTER OG FORMUER
Danmarks Statistik

Denmark – Danish annual

Detailed statistical tables and text on income and property assessments.

08032 INDUSTRI OG ENERGI; STATISTISKE EFTERRETNINGER
Danmarks Statistik

Denmark – Danish monthly 20pp DKr92,00
ISSN No 0108 5468

08033 INDUSTRISTATISTIK
Danmarks Statistik

Denmark – Danish annual 107pp DKr40.98

Report on industrial statistics.

08034 KOMMUNALE FINANSER
Danmarks Statistik

Denmark – Danish annual 133pp DKr65.67
ISSN No 0106 9802

Statistics on local government finance.

08035 KOMPASS REGISTER
Kompass Publishers, UK

Denmark – English/French/German/Spanish/Italian annual £120.00

Comprehensive business directory giving information on over 14,000 companies listed geographically and cross-referenced to a directory of products and services.

08036 KREDITMARKEDSSTATISTIK
Danmarks Statistik

Denmark – Danish bi-monthly DKr382.79
ISSN No 0901 7321

Credit market statistics.

08037 LANDBRUG: STATISTISKE EFTERRETNINGER
Danmarks Statistik

Denmark – Danish monthly 8pp DKr126.00
ISSN No 0108 5522

08038 LANDSBRUGSSTATISTIK
Danmarks Statistik

Denmark – Danish annual 330pp DKr57.38

Report on agricultural statistics.

08039 LEVEVILKAR I DANMARK
Danmarks Statistik

Denmark – Danish 1984

Statistics on living conditions in Denmark.

08040 LON OG INDKOMSTATISTIK
Danmarks Statistik

Denmark – Danish 4-6 times a year
DKr96.72
ISSN No 0107 8771

Statistics on earnings and incomes.

08041 MANEDLIG BESKAEFTIGELSES-OG LØNSTATISTIK FOR INDUSTRI
Danmarks Statistik

Denmark – Danish monthly DKr106.56

Statistcial report on industrial employment and labour costs.

08042 MANEDLIG ORDRE-OG OMSAETNINGSSTATISTIK FOR INDUSTRI
Danmarks Statistik

Denmark – Danish monthly DKr120.49

Statistical report on industrial sales and orders.

08043 MONETARY REVIEW
Danmarks National Bank

Denmark – English quarterly c30pp

Review giving tables and graphs on the current financial situation.

08044 MANEDSBORSEN*
Forlaget Børsen A/S

Denmark – Danish monthly c70pp
DKr207.35

Business and commercial news.

08045 MONTHLY LIST
Kobenhavns Fondsbors

Denmark – Danish/English monthly 40pp
DKr230

Covers the trading rates every trading day and the total amount of trade in each security.

08046 MONTHLY REPORT
Kobenhavns Fondsbors

Denmark – Danish monthly 2pp free

Includes statistical figures for the Stock Exchange.

08047 NATIONALREGNESKABSSTATIS-TIK
Danmarks Statistik

Denmark – Danish annual 180pp DKr73.77
ISSN No 0108-8173

National Accounts Statistics.

08048 NORDISK FORSAKRINGSTIDSKRIFT
Svenska Forsakringsforeningen

08072 **TRANSPORT***
Teknisk Forlag A/S

Denmark – Danish 20 issues a year DKr195.20

Up-to-date information on the transport sector with a special section each month on packing.

08073 **UDENRIGSHANDELEN FORDELT PA VARER OG LANDE**
Danmarks Statistik

Denmark – Danish quarterly DKr737.70

Statistics on external trade by commodities and countries.

08074 **VARESTATISTIK FOR INDUSTRI**
Danmarks Statistik

Denmark – Danish annual

Statistics on manufacturers' sales of commodities.

08075 **VARESTATISTIK FOR INDUSTRI, 4 SERIER**
Danmarks Statistik

Denmark – Danish quarterly DKr94.26

Manufacturers' sales of commodities.

08076 **VEJTRANSPORTEN I TAL OG TEKST**
Automobil–Importørernes Sammenslutning

Denmark – Danish annual 98pp
ISSN No. 0083 5358

Statistics on imports, production and registration of motor vehicles, vehicles in use, traffic, accidents etc.

EUROPE EAST

09001 **BUSINESS EASTERN EUROPE**
Business International

Europe, East – English weekly SF1470

Focuses regularly on the practical problems of financing countertrade, business outlook and developments in each market that affects business.

09002 **CMEA ECONOMIC COOPERATION**
CMEA Bulletin

Bulgaria, Czechoslovakia, GDR, Hungary – English/French/German/Spanish quarterly 1984 129pp US$3
ISBN/ISSN No. 0237-0107

Economic and social policy, technological development in the CMEA member countries, relations with other countries, joint economic organizations.

09003 **COMECON**
National Westminster Bank

Europe, East – English irregular 4pp free

Brief economic report.

09004 **COMECON FOREIGN TRADE DATA**
Macmillan Publishers Ltd, UK

Europe, East – English annual 550pp

Collection of data on balances of payments, indebtedness to the West and exchange rates collected from CMEA statistics, UN foreign trade statistics and Western statistics.

09005 **COMECON REPORTS**
World Reports (UK) Ltd

Europe, East – English quarterly £200

In-depth articles about the economic performance of Comecon countries.

09006 **CONTEMPLATING COMECON**
East European Trade Council, UK

Europe, East – English free

Introductory booklet to commercial practices in the COMECON countries.

09007 **CONTRACTS WITH EAST EUROPE**
East European Trade Council, UK

Europe, East – English £7.50

Guide to contract negotiation with COMECON countries.

09008 **COUNTERTRADE UPDATE: EASTERN EUROPE**
Business International

Europe, East – English quarterly 2 vols SF1550

Vol.1 is a description of countertrade basics, terms and techniques. Vol.2 is a country-by-country survey of countertrade practices.

09009 **COURRIER DES PAYS DE L'EST**
Available from La Documentation Francaise

Europe, East – French monthly FrF41 per issue

Economics and commercial information on Eastern Europe.

09010 **DOING BUSINESS WITH EASTERN EUROPE**
Business International

Europe, East–English quarterly, SF1100 per country

For each country provides analysis of 5-year and annual plans, foreign trade statistics and general business information.

09011 **EASTERN EUROPE AND THE USSR 1985**
Economist Intelligence Unit

Europe, East – English 119pp
ISBN/ISSN No.0267 5919

Contains regional articles and individual country studies.

09012 **EASTERN EUROPE: A BUSINESS PROFILE, 1985**
East European Trade Council

Europe, East – English 24pp

General description of trade with Eastern Europe plus a statistical appendix of trade figures.

09013 **EASTERN EUROPE, TURKEY AND YUGOSLAVIA**
UK Iron and Steel Statistics Bureau

Europe, East – English 1986 with annual statistical summary £25.00 (£28.00 airmail)

Report on the steel industry showing production, consumption and details of imports and exports.

09014 **EAST EUROPE AGRICULTURE**
Agra Europe (London) Ltd

Europe, East – English monthly 1982 £170 UK, £178 Europe, £182 world
ISSN No. 0263-3205

Situation reports, tables and rare information from the USSR and other East European countries.

09015 **EAST EUROPE DIGEST**
London Chamber of Commerce

Europe, East – English monthly 1965 6pp cost on application

Economic conditions and trade.

09016 **EAST EUROPEAN INDUSTRIAL MONITOR**
Business International

Europe, East – English monthly SF1850 each monitor

14 reports covering different industrial sectors, giving data on production and investment plans, export and import figures, plant capacities etc.

09017 **EAST EUROPEAN STATISTICS SERVICE**
East-West

Europe, East – English monthly 10pp

Covers the economy, trade and industrial production and provides detailed statistics.

09018 **ECONOMIC COLLOQUIA**
North Atlantic Treaty Organisation

Europe, East – English/French annual 400pp free

Papers based on the proceedings of the colloquia on various economic topics concerned with Eastern Europe.

09019 **ECONOMIC COOPERATION BETWEEN THE MEMBER COUNTRIES OF CMEA**
Council for Mutual Economic Assistance (CMEA)

Europe, East – English/German/French/ Spanish quarterly

09020 **REGISTER OF COMMERCIAL HOUSES TRADING WITH EASTERN EUROPE**
East European Trade Council

Europe, East – English biannual May 1983 28pp free

List of British-based agency companies, banks, consultants and countertraders offering services to manufacturers wishing to export to Eastern Europe.

09021 **STATISTICAL REVIEW OF TRADE AMONG COUNTRIES HAVING DIFFERENT ECONOMIC AND SOCIAL SYSTEMS**
United Nations Conference for Trade and Development (UNCTAD)

Europe, East – English/French/Spanish annual

Statistical information on trade relations of the socialist countries of East Europe.

09022 **STATISTICHESKIJ EJEGODNIK STRAN–CHLENOV SOVETA EKONOMICHESKOJ VZAIMOPOMOSCI**
V/O Mezhdunarodnaya Kniga/ available from Collets

Europe, East – Russian annual Rub16-40

Statistical yearbook of the CMEA member countries.

09023 **L'URSS ET L'EUROPE DE L'EST**
La Documentation Francaise

Europe, East – French 1987 250pp FrF50

Analysis of political, diplomatic, economic and social events.

09024 **WIRTSCHAFTLICHE ENTWICKLUNG IN OSTEUROPA ZUR JAHRESWENDE**
Verlag Weltarchiv GmbH, FDR/K. Bolz

Europe, East – German annual 300pp DM39.00

Economic development in East Europe.

EUROPE EAST AND WEST

10001 **AGRAFILE**
Agra Europe (London) Ltd

Europe – English monthly 1986 £91 UK, £95 Europe, £98 world
ISBN/ISSN No. 0269 3690

Excerpts from Agra Europe publications, collected separately each month under four titles: dairy products, fruit and vegetables, grain and oilseeds, livestock and meat.

10002 **AGRICULTURAL REVIEW OF EUROPE**
United Nations Economic Commission for Europe

Europe – English annual 1958 cost varies per issue

Includes all types of data on the dairy, meat, grain and produce industries.

10003 **AGRICULTURAL TRADE IN EUROPE**
UNECE

Europe – English annual 1960 US$11

Reviews and analyses recent developments in the import and export of agricultural products within Europe.

10004 **ANNUAL BULLETIN OF COAL STATISTICS FOR EUROPE**
UNECE

Europe – English annual 1966 US$20

Basic data on developments and trends in the field of solid fuels giving statistics for Europe, Canada and the US.

10005 **ANNUAL BULLETIN OF ELECTRIC ENERGY STATISTICS FOR EUROPE**
UNECE

Europe – English annual 1956 US$24

Basic data on developments and trends of electric energy is provided. Also included are statistics on capacity of plants, production, consumption, supplies to customers and consumption.

10006 **ANNUAL BULLETIN OF GAS STATISTICS FOR EUROPE**
UNECE

Europe – English annual 1966 US$26

Basic data on developments and trends, consumption and production of gas in Europe, Canada and the US.

10007 **ANNUAL BULLETIN OF GENERAL ENERGY STATISTICS FOR EUROPE**
UNECE

Europe – English annual 1968 US$25

Basic data on the energy situation as a whole as well as details on the production of energy by form, overall energy balance sheets, deliveries of petroleum products for inland consumption, liquid fuels and nuclear, hydro and geothermal energy.

10008 **ANNUAL BULLETIN OF HOUSING AND BUILDING STATISTICS FOR EUROPE**
UNECE

Europe – English annual 1957 US$18

Information on dwelling construction, materials used and employment in the construction industry. Also included are wholesale price indices of building materials in Europe, Canada and the US.

10009 **ANNUAL BULLETIN OF STEEL STATISTICS FOR EUROPE**
UNECE

Europe – English annual 1973 US$19

Basic data on the development of steel production and trade, consumption and trade of raw materials, movements of scrap, consumption of energy in the steel industry and steel deliveries to consuming industries in European countries, Canada, the US and Japan.

10010 **ANNUAL BULLETIN OF TRANSPORT STATISTICS FOR EUROPE**
UNECE

Europe – English annual 1949 US$19

Statistics and brief studies on transport plus tables on energy consumption for transport. Data covers Europe, Canada and the US.

10011 **ANNUAL REPORT–CEFIC**
Chemical Industries Association Ltd, UK

Europe – English annual £1.00

Annual report including basic economic statistics of the European Council of Chemical Manufacturers Federation.

10012 **ANNUAL REVIEW OF ENGINEERING INDUSTRIES AND AUTOMATION**
UNECE

Europe – English annual 1979 US$27

Analyses data on production, investments, manpower and price indices in Europe.

10013 **ANNUAL REVIEW OF THE CHEMICAL INDUSTRY**
United Nations Economic Commission for Europe

Europe – English annual US$30

10014 **BRAVEREIEN UND MALZEREIEN IN EUROPA**
Verlag Hoppenstedt and Co.

Europe – German annual 700pp DM 275

Breweries and maltsters in Europe.

10015 **COAL SITUATION IN THE ECE REGION AND ITS PROSPECTS**
UN Economic Commission for Europe

Europe – English annual

10016 **CEFIC ENERGY STATISTICS (CONSUMPTION)**
Chemical Industries Association Ltd, UK

Europe – English annual £16

Survey carried out by the European Council of Chemical Manufacturers Federation.

10017 **CURRENT EUROPEAN DIRECTORIES**
CBD Research Ltd
G.P. Henderson (ed.)

Europe – English irregular 1969

Various listings of directories including those covering Europe as a whole, followed by those relating to a specific country, in an A-Z order, an index of titles and an analytical subject index in English, French and German.

Norway, Finland, Sweden, Denmark – Scandinavian/English/German quarterly 1921 90pp SKr40 per year ISSN No 0348-6516

Private and public insurance.

08049 OECD ECONOMIC SURVEYS – DENMARK
OECD

Denmark – English annual 70pp £2.40/ DM12/US$5/FrF24

A detailed analysis of recent developments in demand production, employment, prices and wages, conditions in the money and capital markets and developments in the balance of payments. It includes short-term forecasts as well as analyses of medium-term problems of specific relevance to the elaboration of the country's economic policies.

08050 OFFICIAL LIST
Kobenhavns Fondsbors

Denmark – English/Danish Daily 20-25pp DKr4 per day

Covers trade on the Copenhagen Stock Exchange the previous trading day.

08051 PENGE OG INVESTERING*
Forlaget Børsen A/S

Denmark – Danish monthly c25pp DKr183.00

Financial and monetary news.

08052 PENGE OG KAPITALMARKED: STATISTISKE EFTERRETNINGER
Danmarks Statistik

Denmark – Danish monthly 40pp DKr67.00 ISSN No 0108-5476

08053 PRISSTATISTIK
Danmarks Statistik

Denmark – Danish monthly DKr140.98

Statistical report on prices.

08054 REGNSKABSSTATISTIK FOR INDUSTRIEN
Danmarks Statistik

Denmark – Danish annual 158pp DKr65.57

Statistics on industrial accounts.

08055 REPORT AND ACCOUNTS–DANMARKS NATIONAL BANK*
Danmarks National Bank

Denmark – Danish/English annual c130pp free

Annual reports including statistical tables covering all branches of the economy.

08056 SAMFAERDSEL OG TURISME: STATISTISKE EFTERRETNINGER
Danmarks Statistik

Denmark – Danish monthly 16pp DKr123.00 ISSN No. 0108 5484

08057 SETTING UP IN DENMARK
Copenhagen Handelsbank

Denmark – English/German every other year 1972 40pp free ISBN/ISSN No. 0901-800X

Economic, legal and financial aspects of foreign investment in Denmark

08058 SKATTER OG AFGIFTER
Danmarks Statistik

Denmark – Danish annual 136pp DKr65.57

Detailed statistical tables and text on taxes and duties.

08059 SOCIAL SIKRING OG RETSVAESEN: STATISTISKE EFTERRETNINGER
Danmarks Statistik

Denmark–Danish monthly 14pp DKr32.00

08060 SOCIALSTATISTIK
Danmarks Statistik

Denmark – Danish 6-10 times a year DKr107.38 ISSN No. 0109-372X

Social statistics.

08061 STATISTICS
Danish Bacon and Meat Council

Denmark – English annual 40pp

Statistics on pig production, prices, exports of meat etc.

00062 STATISTIK ARBOG
Danmarks Statistik

Denmark – Danish annual 500pp DKr98.36

Statistical yearbook consisting of tabulations from the Danish Statistical Department and other Danish institutions.

08063 STATISTIK: DANSK ELFORSYNING
Danske Elvaerkers Forening

Denmark – Danish/English annual 48pp

Data on production and consumption, fuel, production plants, forecasting and planning for the electricity industry.

08064 STATISTIK MANEDSOVERSIGT
Danmarks Statistik

Denmark – Danish monthly DKr204.92

An overall view of essential short-term statistics.

08065 STATISTIK OVER REGISTRERINO AF NYE AUTOMOBILIER I DANMARK
Automobil – Importorernes Sammenslutning

Denmark – Danish monthly 16pp ISSN No. 0901 6139

New registrations for cars, vans, lorries and buses.

08066 STATISTISK TIARS-OVERSIGT
Danmarks Statistik

Denmark – Danish annual 180pp DKr45.08

Statistical review giving comparative data for the preceding ten years.

08067 STATISTISKE EFTERRETNINGER
Danmarks Statistik

Denmark – Danish irregular

Statistical news which has articles giving summary results of surveys and census and updated indices and other statistics. Divided into 14 main subject groups.

08068 SUPERMARKEDER OG ANDRE STORE DAGLIGVAREBUTIKKER
Per Press ApS

Denmark – Danish annual 1965 243pp DKr765.00 and postage

Directory of 1184 supermarkets and variety stores in Denmark, 266 discount stores and 193 other food stores with a minimum turnover of 10 million Danish crowns. The directory gives information on turnover, sales area, assortment in main groups, competition and future trends.

08069 TAL OG DATA MEDICIN OG SUNDHEDSVAESEN/FACTS MEDICINE AND HEALTH CARE
Foreningen af Danske Medicinfabrikker

Denmark – Danish/English annual 110 pp ISSN No. 0107 1181

Handbook of the pharmaceutical industry, covering production, foreign trade, investment, employment, consumption.

08070 TAX AND INVESTMENT PROFILE
Touche Ross International, USA

Denmark – English free

Booklet providing information on financial system and legislation including taxation and currency regulations which is frequently updated.

08071 TOURISM IN DENMARK: FACTS AND FIGURES
Danmarks Turistrad

Denmark – English 2pp free

Statistics on tourism in Denmark including tourist receipts, tourism and employment, tourism by nationality and by region.

10018 **DIRECTORY OF EUROPEAN ASSOCIATIONS PART 2 NATIONAL LEARNED, SCIENTIFIC AND TECHNICAL SOCIETIES**
CBD Research Ltd
R.W. Adams

Europe – English/French/German irregular

Information on national, learned, scientific and technical societies, institutes and academies of all countries of Europe. Contents include subject indexes in English, French and German, a main directory of organizations listed under 650 subject headings, listings by country, an index of acronyms and abbreviations and an alphabetical index to names of associations.

10019 **DIRECTORY OF EUROPEAN INDUSTRIAL AND TRADE ASSOCIATIONS**
CBD Research Ltd

Europe – English/French/German irregular 1971 £62.50

Includes industrial and trade associations in all countries of both East and West Europe. Contents include a list of international organizations to which European trade associations are affiliated, subject indexes in English, French and German, a main directory listing organizations by 650 subject headings - listings by country, an index to acronyms and abbreviations and an alphabetical index to names of associations.

10020 **ECONOMIC SURVEY FOR EUROPE**
United Nations

Europe – English annual US$60.00

Each issue provides an in-depth study of some topic relevant to the European economy.

10021 **ELECTRIC POWER SITUATION IN THE ECE REGION**
United Nations Economic Commission for Europe

Europe – English annual

10022 **EUROPEAN ADVERTISING AND MEDIA FORECAST**
Advertising Association

All EEC countries plus USA and Japan – English quarterly 100pp £425.00 p.a. ISSN No.0951 7758

Advertising expenditure plus media developments Europe-wide.

10023 **EUROPEAN COMPANIES: A GUIDE TO SOURCES OF INFORMATION**
CBD Research Ltd
G.P. Henderson (ed.)

Europe – English irregular 1961

A guide to sources on the information available in official records, publications and commercial services on business enterprises. The book describes the sources available and how to use them.

10024 **EUROPEAN DIRECTORY OF MARKETING INFORMATION SOURCES**
Euromonitor

Europe – English occasional 400pp £82.00

Lists 2500 sources of market and business data including (as well as libraries, official publications and research companies) databases, databanks, business and marketing journals and associations, embassies and consulates. In addition, a useful profile of each country portrays its social and economic conditions.

10025 **EUROPEAN MARKETING DATA AND STATISTICS**
Euromonitor

Europe – English annual 268pp £87.00

In addition to the major statistics on economic, social and demographic subjects, it features data on consumer products and standard of living. Areas included are food, drink, tobacco, cosmetics, chemicals, pharmaceuticals, tableware, textiles, clothing, electricals, leisure goods, automotives and travel.

10026 **EUROPEAN TIMBER TRENDS AND PROSPECTS 1980-2020**
United Nations

Europe – English US$120.00 2 vols. Supplement to 'Timber Bulletin': annual subscription US$80.00

10027 **GAS SITUATION AND NATURAL GAS MARKETS IN THE ECE REGION AND ITS PROSPECTS**
United Nations Economic Commission for Europe

Europe – English annual

10028 **JAHRBUCH FOR BERGBAU, ENERGIE, MINERALOL UND CHEMIE**
Verlag Glückauf GmbH, Essen

Europe – German annual c1300pp DM98

Directory giving information on the European energy and mineral industries. Over 5,000 organizations are covered in the following sectors: coal mining in Germany and Europe; metal and minerals in Germany; petroleum and natural gas in Germany and the North Sea; electricity and power in Germany and the European Economic Community; gas in Germany and the EEC; the petroleum industry including refineries and pipe-lines in the EEC. There is also information on European organizations, policies and technical developments in these fields.

10029 **MONTHLY TRAFFIC STATISTICS, PRESS RELEASES**
Association of European Airlines

Air traffic statistics.

10030 **OVERALL ECONOMIC PERSPECTIVE TO THE YEAR 2000**
UN Economic Commission for Europe

Europe – English

Base-line scenario.

10031 **PAN EUROPEAN ASSOCIATIONS: A DIRECTORY OF MULTI-NATIONAL ORGANISATIONS IN EUROPE**
CBD Research Ltd
C.A.P. Henderson (ed.)

Europe – English irregular

Information about multinational associations in Europe, whether of individuals, businesses, societies or governments.

10032 **QUARTERLY BULLETIN OF COAL STATISTICS FOR EUROPE**
United Nations

Europe – English/French quarterly US$9.00

10033 **QUARTERLY BULLETIN OF STEEL STATISTICS FOR EUROPE**
United Nations

Europe – English/French quarterly US$9.00 a copy

10034 **REVIEW OF THE AGRICULTURAL SITUATION IN EUROPE**
United Nations

Europe – English annual 2 vols

Covers grain, livestock, meat, dairy products and eggs.

10035 **STATISTICAL INDICATORS OF SHORT-TERM ECONOMIC CHANGES IN ECE COUNTRIES**
United Nations

Europe – English monthly 1959 Subscription US$45, 1 issue US$6

An up-to-date overall picture of short-term economic trends in Europe, Canada and the USA.

10036 **STATISTICS EUROPE: SOURCES FOR SOCIAL, ECONOMIC AND MARKET RESEARCH**
CBD Research Ltd
R. Leigh (ed.)

Europe – English irregular 1968 320pp £47.50

An up-to-date guide to sources of statistical information for all 33 countries of West Europe and East Europe. Also includes a descriptionn of the statistical activities and publications of international organizations covering the whole of Europe or major groups of countries.

10037 **STATISTICS OF ROAD TRAFFIC ACCIDENTS IN EUROPE**
UNECE

Europe – English annual 1960 US$12.50

Includes data on causes, types and results of accidents in Europe, Canada and the US.

10038 **STEEL MARKET**
UN Economic Commission for Europe

Europe–English annual US$19.00

EUROPE WEST

11001 ANNUAL REPORT–EFTA
European Free Trade Association

Europe, West – English/French/German annual free
ISSN No. English 0258-3844; French 0258-0756; German 0258-3852

11002 BUSINESS EUROPE
Business International

Europe, West – English fortnightly SF750

Looks at national and EEC-related issues, trends and policies. Includes business outlooks for 16 European countries, labour cost surveys of sectoral prospects for major countries.

11003 EFTA TRADE
European Free Trade Association

Europe, West – English/French/German annual 112pp free
ISSN No. 0531-4119

Specialist economic publication containing comparative data of EFTA's trade.

11004 ECONOMIC INTEGRATION AND FREE TRADE IN A CHANGING WORLD ECONOMY
European Free Trade Association

Europe, West – English/French/German 1980 free

Text of speeches delivered at EFTA's twentieth anniversary meeting.

11005 THE EUROPEAN ECONOMY: GROWTH AND CRISIS
Oxford University Press

Europe, West – English 1982 670pp £12.50
ISBN/ISSN No. 019 877119 3

Covers applied economics, European economics and modern economic history.

11006 EUROPEAN FREE TRADE ASSOCIATION
European Free Trade Association

Europe, West – English 1987 c160pp free

Detailed account of EFTA's history and achievements.

11007 EUROPEAN TAXATION
International Bureau of Fiscal Documentation

Europe, West – English monthly 1960 DF750, binder DF40

[illegible] decisions on European Taxation.

11008 EXECUTIVE FOCUS/EUROPE
Business International

Europe, West – English monthly SF750

An in-depth look at the major issues affecting business in Europe with particular emphasis on the single European market.

11009 FOUNDRY DIRECTORY AND REGISTER OF FORGES
Metal Bulletin Books Ltd

Europe, West – English biennial 1959 286pp £25.00
ISBN No. 0 900 542 94 2

Includes alphabetical index to foundries and forges in the UK and West Europe, buyers' guide to UK castings and forgings, foundries in West Europe, suppliers of equipment.

11010 FREE TRADE AGREEMENTS OF THE EFTA COUNTRIES WITH THE EUROPEAN COMMUNITIES
European Free Trade Association

Europe, West – English/French/German free

Text of the EFTA agreements of 1972 and subsequent similar agreements.

11011 GUIDES TO EUROPEAN TAXATION: THE TAXATION OF COMPANIES IN EUROPE
International Bureau of Fiscal Documentation

Europe, West – English updated 6 times a year DF1600, updating service DF650

Analysis and discussion of all taxes levied on companies in West European countries.

11012 GUIDES TO EUROPEAN TAXATION: VOL.1–THE TAXATION OF PATENT ROYALTIES, DIVIDENDS, INTEREST IN EUROPE
International Bureau of Fiscal Documentation

Europe, West – English updated 3 times a year DF630, updates DF320

Analyses taxation on income flowing between companies from one country to another.

11013 GUIDES TO EUROPEAN TAXATION: VOL.4–VALUE ADDED TAXATION IN EUROPE
International Bureau of Fiscal Documentation

Europe, West – English updated 4 times per year DF840, updating service DF340

Analyses and survey of VAT in 14 West European countries (including Portugal and Spain).

11014 LES INVESTISSEMENTS DIRECTS ETATS-UNIS/EUROPE NOTES ET ETUDES DOCUMENTAIRE NO 4771
La Documentation Francaise

Europe, West – French 1984 116pp FrF50
ISSN No. 0029 4004

Covers direct investment between the US and Europe.

11015 LES PAYS D'EUROPE OCCIDENTALE
La Documentation Francaise

Europe, West – French annual 1980 276pp FrF48
ISSN No. 0029-4004

Review of political and economic social life in the 17 countries of Western Europe.

11016 FONTI STATISTICHED ECONOMIA DEI PAESI MEDITERRANEI STATISTICHE ED ECONOMIA
Istituto di Ricerche sull'economia mediterranea

Europe, West – Italian/English/German 1987 350-400pp Free on request

Economy and statistics of Mediterranean countries.

11017 STOCKHOLM CONVENTION
European Free Trade Association

Europe, West – English/French bilingual paperback edition free

English/French bilingual loose-leaf edition. Full text of the Stockholm Convention (including the full text of Annex B, on origin rules) with regular updating service supplying amendments SF60.00.

EEC

12001 **ABECOR COUNTRY REPORT – EEC**
Abecor

European Communities – English 1986 2pp free

Brief economic report.

12002 **AGRICULTURE–STATISTICAL YEARBOOK**
European Community

European Communities – multilingual-tables in French and English annual 260pp ECU20.90

Contains the most important data published in the specialized agricultural statistical yearbook including land use, structure of agricultural holdings, crop production, animal production, prices and price indices, agricultural accounts, forestry and fisheries.

12003 **AGRICULTURAL INCOME**
European Community

European Communities – English annual 100pp ECU9

Compares changes in agricultural income between the current and previous year overall and by country.

12004 **AGRICULTURAL MARKETS–PRICE**
European Community

European Communities – multilingual 10 issues per year 1981 ECU41.21

12005 **AGRICULTURAL PRICES**
European Community

European Communities – German/English/French/Italian annual 300pp ECU18.50

Gives selling price in ECU and the national currency for crop products, wine, animals and meat, animal products and purchase prices of the meat and agricultural production industry. Feedingstuffs, fertilizers, motor fuels and fuels for heating.

12006 **AGRICULTURAL PRICES, QUARTERLY**
European Community

European Communities – quarterly 1983 microfiche

Contains monthly agricultural price series covering the preceding two years.

12007 **ANIMAL PRODUCTION–QUARTERLY STATISTICS**
European Community

European Communities – English/French quarterly 110pp ECU50.90

Gives monthly, quarterly and annual data on meat/eggs and poultry/milk and milk products for both production and external, plus an annexe on supply balance sheets with survey results and forecasts.

12008 **ANNUAL REPORT–CEDEFOP**
European Centre for the Development of Vocational Training

European Communities – multilingual annual 84pp free

A description of the activities of CEDEFOP including a list of members of staff.

12009 **ANNUAL REPORT-EFTA**
European Free Trade Association

European Communities – English annual free

12010 **BALANCE OF PAYMENTS–GEOGRAPHICAL BREAKDOWN**
European Community

European Communities – English/French annual 209pp ECU17.60

Part 1 gives a geographical breakdown for each member state, plus the US and Japan and the EC as a whole. Part 2 gives tables for selected items, e.g. goods and services, unrequited transfers, long-term capital, basic balance.

12011 **BALANCE OF PAYMENTS–GLOBAL DATA**
European Community

European Communities – English/French annual 65pp ECU7.78

Data on global balance of payments (annual flows) for each member state and for the community as a whole. Tables covering individual topics such as goods and services, current account capital and reserves.

12012 **BALANCE OF PAYMENTS–GLOBAL DATA**
European Community

European Communities – English/French quarterly 125pp ECU27.70 per sub

Data on the overall balance of payments (quarterly and annual flows) for each member state, for the community as a whole and for the US and Japan. Also comparative tables for the main balances of the balances of payments of industrialized countries.

12013 **BASIC STATISTICS OF THE COMMUNITY**
European Community

European Communities – multilingual annual 293pp ECU7

Basic statistics of the EEC compared with other European countries, Canada, US, Japan and USSR.

12014 **BULLETIN OF THE ECONOMIC AND SOCIAL COMMITTEE OF THE EUROPEAN COMMUNITIES**
European Communities

European Communities – multilingual monthly c60pp ECU28

Summarizes world events in so far as they affect the EEC, and also gives information on current legislation, policies and trends in the EEC.

12015 **BULLETIN OF ENERGY PRICES**
European Community

European Communities – English/French twice a year 85pp ECU8.10

Summarizes recent price information for all principal energy sources. Covers both import and consumer prices.

12016 **BULLETIN OF THE EUROPEAN COMMUNITIES**
European Community

European Communities–multilingual monthly + indexes 150pp ECU80.90, 1 copy ECU7

Covers main events, developments in community policy, external relations, financing of community activities, European political cooperation, relations between the Community's institutions and activities of the institutions.

12017 **BULLETIN OF THE EUROPEAN COMMUNITIES SUPPLEMENT**
European Community

European Communities – irregular

These appear in a separate series and are numbered independently. They generally feature official texts adopted by the Communities, e.g. communications to the council, programmes, reports, proposals.

12018 **THE C.A.P. MONITOR**
Agra Europe (London) Ltd

European Communities – English monthly £368 UK, £385 Europe, £396 world

A regular updated loose-leaf guide to the Common Agricultural policy of the European Community.

12019 **CARRIAGE OF GOODS–INLAND WATERWAYS**
European Community

European Communities – multilingual annual 168pp ECU12.80

Traffic of goods by inland waterways with the European Communities by country, by type of vessel and by type of goods.

12020 **CARRIAGE OF GOODS–RAILWAYS**
European Communities

European Communities – multilingual annual 150pp ECU17.50

Statistics on goods transported by rail in to the EEC by member states and by type of goods.

12021 **CARRIAGE OF GOODS–ROAD**
European Community

European Communities – multilingual annual 110pp ECU12.80

Statistics on goods traffic by road, carried on vehicles registered in member states.

12022 **COMPETITION LAW IN THE EEC AND ECSC APPLICABLE TO STATE AIDS**
European Community

European Communities – English occasional 261pp ECU6.70

A compilation of council regulations, statutory decisions and notices from the community relating to competition.

12023 **COMPLETING THE INTERNAL MARKET**
European Community

European Communities – multilingual 1985 37pp

White paper from the Commission for the European Council on the Single European Market.

12024 **CONSUMER PRICE INDEX**
European Community

European Communities – monthly ECU46.50, subscription ECU4.40 per copy

Consumer price indices for individual member states and the EEC as a whole. A quarterly supplement provides a detailed breakdown of consumer prices by product for each market with a time series of up to six years.

12025 **LES COOPERATIVES OUVRIERES DE PRODUCTION EN FRANCE ET DANS LA CEE NOTES DE ETUDES DOCUMENTAIRES NO 4690-91**
La Documentation Francaise

European Communities – French 1982 192pp FrF50
ISSN No. 0029 4004

Covers workers' cooperatives in the European Community.

12026 **THE COURIER**
European Community

European Communities – English/French bimonthly 140pp

Magazine for developing countries linked by association agreements to the community. Deals with community affairs and development policy.

12027 **CROP PRODUCTION**
European Community

European Communities – English/French/German/Italian quarterly 90pp ECU15.00

Current information on: production of crops, fruit and vegetables, area sown, stocks and deliveries of cereals and potatoes, meterology, supply balances for crop products.

12028 **CROP PRODUCTION–QUARTERLY STATISTICS GLOSSARIUM**
European Community

European Communities – multilingual annual 30pp

Glossary of terms used in Crop Production Quarterly Statistics.

12029 **DEMOGRAPHIC STATISTICS**
European Community

European Communities – multilingual occasional 220pp ECU18.50

A series of thematical tables on population change, population of states, population by sex and age, births, marriages and deaths and international comparisons. The rest of the book contains country tables which include forecast data.

12030 **DIRECTORY OF THE COMMISSION OF THE EUROPEAN COMMUNITIES**
European Community

European Communities – multilingual irregular 124pp ECU3.50

Studies of the services of the Commission of the European Communities.

12031 **DIRECTORY OF EUROPEAN AGRICULTURAL ORGANISATIONS**
European Community

European Communities – occasional 718pp ECU67.10

12032 **ECU–EMS INFORMATION**
European Community

European Communities – monthly 10pp ECU25.70, subscription 1 copy ECU4

Statistical data and information on the European Monetary System and the ECU exchange rates.

12033 **EEC**
National Westminster Bank

European Communities – English irregular 4pp free

Brief economic report.

12034 **EEC: CHECKLIST OF SELECTED SECONDARY LEGISLATION AND BACKGROUND INFORMATION**
British Bankers Association

European Communities – English annual £25.00

Synopsis of EEC regulations which affect banking.

12035 **EEC COMPETITION RULES**
European Community

European Communities – 62pp

Guide to small and medium-sized enterprises on competition rules.

12036 **EEC DAIRY FACTS AND FIGURES**
Milk Marketing Board, UK

European Communities – English annual £6.00

Description of the main features of EEC institutions and regulations relevant to the dairy industry. There are comparative tables for herd structure, prices, supplies and trade.

12037 **E F NEWS**
European Foundation for the Improvement of Living and Working Conditions

European Communities – multilingual bi-monthly free

A bi-monthly newsletter which, in addition to highlighting the activities of the foundation, selectively covers other work being done in Europe on themes relevant to the foundation's aims.

12038 **E G MAGAZIN**
Nomos Verlagsgesellschaft

European Communities – German 10 times a year DM40

A European-wide coverage of economics, law, politics and culture. Each issue concentrates on a particular theme.

12039 **EIB INFORMATION**
European Community

European Communities – English/German/ Danish/Dutch quarterly free

Newsletter of the European Investment Bank.

12040 **ERDF IN FIGURES**
European Community

European Regional Development Fund.

12041 **EARNINGS–INDUSTRY AND SERVICES**
European Community

European Communities – English/Spanish/ German/Italian twice a year 227pp ECU22.28 subscription

Statistics on earnings of manual workers in industry, of non-manual workers in industry and of earnings in services by country and by industrial group.

12042 **ECONOMIC AND SOCIAL CONSULTATIVE ASSEMBLY ANNUAL REPORT**
European Community

European Communities – multilingual annual 117pp ECU4.04

Reviews the work of the Committee and describes its structure and membership.

12043 **ECONOMIC AND SOCIAL SITUATION OF THE COMMUNITY**
European Communities

European Communities – multilingual 44pp ECU4

Covers the committee opinion on the economic situation and social development within the EC.

12044 **ECONOMIC ACCOUNTS FOR AGRICULTURE, FORESTRY, UNIT VALUES**
European Community

European Communities – Introduction multilingual, table in French/English annual 122pp ECU17.40

The publication contains 2 types of tables: giving a comparative picture of the main national accounts and aggregates over 7 years and detailed tables by country for a period of 5 years in national currencies.

12045 **ELECTRICITY PRICES**
European Community

European Communities – English/French annual 90pp ECU11.50

Contains the most recent prices and a time series. Provides data for industrial and for household prices by member state.

12046 **EMPLOYMENT & UNEMPLOYMENT**
European Community

European Communities – multilingual annual 227pp ECU19.60

Includes such data as populations, working population and employment, employees in employment by industry, unemployment, skills and working hours.

12047 **ENERGY–MONTHLY STATISTICS**
European Community

European Communities – German/English/ French monthly ECU53.50 subscription, ECU5.10 1 copy

Includes data on coal, hydrocarbons, electrical energy, petroleum balance sheets, energy balance sheets, climatic conditions and prices. Includes import/ export and production by product and by country.

12048 **ENERGY & STATISTICAL YEARBOOK**
European Community

European Communities – Danish/Greek/ English/French/Dutch annual 200pp ECU20.90

Statistical information on the energy and economy in the community and member states, structured around the energy balance sheets for the last year.

12049 **ENERGY IN EUROPE**
European Community

European Communities – multilingual 3 times a year 1985 78pp ECU35 subscription, ECU12.70 1 issue

Energy policies and trends in the European Community.

12050 **EURATOM SUPPLY AGENCY–ANNUAL REPORT**
European Community

European Communities – English annual 49pp ECU5.80

12051 **EUROBAROMETER–PUBLIC OPINION IN THE EUROPEAN COMMUNITY**
European Community

European Communities – multilingual bi-annual 1974 150pp

Twice-yearly opinion poll published in the official Community languages.

12052 **EUROFISH REPORT**
Agra Europe (London) Ltd, UK

European Communities – English semi-monthly £347 UK, £370 Europe, £380 world

Review of European fishing and world fisheries. Coverage of EEC legislation and common fisheries policy.

12053 **THE EUROPEAN COMMUNITY'S FISHERY POLICY**
European Community

European Communities – occasional 77pp

Survey of the fisheries situation, resources, consumption, economic importance of the fishing industry, justification for a European policy and its aims; fisheries in the international context.

12054 **THE EUROPEAN COMMUNITY–THE MEDITERRANEAN BASIN**
European Communities

European Communities – 1985 175pp

Study on the consequences of the process of enlargement both for the Mediterranean zone and for the community itself.

12055 **EUROPEAN DOCUMENTATION**
European Community

European Communities – 30-90pp

In-depth coverage of the main community policies such as the internal market, the economy, environmental policy, European unification, agricultural policy, the ECU, social policy.

12056 **EUROPA TRANSPORT–ANALYSIS & FORECASTS**
European Community

European Communities – English (available multilingual) annual 26pp ECU2.24

Observations of general trends in transport activity, including modal and geographical analysis.

12057 **EUROPA TRANSPORT–MARKET DEVELOPMENTS**
European Community

European Communities – multilingual quarterly + 2 annual studies 70pp ECU3.35

General assessment of main trends of period under review with results mainly in tabular and graphical form of statistical information on the international intra-Community transport of goods.

12058 **EUROPA TRANSPORT–OBSERVATIONS OF TRANSPORT MARKETS**
European Communities

European Communities – multilingual 4 issues and 2 annual studies 115pp ECU19.70

12059 **EUROPE IN FIGURES**
European Community

European Communities –multilingual 64pp ECU5

Covers 30 subjects covering the entire socio-economic situation in the European Community and comparing it with that of the US and Japan.

12060 **EUROPEAN AGRICULTURE PRICE INDICES AND GLOSSARIUM**
European Community

European Communities – multilingual annual 50pp

Glossary of terms used in European Agricultural Price Indices.

12061 **EUROPEAN COMMUNITIES AGRICULTURAL PRICE INDICES: MONTHLY RESULTS, HALF YEARLY STATISTICS**
European Community

European Communities – French/English biannual 110pp ECU34.70

The EC Agricultural Price Indlces (output and input) comprises the EC Index of producer prices of agricultural products and the EC Indices of producers' prices of the means of agricultural production.

12062 **EUROPEAN COMMUNITY – ASIAN TRADE: A STATISTICAL ANALYSIS**
European Community

European Communities - English/French occasional 266pp ECU9.30

Analysis of the evaluation of the geographical and product distribution of trade between the EC and the Asian countries.

12063 **EUROPEAN ECONOMY**
European Community

European Communities – English quarterly 220pp ECU58.00 p.a.

Economic trends, planning and reports for the European Community as a whole.

12064 **EUROPEAN ECONOMY–SUPPLEMENT: SERIES A–RECENT ECONOMIC TRENDS**
European Community

European Communities – English 11 issues a year 8pp ECU23.50 p.a.

12065 **EUROPEAN ECONOMY–SERIES B: ECONOMIC PROSPECTS–BUSINESS SURVEY RESULTS AND CONSUMER SURVEY RESULTS**
European Community

European Communities – 11 issues a year ECU23.50

12066 **EUROPEAN FILE**
European Communities

European Communities–multilingual fortnightly 12pp free

Consists of short reviews, and takes a brief look at some community topics.

12067 **EUROPEAN INVESTMENT BANK–ANNUAL REPORT**
European Communities

European Communities – annual 120pp

A review of the year's activities, particularly loans granted within the community and elsewhere, along with the relevant statistics.

12068 **EUROPEAN INVESTMENT BANK–KEY FACTS**
European Community

European Communities – English leaflet free

Information leaflet.

12069 **THE EUROPEAN ORCHARD–1977 & 1982 SURVEYS–ANALYSES AND FORECASTS**
European Community

European Communities – introduction in German/French/English/Italian, text in French occasional 117pp ECU6.69

Reports the results of two surveys on fruit tree plantation for the production of dessert apples and pears, peaches and oranges, intended entirely and mainly for sale.

12070 **EUROPEAN REGIONAL DEVELOPMENT FUND–ANNUAL REPORT**
European Community

European Communities – annual 165pp ECU9.50

Describes the work and distribution of the fund, the type of projects provided and how they are managed.

12071 **EUROSTAT NEWS**
European Community

European Communities – Danish/English/ French quarterly 30pp ECU53.50

News and general information on the Statistical Office of the European Communities.

12072 **EUROSTAT REVIEW**
European Community

European Communities – English/French/ German annual 221pp ECU16.20

Compendium of the most important community statistics over a 10-year period.

12073 **EUROSTATISTICS: DATA FOR SHORT-TERM ECONOMIC ANALYSIS**
European Community

European Communities – English/French/ German 11 times a year 110pp ECU53.50, ECU54 1 copy

Reviews the main quantitative data relating to the community and its member states: economy, employment, industrial production, sample surveys, external trade, prices, finance, balance of payments.

12074 **EXPRESS MONITOR**
AGRA Europe (London) Ltd

European Communities – English weekly 1987 £330 UK, £346 Europe ISBN/ISSN No. 0951 2063

Detailed reports, summaries and commentary on EEC legislation with advance notification of proposed new regulations and reports from management committees.

12075 **EXTERNAL TRADE–ANALYTICAL TABLE–NIMEXE**
European Communities

European Communities – annual number of pages varies per volume ECU704

Foreign trade statistics relating to all the goods entering and leaving the community or available among members. There are separate volumes for export and import and the data is classified by product. Volume and value figures are both given.

12076 **EXTERNAL TRADE–MONTHLY STATISTICS**
European Communities

European Communities – English/French monthly 120pp ECU111 subscription, ECU10.20 1 copy

Contains a general summary of trade by country and trade by commodity, trends in trade by country and trade by commodity, trade by partner countries and trade of main non-community countries.

12077 **EXTERNAL TRADE–STATISTICAL YEARBOOK**
European Communities

European Communities – multilingual annual 75pp ECU8.70

Special information is given on the trade of Spain and Portugal from 1977.

12078 **EXTERNAL TRADE STATISTICS: USERS GUIDE**
European Community

European Communities – occasional 64pp

12079 **FAMILY BUDGETS-COMPARATIVE TABLES:GERMANY, FRANCE, ITALY, UNITED KINGDOM**
European Communities

Germany/France/Italy/UK – English/French occasional 197pp ECU4.42

Data on households and accommodation, average annual expenditure of household and average quantitative consumption of selected items. Each section is subdivided by socio-economic category, by type of household, by income group, by region and by urban/rural location.

12080 **FAMILY BUDGETS–COMPARATIVE TABLES: NETHERLANDS, BELGIUM, IRELAND, DENMARK, GREECE, SPAIN**
European Communities

Belgium, Ireland, Denmark, Greece, Spain – German/English/French/Dutch occasional 279pp ECU5.53

Data on households and accommodation, average annual expenditure of household and average quantitative consumption of selected items. Each section is subdivided by socio-economic category, by type of household, by income group, by region and by urban/rural location.

12081 **FARM ACCOUNTANCY DATA NETWORK: HANDBOOK OF LEGISLATION–INSTRUCTIONS–NOTES FOR GUIDANCE**
European Community

European Communities – occasional 26pp ECU9.88

Two parts.

12082 **FARM STRUCTURE - METHODOLOGY OF COMMUNITY SURVEYS**
European Communities

European Communities – English 1986 290pp ECU15.70

Defines the methodology used to carry out the 1983, 1985 and 1987 surveys of farm structure.

12083 **FARM STRUCTURE SURVEY–ANALYSIS OF RESULTS**
European Communities

European Communities – English/French/ German occasional pages vary per analysis cost varies per analysis

A series of brief analyses of the Farm Structure Survey covering: economics, size and other principal activities/type of farming/agriculture labour force/structure of dairy products/regional aspects of agricultural holdings. Last issued as a separate publication.

12084 **FARM STRUCTURE SURVEY–MAIN RESULTS**
European Communities

European Communities – French/English/ German introduction irregular 1967 30pp ECU11.60

Results of the survey are given by: member of state, by size, classes of holdings, by farm types and by regions with a sector on historical results.

12085 **FINANCIAL REPORT–EUROPEAN COAL & STEEL COMMUNITY**
European Community

European Communities – annual 80pp free

12086 **FISHERIES–STATISTICAL YEARBOOK**
European Community

European Communities – annual 119pp

12087 **FOREIGN TRADE–THIRD COUNTRIES–STATISTICAL YEARBOOK**
European Communities

European Communities – annual ECU29.60

Vol. A ACP (African, Caribbean and Pacific) countries, Vol. B Mediterranean countries. Imports and exports in both volumes supplied giving principal products and groupings of products by principal partner and trading zones. Products are classified to SITC Rev. 1.

12088 **FORESTRY STATISTICS**
European Communities

European Communities – multilingual irregular 117pp ECU11.60

Data on forest structure, wood production by type, raw wood balances, pulpwood balance sheets, intra-community trade in raw wood and supply sheets of main wood products by country, consumption of pulpwood and number of forest fires.

12089 **GAS PRICES**
European Communities

European Communities – English annual 100pp ECU11.60

Updating of the annual inquiries with a time series back to 1980.

12090 **DER GEMEINSAME AGRARMARKT**
Nomos Verlagsgesellschaft

European Communities – German looseleaf DM198

Covers the Common Agricultural Policy.

12091 **GENERAL GOVERNMENT ACCOUNTS AND STATISTICS**
European Communities

European Communities – multilingual, tables in English/French annual 327pp ECU16.20

This series on the statistics of general government shows the total of general government transactions by subsectors (central and local government, social security) together with an analysis of the revenue and expenditure of this sector. The volume also contains details of the product of various national taxes.

12092 **GENERAL REPORT ON THE ACTIVITIES OF THE EUROPEAN COMMUNITY IN ...**
European Community

European Communities – multilingual annual 400pp ECU9.50

Review of Community activities over the past year.

12093 **GOVERNMENT FINANCING OF RESEARCH AND DEVELOPMENT**
European Community

European Communities – English annual 114pp ECU14

Analysis of trends in the financing of research and development in the member states and analysis by objective.

12094 **GRANTS AND LOANS FROM THE EUROPEAN COMMUNITY**
European Community

European Communities – 140pp

The community's system of loans and grants, how it works and how to have recourse to it.

12095 **GREEN EUROPE**
AGRA Europe (London) Ltd

European Communities – English monthly 1963 £466 UK, £504 Europe, £516 world ISSN No. 0141 2213

Background information on CAP and other matters affecting agriculture and allied industries.

12096 **GREEN EUROPE**
European Community

European Communities – English irregular 60pp ECU1.20 per copy ISSN No. 0250-5886

Newsletter on the common agricultural policy.

12097 **INDUSTRIAL PRODUCTION–QUARTERLY STATISTICS**
European Community

European Communities – English/French/ German quarterly 200pp ECU28

Statistics of industrial production by product. Annual and quarterly data on production of industrial products in member states of the EC.

12098 **INDUSTRIAL TRENDS: MONTHLY STATISTICS**
European Community

European Communities – English/German/ French monthly 70pp ECU46.50

Indices of industrial production, turnover, orders received, number of employees, gross wages and salaries by branch of industry, as well as indices of the value of export and import. A special chapter is devoted to the building and civil engineering sector.

12099 **INDUSTRY–STATISTICAL YEARBOOK**
European Community

European Communities – Introduction in all EEC languages/tables in French/English annual 140pp ECU22.10

A selection of the most important statistics about industry concerning structure, activity, investments, size of enterprises, industrial products, short-term indicators and external trade as well as comparative tables between EC, US and Japan.

12100 **INFORMATION MARKET**
European Community

European Communities – multilingual quarterly 10pp free

This newsletter is published as a special supplement to Euroabstracts.

12101 **AN INTRODUCTION TO THE LAWS AND INSTITUTIONS OF THE EUROPEAN COMMUNITIES**
Butterworth & Co. (Publishers) Ltd, UK
D. Lasok and J. Bridge

European Communities – English 4th edition 1987 520pp £23.00 hard £15.95 soft
ISBN No. 0 406 26880 0 hard
ISBN No. 0 406 26881 9 soft

Provides a clear exposition of the framework of the European Communities.

12102 INVESTMENT IN THE COMMUNITY COALMINING AND IRON & STEEL INDUSTRIES: SURVEY
European Community

European Communities – English/French/German annual 102pp ECU18.50

Data on capital expenditure and production in each of the industries and their subdivisions.

12103 IRON & STEEL–MONTHLY
European Community

European Communities – German/English/French/Italian monthly 22pp ECU37 subscription, ECU3.50 1 copy

Data on production of pig iron, crude steel and for the various finished solid products, new orders for ordinary steels, production and special steel and foreign and internal trade and employment within the industry.

12104 IRON & STEEL–QUARTERLY STATISTICS
European Community

European Communities – German/English/French quarterly 77pp ECU72 subscription, ECU19.60 1 copy

Includes employment, production, works deliveries, receipts and stocks, trade and consumption.

12105 IRON & STEEL–STATISTICAL YEARBOOK
European Community

European Communities – multilingual annual 149pp ECU23.10

Data on economic and industrial background, employment in the industry, production of raw materials, and iron and steel, works deliveries, foreign trade, consumption, investment, price and wages.

12106 JOURNAL OF COMMON MARKET STUDIES
Basil Blackwell UK, Publisher

European Communities – English quarterly c90pp per issue £22.00 p.a.

Articles on economic and political developments in common market countries.

12107 LABOUR COSTS
European Communities

European Communities – multilingual occasional 1966 2 vols ECU11.40

12108 LABOUR FORCE SURVEY
European Community

European Communities – multilingual annual 165pp ECU7

Facts and figures on population, labour forces, workers, the unemployed, weekly working hours and categories of activity by region.

12109 MILK PRODUCTS
AGRA Europe (London) Ltd

European Communities – English ten issues per year 1986 £154 UK, £165 Europe, £170 world
ISSN No. 0950 3730

A report on EC butter, cheese and milk production and markets with graphs and tables covering principal dairying nations of Europe and the world.

12110 MONEY AND FINANCE
European Community

European Communities – English/French quarterly 97pp ECU37 subscription, ECU10.40 1 copy

Data on structural indicators such as financial accounts, money supply, public finance, interest rates and exchange rates. Data on the European Monetary System and current financial indicators, e.g. share prices.

12111 NATIONAL ACCOUNTS ESA–AGGREGATES
European Communities

European Communities – English/French/Dutch annual 133pp ECU11.60

European system of integrated economic accounts-comparison between the member states, the US and Japan.

12112 NATIONAL ACCOUNTS ESA–DETAILED TABLES BY BRANCH
European Communities

European Communities – English/French annual 173pp ECU10.50

Operation on goods and services, value added, earnings of employees, gross fixed capital formation, final consumption of households.

12113 NATIONAL ACCOUNTS ESA–DETAILED TABLES BY SECTOR
European Community

European Communities – English/French annual 385pp ECU27.70

Detailed data for the community and the member states on flows of income between institutional sectors and their financial transactions.

12114 NEWSLETTER: NEW TECHNOLOGIES AND INNOVATION POLICY
European Community

European Communities – multilingual irregular 10pp ECU22

Reports on the community's policy on new technology, research and development and innovations.

12115 OFFICIAL JOURNAL OF THE EUROPEAN COMMUNITIES–SERIES C: INFORMATION AND NOTICES, SERIES L: LEGISLATION
European Community

European Communities – multilingual daily varies per issue ECU337 hardcopy, ECU233.40 microfilm, also available in microfiche

12116 OPERATION OF THE EUROPEAN COMMUNITY CONCERNING SMALL AND MEDIUM-SIZED ENTERPRISES PRACTICAL HANDBOOK
European Community

European Community – English irregular 214pp ECU17

12117 OPERATION OF NUCLEAR POWER STATIONS
European Community

European Communities – English/French annual 126pp ECU10.20

General data on nuclear plant operations followed by operational characteristics for individual plants by month, year and a historical time series.

12118 POUR UN ROLE ACTIF DE LA CEE SUR LA SCENE AGRICOLE INTERNATIONALE
La Documentation Francaise

European Communities – French irregular 184pp FrF55

An analysis of countries exporting agricultural products.

12119 PRACTICAL GUIDE TO THE USE OF THE EUROPEAN COMMUNITIES SCHEME OF GENERALISED TARIFF PREFERENCES
European Communities

European Communities – English 1986 369pp ECU12.44

12120 QUARTERLY NATIONAL ACCOUNTS/ESA
European Communities

European Communities – English quarterly 10pp ECU9.30 subscription, ECU2.50 1 copy

Contains indices and GDP.

12121 RAW MATERIALS: EC SUPPLY 1975-83
European Community

European Communities – German/English/French occasional 73pp ECU5.66

Gives general statistics on raw materials.

12122 **REGIONAL ACCOUNTS ESA–DETAILED TABLES BY BRANCH**
European Communities

European Communities – multilingual annual 107pp ECU11.37

Section A contains summary tables including a time series for gross value added, population, employment and GDP. Section B contains detailed tables by branch for the latest year.

12123 **REGIONS–THE COMMUNITY'S FINANCIAL PARTICIPATION IN INVESTMENTS**
European Community

European Communities – annual 87pp ECU5.80

12124 **THE REGIONS OF THE ENLARGED COMMUNITY**
European Communities

European Communities – occasional 1980 270pp ECU23.30

A periodic report on the social and economic situation in the region of the community and industry, a statement of the regional policy committee.

12125 **REGIONS–STATISTICAL YEARBOOK**
European Community

European Communities – multilingual annual 233pp ECU23.20

Contains comparable statistics which are the most representative of the social and economic situation in the EC such as demography, employment and unemployment, living standards, transport, industry, energy, agriculture and economic aggregates.

12126 **REGIONS IN THE EUROPEAN COMMUNITY**
Oxford University Press

European Communities – English 1985 265pp £22.50
ISBN No. 019 827476 9

European studies and comparative government.

12127 **REPORT IN COMPETITION POLICY**
European Community

European Communities – multilingual annual 286pp ECU11.60

Overall survey of the policy during the previous year, its application to companies, state aids, adjustments of national monopolies of either a commercial or public nature.

12128 **REPORT OF ACTIVITIES–MONETARY COMMITTEE OF THE EUROPEAN COMMUNITIES**
European Community

European Communities – annual 14pp ECU4.60

12129 **REPORT ON THE AGRICULTURAL SITUATION IN THE COMMUNITY**
European Community

European Communities – English annual 486pp ECU25.50

Analyses and statistics on the general situation, factors of production, the structures and situation of the markets for agricultural products, obstacles to the common agricultural market, the position of consumers and producers and the financial aspects. The general prospects and market outlook for agricultural products are also dealt with.

12130 **REPORT ON SOCIAL DEVELOPMENTS**
European Community

European Communities – multilingual annual 268pp ECU21

European Commission's review of social events during the past year in the Europe of 12, reflecting the views of government experts and spokesmen for the various groups in European Society.

12131 **RESULTS OF THE BUSINESS SURVEY CARRIED OUT AMONGST MANAGEMENTS IN THE COMMUNITY**
European Community

European Communities – Danish/German/English/French/Italian/Dutch monthly 50pp ECU46.20

Based on the questionnaire to 20,000 enterprises. Questions asked mostly include level of production, stocks, prices, order book and expectations, quarterly questions include those on employment, limits on production capacity, new orders, duration of assured production and capacity utilates. A half-year investment survey is also carried out.

12132 **SOCIAL EUROPE–GENERAL REVIEW**
European Community

European Communities – English 3 issues per year 140pp ECU28, ECU10.20 1 copy

This review and its supplements cover the community's principal measures, policies and studies on employment, social affairs, education, health and safety, professional training as well as the main events taking place in the field of employment in the member states along with latest statistical data.

12133 **STATISTICAL YEARBOOK: TRANSPORT, COMMUNICATIONS, TOURISM**
European Community

European Communities – multilingual occasional 196pp ECU26.68

The yearbook contains in detail the most important data on infrastructure, mobile equipment, the distances travelled by the various modes of transport and selected data for traffic accidents, post and telecommunications and tourism.

12134 **STEEL CONSUMPTION BY USER BRANCH**
European Community

European Communities – English/French/German 1970-84 76pp ECU5.80

Detailed statistics on overall community steel consumption by steel product and user branch.

12135 **STRUCTURE AND ACTIVITY OF INDUSTRY–ANNUAL ENQUIRY–MAIN RESULTS**
European Community

European Communities – German/English/French annual 300pp ECU21

The main results of the coordinated annual inquiry into industrial activity. It gives annually the results for the most important economic variables of the inquiry which are: employment, value added products, value labour costs. The tables are presented first by variable and then by industrial activity arranged according to NACE.

12136 **STRUCTURE AND ACTIVITY OF INDUSTRY–DATA BY SIZE OF ENTERPRISE**
European Community

European Communities – English/French/German biannual ECU6.73

The results of the coordinated annual inquiry into industry for the five most important variables by three classes of size of enterprise.

12137 **SUPPLEMENT TO THE OFFICIAL JOURNAL OF THE EUROPEAN COMMUNITIES, SERIES S**
European Economic Community

European Communities – multilingual daily ECU150.20
ISSN No. 0378-7273

Publication of notices of public works, contracts and public supply contracts and invitations to tender of the European Development Fund.

12138 **TRADE: EC–DEVELOPING COUNTRIES– MANUFACTURED PRODUCTS–ANALYSIS**
European Community

European Communities – English/French occasional 418pp ECU11.60

Analyses the development and structure of the European Community's trade in manufactured products with developing countries.

12139 **TRANSPORT AND EUROPEAN INTEGRATION**
European Communities
Carlo Degli Abbati

European Communities – English occasional ECU15.48

Covers all modes of transport and European transport policy administered by the international institutions.

12140 TRENDS IN THE DISTRIBUTIVE TRADES, RETAILS SALES, REGISTRATION OF CARS
European Communities

European Communities – English/French monthly 10pp ECU18.50 subscription, ECU2.40 1 copy

Data on retail trade value and on registration of private and commercial cars by country.

12141 UNEMPLOYMENT – MONTHLY BULLETIN
European Communities

European Communities – English monthly 14pp ECU 23.50 subscription, ECU 3.40 per copy

12142 VOCATIONAL TRAINING BULLETIN
European Centre for the Development of Vocational Training

European Communities–multilingual 3 issues per year 64pp ECU8 subscription

Articles on vocational training and on particular projects throughout the European Community.

FINLAND

13001 **THE 3000 LARGEST COMPANIES IN FINLAND**
Company Facts Ltd

Finland – Finnish/Swedish/English annual 175pp Fmk385
ISSN No. 0784 0012

13002 **ABECOR COUNTRY REPORT – FINLAND**
Abecor

Finland – English 1986 2pp free

Brief economic report.

13003 **ANNUAL REPORT – FINNAIR OY**
Finnair Oy

Finland – Finnish/English annual 40pp

Financial results of Finnair.

13004 **ANNUAL REPORT (KANSALLIS-OSAKE-PANKKI)**
Kansallis-Osake-Pankki

Finland – Finnish/English annual

Annual report of the bank.

13005 **AGRICULTURE AND FORESTRY: ECONOMY STATISTICS OF AGRICULTURE AND FORESTRY (OSF XXXIX)**
Central Statistical Office of Finland

Finland – Finnish/Swedish/English irregular 1979 81pp
ISSN No. 0356 2913

13006 **AUTOMOBILES AND HIGHWAYS IN FINLAND**
Finnish Road Association

Finland – Finnish/English annual 115pp
ISSN No. 0567 1795

13007 **BANK OF FINLAND ANNUAL STATEMENT**
Bank of Finland

Finland – Swedish/English/Finnish annual 1866 Fmk10

Annual report of the Bank of Finland.

13008 **BANK OF FINLAND MONTHLY BULLETIN**
Bank of Finland

Finland – English monthly 30pp free

Basic statistics and key economic indicators and articles in the economy.

13009 **BANK OF FINLAND YEAR BOOK**
Bank of Finland

Finland – Finnish/Swedish/English annual Fmk60

13010 **BANKING TECHNOLOGY AND PAYMENT SYSTEMS IN FINLAND**
Finnish Bankers' Association

Finland – English/Finnish annual November 1985 20pp free

Banking technology and payment systems in Finland.

13011 **BANKS: BANK OF FINLAND, POST OFFICE BANK, COMMERCIAL BANKS, MORTGAGE BANKS, SAVINGS BANKS, COOPERATIVE BANKS, FOREIGN-OWNED BANKING INSTITUTIONS (STATISTICAL REPORT RT, FINANCING)**
Central Statistical Office of Finland

Finland – Finnish/Swedish monthly 1974 22pp Fmk120.00
ISSN No. 0355 2322

13012 **BANKS: COMMERCIAL BANKS, COOPERATIVE BANKS, SAVINGS BANKS, MORTGAGE BANKS AND FOREIGN-OWNED INSTITUTIONS (OSF VII)**
Central Statistical Office of Finland

Finland – Finnish/Swedish/English annual 1874 40pp Fmk55
ISSN No. 0355 2454

13013 **BANKS: STATE OF SAVINGS BANKS AND COOPERATIVE BANKS, BONDS AND DEBENTURES OWNED BY BANKS (STATISTICAL REPORT RT, FINANCING)**
Central Statistical Office of Finland

Finland – Finnish/Swedish quarterly 1975 3pp Fmk40 ISSN No. 0355 2322

13014 **BLUE BOOK: DIRECTORY OF THE ECONOMIC LIFE IN FINLAND**
Sininen Kirja Oy

Finland – Finnish/Swedish/English annual 1050pp Fmk820
ISSN No. 0782-2553

13015 **BUILDING CONSTRUCTION STATISTICS (STATISTICAL REPORT RA, CONSTRUCTION)**
Central Statistical Office of Finland

Finland – Finnish/Swedish quarterly 1967 15pp Fmk60
ISSN No. 0355 2314

13016 **BUILDING COST INDICES (INDEX REPORT RK)**
Central Statistical Office of Finland

Finland – Finnish/Swedish monthly 1964 6pp Fmk80
ISSN No. 0355 239X

13017 **BUILDING PERMITS GRANTED (STATISTICAL REPORT RA, CONSTRUCTION)**
Central Statistical Office of Finland

Finland – Finnish/Swedish monthly 1967 2pp Fmk80
ISSN No. 0355 2314

13018 **BULLETIN OF STATISTICS–QUARTERLY**
Central Statistical Office of Finland

Finland – Finnish/English quarterly 120pp Fmk160 per year

13019 **BULLETIN ON BANKRUPTCIES**
Central Statistical Office of Finland

Finland – Finnish monthly 1986 8pp Fmk180
ISSN No. 0783 716X

13020 **BUILDING CONSTRUCTION STATISTICS (OSF XVIII C)**
Central Statistical Office of Finland

Finland – Finnish/Swedish/English annual 1960 (1961) 180pp Fmk60
ISSN No. 0355 2152

13021 **BULLETIN OF STATISTICS-MONTHLY**
Central Statistical Office of Finland

Finland – Finnish/Swedish monthly 1982 7pp Fmk30
ISSN No. 0781 7584

Rapid information on indices, employment and unemployment.

13022 **CLOTHING INDUSTRY YEAR BOOK**
Central Association of the Finnish Clothing Industry

Finland – Finnish/Swedish annual 34pp free

Statistics on production, foreign trade and labour market.

13023 **CONSTRUCTION OF DWELLINGS (OSF XVII D)**
Central Statistical Office of Finland

Finland – Finnish/Swedish/English annual 1966 (1968) 66pp Fmk36
ISSN No. 0355 2152

13024 **CONSTRUCTION OF DWELLINGS (STATISTICAL REPORT RA, CONSTRUCTION)**
Central Statistical Office of Finland

Finland – Finnish/Swedish quarterly 1966 5pp
ISSN No. 0355 2314

13025 **CONSUMER PRICE INDEX (1985=100) (INDEX REPORT KH)**
Central Statistical Office of Finland

Finland – Finnish/Swedish monthly 1957 2pp Fmk60
ISSN No. 0355 2381

13026 **CONSUMER PRICE STATISTICS (STATISTICAL REPORT HI, PRICES)**
Central Statistical Office of Finland

Finland – Finnish/Swedish quarterly 1968 6pp Fmk40
ISSN No. 0355 2241

13027 **COST INDICES OF ROAD AND LAND CONSTRUCTION (INDEX REPORT TR)**
Central Statistical Office of Finland

Finland – Finnish/Swedish monthly 1969 2pp Fmk60
ISSN No. 0355 2411

13028 **COUNTRY PROFILES–FINLAND**
Economist Publications Ltd

Finland – English annual 40pp £25 UK, subscription varies in rest of world

Resumé of politics, economy and industry including statistical summaries.

13029 **COUNTRY REPORTS–FINLAND**
Economist Publications Ltd

Finland – English quarterly 25pp £58 UK, subscription varies in rest of world

Economic policies and development plans, trends in production and demand, monetary and fiscal conditions, wages and prices, merchandise trade, invisibles, capital flows, exchange rates and foreign debt plus a forecast of the economic prospects.

13030 **CREDIT FLOW STATISTICS (STATISTICAL REPORT RT, FINANCING)**
Central Statistical Office of Finland

Finland – Finnish/Swedish quarterly 1979 20pp Fmk40
ISSN No. 0355 2322

13031 **CREDIT MARKET STATISTICS (STATISTICAL REPORT RT, FINANCING)**
Central Statistical Office of Finland

Finland – Finnish/Swedish annual 1969 51pp Fmk48
ISSN No. 0355 2322

13032 **DWELLING UNITS AND FAMILIES (STATISTICAL REPORT VA, POPULATION)**
Central Statistical Office of Finland

Finland – Finnish/Swedish annual 1977 82pp Fmk62
ISSN No. 0355 2365

13033 **EARNINGS OF EMPLOYEES IN BUSINESS (STATISTICAL REPORT PA, WAGES)**
Central Statistical Office of Finland

Finland – Finnish/Swedish annual 1967 50pp Fmk40
ISSN No. 0355 2306

13034 **EARNINGS OF FARM WORKERS (STATISTICAL REPORT PA, WAGES)**
Central Statistical Office of Finland

Finland – Finnish/Swedish quarterly 1966 12pp Fmk35
ISSN No. 0355 2306

13035 **EARNINGS OF GOVERNMENT WORKERS AND EMPLOYEES PAID FOR THE HOUR (STATISTICAL REPORT PA, WAGES)**
Central Statistical Office of Finland

Finland – Finnish/Swedish five issues per year 1966 7pp Fmk35
ISSN No. 0355 2306

13036 **EARNINGS OF INDUSTRIAL EMPLOYEES (STATISTICAL REPORT PA, WAGES)**
Central Statistical Office of Finland

Finland – Finnish/Swedish annual 1977 50pp Fmk40
ISSN No. 0355 2306

13037 **EARNINGS OF INDUSTRIAL AND HOUSE CONSTRUCTION WORKERS (STATISTICAL REPORT PA, WAGES)**
Central Statistical Office of Finland

Finland – Finnish/Swedish quarterly 1966 4pp Fmk70
ISSN No. 0355 2306

13038 **EARNINGS OF NON-PROFIT INSTITUTIONS SERVING HOUSEHOLDS (STATISTICAL REPORT PA, WAGES)**
Central Statistical Office of Finland

Finland – Finnish/Swedish annual 1966 50pp Fmk40
ISSN N0. 0355 2306

13039 **EARNINGS OF TRANSPORT WORKERS (STATISTICAL REPORT PA, WAGES)**
Central Statistical Office of Finland

Finland – Finnish/Swedish quarterly 1966 10pp Fmk60
ISSN No. 0355 2306

13040 **EARNINGS OF WORKERS, EMPLOYED BY THE STATE UNDER WORKING CONTRACT (STATISTICAL REPORT PA, WAGES)**
Central Statistical Office of Finland

Finland – Finnish/Swedish annual 1966 50pp Fmk35
ISSN No. 0355 2306

13041 **EARNINGS OF WORKERS IN FORESTRY (STATISTICAL REPORT PA, WAGES)**
Central Statistical Office of Finland

Finland – Finnish/Swedish quarterly 1966 17pp Fmk35
ISSN No. 0355 2306

13042 **EARNINGS OF WORKERS PAID FOR THE HOUR IN COMMUNES AND COMMUNAL FEDERATIONS (STATISTICAL REPORT PA, WAGES)**
Central Statistical Office of Finland

Finland – Finnish/Swedish annual 1966 150pp Fmk65
ISSN No. 0355 2306

13043 **ECONOMIC SURVEY: FINLAND**
Ministry of Finance Economics Dept.

Finland – English annual 136pp Fmk40
ISSN No. 0430 5227

13044 **ENERGY REVIEW**
Ministry of Trade and Industry

Finland – Finnish/Swedish/English quarterly 48pp
ISSN No. 0356 9276

13045 **ENERGY STATISTICS (OSF XLII)**
Ministry of Trade and Industry

Finland – Finnish/Swedish/English annual 1981 125pp Fmk40
ISSN No. 0359 7539

13046 **ENTERPRISE AND ESTABLISHMENT REGISTER: ESTABLISHMENTS (STATISTICAL REPORT YR, ENTERPRISES)**
Central Statistical Office of Finland

Finland – Finnish/Swedish every two years 1968 120pp Fmk50
ISSN No. 0355 2373

13047 **ENTERPRISE AND INCOME STATISTICS OF FARM ECONOMY (STATISTICAL REPORT KT, NATIONAL ACCOUNTS)**
Central Statistical Office of Finland

Finland – Finnish/Swedish/English table headings annual 1967 220pp Fmk65
ISSN No. 0355 2276

13048 **ENVIRONMENTAL STATISTICS 1986 (OSF)**
Central Statistical Office of Finland

Finland – Finnish/Swedish/English irregular 1972 200pp Fmk72

13049 **ESTIMATED POPULATION BY MUNICIPALITIES (31ST DECEMBER REPORT VA, POPULATION)**
Central Statistical Office of Finland

Finland – Finnish/Swedish annual 1983 13pp Fmk12
ISSN No. 0355 2365

13050 **FARM ECONOMY STATISTICS: ENTERPRISE AND INCOME STATISTICS OF FARM ECONOMY (OSF XXXIX)**
Central Statistical Office of Finland

Finland – Finnish/Swedish/English table headings annual 1973 206pp Fmk62
ISSN No. 0356 2913

Statistics on enterprise and income relevant to farms.

13051 **FARM REGISTER (OSF XLIII)**
National Board of Agriculture

Finland – Finnish/Swedish/English annual 1980 137pp Fmk41
ISSN No. 0781 075X

13052 **FINANCIAL STATEMENTS STATISTICS OF CONSTRUCTION (STATISTICAL REPORT YR, ENTERPRISES)**
Central Statistical Office of Finland

Finland – Finnish/Swedish/tables annual 1967 42pp Fmk28
ISSN No. 0355 2373

13053 **FINANCIAL STATEMENTS STATISTICS OF INDUSTRIAL ENTERPRISES (SIC 2, 3, 4) (STATISTICAL REPORT YR, ENTERPRISES)**
Central Statistical Office of Finland

Finland – Finnish/Swedish/tables and list of words in English annual 1974 50pp Fmk32
ISSN No. 0355 2373

13054 **FINANCIAL STATEMENTS STATISTICS OF TRANSPORT AND COMMUNICATIONS (STATISTICAL REPORT YR, ENTERPRISES)**
Central Statistical Office of Finland

Finland – Finnish/Swedish list of words in English+summary annual 1961 55pp Fmk25
ISSN No. 0355 2373

13055 **FINANCIAL STATEMENTS STATISTICS OF WHOLESALE AND RETAIL TRADE (STATISTICAL REPORT YR, ENTERPRISES)**
Central Statistical Office of Finland

Finland – Finnish/Swedish/summary, list of words and tables in English annual 1969 77pp Fmk45
ISSN No. 0355 2373

13056 **FINANCING OF HIRE PURCHASE TRADE (STATISTICAL REPORT RT, FINANCING)**
Central Statistical Office of Finland

Finland – Finnish/Swedish quarterly 1971 12pp Fmk40
ISSN No. 0355 2322

13057 **FINLAND**
UK Iron and Steel Statistics Bureau

Finland – English with annual statistical summary 1986 £25

Report on the steel industry showing production, consumption and details of imports and exports.

13058 **FINLAND IN FIGURES**
Central Statistical Office of Finland

Finland – English/Finnish/Swedish/German/Russian/French/Spanish/Arabic annual 32pp Fmk4
ISSN No. 0357 0371

13059 **FINLAND'S BALANCE OF PAYMENTS (STATISTICAL REPORT KT, NATIONAL ACCOUNTS)**
Central Statistical Office of Finland

Finland – Finnish/Swedish/English annual (timescale covering 10 years) 1967 39pp Fmk43
ISSN No. 0355 2276

13060 **FINNISH BANKING SYSTEM**
Finnish Bankers' Association

Finland – English/Swedish/Finnish biennial November 1978 40pp free

The banking system in Finland.

13061 **FINNISH BUSINESS REPORT**
Kauppalehti Oy

Finland – English monthly 30pp US$35
ISSN No. 0780 4652

13062 **FINNISH METAL AND ENGINEERING INDUSTRY**
Federation of Finnish Metal and Engineering Industries

Finland – English/German annual 41pp

Statistics on production, foreign trade and manpower.

13063 **FINNISH BOND ISSUES**
Bank of Finland

Finland – Finnish/Swedish/English annual 1962 Fmk50

13064 **FINANCIAL MARKETS IN FINLAND**
Bank of Finland

Finland – English irregular free

13065 **FOREIGN TRADE (OSF I A)**
Board of Customs

Finland – Finnish/Swedish/English annual 1856 Vol.I 660pp, Vol.II 170pp, Vol.III 270pp Fmk340 vol.I, Fmk55 vol.II, Fmk140 vol.III
ISSN No. 0355-0249

Vol.I: foreign trade in terms of the harmonised system; vol.II: special statistics relating to foreign trade and customs administration; vol.III: foreign trade by commodities and categories of goods as well as annual statistics on total trade by countries in terms of the SITC.

13066 **FOREIGN TRADE (OSF I A)**
Board of Customs

Finland – Finnish/Swedish/English monthly 1904 67pp Fmk265
ISSN No. 0041-6177

Trade with selected countries and regions by SITC/by countries of origin/imports and exports by harmonized system groups and sub headings. Detailed monthly statistics in accordance with the subclassification of the harmonized system by countries are obtainable only on microfiche.

13067 **FORSAKRINGSTIDNING**
Vakuutussanomia Oy

Finland – Swedish 5 issues per year 1935 40pp Fmk150 per year
ISSN No. 0355 7308

Finnish insurance industry.

13068 **GROWTH POLICIES IN A NORDIC PERSPECTIVE 1987**
Institute of Industrial Economics

Norway, Sweden, Finland, Denmark – English 1984
ISBN No. 91 7204 276-1

Economic policies and outlook.

13069 **HEALTH CARE IN FINLAND**
Ministry of Social Affairs and Health

Finland – Swedish/English/German/French 1986 39pp

Brief review of bases of health policy and health care costs in Finland.

13070 **HEALTH SERVICES: YEARBOOK OF NATIONAL BOARD OF HEALTH (OSF XI)**

Finland – Finnish/Swedish/summary in English irregular 1884 280pp Fmk120
ISSN. No. 0303 2442

13071 **HINTS TO EXPORTERS**
Department of Trade and Industry

Finland – English annual

Practical guide for businessmen giving general information, useful addresses, methods of doing business and relevant regulations.

13072 **HOUSEHOLD SURVEY 1981 (STATISTICAL SURVEYS NO 71)**
Central Statistical Office of Finland

Finland – Finnish/Swedish/English every 5 years 1971 Vol.I 179pp, Vol.II 180pp, Vol.III 130pp Fmk45 vol.I, Fmk54 vol.II, Fmk38 vol.III
ISSN No. 0355 208X

Vol. I household consumption expenditure
Vol. II households in separate phases of life
Vol. III quality survey.

13073 **HOUSEHOLD SURVEY 1985**
Central Statistical Office of Finland

The results were published in 7 volumes during 1988.

13074 **HOW THE FINNS SPENT THEIR HOLIDAY IN ...**
Finnish Tourist Board
Markku Heiskanen

Finland – English irregular 24pp free
ISBN/ISSN No. 951-99829-9-X/0355-6204

13075 **INCOME DISTRIBUTION STATISTICS (OSF XLI)**
Central Statistical Office of Finland

Finland – Finnish/Swedish/English annual 1978 110pp Fmk50
ISSN No. 0358 2825

13076 **INCOME DISTRIBUTION STATISTICS: (PRELIMINARY DATA STATISTICAL REPORT TU, INCOME)**

Finland – Finnish/Swedish annual 1977 18pp Fmk20
ISSN No. 0355 2349

13077 **INDEX OF INDUSTRIAL PRODUCTION (STATISTICAL REPORT TE, INDUSTRY)**
Central Statistical Office of Finland

Finland – Finnish/Swedish monthly 1969 6pp Fmk100
ISSN No. 0355 2330

13078 **INDUSTRIAL STATISTICS (OSF XVIII A)**
Central Statistical Office of Finland

Finland – Finnish/Swedish/table headings in English annual 1884 Vol.1 284pp, Vol.2 494pp, Vol.3 100pp Fmk90, Fmk150, Fmk35
ISSN No. 0071 5344

Vol.1 Data by brand, Vol.2 Product data, Vol.3 Energy Statistics.

13079 **INFORMATION TECHNOLOGY AND WORK IN FINLAND (STUDIES NO. 125)**
Central Statistical Office of Finland

Finland – English 1987 131pp Fmk60
ISBN No. 951 47 0133X/0355 2071

13080 **INPUT-OUTPUT STUDY 1982: PRELIMINARY DATA (STATISTICAL REPORT KT 1985:4)**
Central Statistical Office of Finland

Finland – Finnish/Swedish/English irregular 1956 43pp
ISSN No. 0355 2276

13081 **INPUT PRICE INDEX OF REBUILDING 1985=100 (STUDIES NO 1[illegible]1)**
Central Statistical Office of Finland

Finland – Finnish/Swedish/English summary 1987 50pp Fmk26
ISBN No. 951-47 0404S/0355 2071

13082 **INSURANCE COMPANIES IN FINNISH SOCIETY**
Federation of Finnish Insurance Companies

Finland – English every two years 1983 20pp free

Finnish insurance industry.

13083 **INSURANCE IN FINLAND**
Vakuutussanomia Oy

Finland – English 2 issues per year 40pp free
ISSN No. 0356-9993

Finnish insurance industry.

13084 **INSURANCE COMPANIES (OSF XXIIA)**
Ministry of Social Affairs and Health

Finland – Finnish/Swedish/English annual 1892 280pp Fmk113
ISSN No. 0356 4436

13085 **INTERNAL MIGRATION BY MUNICIPALITY (STATISTICAL REPORT VA, POPULATION)**
Central Statistical Office of Finland

Finland – Finnish/Swedish annual 1969 140pp Fmk50
ISSN No. 0355 2365

13086 **KANSALLIS-OSAKE-PANKKI ECONOMIC REVIEW**
Kansallis-Osake-Pankki

Finland – English free

Economic review.

13087 **KAUPPAKAMARI**
Central Chamber of Commerce

Finland – Finnish/Swedish 10 per year 1921 50pp Fmk250
ISSN No. 0781-6375

Chamber of Commerce monthly journal.

13088 **KAUPPALEHTI**
Kauppalehti Oy

Finland – Finnish daily (5 per week) 35pp Fmk712
ISSN No. 0451 5560

13089 **LABOUR DISPUTES (STATISTICAL REPORT TY, LABOUR FORCE)**
Central Statistical Office of Finland

Finland – Finnish/Swedish/English quarterly and annual 1971 6 and 47pp Fmk55, Fmk 35
ISSN No. 0355 2357

13090 **LABOUR FORCE SURVEY (OSF XL)**
Central Statistical Office of Finland

Finland – Finnish/Swedish/English annual 1976 100pp Fmk54
ISSN No. 0781 5611

13091 **LABOUR FORCE SURVEY (STATISTICAL REPORT TY, LABOUR FORCE)**
Central Statistical Office of Finland

Finland – Finnish/Swedish monthly and quarterly 1969 2 and 16pp Fmk60, Fmk65
ISSN No. 0355 2357

13092 **LABOUR FORCE SURVEY: ANNUAL INTERVIEW (STATISTICAL REPORT TY, LABOUR FORCE)**
Central Statistical Office of Finland

Finland – Finnish/Swedish annual 1977 112pp Fmk45
ISSN No. 0357 2357

13093 **LABOUR REPORTS**
Ministry of Labour Planning Department

Finland – Finnish/Swedish/English quarterly 64pp Fmk120
ISSN No. 0430 5280

13094 **LANDERBERICHT FINNLAND**
Federal Statistical Office of Germany

Finland – German irregular DM7.90

Statistical survey of Finland including such areas as demography, geography, education, employment, agriculture, production, overseas trade, transport, tourism, finance, wages and prices and national accounts.

13095 **LIFE TABLES (STATISTICAL REPORT VA, POPULATION)**
Central Statistical Office of Finland

Finland – Finnish/Swedish annual 1971 13pp Fmk12
ISSN No. 0355 3565

13096 **LISTED COMPANIES IN FINLAND**
Kansallis-Osake-Pankki

Finland – Finnish/English annual 192pp
ISSN No. 0357 5691

13097 **LIVING CONDITIONS IN FINLAND 1984 (STATISTICAL SURVEYS NO 74)**
Central Statistical Office of Finland

Finland – Finnish/Swedish/English irregular 1977 284pp Fmk89
ISSN No. 0355 208X

13098 **LONG DISTANCE LORRY TRAFFIC (STATISTICAL REPORT L1, TRANSPORT)**
Central Statistical Office of Finland

Finland – Finnish/Swedish annual 1965 12pp Fmk15
ISSN No. 0355 2284

13099 **LOOK AT FINLAND**
Finnish Tourist Board

Finland – English 4 issues a year c60pp

Contains articles about political and economic developments, industry and commerce.

13100 **MERENKULUN TILASTOJA/ SJOFARTSSTATISTIK**
Finnish Shipowners' Association

Finland – Finnish/Swedish annual 1984 50pp free
ISBN No. 0783-7364

Finnish merchant fleet: age, size, structural changes, financing, ships on order/laid up, manning costs, wages, working hours; passenger traffic.

13101 **METSATEOLLISUUDEN VUOSIKIRJA**
Suomen Metsateollisuuden Keskusliitto

Finland – Finnish annual 40pp free

Statistics on wood industry.

13102 **MONTHLY BULLETIN***
Bank of Finland

Finland – English monthly c30pp free

Basic statistics and key economic indicators and articles on the economy.

13103 **MONTHLY REVIEW OF AGRICULTURAL STATISTICS**
National Board of Agriculture

Finland – Finnish/Swedish/English 25pp

ISSN No. 0430 5329

13104 **MOTOR VEHICLES (STATISTICAL REPORT L1, TRANSPORT AND ACCOMMODATION)**
Central Statistical Office of Finland

Finland – Finnish/Swedish annual 1969 47pp Fmk25
ISSN No. 0355 2284

13105 **MUNICIPAL FINANCES (OSF XXXI)**
Central Statistical Office of Finland

Finland – Finnish/Swedish/English annual 1910 50pp Fmk40
ISSN No. 0430 5566

13106 **NATIONAL ACCOUNTS (STATISTICAL REPORT KT, NATIONAL ACCOUNTS)**
Central Statistical Office of Finland

Finland – Finnish/Swedish (English table headings in annual pub.) quarterly and annual 1964 quarterly 10pp, annual 200pp Fmk90
ISSN No. 0355 2276

13107 **NATIONAL BUDGET FOR ....: FINLAND**
Ministry of Finance Economics Dept

Finland – English annual 44pp Fmk20
ISSN No. 0532 9280

13108 **NAVIGATION: SHIPPING BETWEEN FINLAND AND FOREIGN COUNTRIES**
National Board of Navigation

Finland – Finnish/Swedish/English annual 1918 84pp Fmk35
ISSN No. 0430 5582

13109 **NAVIGATION: MERCHANT FLEET (OSF I BA)**
National Board of Navigation

Finland – Finnish/Swedish/English annual 1918 56pp Fmk17
ISSN No. 0430 5574

13110 **NORDISK FORSAKRINGSTIDSKRIFT**
Svenska Forsakringsforeningen

Norway, Finland, Sweden, Denmark – Scandinavian/English/German quarterly 1921 90pp Skr40 p.a.
ISSN No. 0348-6516

Private and public insurance.

13111 **OECD ECONOMIC SURVEYS–FINLAND**
OECD

Finland – English annual 70pp £2.40, DM12, US$5, FrF24

A detailed analysis of recent developments in demand, production, employment, prices and wages, conditions in the money and capital markets and developments in the balance of payments. It includes short-term forecasts as well as analyses of medium-term problems of specific relevance to the elaboration of the country's economic policies.

13112 **POPULATION VOLUME 1, STRUCTURE OF POPULATION AND VITAL STATISTICS. WHOLE COUNTRY AND PROVINCES (OSF VI A)**
Central Statistical Office of Finland

Finland – Finnish/Swedish/English annual 1941 110pp Fmk48
ISSN No. 0430 5612

13113 **POPULATION. VOLUME 2, STRUCTURE OF POPULATION BY MUNICIPALITY (OSF VI A)**
Central Statistical Office of Finland

Finland – Finnish/Swedish/English annual 1941 80pp Fmk42
ISSN No. 0430 5612

13114 **POPULATION VOLUME 3, VITAL STATISTICS BY MUNICIPALITY (OSF VI A)**
Central Statistical Office of Finland

Finland – Finnish/Swedish/English annual 1941 165pp Fmk55
ISSN No. 0430 5612

13115 **POPULATION CENSUS 1985 (OSF)**
Central Statistical Office of Finland

Finland – Finnish/Swedish/English every 5 years 1950 cost to be announced

Vol.1 Data by municipalities; vol.2 Household-dwelling units and families; vol.3 Housing conditions; vol.4 Dwelling and building stock; vol.5 Occupation and industry.

13116 **POPULATION MOVEMENTS (STATISTICAL REPORT, VA POPULATION)**
Central Statistical Office of Finland

Finland – Finnish/Swedish quarterly 1968 63pp Fmk100
ISSN No. 0355 2365

13117 **POPULATION PROJECTION BY MUNICIPALITIES 1984-2010 (STATISTICAL REPORT VA 1985:10)**
Central Statistical Office of Finland

Finland – Finnish/Swedish/English 103pp Fmk50
ISSN No. 0355 2365

13118 **POSTS AND TELECOMMUNICATIONS (OSF XIII)**
General Directorate of Posts and Telecommunications

Finland – Finnish/Swedish/English annual 1885 174pp
ISSN No. 0355 1083

13119 **PRELIMINARY DATA ON INDUSTRIES (STATISTICAL REPORT TE, INDUSTRY)**
Central Statistical Office of Finland

Finland – Finnish/Swedish annual 1968 78pp Fmk45
ISSN No. 0355 2357

13120 **PRICE REPORT**
National Board of Trade and Consumer Interests

Finland – Finnish monthly 29pp
ISSN No. 0359 0917

13121 **PRICES OF DWELLINGS (STATISTICAL REPORT AS, HOUSING)**
Central Statistical Office of Finland

Finland – Finnish quarterly 1985 21pp Fmk110
ISSN No. 0782 9868

13122 **PRODUCER PRICE INDICES (INDEX REPORT TH)**
Central Statistical Office of Finland

Finland – Finnish/Swedish monthly 1968 10pp Fmk60
ISSN No. 0355 2403

13123 **PRODUCER PRICE INDICES 1980=100 (STUDIES NO 105)**
Central Statistical Office of Finland

Finland – Finnish/English summary 1984 106pp Fmk28
ISBN/ISSN No. 951 46 7722 6/0355 2071

13124 **QUARTERLY STATISTICS FOR SOCIAL INSURANCE INSTITUTION**
Social Insurance Institution

Finland – Finnish/Swedish quarterly 50pp free
ISSN No. 0355 0060

13125 **RAILWAY STATISTICS (OSF XX)**
Railway Board

Finland – Finnish/Swedish/English annual 1871 150pp Fmk55
ISSN No. 0357 0339

13126 **REGIONAL ACCOUNTING: PRODUCTION, EMPLOYMENT AND GROSS DOMESTIC FIXED CAPITAL FORMATION BY PROVINCES IN 1982 (STATISTICAL SURVEYS NO. 77)**
Central Statistical Office of Finland

Finland – Finnish/Swedish/English irregular 1960 116pp Fmk35
ISBN/ISSN No. 951 46 9102 4/0355 208X

13127 **REGIONAL STATISTICS ON CREDITS OUTSTANDING (STATISTICAL REPORT RT, FINANCING)**
Central Statistical Office of Finland

Finland – Finnish/Swedish annual 1979 28pp
ISSN No. 0355 2322

13128 **REGISTERED NEW VEHICLES (STATISTICAL REPORT L1, TRANSPORT) AND ACCOMMODATION**
Central Statistical Office of Finland

Finland – Finnish/Swedish monthly and annual 1969 1 and 2pp Fmk90
ISSN No. 0355 2284

13129 **REGISTERED POPULATION BY COMMUNES (STATISTICAL REPORT VA, POPULATION)**
Central Statistical Office of Finland

Finland – Finnish/Swedish annual 1969 14pp Fmk12
ISSN No. 0355 2365

13130 **RENT SURVEY (STATISTICAL REPORT AS, HOUSING)**
Central Statistical Office of Finland

Finland – Finnish/Swedish annual 1966 10pp Fmk30
ISSN No. 0782 9868

13131 **ROAD AND WATERWAY CONSTRUCTION (OSF XIX)**
National Board of Public Roads and Waterways

Finland – Finnish/Swedish/English annual 1885 111pp Fmk33
ISSN No. 0355 6131

13132 **SOCIAL EXPENDITURE AND ITS FINANCING IN FINLAND 1986-2000**
Ministry of Social Affairs and Health

Finland – Finnish/English 1986 19pp

A summary of the social expenditure and of the ensuing financial challenges by the year 2000.

13133 **SOCIAL EXPENDITURE IN 1984 AND 1985 (MINISTRY OF SOCIAL AFFAIRS AND HEALTH, PLANNING DEPARTMENT, PUBLICATIONS 3:1987)**
Ministry of Social Affairs and Health

Finland – Finnish/Swedish/English 1987 110pp
ISSN No. 0784-0853

Calculations of social expenditure in 1984 and 1985 and development trends from the year 1975.

13134 **SOCIAL INSURANCE IN FINLAND**
Ministry of Social Affairs and Health

Finland – Swedish/English/German/French 1986 48pp

Brief introduction to social insurance systems in Finland.

13135 **SOCIAL WELFARE IN FINLAND**
Ministry of Social Affairs and Health

Finland – English/Swedish/German/French 1986 32pp

Brief account of social welfare and its financial implications.

13136 **STANDARD INDUSTRIAL CLASSIFICATION (SIC) (HANDBOOKS NO 4, 2ND REV EDITION)**
Central Statistical Office of Finland

Finland – Finnish 1987 236pp Fmk80
ISBN/ISSN No. 951 47 0325 1/0355 2063

13137 **STATE EXPENDITURE BY PROVINCES (STATISTICAL REPORT JT, GENERAL GOVERNMENT)**
Central Statistical Office of Finland

Finland – Finnish/Swedish annual 1980 24pp Fmk13
ISSN No. 0359 081X

13138 **STATE REVENUE BY PROVINCES (STATISTICAL REPORT JT, GENERAL GOVERNMENT)**
Central Statistical Office of Finland

Finland – Finnish/Swedish annual 1982 10pp Fmk8
ISSN No. 0359 081X

13139 **STATEMENT OF THE BANK OF FINLAND**
Bank of Finland

Finland – Finnish 4 a month free

The balance sheet and the statement of note issue from the Bank of Finland.

13140 **STATISTICAL YEARBOOK OF FINLAND**
Central Statistical Office of Finland

Finland – Finnish/Swedish/English annual 1879 520pp Fmk215
ISSN No. 0081 5063

Data on population, agriculture, industry, business and commerce, transport, prices and incomes, consumption, social services.

13141 **STATISTICS ON BONDS AND DEBENTURES (STATISTICAL REPORT RT, FINANCING)**
Central Statistical Office of Finland

Finland – Finnish/Swedish quarterly 1976 7pp Fmk40
ISSN No. 0355 2322

13142 **STATISTICS OF INCOME AND PROPERTY (OSF IV B)**
Central Statistical Office of Finland

Finland – English/Swedish/Finnish annual 1920 100pp Fmk45
ISSN No. 0780 9352

13143 **STATISTICS ON INCOME AND PROPERTY: PRELIMINARY DATA (STATISTICAL REPORT TU, INCOME)**
Central Statistical Office of Finland

Finland – Finnish/Swedish annual 1969 29pp Fmk20
ISSN No. 0355 2349

13144 **STATISTICS ON ADVANCES AND DEPOSITS (STATISTICAL REPORT RT, FINANCING)**
Central Statistical Office of Finland

Finland – Finnish/Swedish monthly 1971
2pp Fkm60
ISSN No. 0355 2322

13145 **STATISTICS ON CREDITS OUTSTANDING (STATISTICAL REPORT RT, FINANCING)**
Central Statistical Office of Finland

Finland – Finnish/Swedish annual 1971
45pp Fmk30
ISSN No. 0355 2322

13146 **STATISTICS ON EARNINGS**
Central Statistical Office of Finland

Finland – Finnish annual 1985/86 190pp
Fmk70

Summary publication on various earnings statistics and wage and salary indices.

13147 **STATISTICS ON INTEREST RATES (STATISTICAL REPORT RT, FINANCING)**
Central Statistical Office of Finland

Finland – Finnish/Swedish quarterly 1972
20pp Fmk40
ISSN No. 0355 2322

13148 **STOCKS OF COMMERCIAL ENTERPRISES (STATISTICAL REPORT YR, ENTERPRISES)**
Central Statistical Office of Finland

Finland – Finnish/Swedish quarterly 1978
3pp Fmk60
ISSN No. 0355 2373

13149 **STOCKS OF INDUSTRIAL ENTERPRISES (STATISTICAL REPORT YR, ENTERPRISES)**
Central Statistical Office of Finland

Finland – Finnish/Swedish quarterly 1974
5pp Fmk60
ISSN No. 0355 2373

13150 **SUHDANNE**
Elinkeinoelaman-Tutkimuslaitos (ETLA)

Finland – Finnish with English summary and headings quarterly 150-160pp Fmk260 plus postage
ISSN No. 0303 8130

Domestic development, international developments, short-term economic prospects. Contains assessments of economic prospects for the next 5-year period and other comprehensive short-term forecasts.

13151 **SUOMEN VAKUUTUSVUOSIKIRJA, FORSAKRINGSARSBOK FOR FINLAND**
Finnish Insurance Society

Finland – Finnish/Swedish annual 1912
170pp Fmk90
ISSN No. 0356 7826 (Finnish), 0356 7834 (Swedish)

Finnish insurance industry (companies, associations, directors, statistics, English glossary).

13152 **TALOUSELAMA**
Talouselama Oy

Finland – Finnish weekly 94pp Fmk520
ISSN No. 0356 5106

13153 **THE TEXTILE INDUSTRY YEARBOOK**
Association of Finnish Textile Industries

Finland – Finnish/Swedish/English annual
36pp free

Statistics on production, foreign trade and employment.

13154 **TIME SERIES ON WHOLESALE AND RETAIL TRADE 1968-1985 (STUDIES NO 130)**
Central Statistical Office of Finland

Finland – Finnish/Swedish 1987 101pp
Fmk60
ISBN/ISSN No. 951 47 0093 7/0355 2071

13155 **TOURISM STATISTICS**
Finnish Tourist Board

Finland – Finnish/Swedish/English annual
1975

Statistical survey of the tourist industry.

13156 **UNION BANK OF FINLAND ANNUAL REPORT**
Union Bank of Finland

Finland – English annual 40pp free

13157 **UNITAS: ECONOMIC QUARTERLY REVIEW**
Union Bank of Finland

Finland – English/Finnish/German/Swedish quarterly 30pp free
ISSN No. 0041 7130

13158 **VAKUUTUSSANOMAT**
Vakuutussanomia Oy

Finland – Finnish 10 per year 1904 40pp
Fmk150 p.a.
ISSN No. 0355 7294

Finnish insurance industry.

13159 **VARUSTAMOYHDISTYKSEN KATSAUS/REDERIFORENINGENS BULLETIN**
Finnish Shipowners' Association

Finland – Finnish/Swedish 6 per year 1985
30pp free
ISSN No. 0782-7598

Finnish shipping topics of the day.

13160 **WAGE AND SALARY INDEX 1980=100 (STUDIES NO 124)**
Central Statistical Office of Finland

Finland – Finnish/English summary 1986
68pp Fmk35
ISBN No. 951 46 931 75/0355 2071

13161 **WAGE AND SALARY INDEX (INDEX REPORT AT)**
Central Statistical Office of Finland

Finland – Finnish/Swedish quarterly 1979
4pp Fmk35
ISSN No. 0357 7207

13162 **WHOLESALE AND RETAIL TRADE (STATISTICAL REPORT KA, TRADE)**
Central Statistical Office of Finland

Finland – Finnish/Swedish monthly and annual 1968 5 pp Fmk90, Fmk22
ISSN No. 0355 255X

13163 **WORKING ENVIRONMENT IN FINLAND**
Ministry of Social Affairs and Health

Finland – Swedish/English/German/French
1987 39pp

Brief review of trends in working conditions and the labour market and labour protection in Finland.

13164 **YEARBOOK OF FARM STATISTICS (OSF III)**
National Board of Agriculture

Finland–Finnish/Swedish/English annual
1869 280pp Fmk86
ISSN No. 0781 7927

13165 **YEARBOOK OF FOREST STATISTICS (OSF XVII A)**
Finnish Forest Research Institute

Finland – Finnish/Swedish/English annual
1968 238pp Fmk94
ISSN No. 0359 968X

13166 **YEARBOOK OF TRANSPORT STATISTICS (OSF XXXVI)**
Central Statistical Office of Finland

Finland – Finnish/Swedish/English annual
1958 142pp Fmk68
ISSN No. 0430 5272

FRANCE

14001 **THE AGRICULTURE OF FRANCE AND HUNGARY 1980–1982**
Statistical Publishing House (Hungary)

France – Hungarian Ft76

Review of agriculture in France and Hungary.

14002 **ANNALES D'ECONOMIE ET DE STATISTIQUE**
Institut National de la Statistique et des Etudes Economiques

France – French quarterly FrF385

Results of economic research.

14003 **ANNALES DES MINES***
Gedim

France – French with summaries in English/German/Spanish/Russian monthly c200pp FrF240.00

Review and statistics on the energy and metals industries.

14004 **L'ANNEE BOURSIER***
Chambre Syndicale des Agents de Change

France – French annual since 1962 FrF72.00 in Europe FrF79.00 in US FrF82.00 in Japan

Annual report of the stock exchange which contains the figures, statistics and graphs concerning the activity of the market during the year.

14005 **ANNUAIRE ABREGE DES STATISTIQUES***
Direction Generale des Douanes et Droits Indirects

France – French annual c300pp FrF60.00

Pocket book which summarizes movements in foreign trade for the preceding year.

14006 **ANNUAIRES DESFOSSES***
Cote Desfosses

France – French annual 2 vols £65.00

Official directory of the Paris stock exchange.

14007 **ANNUAIRE DE STATISTIQUE AGRICOLE**
Ministere de l'Agriculture

France – French annual FrF490.00 paper, FrF105.00 microfiche

Statistics on matters pertaining to agriculture such as climate, agricultural labour, technology and training. Specific data on production.

14008 **ANNUAIRE DE STATISTIQUE INDUSTRIELLE**
Ministere de l'Industrie

France – French annual FrF400

Detailed production, import and export data by NAP code.

14009 **ANNUAIRE PROVISOIRES DE STATISTIQUE AGRICOLE. RESULTATS**
Ministere de l'Agriculture

France – French annual FrF60.00 paper FrF18.00 microfiche

The ministry's provisional estimates of production; vegetable production and livestock are analysed by department and by region.

14010 **ANNUAIRE RETROSPECTIF CEREALES**
Ministere de l'Agriculture
Ministere de l'Agriculture SCEES

France – French irregular FrF75 paper FrF25 microfiche

Data on area and production of cereals for the last 150 years.

14011 **ANNUAIRE RETROSPECTIF DE STATISTIQUE AGRICOLE: LEGUMES FRAIS**
Ministere de l'Agriculture

France – French annual FrF75 paper, Frf25 microfiche

Data on about 50 types of vegetable production for the last 20 years.

14012 **ANNUAIRE RETROSPECTIF DE STATISTIQUE AGRICOLE: PLANTES SARCLEES, LEGUMES SECS OLEAGINEUX, TEXTILES, CULTURES DIVERSES**
Ministere de l'Agriculture
Ministere de l'Agriculture SCEES

France – French irregular FrF75 paper, FrF25 microfiche

Data on area and production of various crops for the last 150 years.

14013 **ANNUAIRE STATISTIQUE DE LA FRANCE**
Institut National de la Statistique et des Etudes Economiques

France – French annual 900pp FrF460 ISBN No. 2110640634

Detailed statistics on population, the economy and social trends, including long time series.

14014 **ARCHIVES ET DOCUMENTS**
Institut National de la Statistique et des Etudes Economiques

France – French cost variable

A series similar to the "Collections de l'INSEE' but more specialized and providing a greater level of detail. About 30 are produced each year, each one on a specific subject and together covering all aspects of economic and social life.

14015 **LA BALANCE DES PAIEMENTS DE LA FRANCE**
Banque de France

France – French annual

Detailed analysis of France's balance of payments, giving quarterly figures.

14016 **LA BANQUE DE FRANCE ET LA MONNAIE**
Banque de France

France – French irregular 180pp FrF50

Review of the French financial system, covering the following topics: money, the money supply, the financial system, the objectives of monetary policy, the instruments employed in achieving it, the role of the Banque de France in the financial system.

14017 **BULLETIN DU CENTRE D'ETUDES DE L'EMPLOI (CEE)***
Centre d'Etudes de l'Emploi

France – French quarterly FrF13.00

Information on all aspects of employment and labour designed to present the results of official studies to the general public.

14018 **BULLETIN DES INDICES DE COURS***
Chambre Syndicale des Agents de Change

France – French daily with a weekly supplement FrF355.00 in Europe FrF540.00 in US FrF625.00 in Japan

Daily indices of French stocks showing the general index, and the index of industrial stocks given in 9 sectors and 35 subsectors. The weekly supplement gives the index of 68 constituent sections.

14019 **BULLETIN DE STATISTIQUE AGRICOLE**
Ministere de l'Agriculture

France – French bi-monthly FrF80.00 paper FrF18.00 microfiche each, annual FrF400.00 paper FrF90.00 microfiche

Statistics for the whole country covering every aspect of the agricultural industry. Topics covered include labour, equipment, prices, food industry, tobacco, salt, financial structure, methods of transporting produce and marketing.

14020 **BULLETIN MENSUEL DE STATISTIQUE**
Institut National de la Statistique et des Etudes Economiques

France – French monthly FrF300

Monthly statistical bulletin.

14021 **BULLETIN MENSUEL DE STATISTIQUE INDUSTRIELLE**
Ministere de l'Industrie

France – French monthly FrF400

Monthly statistics on variables, such as deliveries, consumption, stocks held, in industry.

14022 **BULLETIN TRIMESTRIEL DE LA BANQUE DE FRANCE**
Banque de France

France – French quarterly FrF130 annually

Bulletin designed for the professional financial world. It consists of 4 parts: 'Actualité' report on the current economic situation; 'Etudes' technical analytic articles; statistical tables; and the official bulletin of the bank.

14023 **CAHIERS DE STATISTIQUE AGRICOLE**
Ministere de l'Agriculture

France – French bi-monthly FrF50 each FrF250.00 annually

Articles on topical research or projects in the agricultural field.

14024 **LES CAHIERS ECONOMIQUES ET MONETAIRES**
Banque de France

France – French irregular 1975 cost various

Each issue consists of a number of articles on a specific economic or monetary topic.

14025 **CHIFFRES CLES DE L'INDUSTRIE FRANCAISE**
Ministere de l'Industrie

France – French annual 216pp FrF65

Key figures for French industry including its relevance to both domestic and world economy, covering production, investment, foreign exchange.

14026 **COLLECTIONS DE L'INSEE**
Institut National de la Statistique et des Etudes Economiques

France – French frequent FrF2350 (for all 5 series)

Five series of reports in detail on main economic and social developments. Series C: Comptes et planification; national accounts in total and by sector. Series D. Demographie et emploi; covering population, activity rates, labour force. Series E: Enterprises: including reports on commercial, agricultural and industrial structure. Series M: Menages; household composition, income and expenditure, housing conditions. Series R: regional development, regional accounts, population, labour force and public finance. Some of these reports are entered individually elsewhere in this section.

14027 **COLLECTIONS DE STATISTIQUE AGRICOLE SERIE ETUDES**
Ministere de l'Agriculture

France – French irregular each: FrF95.00 paper FrF25.00 microfiche, subscription for 10 numbers: FrF840.00 paper FrF190.00 microfiche

Series of reports containing statistics on all aspects of agriculture.

14028 **LE COMMERCE EN FRANCE EN 198...**
Institut National de la Statistique et des Etudes Economiques (INSEE)

France – French annual c160pp

Statistics on commerce giving margins, revenue, expenditure, turnover and employment. Data on retailing analysed by type of outlet and other data analysed by type of trade.

14029 **COMMENTAIRES ANNUELS***
Direction Generale des Douanes et Droits Indirects

France – French annual FrF60.00

Detailed analysis of the foreign trade statistics of the preceding three years.

14030 **COMMENTAIRES TRIMESTRIELS DU COMMERCE EXTERIEUR DE LA FRANCE***
Direction Generale des Douanes et Droits Indirects

France – French quarterly FrF75.00

Quarterly statistics on foreign trade.

14031 **COMMERCE EXTERIEUR DE LA FRANCE**
Centre Francais du Commerce Exterieur

France – French annual c50pp FrF100.00

Figures for foreign trade.

14032 **COMPTE RENDU ANNUEL DES OPERATIONS DE LA BANQUE DE FRANCE**
Banque de France

France – French annual free

Annual accounts of the Banque de France including an analysis of French financial policy.

14033 **LES COMPTES DE L'AGRICULTURE FRANCAISE EN 198...**
Institut National de la Statistique et des Etudes Economiques (INSEE)

France – French annual c200pp

Agricultural accounts giving data on supply and demand of agricultural products, revenue and expenditure and overseas trade.

14034 **LES COMPTES DE LA SECURITE SOCIALE; RESULTATS 1986 – PREVISIONS 1987-88; RAPPORT JUILLET 1987**
La Documentation Francaise

France – French annual 1986 124pp FrF70 ISBN No. 2 11 01838 0

Financial data on the social security system.

14035 **LES COMPTES FINANCIERS NATIONAUX**
Banque de France

France – French annual

Statistics on national accounts.

14036 **LES CONSOMMATIONS D'ENERGIE DANS L'INDUSTRIE EN 1985 TRAITS FONDAMENTAUX DU SYSTEME INDUSTRIEL FRANCAIS**
La Documentation Francaise

France – French annual 1980 190pp FrF71 ISBN No. 02447118

The use of major forms of energy in French industry.

14037 **COTES DESFOSSES***
Côte Desfosses

France – French daily FrF101.00

Financial newspaper giving daily a complete list of Stock Exchange prices.

14038 **COUNTRY PROFILES**
Economist Publications Ltd

France – English annual 40pp £25 UK, subscription varies in rest of world

Resumé of politics, economy and industry including statistical summaries.

14039 COUNTRY REPORTS
Economist Publications Ltd

France – English quarterly 25pp £58 UK subscription varies in rest of world

Economic policies and development plans, trends in production and demand, monetary and fiscal conditions, wages and prices, merchandise, trade, invisibles, capital flows, exchange rates and foreign debt plus a forecast of the economic prospects.

14040 COURRIER DES STATISTIQUES
Institut National de la Statistique et des Etudes Economiques

France – French quarterly FrF115

Report on statistical research, publications, forthcoming events etc.

14041 DEFIS A L'ECONOMIE FRANCAISE: DOSSIERS DU GROUPE: PERSPECTIVES MACROECONOMIQUES A MOYEN TERME
La Documentation Francaise

France – French 272pp FrF120
ISBN/ISSN No. 2 11 001715 5

Decisive factors in the economic development of France in the next 10 years.

14042 DOING BUSINESS IN FRANCE
Delegation a l'Amenagement du Territoire et a l'Action Regionale (DATAR)

France – English 1985 48pp free

Description of company law, taxation, labour law, foreign trade and exchange control and distribution and licensing.

14043 DONNEES SOCIALES
Institut National de la Statistique et des Etudes Economiques

France – French every 3 years 400pp

Data on social trends.

14044 ECOFLASH
Institut National de la Statistique et des Etudes Economiques

France – French monthly 1985 FrF72
ISSN No. 0296 4449

Summary tables and graphs on a variety of economic and social issues. Each issue concentrates on a particular subject.

14045 ECONOMIE ET STATISTIQUE
Institut National de la Statistique et des Etudes Economiques

France – French monthly FrF375

Monthly economic and statistical review.

14046 ENQUETE ANNUELLE D'ENTERPRISE
Ministere de l'Industrie

France – French annual 6 vols cost various

Vol.1 provisional results of the industrial section; vol.2 details on 40 industrial sectors; other 4 volumes give detailed results on 250 sectors.

14047 L'ENQUETE ANNUELLE SUR LE COMPORTEMENT DES ENTERPRISES INDUSTRIELLES
Banque de France

France – French annual

A survey of 3000 companies with aggregated data on turnover, exports, investments etc. Also forecasts for investment intentions.

14048 ENQUETE MENSUELLE DE CONJONCTURE
Banque de France

Results of surveys held by each branch of the Banque de France giving current information on economic trends in industry, production, orders, stocks, prices, employment.

14049 ENQUETE SUR L'EMPLOI
Institut National de la Statistique et des Etudes Economiques (INSEE)

France – French annual 270pp

Survey of employment and unemployment with information on occupational structures, patterns of qualifications and age, hours of work and duration of employment.

14050 L'ENQUETE SUR L'EVOLUTION DES TRESORERIES, DE L'EPARGNE ET DU CREDIT
Banque de France

France – French annual

Results of an enquiry based on bank branches looking at the demand for money, credit and savings.

14051 L'EQUIPEMENT DES MENAGES AU DEBUT DE 198...
Institut National de la Statistique et des Etudes Economiques (INSEE)

France – French biennial c50pp

Data on consumer durables analysed by household and by region.

14052 L'ETUDE SUR LA SITUATION FINANCIERE DES REGIONS
Banque de France

France – French annual

Statistics on the financial and banking sectors in the regions.

14053 ETUDES SECTORELLES
Ministere de l'Industrie

France – French irregular FrF85 each

Each study covers a different industrial sector (e.g. textiles and clothing), and looks at its structure, international position, evolution and problems.

14054 FASCICULES DE RESULTATS DE LA CENTRALE DE BILANS
Banque de France

France – French annual FrF30

An analysis of the performance of companies and industrial sectors giving data on size, number of employees, value added, and various financial ratios.

14055 LE FER-BLANC EN FRANCE ET DANS LE MONDE
Chambre Syndicale des Producteurs de Fer-Blanc et de Fer-Noir

France – French annual 20pp

Data on tin plate in France, with statistics on production, deliveries, imports and exports.

14056 FICHES BANQUES*
Dafsa

France – French annual

Analysis of both French and foreign banks established in France, and other financial institutions covering 68 establishments. The information includes key personnel, organization, activities, financial status.

14057 FRANCE
UK Iron and Steel Statistics Bureau

France – English 1986 with annual statistical summary £25

Report on the steel industry showing production, consumption and details of imports and exports.

14058 FRANCE AND YOU; THE ECONOMIC ENVIRONMENT
Delegation a l'Amenagement du Territoire et a l'Action Regionale (DATAR)

France – English 1986 24pp free

Details of economic policy, foreign trade, government incentives and human resources.

14059 FRANCE: PERSPECTIVES SECTORIELLES
Credit Lyonnais

France – French annual 80pp

A review of major industrial sectors giving figures on turnover, production, import and export for each sector.

14060 GRAPH AGRI (NATIONAL): ANNUAIRE DE GRAPHIQUES AGRICOLES
Ministere de l'Agriculturre

France – French annual 1979 FrF110
ISSN No. 242 2085

The development of agriculture over the last 10 years in the form of charts and graphs.

14061 GRAPH AGRI REGIONS
Ministere de l'Agriculture

France – French irregular 1983 FrF100

Statistical data on agriculture at a regional level.

14062 GRAPHIQUES DE LA BOURSE DE PARIS*
Chambre Syndicale des Agents de Change

France – French bi-monthly

Charts giving up-to-date graphic representation of shares traded on the French stock exchange. Each chart gives the following information: prices quoted during an 8-12 month period; the moving average based on 200 days; the volume of transactions during a period of 8-12 months; a yearly range chart giving highest, lowest and latest prices since 1962.

14063 HINTS TO EXPORTERS
Department of Trade and Industry

France – English annual

Practical guide for businessmen giving general information, useful addresses, methods of doing business and relevant regulations.

14064 HUMAN RESOURCE MANAGEMENT IN FRANCE
Delegation a l'Amenagement du Territoire et a l'Action Regionale (DATAR)

France – English 1986 free

Data on employment, working conditions, salaries, benefits and industrial relations.

14065 L'IMPLANTATION ETRANGERE DANS L'INDUSTRIE
Ministere de l'Industrie

France – French annual FrF85

Statistical report on foreign ventures in French industry. Data by sector, by origin and by region.

14066 L'INDUSTRIE ET LES REGIONS
Ministere de l'Industrie

France – French annual FrF85

Regional details on industrial sectors – manpower, investment, wages.

14067 L'INDUSTRIE ET DES REGIONS EN 1985: TRAITS FONDAMENTAUX DU SYSTEME INDUSTRIEL FRANCAIS
La Documentation Francaise

France – French irregular 1981 252pp FrF71
ISSN No. 0 2447118

Detailed statistics on regional industrial structure.

14068 INDUSTRIES AGRICOLES ET ALIMENTAIRES (SERIES S)
Ministere de l'Agriculture

France – French irregular 1974 FrF60 paper FrF18 microfiche
ISSN No. 02436647

Data on agriculture and food industries.

14069 INDUSTRIES ELECTRIQUES ET ELECTRONIQUES
Federation des Industries Electriques et Electroniques

France – French quarterly 8pp

Newsletter of the FIEE giving information on the electrical and electronics sectors in France.

14070 INDUSTRIES FRANCAISES DES EQUIPEMENTS POUR VEHICULES
Federation des Industries des Equipements pour Vehicules

France – French/English 1986 24pp

Booklet giving information on the vehicle equipment industry with statistics for turnover and exports, for the automobile, motor cycle and bicycle industries.

14071 INFORMATIONS RAPIDES
Institut National de la Statistique et des Etudes Economiques

France – French 200 a year FrF1360

Notes on current economic developments.

14072 INFORMATIONS RAPIDES–COMMERCE EXTERIEUR AGRO-ALIMENTAIRE
Ministere de l'Agriculture

France – French monthly FrF18.00 each FrF180.00 annual

Current statistics on agricultural and food exports covering live animals, carcases, dairy products, vegetables, fruit, cereals, grain, oil, sugar, drinks including wine.

14073 INFORMATIONS RAPIDES–FRUITS
Ministere de l'Agriculture

France – French irregular FrF13.00 each FrF140.00 annually

Statistics on the production of peaches, apples, pears, plums and table grapes.

14074 INFORMATIONS RAPIDES–LEGUMES
Ministere de l'Agriculture

France – French irregular FrF13.00 each FrF280.00 annually

Statistics on vegetable production covering artichokes, carrots, melons, cauliflowers, early potatoes, salads, tomatoes.

14075 INFORMATIONS RAPIDES–SITUATION AGRICOLE
Ministere de l'Agriculture

France – French monthly FrF13.00 each FrF125.00 annually

Figures on the national agricultural situation.

14076 INFORMATIONS RAPIDES–STATISTIQUES DES ENTREPRISES
Ministere de l'Agriculture

France – French irregular c10pp FrF18.00 each FrF90.00 annually

Synthesis of current statistics on the agriculture and food industries, in particular the results of surveys of productive capacity.

14077 INFORMATIONS RAPIDES – VITICULTURE
Ministere de l'Agriculture

France – French irregular FrF15.00 each FrF50.00 annual

Statistics on viniculture.

14078 INFORMATIONS RAPIDES–PRODUCTION ANIMALE
Ministere de l'Agriculture

France – French weekly 1977 FrF11 each FrF470 annual
ISSN No. 223 4912

Weekly data on slaughtering, prices etc. of cattle and pigs.

14079 INFORMATIONS RAPIDES–SECTEUR AVICOLE
Ministere d l'Agriculture

France – French monthly 1977 FrF12 each FrF125 annual
ISSN No. 223 4920

Data on the poultry industry including foreign trade.

14080 INFORMATIONS RAPIDES–STATISTIQUES LAITIERES
Ministere de l'Agriculture

France – French monthly 1977 FrF20 each FrF200 annual
ISBN/ISSN No. 223 4939

Statistics on the dairy industry including foreign trade, stocks, national and regional prices.

14081 INFORMATION STATISTIQUES SUR L'INDUSTRIE DE LA REGION
Ministere de l'Industrie

France – French annual FrF85

Data for each region on employment, investment, public sector, energy use and foreign investment. In 21 parts.

14082 **INGENERIE, ETUDES ET CONSEILS**
Ministere de l'Industrie

France – French annual FrF85

Engineering data on size, production and exports.

14083 **INVESTMENT INCENTIVES IN FRANCE**
Delegation a l'Amenagement du Territoire et a l'Action Regionale (DATAR)

France – English 1984 16pp free

Details of regional development grants and small business grants.

14084 **KEY ECONOMIC INDICATORS**
Credit Lyonnais

France – English monthly

Statistics on industrial production, employment, foreign trade, money market etc. Also includes takes for other major developed countries.

14085 **KOMPASS REGISTER**
Kompass Publishers, UK

France – French/English/German/Spanish/Italian annual £145.00

Comprehensive business directory giving information on over 41,000 companies listed geographically and cross-referenced to a directory of products and services.

14086 **LETTRE MENSUELLE DE CONJONCTURE***
La Chambre de Commerce et d'Industrie de Paris

France – French monthly

Newsletter of economic activity.

14087 **LA LETTRE MENSUELLE REGIONALE**
Banque de France

France – French monthly

Economic trends for each region.

14088 **LE MARCHE MONETAIRE**
Banque de France

France – French 1981 4pp free

Report on the money market.

14089 **MONITEUR DU COMMERCE INTERNATIONAL (MOCI)***
Centre Francais du Commerce Exterieur

France – French weekly FrF810.00 in France monthly FrF920.00 overseas

Loose-leaf publicationm providing weekly reports on current developments in external trade with monthly updates of current regulations.

14090 **LA MONNAIE EN 19-**
Banque de France

France – French annual free

Summary of chief statistics relevant to financial situation followed by a brief commentary.

14091 **LES MUTATIONS DU SYSTEME FINANCIER FRANCAIS NOTES ET ETUDES DOCUMENTAIRES NO. 4820**
La Documentation Francaise

France – French 1986 144pp FrF50
ISSN No. 0029-4004

Covers changes in the French financial system.

14092 **NEWSLETTER FROM FRANCE***
DATAR

France – English/Spanish/German quarterly free

Newsletter covering current developments in the economy.

14093 **LA NOTE DE CONJONCTURE REGIONALE**
Banque de France

France – French twice a year

Economic trends for each region.

14094 **NOTE MENSUELLE D'INFORMATION DE LA DIRECTION DES TRANSPORTS TERRESTRES***
Ministere des Transports

France – French monthly c20pp FrF90.00

Up-to-date information on all aspects of land transport.

14095 **NOTES BLEUES***
Ministere de l'Economie et Ministere du Budget

France – French frequent free

Booklets summarizing current statistics in an easily comprehensible form. All aspects of the economy and finance are covered.

14096 **NOTES D'INFORMATION***
La Chambre de commerce et d'Industrie de Paris

France – French frequent FrF6.00-10.00

Frequent brief newsletters on a variety of commercial and financial topics such as current legislation and regulations relevant to trade.

14097 **LES NOTES DU SERVICE DE L'INFORMATION**
Banque de France

France – French irregular free

Short studies on a variety of topics, mainly money, credit and the activities of the Banque.

14098 **LES NOTES FINANCIERES ANNUELLES REGIONALES**
Banque de France

France – French

Analyses the financial situation in each region.

14099 **PERSPECTIVES DU FINANCEMENT DE L'ECONOMIE FRANCAISE**
La Documentation Francaise

France – French 3 vols.

14100 **POPULATION***
INED

France – French quarterly [illegible]
FrF110.00

Report of demographic surveys and investigations.

14101 **POPULATIONS ET SOCIETES***
INED

France – French monthly 2pp FrF16

Condensed information on economic and demographic events.

14102 **PRATIQUES CULTURELLES DES FRANCAIS: DESCRIPTION SOCIO-DEMOGRAPHIQUE: EVOLUTION 1973-1981**
Ministere de la Culture

France – French 1982 400pp FrF92
ISBN No. 2247003931

A survey of how the French spend their leisure time etc. Data on reading, watching TV, use of audio visual equipment, trips out.

14103 **PREMIER RESULTATS**
Institut National de la Statistique et des Etudes Economiques

France – French 20 issues a year 4pp FrF8 an issue
ISSN No. 0758-7724

Preliminary results from INSEE studies which appear in depth in other INSEE publications at a later date.

14104 **PREVISIONS GLISSANTES DETAILLEES HORIZON 1991**
BIPE/INSEE

France – French annual 1979 various

Issued in 9 parts, each covering different industrial sectors (metalworking, chemicals, plastics, printing etc.). Gives detailed statistics on production, employment, finance as well as forecasts.

14105 **PRINCIPAUX MECANISMES DE DISTRIBUTION DU CREDIT**
Banque de France

France – French irregular 150pp FrF35

Detailed review of credit mechanisms.

14106 **PRODUCTION ANIMALE (SERIE S)**
Ministere de l'Agriculture

France – French irregular 1975 FrF60 paper FrF18 microfiche
ISSN No. 02436566

Data on animal production.

14107 **PRODUCTION VEGETALES ET FORESTIERES (SERIE S)**
Ministere de l'Agriculture

France – French irregular 1975 Fr60 paper FrF18 microfiche
ISSN No. 07553218

Data on vegetable and forestry production.

14108 **PROPRIETE ET POUVOIR DANS L'INDUSTRIE VOL.1: LE SECTEUR PUBLIC; VOL.2: LE SECTEUR PRIVE**
La Documentation Francaise

France – French 1987 2 vols. FrF50
ISBN No. 0029-4004

14109 **RAPPORT ANNUEL DE LA COMMISSION BANCAIRE**
Banque de France

France – French annual FrF150.00

Report of the commission on banking control. Reviews relevant legislation and gives the financial statements of all registered banks.

14110 **RAPPORT ANNUEL–UNION DES INDUSTRIES CHIMIQUES***
Union des Industries Chimiques

France – French annual c50pp free

Annual report of the federation of chemical industries.

14111 **RAPPORT ANNUEL DU CONSEIL NATIONAL DU CREDIT**
Banque de France

France – French annual FrF70.00

Overview of the financial situation followed by a detailed analysis of statistics relevant to finance, banking and other credit institutions. Contains many statistical tables.

14112 **RAPPORT SUR LES COMPTES DE LA NATION**
Institut National de la Statistique et des Etudes Economiques

France – French annual c4 vols

Detailed report on national accounts.

14113 **RECENSEMENT GENERAL DE LA POPULATION 1982**
Institut National de la Statistique et des Etudes Economiques

France – French various

Results of the latest census published in a number of volumes.

14114 **RESEAU D'INFORMATION COMPTABLE AGRICOLE EN 198_**
Institut National de la Statistique et des Etudes Economiques

France – French annual c205pp FrF35.00

Detailed analysis of agricultural accounts giving information on output, value added, cost of materials, revenue, capital, investment, profitability. Analysed by size of holding, main activity and region.

14115 **RESULTATS MENSUELLES DES ENQUETES DE BRANCHE**
Ministere de l'Industrie

France – French monthly FrF270 per sector

The series covers 8 industrial sectors with data for products in those sectors on production, deliveries, stocks, imports and exports.

14116 **RESULTATS TRIMESTRIELS DES ENQUETES DE BRANCHE**
Ministere de l'Industrie

France – French quarterly and annual supplement FrF180

Market information on 14 major sectors.

14117 **LA REVUE ANNUELLE DE L'EVOLUTION DES PRINCIPALES BRANCHES D'ACTIVITE**
Banque de France

France – French annual

Reviews industrial and commercial activity with data on production, overseas trade and investments.

14118 **REVUE FRANCAISE DES AFFAIRES SOCIALES***
Ministere du Travail et de la Participation

France – French quarterly c150pp FrF250.00

Articles on a variety of subjects connected with labour and social security. The publication is accompanied by monthly bulletins of labour statistics and supplements giving other relevant statistics.

14119 **LES SALAIRES DANS L'INDUSTRIE, LE COMMERCE ET LES SERVICES EN 198_**
Institut National de la Statistique et des Etudes Economiques

France – French annual c168pp

Statistics on salaries in industry, commerce and services excluding agriculture and the public sector. Figures are given for establishments by activity, number of employers, salary bill. Salaries are analysed by industry, occupation and region.

14120 **SIDERURGIE FRANCAISE EN 19...**
Chambre Syndicale de la Siderurgie Francaise

France – French annual c50pp free

Annual report of the French steel industry.

14121 **SITUATION AGRICOLE AU FRANCE–COMMERCE EXTERIEUR BOIS ET DERIVES**
Ministere de l'Agriculture

France – French quarterly 1981 FrF33 each FrF120 annual
ISSN No. 243 8283

Statistics on imports and exports of the timber industry by volume and value.

14122 **SITUATION AGRICOLE EN FRANCE–CONJONCTURE GENERALE**
Ministere de l'Agriculture

France – French monthly 1979 FrF40 each FrF400 annual
ISSN No. 2225220

A digest of economic information on agriculture and the food industry.

14123 **SITUATION AGRICOLE EN FRANCE NOTE DE CONJONCTURE – PRODUCTION ANIMALE**
Ministere de l'Agriculture

France – French monthly FrF40.00 each FrF400.00annually

Statistics of production, consumption, export, prices of cattle, sheep, pigs, cows, horses and all types of meat.

14124 **SITUATION AGRICOLE EN FRANCE NOTE DE CONJONCTURE–PRODUCTION AVICOLE**
Ministere de l'Agriculture

France – French quarterly FrF43.00 each FrF160 annually

Statistics on poultry production, marketing and exports.

14125 **SITUATION AGRICOLE EN FRANCE NOTE DE CONJONCTURE–PRODUCTION BOVINE**
Ministere de l'Agriculture

France – French quarterly FrF33.00 each FrF120.00 annually

Statistics accompanied by a commentary on cattle production.

14126 **SITUATION AGRICOLE EN FRANCE NOTE DE CONJONCTURE–PRODUCTION PORCINE**
Ministere de l'Agriculture

France – French quarterly FrF45.00 each FrF120.00 annually

Statistics on pig production.

14127 **SITUATION AGRICOLE EN FRANCE NOTE DE CONJONCTURE–PRODUCTION VEGETALE**
Ministere de l'Agriculture

France – French monthly FrF40.00 each FrF400.00 annually

Satistics on the production, marketing and export of all types of vegetable produce.

14128 **SITUATION DE L'INDUSTRIE FRANCAISE**
Institut National de la Statistique et des Etudes Economiques

France – French annual

Statistics on French industry.

14129 **LA SITUATION DEMOGRAPHIQUE**
Institut National de la Statistique et des Etudes Economiques

France – French annual

Population statistics, giving births, deaths, marriages, divorces nationally and regionally.

14130 **LA SITUATION DU MARCHE VITICOLE (BULLETIN DE CONJONCTURE) THE ANALYSIS OF WINE MARKET**
Institut National de la Recherche Agronomique

France – French 3 per annum 1966 120-220pp FrF153 p.a.

Viticulture in France and Europe.

14131 **STATISTIQUE AGRICOLE ANNUELLE**
Ministere de l'Agriculture

France–French annual 1987 FrF120 paper FrF36 microfiche
ISSN No. 0244-5271

Statistics on land utilization and agricultural product by department.

14132 **STATISTIQUE DE LA FORMATION PROFESSIONELLE CONTINUE FINANCEE PAR LES ENTREPRISES (TRAITMENT DES DECLARATIONS D'EMPLOYEURS 1984-1985-1986)**
La Documentation Francaise

France – French 116pp FrF90
ISBN No. 2 11 001738 4

Statistics on employers' financing of professional training.

14133 **STATISTIQUES DU COMMERCE EXTERIEUR IMPORTATIONS-EXPORTATIONS***
Direction Generale des Douanes et Droits Indirect

France – French annual c1,000pp FrF160.00

Statistics on imports and exports classified by countries of origin or destination and also by product.

14134 **STATISTIQUES ET ETUDES FINANCIERES***
Ministere de l'Economie et Ministere du Budget

France – French monthly c200pp FrF180.00

Detailed analysis of current economic situation including statistics and relevant legislation.

14135 **STATISTIQUES DE L'INDUSTRIE FRANCAISE DES PATES, PAPIERS ET CARTON**
Confederation Francaise de l'Industrie des Papiers, Cartons et Celluloses

France – French annual c35pp

Statistics on production, consumption, import and export of paper, board and packaging.

14136 **STATISTIQUES ET INDICATEURS DES REGIONS FRANCAISES**
Institut National de la Statistique et des Etudes Economiques

France – French annual c600pp

Socio-economic indicators for regions covering population, economically active population, agriculture, industry, services, communications, distributive trades, education, household finance.

14137 **STATISTIQUES MENSUELLES DE LA BOURSE DE PARIS***
Chambre Syndicale des Agents de Change

France – French monthly

Monthly statistics of the Paris stock exchange containing information on market activity, prices, and tables of statistics for each stock traded on the forward market and for the 50 most active stocks traded on the cash market only.

14138 **STATISTIQUES MONETAIRES ANNUELLES**
Banque de France

France – French annual FrF110

Current and time series data on money supply, credit and savings.

14139 **STATISTIQUES MONETAIRES MENSUELLES**
Banque de France

France – French monthly

Provisional statistics on money supply, financial assets, interest rates, money markets etc.

14140 **STATISTIQUES MONETAIRES TRIMESTRIELLES**
Banque de France

France – French quarterly

Similar to 'Statistiques Monetaires Mensuelles' but providing more detail.

14141 **STRUCTURES ET ENVIRONMENT DES EXPLOITATIONS (SERIE S)**
Ministere de l'Agriculture

France – French irregular 1975 FrF60 paper FrF18 microfiche
ISBN/ISSN No. 0243 8585

Data on the structure of agricultural units.

14142 **SUMMARY OF FRENCH COMPANY LAW**
Delegation a l'Amenagement du Territoire et l'Action Regionale (DATAR)

France – English/Spanish/German 1986 free

Major forms of companies and bankruptcy procedure.

14143 **SUMMARY OF FRENCH TAX SYSTEM**
Delegation a l'Amenagement du Territoire et l'Action Regionale (DATAR)

France – English/Spanish/German 1986 free

Various types of taxes, both corporate and personal, and tax benefits.

14144 **SYNTHESES STATISTIQUES, COMPTES ET REVENUES (SERIE S)**
Ministere de l'Agriculture

France – French irregular 1974 FrF60 paper FrF18 microfiche
ISSN No. 0244 5271

Data on the accounts of the agricultural sector, including income, expenditure and external trade.

14145 **TABLEUX DE CONSOMMATION D'ENERGIE EN FRANCE 1987**
La Documentation Francaise

France – French irregular 1982 131 pp FrF90
ISSN No. 2 11 17 48 8

Energy development over the last 12 years and the part played by each form of energy.

14146 **TABLEAUX DE L'ECONOMIE FRANCAISE**
Institut National de la Statistique et des Etudes Economiques

France – French annual FrF38

ISBN/ISSN No. 211 0640642

A survey of the French economy intended for general use.

14147 **TAX AND INVESTMENT PROFILE**
Touche Ross International, US

France – English free

Survey covering investment, trade, labour, business practices, financial system. Frequently updated.

14148 **TENDANCES DE LA CONJONCTURE**
Institut National de la Statistique et des Etudes Economiques

France – French monthly FrF590

Economic indicators, published in 2 volumes with 3 supplements.

14149 **TRAFFIC MARITIME DU PORTE DE MARSEILLE**
Porte Autonomie de Marseille

France – French/English monthly

Statistics on the port of Marseilles.

14150 **LES TRANSPORTS EN FRANCE**
Institut National de la Statistique et des Etudes Economiques

France – French annual c150pp

Statistics on all forms of transport giving traffic, revenue and costs. Covers road, rail, air and sea transport.

14151 **TRAVAIL ET EMPLOI***
Ministere du Travail et de la Participation

France – French quarterly FrF70.00

Articles and research reports on all aspects of labour and its relevance to the economy.

FEDERAL GERMAN REPUBLIC

15001 ABC Geographical Gazetteer of the German Economy
ABC–Verlagshaus

Germany, West – German 1150pp

Places of any industrial importance. Includes economic and communications data from official sources.

15002 ABC Industrial Information and References
ABC–Verlagshaus

Germany, West – German 7000pp (4 volumes)

Register of manufacturers in Germany and West Berlin covering 68 industrial groups and subdivisions.

15003 ABECOR COUNTRY REPORT – FEDERAL REPUBLIC OF GERMANY
Abecor

Germany, West – English 1986 2pp free

Brief economic report.

15004 ABSATZ VON BIER (2140921)
W. Kohlhammer GmbH

Germany, West – German monthly DM1.60

Statistics on sales of beer.

15005 ABSCHLUSSE DER AKTIENGESELLSCHAFTEN (2020210)
W. Kohlhammer GmbH

Germany, West – German annual DM16.50

Figures for the balances of joint stock companies.

15006 ABSCHLUSSE DER ÖFFENTLICHEN VERSORGUNGS- UND VERKEHRS-UNTERNEHMEN (2020300)
W. Kohlhammer GmbH

Germany, West – German annual DM12.00

Figures giving the balances of public utilities and transport.

15007 AGRARBERICHT DER BUNDESREGIERUNG
Bundesministerium fur Ernahrung, Landwirtschaft und Forsten

Germany, West – German annual free

Annual report on German agriculture.

15008 AKTIENMARKTE (2090200)
W. Kohlhammer GmbH

Germany, West – German monthly DM3.20

Statistics on share markets.

15009 AMTLICHE NACHRICHTEN DER BUNDESANSTALT FUR ARBEIT
Bundesanstalt fur Arbeit

Germany, West – German monthly and annual 70-370pp DM100

Labour market.

15010 ANGESTELLTENVERDIENSTE IN INDUSTRIE UND HANDEL
W. Kohlhammer GmbH

Germany, West – German quarterly DM11.20

Earnings of salaried employees in industry and commerce.

15011 ANNUAL REPORT–DEUTSCHE BUNDESBANK
Deutsche Bundesbank

Germany, West – German/English annual free

15012 ARBEITERVERDIENSTE IN DER INDUSTRIE (2160210)
W. Kohlhammer GmbH

Germany, West – German quarterly DM8.00

Earnings of wage earners in industry.

15013 ARBEITERVERDIENSTE IN DER LANDWIRTSCHAFT–ARBEITNEHMERVERDIENSTE IN INDUSTRIE UND HANDEL (2160100)
W. Kohlhammer GmbH

Germany, West – German annual DM1.60

Earnings of labour in agriculture: earnings of employees in industry and commerce.

15014 ARBEITS-UND SOZIALSTATISTIK*
Bundesminister fur Arbeit und Sozialordnung

Germany, West – German annual DM12.50

Social and labour statistics.

15015 ARBEIT UND SOZIALPOLITIK
Nomos Verlagsgesellschaft

Germany, West – German monthly DM90

Journal covering labour and social policy.

15016 ARBEITSKOSTEN IM GROSS -UND EINZELHANDEL SOWIE IM BANK - UND VERSICHERUNGSGEWERBE

Germany, West – German quadrennial DM13.50
ISSN No. 2163202

Labour costs in wholesale and retail trade as well as in banking and insurance.

15017 ARBEITSKOSTEN IM PRODUZIERENDEN GEWERBE
W. Kohlhammer GmbH

Germany, West – German quadrennial DM19.50
ISBN/ISSN No. 2163201

Labour costs in production industries.

15018 ARBEITSKRAFTE
W. Kohlhammer GmbH

Germany, West – German annual DM10.50
ISSN No. 2030220

Labour force.

15019 AUSFUHR NACH VERBRAUCHS- UND KAUFERLANDERN UND WARENGRUPPEN (2070320)
W. Kohlhammer GmbH

Germany, West – German annual DM21.50

Exports by countries of consumption and of purchase and by commodity groups: foreign trade in selected commodities.

15020 AUSGEWAHLTE ZAHLEN FUR DIE AGRARWIRTSCHAFT BETRIEGS-ARBEITS-UND EINKOMMENSVERHALTNISSE BETRIEBE (2030100)
W. Kohlhammer GmbH

Germany, West – German annual DM19.50

Selected figures on agriculture, structure of holdings, operating conditions and incomes, and details of holdings.

15021 **AUSGEWAHLTE ZAHLEN FUR DIE BAUWIRTSCHAFT (1020200)**
W. Kohlhammer GmbH

Germany, West – German monthly DM11.10

Selected figures for the construction industry including building permits, buildings completed, and construction orders.

15022 **AUSGEWAHLTE ZAHLEN ZUR ENERGIEWIRTSCHAFT**
W. Kohlhammer GmbH

Germany, West – German monthly/annual 50/68pp DM9.50, DM10.50
ISSN No. 1020220

Power production.

15023 **AUSLANDER (2010200)**
W. Kohlhammer GmbH

Germany, West – German annual DM10.50

Statistics on aliens.

15024 **AUSSENHANDEL NACH DEM INTERNATIONALEN WARENVERZEICHNIS FUR DEN AUSSENHANDEL (SITC REV II) UND LANDERN (SPEZIALHANDEL)**
W. Kohlhammer GmbH

Germany, West – German annual DM25.50
ISBN/ISSN No. 2070700

Foreign trade according to the Standard International Trade Classification (SITC Rev II) and by countries–special trade.

15025 **AUSSENHANDEL NACH LANDERN UND GUTERGRUPPEN DER PRODUKTIONSSTATISTIKEN (SPEZIALHANDEL)**
W. Kohlhammer GmbH

Germany, West – German annual DM15.00

Foreign trade by countries and commodity groups of industry statistics.

15026 **AUSSENHANDEL NACH WAREN UND LANDERN (SPEZIALHANDEL)**
W. Kohlhammer GmbH

Germany, West – German monthly DM27.00
ISBN/ISSN No. 2070200

Foreign trade by commodities and countries–special trade.

15027 **AUSSERBETRIEBLICHE EINKOMMEN UND ARBEITSVERHALTNISSE FUR AUSGEWAHLTE BETRIEBSGRUPPEN**

Germany, West – German biennial DM20.60
ISSN No. 2030217

Outside income and working conditions for selected groups of holdings.

15028 **BADEN-WURTTEMBERGISCHE WERTPAPIERBORSE ZU STUTTGART AMTLICHES KURSBLATT**
Baden-Wurttembergische Wertpapierborse zu Stuttgart

Germany, West – German weekly DM520 p.a.

Stock market in Stuttgart.

15029 **DIE BANK (20.004)**
Bank Verlag Koln

Germany, West – German frequent DM86.45

Journal giving information on banking developments and trends.

15030 **BANKEN–JAHRBUCH**
Verlag Hoppenstedt & Co.

Germany, West – German annual 1982 1300pp DM410

Information on 1600 banking, credit and finance companies in West Germany.

15031 **BANKEN–ORTSLEXIKON**
Verlag Hoppenstedt & Co.

Germany, West – German annual with monthly updating c2,300pp DM450 basic work without updating; subscription DM80 basic work plus approx. DM100 per month for updatings

Directory of German banking firms giving over 44,000 branches with full information on personnel, activities and financial position.

15032 **BANKWESEN IN DER BUNDESREPUBLIK DEUTSCHLAND (22.004)**
Bank Verlag Koln

Germany, West – German/English/French 1983 48pp DM3.80

Account of the German banking system.

15033 **BAUMOBSTFLACHEN**
W. Kohlhammer GmbH

Germany, West – German quinquennial DM12.20
ISSN No. 2030314

Areas of fruit trees.

15034 **BAUTATIGKEIT (2050100)**
W. Kohlhammer GmbH

Germany, West – German annual DM12.00

Statistics on activities in the building industry.

15035 **BEKLEIDUNGSGEWERBE**
IFO Institut fur Wirtschaftsforschung

Germany, West – German irregular 233pp DM74

Clothing industry.

15036 **BERICHT UBER DIE VERBESSERUNG DER AGRARSTRUKTUR IN DER BUNDESREPUBLIK DEUTSCHLAND**
Bundesministerium fur Ernahrung, Landwirtschaft und Forsten

Germany, West – German annual free

Yearly report on improvements in German agriculture.

15037 **BERICHT UBER VIEH UND FLEISCH**
Bundesministerium fur Ernahrung, Landwirtschaft und Forsten

Germany, West – German weekly free

Weekly report of the meat industry.

15038 **BESCHAFTIGTE UND UMSATZ IM EINZELHANDEL (MESSZAHLEN) (2060310)**
W. Kohlhammer GmbH

Germany, West – German monthly DM4.80

Figures for persons engaged and turnover in the retail trade–index numbers.

15039 **BESCHAFTIGTE UND UMSATZ IM GASTGEWERBE (MESSZAHLEN) (2060410)**
W. Kohlhammer GmbH

Germany, West – German monthly DM1.60 annual

Persons engaged and turnover in the hotel and restaurant industry–index numbers.

15040 **BESCHAFTIGTE UND UMSATZ IM GROSSHANDEL (MESSZAHLEN) (2060110)**
W. Kohlhammer GmbH

Germany, West – German monthly DM4.80 annual

Statistics on employees and turnover in wholesale trade.

15041 **BESCHAFTIGUNG, UMSATZ UND ENERGIEVERSORGUNG DER UNTERNEHMEN UND BETRIEBE IM BERGBAU UND IM VERARBEITENDEN GEWERBE**
W. Kohlhammer GmbH

Germany, West – German annual DM12.00
ISSN No. 2040411

Employment, turnover and power supply of enterprises and local units in mining and manufacturing.

15042 BESCHAFTIGUNG, UMSATZ, INVESTITIONEN UND KOSTENSTRUKTUR DER UNTERNEHMEN IN DER ENERGIE- UND WASSERVERSORGUNG (2040610)
W. Kohlhammer GmbH

Germany, West – German annual DM12.00

Cost structure in the power and water supply industries.

15043 BESCHAFTIGUNG, UMSATZ UND INVESTIONEN DER UNTERNEHMEN IM BAUGEWERBE (2040520)
W. Kohlhammer GmbH

Germany, West – German annual DM7.50

Statistics on employment, turnover and investment in the building industry.

15044 BESCHAFTIGUNG, UMSATZ UND INVESTITIONEN DER UNTERNEHMEN IM BERGBAU UND IM VERARBEITENDEN GEWERBE (2040421)
W. Kohlhammer GmbH

Germany, West – German annual DM14.30

Statistics for employment, turnover and investments in the mining and manufacturing industries.

15045 BESCHAFTIGUNG, UMSATZ UND INVESTITIONEN DER UNTERNEHMEN IN DER ENERGIE- UND WASSERVERSORGUNG (2040610)
W. Kohlhammer GmbH

Germany, West – German annual DM12.00

Statistics on employment, turnover and investment in power and water supply industries.

15046 BESCHAFTIGUNG, UMSATZ, WARENEINGANG, LAGERBESTAND UND INVESTITIONEN IM EINZELHANDEL
W. Kohlhammer GmbH 2060320

Germany, West – German annual DM10.50

Purchases of goods, stock and gross proceeds in retail trade.

15047 BESITZVERHALTNISSE, GRUNDSTUCKSVERKEHT: FACHLICHE VORBILDUNG DER BETRIEBSLEITER (2030216)
W. Kohlhammer GmbH

Germany, West – German biennial DM13.50

Statistics on land tenure, transactions of real property, and technical qualifications of farm operators.

15048 BESTAND AN WOHNUNGEN
W. Kohlhammer GmbH

Germany, West – German annual DM7.50
ISSN No. 2050300

Housing.

15049 BETRIEBSGROSSENSTRUKTUR
W. Kohlhammer GmbH

Germany, West – German annual DM6.00
ISSN No. 2030211

Size structure of holdings.

15050 BETRIEBSSYSTEME UND STANDARDBETRIEBSEINKOMMEN
W. Kohlhammer GmbH

Germany, West – German biennial DM15.00

Operating systems and standard income of holdings.

15051 BEVOLKERUNG GESTERN, HEUTE UND MORGEN
W. Kohlhammer GmbH

Germany, West – German irregular 212pp DM10.50
ISSN No. 1021100

The population of West Germany, including model computations for future development up to 2030.

15052 BEVOLKERUNGSSTRUKTUR UND WIRTSCHAFTSKRAFT DER BUNDESLANDER (1010700)
W. Kohlhammer GmbH

Germany, West – German annual DM20.60

Major demographic and economic data by region.

15053 THE 300 BIGGEST GERMAN FIRMS
German Chamber of Industry and Commerce

Germany, West – English £8.00

Up-to-date information designed for the use of businessmen.

15054 BILDUNG IM ZAHLENSPIEGEL
W. Kohlhammer GmbH

Germany, West – German annual 156pp DM16.50
ISSN No. 1020100

Statistics of education.

15055 BINNENSCHIFFAHRT (2080400)
W. Kohlhammer GmbH

Germany, West – German monthly DM4.80 annual DM19.50

Statistics on inland water transport.

15056 BMELF INFORMATIONEN
Bundesministerium fur Ernahrung, Landwirtschaft und Forsten

Germany, West – German weekly free

Current information issued by the German Ministry of Agriculture.

15057 BODENNUTZUNG DER BETRIEBE
W. Kohlhammer GmbH

Germany, West – German biennial DM10.50
ISSN No. 2030212

Land use of holdings.

15058 BODENNUTZUNG UND PFLANZLICHE ERZEUGUNG
W. Kohlhammer GmbH

Germany, West – German annual DM12.00
ISSN No. 2030300

Land use and vegetable production.

15059 BRAUWIRTSCHAFT (2140922)
W. Kohlhammer GmbH

Germany, West – German annual DM3.20

Finance and taxes in the brewing industry.

15060 BRITISH–GERMAN TRADE
German Chamber of Industry and Commerce

Germany, West – English monthly £20.00

Official magazine of the chamber.

15061 BUNDESARBEITSBLATT
W. Kohlhammer GmbH

Germany, West – German monthly 135pp
ISSN No. 007 5868

Labour and social statistics.

15062 BUNDESREPUBLIK DEUTSCHLAND IN ZAHLEN
W. Kohlhammer GmbH

Germany, West – German annual 6-10pp

The Federal Republic of Germany in figures.

15063 CHAMBERS OF INDUSTRY AND COMMERCE IN GERMANY
German Chamber of Industry and Commerce

Germany, West – English free

15064 CHEMISCHE INDUSTRIE
IFO–Institut fur Wirtschaftsforschung

Germany, West – German irregular 429pp DM142

Chemical industry.

15065 COUNTRY PROFILES–WEST GERMANY
Economist Publications Ltd

Germany, West – English annual 40pp £25 UK, subscription varies in rest of world

Resumé of politics, economy and industry including statistical summaries.

15066 **COUNTRY REPORTS–WEST GERMANY**
Economist Publications Ltd

Germany, West – English quarterly 25pp £58 UK, subscription varies in rest of world

Economic policies and development plans, trends in production and demand, monetary and fiscal conditions, wages and prices, merchandise, trade, invisibles, capital flows, exchange rates and foreign debt plus a forecast of the economic prospects.

15067 **DEUTSCH-AMERIKANISCHE GESCHAFTSBEZIEHUNGEN/ GERMAN AMERICAN BUSINESS CONTACTS**
Verlag Hoppenstedt & Co.

Germany, West – German/English annual DM198

German companies and their American counterparts, companies in the US with their German counterparts.

15068 **DEUTSCHE BANK BULLETIN**
Deutsche Bank

Germany, West – English quarterly 16pp ISSN No. 0722 3250

Current economic and monetary issues.

15069 **DER DEUTSCHE MASCHINEN–UND ANLAGENBAU**
Verlag Hoppenstedt & Co.

Germany, West – German every three years 500pp DM135

German machinery manufacturers and plantmakers.

15070 **DIE DEUTSCHE VERSICHERUNGSWIRTSCHAFT JAHRBUCH**
Gesamtverband der Deutschen Versicherungswirtschaft eV

Germany, West – German/English annual 1981 140pp DM3.00
ISSN No. 0722 1118

Insurance, business development, capital investments, claims.

15071 **DIE DEUTSCHE WIRTSCHAFT IM STRUKTURWANDEL**
Institut fur Weltwirtschaft an der Universitat Kiel

Germany, West – German 1981 368pp DM58.00

Report on current structural changes in the economy.

15072 **LE DEUTSCHEMARK**
La Documentation Francaise/G. Moine

Germany, West – French 1981 FrF50

Detailed analysis of the monetary situation in FRG including statistical tables on all aspects of the economy and a bibliography.

15073 **DRUCKEREI-UND VERVIELFALTIGUNGSINDUSTRIE**
IFO–Institut fur Wirtschaftsforschung

Germany, West – irregular 110pp DM38.60

Printing and copying industry.

15074 **DUNGEMITTELVERSORGUNG (2040820)**
W. Kohlhammer GmbH

Germany, West – German monthly DM1.60 annual DM4.50

Statistics on fertilizer supplies.

15075 **THE ECONOMIC SITUATION IN THE FEDERAL REPUBLIC OF GERMANY**
Federal Minister of Economics

Germany, West – English monthly 50pp

Economic development, manufacturing, construction, employment, labour, trade, interest rates, wages and prices.

15076 **EINFUHR NACH HERSTELLUNGS- UND EINKAUFSLANDERN UND WARENGRUPPEN (2070310)**
W. Kohlhammer GmbH

Germany, West – German annual DM19.50

Statistics on imports by countries of production and of sale and by commodity groups.

15077 **EINHEIMISCHE ROHSTOFFE-STEINE, ERDEN UND INDUSTRIE MINERALE**
Bundesminister fur Wirtschaft

Germany, West – German 1987 48pp free

Booklet reviewing domestic raw materials and their use in industry.

15078 **EINKOMMENSTEUER (2140710)**
W. Kohlhammer GmbH

Germany, West – German triennial DM14.40

Figures on income tax.

15079 **EINNAHMEN UND AUSGABEN AUSGEWAHLTER PRIVATER HAUSHALTE (2150100)**
W. Kohlhammer GmbH

Germany, West – German monthly DM3.20 annual DM15.00

Income and expenditure of selected private households.

15080 **EISEN UND STAHL (EISENERZBAU, EISENSCHAFFENDE INDUSTRIE, EISEN-, STAHL- UND TEMPERGIESSERIE)**
W. Kohlhammer GmbH

Germany, West – German quarterly DM16.00
ISSN No. 2040810

Iron and steel.

15081 **EISENBAHNVERKEHR, STRASSENBAHNVERKEHR (2080200)**
W. Kohlhammer GmbH

Germany, West – German monthly DM3.20 annual DM19.50

Statistics for road and rail transport.

15082 **ELECTROTECHNISCHE INDUSTRIE**
IFO–Institut fur Wirtschaftsforschung

Germany, West – German irregular 261pp DM84

Electrical engineering industry.

15083 **EMPLOYEES OF BRITISH FIRMS IN WEST GERMANY: INCOME TAX AND SOCIAL SECURITY**
German Chamber of Industry and Commerce

Germany, West – English £10.00

15084 **ENTREPRISES ALLEMANDES ET COOPERATION INDUSTRIELLE A L'ECHELLE EUROPEENNE**
La Documentation Francaise

Germany, West – French irregular 162pp FrF80
ISBN No. 2 11 001580 2

A study of German companies and industrial politics.

15085 **DIE ENTWICKLUNG DES PERSONENVERKEHRS IN DEN REGIONEN DER BUNDESREPUBLIK DEUTSCHLAND BIZ ZUM JAHRE 2000**
Duncker & Humblot GmbH

Germany, West – German irregular 1983 156pp DM76

Projection of passenger traffic in Germany to the year 2000.

15086 **ERZEUGUNG VON GEFLUGEL**
W. Kohlhammer GmbH

Germany, West – German semi-annual DM3.20
ISSN No. 2030423

Poultry production.

15087 **EXPORTING TO WEST GERMANY–DOCUMENTATION AND LEGAL ASPECTS**
German Chamber of Industry and Commerce

Germany, West – English £20.00

Practical information in an abridged form for the use of businessmen.

15088 **FEATURES OF THE GERMAN MARKET**
German Chamber of Industry and Commerce

Germany, West – English £3.00

15089 **FINANZIERUNG MIT RISIKOKAPITAL**
Institut fur Mittelstandsforschung

Germany, West – German, English summary 1986 265pp DM68
ISBN No. 3 7910 5015 X

Test of the hypothesis of a positive correlation between investments of starting and existing companies and the amount of equity capital available. Obstacles in the German tax system and capital market hindering the efficient allocation of risk capital.

15090 **FOREIGN TRADE ACCORDING TO THE STANDARD INTERNATIONAL TRADE CLASSIFICATION (SITC)–SPECIAL TRADE (6370010)**
W. Kohlhammer GmbH

Germany, West – English annual DM22.50

15091 **FOREIGN TRADE WITH THE DEVELOPING COUNTRIES–SPECIAL TRADE (2070510)**
W. Kohlhammer GmbH, Stuttgart

Germany, West – English/German annual DM16.50

15092 **FOREIGN TRADE WITH SELECTED COMMODITIES (2070320)**
W. Kohlhammer GmbH, Stuttgart

Germany, West – English/German annual DM22.50

15093 **FORSCHUNG IM GESCHÄFTSBEREICH DES BUNDESMINISTERS FUR ERNÄHRUNG, LANDWIRTSCHAFT UND FORSTEN–JAHRESBERICHT**
Bundesministerium fur Ernährung, Landwirtschaft und Forsten

Germany, West – German annual on request

Annual report of agricultural research.

15094 **FUTTERWIRTSCHAFT IN DER BUNDESREPUBLIK DEUTSCHLAND**
Bundesministerium fur Ernahrung, Landwirtschaft und Forsten

Germany, West – German annual free

Review of the feed industry.

15095 **DAS GASVERSORGUNGSNETZ ERDGAS–UND FERNGASLEITUNGEN**
Verlag Gluckauf

Germany, West – German 1987 DM48.00

Gas network of Germany.

15096 **GEBIET UND BEVÖLKERUNG (2010100)**
W. Kohlhammer GmbH

Germany, West – German quarterly DM4.80 annual DM19.50

There are two series of figures in these publications. One gives data for the state and development of the population, the other classifies population by administrative units.

15097 **GEMUSEANBAUFLACHEN**
W. Kohlhammer GmbH

Germany, West – German annual DM3.00
ISSN No. 2030313

Areas of vegetable cultivation.

15098 **GENERAL CONDITIONS OF SALE, ACCORDING TO GERMAN LAW**
German Chamber of Industry and Commerce

Germany, West – English £20.00

15099 **DIE GENOSSENSCHAFTEN IN DER BUNDESREPUBLIK DEUTSCHLAND**
Deutsche Genossenschaftsbank (DG Bank)

Germany, West – German annual 1966 50pp DM30

Cooperatives in West Germany.

15100 **GERMAN AGENCY LAW**
German Chamber of Industry and Commerce

Germany, West – English £20.00

15101 **GERMAN AND BRITISH ECONOMY**
German Chamber of Industry and Commerce

Germany, West – English monthly £20 DM80 annual subscription

Comparative economic statistics.

15102 **GERMAN COMPANIES IN GREAT BRITAIN–FIRST CHOICE**
German Chamber of Industry and Commerce

Germany, West – English free

15103 **GERMAN INSURANCE INDICATORS**
Gesamtverband der Deutschen Versicherungswirtschaft eV

Germany, West – English annual 1982 60pp DM3
ISSN No. 0723 6972

Figures and tables about business development taken from GDV Year Book or based on yearbook charts.

15104 **THE GERMAN LABOUR LAW**
German Chamber of Industry and Commerce

Germany, West – English £20.00

15105 **THE GERMAN LIMITED COMPANY**
German Chamber of Industry and Commerce

Germany, West – English £12.00

15106 **GERMAN SUBSIDIARY COMPANIES IN THE UNITED KINGDOM**
German Chamber of Industry and Commerce

Germany, West – English £18.00

15107 **GERMAN TAX LAW**
German Chamber of Industry and Commerce

Germany, West – English 1986 £15.00

15108 **GERMANY**
UK Iron and Steel Statistics Bureau

Germany, West – English 1986 with annual statistical summary £25.00

Report on the steel industry showing production, consumption and details of imports and exports.

15109 **GERMANY (WEST)**
National Westminster Bank

Germany, West – English irregular 4pp free

Brief economic report.

15110 **GESETZLICHE UNFALLVERSICHERUNG IN DER BUNDESREPUBLIK DEUTSCHLAND–STATISTISCHER UND FINANZIELLER BERICHT***
Bundesminister fur Arbeit und Sozialordnung

Germany, West – German annual DM15.00

Statistical and financial report on accident insurance.

15111 **DIE GROSSE 500**
Hermann Luchterhand Verlag

Germany, West – German looseleaf

Continuously updated survey of 500 leading firms giving full address, activities, financial information and chief personnel.

15112 **GRUNDUNGS–FINANZIERUNG DURCH DEN STAAT. FAKTEN, ERFOLG, WIRKUNGEN**
Institut fur Mittelstandsforschung

Germany, West – German 1987 350pp DM74
ISBN No. 3 7910 5017 6

Start-up policy in Germany. Influences of public support on the new firms' development.

15113 **GUTERVERKEHR DER VERKEHRSZWEIGE (2080100)**
W. Kohlhammer GmbH

Germany, West – German quarterly DM8.00 annual DM12.00

Statistics on goods transport classified by branch of transport.

15114 **HANDBUCH DER DEUTSCHEN AKTIENGESELLSCHAFTEN**
Verlag Hoppenstedt & Co.

Germany, West – German fortnightly DM1750

Information on about 2,400 companies including foreign enterprises which deal on the German stock exchange. Details given include address, brief history, main product or service, financial structure and market share.

15115 **HANDBUCH DER GROSSUNTERNEHMEN**
Verlag Hoppenstedt & Co.

Germany, West – German annual c2,500pp DM550

Directory of over 20,000 wholesale enterprises giving financial information, description of products, and organization of the firm.

15116 **HANDEL MIT DEN OSTBLOCKLANDERN (2070600)**
W. Kohlhammer GmbH

Germany, West – German biennial DM9.00

Trade between the Federal Republic of Germany and the Eastern bloc countries.

15117 **HAUSHALTSGELD-WOHER, WOHIN? (1040300)**
W. Kohlhammer GmbH

Germany, West – German 1987 DM6.00

Summary results of continuous family budget surveys.

15118 **HINTS TO EXPORTERS**
Department of Trade and Industry

Germany, West – English annual

Practical guide for businessmen giving general information, useful addresses, methods of doing business and relevant regulations.

15119 **HOCHSEE-UND KUSTENFISCHEREI: BODENSEEFISCHEREI (2030450)**
W. Kohlhammer GmbH

Germany, West – German monthly DM2.30 annual DM5.70

Statistics for sea and inland fisheries including that of Lake Constance.

15120 **HOLZWIRTSCHAFT IM WANDEL**
Wirtschafts und Sozialwissenschaftliches Institut des Deutschen Gewerkschaftsbundes GmbH

Germany, West–German irregular 176pp DM20
ISBN No. 3 7663 0977 3

Study of the wood industry includes data on production, employment and growth prospects.

15121 **HOPPENSTEDT AKTIENANALYSEN**
Verlag Hoppenstedt & Co.

Germany – German continuous DM6400 p.a.

Share analysis.

15122 **HOPPENSTEDT BORSENFUHRER**
Verlag Hoppenstedt & Co.

Germany, West – German quarterly DM67.50 quarterly

Guide to the Stock Exchange analysing the progress of over 196 firms giving detailed information on their financial state.

15123 **HOPPENSTEDT CHARTS–SPEZIALWERTE**
Verlag Hoppenstedt & Co.

Germany – German weekly DM45 per month

Supplements standard securities tables with a further 180 German special (minor) stocks.

15124 **HOPPENSTEDT CHARTS–STANDARDWERTE**
Verlag Hoppenstedt & Co.

Germany – German weekly DM63 per month

Standard securities. Contains 120 price-turnover charts of German blue-chip companies.

15125 **HOPPENSTEDT INVESTMENT SERVICE**
Verlag Hoppenstedt & Co.

Germany, West – German monthly DM37.00 monthly

Information on German stocks giving up-to-date details of interest to the investor.

15126 **IAW–MITTEILUNGEN (IAW REVIEW)**
Institut fur Angewandte Wirtschaftsforschung (IAW)

Germany, West – German 3 times a year 1972 40pp
ISSN No. 0173 5454

Economic theory, politics and statistics.

15127 **IFO–BRANCHENSERVICE**
IFO–Institut fur Wirtschaftsforschung

Germany, West – German monthly DM150 per sector

Key economic information from government statistics, investment surveys and associations relating to more than 20 individual sectors.

15128 **IFO-DIGEST**
IFO–Institut fur Wirtschaftsforschung

Germany, West – English quarterly c40pp DM80.00 annually

Digest of economic trends in the Federal Republic of Germany including analysis and forecasting, business cycle indicators, industry reports, and abstracts of current research of the institute.

15129 **IFO-SCHNELLDIENST**
Duncker & Humblot GmbH

Germany, West – German 3 times per month 1948 20pp DM220 p.a.
ISSN No. 0018 974X

Current awareness journal covering industry, economic trends etc.

15130 **IFO-SPIEGEL DER WIRTSCHAFT–STRUKTUR UND KONJUNKTUR IN BILD UND ZAHL**
IFO–Institut fur Wirtschaftsforschung

Germany, West – German/English annual 1973 130pp DM120
ISBN No. 3 88512 010 0

Statistics on the economy.

15131 **IMPORT OF GERMAN WINE TO THE UNITED KINGDOM**
German Chamber of Industry and Commerce

Germany, West – English £5.00

15132 **INDEX DER GROSSHANDELS-VERKAUFSPREISE (2170600)**
W. Kohlhammer GmbH

Germany, West – German monthly DM4.80

Index of selling prices in wholesale trade.

15133 **INDEX DER GRUNDSTOFFPREISE (2170300)**
W. Kohlhammer GmbH

Germany, West – German monthly DM2.30 annual DM4.30

Price index for basic materials.

15134 INDEX DER TARIFLOHNE UND - GEHALTER
W. Kohlhammer GmbH

Germany, West – German quarterly DM480
ISSN No. 2160430

Index of agreed wages and salaries.

15135 INDIKATOREN ZUR WIRTSSCHAFTSENTWICKLUNG (1010600)
W. Kohlhammer GmbH

Germany, West – German monthly DM14.30

Tables of [illegible], seasonally adjusted time series.

15136 INDIZES DES AUFTRAGSEINGANGS, DES UMSATZES UND DES AUFTRAGSBESTANDS FUR DAS VERARBEITENDE BEWERBE UND FUR DAS BAUHAUPTGEWERBE (2040220)
W. Kohlhammer GmbH

Germany, West – German monthly DM7.90

Indices of orders received and unfilled orders for manufacturing and building industries.

15137 INDIZES DER PRODUKTION UND DER ARBEITSPRODUKTIVITAT, PRODUKTION AUSGEWAHLTER ERZEUGNISSE IM PRODUZIERENDEN GEWERBE
W. Kohlhammer GmbH

Germany, West – German monthly DM9.50
ISSN No. 2040210

Indices of production and of labour productivity, production of selected commodities in production industries.

15138 INDUSTRIAL ESTATES AS INSTRUMENT OF SMALL BUSINESS PROMOTION BY LOCAL AUTHORITIES
Institut fur Mittelstandsforschung

Germany, West – German/English summary 1986 285pp DM68
ISSN No. 3 7910 5005 2

Survey among all private and public authorities running industrial estates in West Germany. Success factors and developments of firms, located in industrial estates, consequences for future locations, also science parks.

15139 INDUSTRIE DER STEINE UND ERDEN
IFO–Institut fur Wirtschaftsforschung

Germany, West – German irregular 134pp DM48

Stone and earth industry.

15140 INTERNATIONAL TRANSACTIONS UNDER GERMAN VAT LAW
German Chamber of Industry and Commerce

Germany, West – English £14.00

15141 INVESTIONEN FUR UMWELTSCHUTZ IM PRODUZIERENDEN GEWERBE (2190300)
W. Kohlhammer GmbH

Germany, West – German annual DM15.00

Investment for environmental protection in production industries.

15142 JAHRBUCH FUR FREMDENVERKEHR
Deutsches Wirtschaftswissenschaftliches Institut fur Fremdenverkehr an der Universitat Munchen

Germany, West – German annual

Tourism.

15143 JAHRESBERICHT UBER DIE DEUTSCHE FISCHWIRTSCHAFT
Bundesministerium fur Ernährung, Landwirtschaft und Forsten

Germany, West – German annual on request

Annual report on the German fishing industry.

15144 JAHRESBERICHT DES VDR
Verband Deutscher Reeder (VDR)

Germany, West – German annual 1971 35pp free

Annual report of the Merchant Shipping Federation.

15145 JAHRESSCHAU DER DEUTSCHEN INDUSTRIE
ABC–Verlagshaus

Germany, West – German annual

Annual review of industries including clothing and lingerie; chemicals; iron, sheet metal and metal working; electrical and electronics; foundry; plastics; furniture; food and beverages and textiles.

15146 KAUFWERTE FUR BAULAND (2170500)
W. Kohlhammer GmbH

Germany, West – German quarterly DM4.80 annual DM9.00

Purchase values for building land.

15147 KAUFWERTE FUR LANDWIRTSCHAFTLICHEN GRUNDBESITZ
W. Kohlhammer GmbH

Germany, West – German annual DM3.00
ISBN/ISSN No. 2070240

Purchasing values of agricultural property.

15148 KEHRWIEDER
Verband Deutscher Reeder (VDR)

Germany, West – German monthly 1957 28pp DM2

Journal covering merchant shipping.

15149 KIELER KURZBERICHTE
Institut fur Weltwirtschaft an der Universitat Kiel

Germany, West – German monthly 40pp free

Brief economic reports.

15150 KOHLENBERGBAU IN DER ENERGIEWIRTSCHAFT DER BUNDESREPUBLIK DEUTSCHLAND
Verlag Gluckauf GmbH

Germany, West – German annual c110pp DM26.00

Analysis of the position of the coal industry in the energy sector of the economy of Germany.

15151 KOMPASS REGISTER
Kompass Publishers, UK

Germany, West – German/English/French/Spanish/Italian annual £145.00

Comprehensive business directory giving information on over 38,000 companies listed geographically and cross-referenced to a directory of products and services.

15152 KONTEN UND STANDARDTABELLEN (2180100)
W. Kohlhammer GmbH

Germany, West – German annual DM25.50

Accounts and standard tables.

15153 KORPERSCHAFTSTEUER (2140720)
W. Kohlhammer GmbH

Germany, West – German triennial DM10.30

Figures for corporation tax.

15154 KOSTENSTRUKTUR IM EINZELHANDEL (2020130)
W. Kohlhammer GmbH

Germany, West – German quadrennial DM13.60

Cost structure in the retail trade.

15155 KOSTENSTRUKTUR IM GASTGEWERBE (2020140)
W. Kohlhammer GmbH

Germany, West – German quadrennial DM7.00

Cost structure in the following sectors: hotels and restaurants.

15156 **KOSTENSTRUKTUR DES GEWERBLICHEN GUTERKRAFTVERKEHRS, DER SPEDITIONEN UND LAGEREIEN, DER BINNENSCHIFFAHRT UND DER SEE UND KUSTENSCHIFFAHRT: (2020452)**
W. Kohlhammer GmbH

Germany, West – German quadrennial DM9.00

Cost structure in the following sectors: commercial goods transport, shipping and warehousing.

15158 **KOSTENSTRUKTUR BEI HANDELSVERTRETERN UND HANDELSMAKLERN**
W. Kohlhammer GmbH

Germany, West – German quadrennial DM11.10
ISSN No. 2020122

Cost structure of commercial representatives and agents.

15159 **KOSTENSTRUKTUR IM HANDWERK (2020110)**
W. Kohlhammer GmbH

Germany, West – German quadrennial DM18.70

Cost structure in the following sectors: handicrafts, wholesale trade, commercial representatives and publishing.

15160 **KOSTENSTRUKTUR DER NICHTBUNDESEIGENEN EISENBAHNEN, DES STADTSCHNELLBAHN-, STRASSENBAHN- UND OMNIBUSVERKEHRS, DER REISEVERANSTALTUNG UND -VERMITTLUNG**
W. Kohlhammer GmbH

Germany, West – German quadrennial DM8.90

Cost structure of privately owned transport and travel.

15161 **KOSTENSTRUKTUR BEI RECHTSANWÄLTEN UND ANWALTSNOTAREN, BEI WIRTSCHAFTSPRÜFERN, STEUERBERATERN UND STEUERBEVOLLMÄCHTIGTEN, BEI ARCHITEKTEN UND BERATENDEN INGENIEUREN**
W. Kohlhammer GmbH

Germany, West – German quadrennial DM13.50

Cost structure in the following professions: lawyers and public notaries, auditors, tax consultants, engineers and architects, and also in incorporated enterprises.

15162 **KOSTENSTRUKTUR DER UNTERNEHMEN IM BAUGEWERBE**
W. Kohlhammer GmbH

Germany, West – German annual DM12.00

Cost structure in the building industry.

15163 **KOSTENSTRUKTUR DER UNDERNEHMEN IM BERGBAU, GRUNDSTOFF-UND PRODUKTIONSGUTERGEWERBE (2040431)**
W. Kohlhammer GmbH

Germany, West – German annual DM13.50

Cost structure in mining, primary and production industries.

15164 **KOSTENSTRUKTUR DER UNTERNEHMEN IM VERBRAUCHSGÜTER PRODUZIERENDEN GEWERBE UND IM NAHRUNGS-UND GENUSSMITTELGEWERBE: BAUGEWERBE (2040433)**
W. Kohlhammer GmbH

Germany, West – German annual DM15.00

Cost structures in the consumer goods, food, tobacco and beverages industries and also the building industry.

15165 **KRITISCHE WACHSTUMSSCHWELLEN IN DER UNTERNEHMENSENTWICKLUNG**
Institut fur Mittelstandsforschung

Germany, West – German/English summary 1985 490pp DM78
ISBN No. 3 7910 5007 9

Longitudinal study of 450 medium-sized industrial companies and classification of determinants influencing growth. Consequences of success or reasons for lack of success.

15166 **LABOUR LEASING TO GERMANY**
German Chamber of Industry and Commerce

Germany, West – German/English £40.00
Practical up-to-date information of interest to foreign businessmen.

15167 **LANDWIRTSCHAFTLICH GENUTZTE FLACHEN**
W. Kohlhammer GmbH

Germany, West – German annual DM3.00
ISSN No. 2030312

Agriculturally used areas.

15168 **LANDWIRTSCHAFTLICHE ERZEUGEERPREISE. ZUKAUFPREISE UND ABSATZWEGE**
Bundesministerium fur Ernahrung, Landwirtschaft und Forsten

Germany, West – German annual free

Details of costs and marketing in the agricultural industry.

15169 **LANGE REIHEN ZUR WIRTSCHAFTSENTWICKLUNG (1010500)**
W. Kohlhammer GmbH

Germany, West – German biennial DM19.50

Basic data on population and employment in addition to long-term statistics on all aspects of the economy.

15170 **LEDERVERARBEITUNG**
IFO–Institut fur Wirtschaftsforschung

Germany, West – German irregular 116pp DM48

Leather working industry.

15171 **LEISTUNG IN ZAHLEN**
Bundesminister fur Wirtschaft

Germany, West – German annual c120pp free

Summary of statistics dealing with all aspects of the economy.

15172 **LOHNSTEUER (2140730)**
W. Kohlhammer GmbH

Germany, West – German triennial DM15.00

Figures on wage tax.

15173 **LUFTVERKEHR (2080600)**
W. Kohlhammer GmbH

Germany, West – German monthly DM6.40 annual DM16.50

Statistics on air transport.

15174 **MEMBERS 1986/87**
German Chamber of Industry and Commerce

Germany, West – English £35.00

15175 **MESSEN REGELN AUTOMATISIEREN**
Verlag Hoppenstedt & Co.

Germany, West – German/English annual 750pp DM25

Details on companies involved in the area of automation/mechanization, testing and measuring instruments.

15176 **MESSZAHLEN FUR BAULEISTUNGSPREISE UND PREISINDIZES FUR BAUWERKE (2170400)**
W. Kohlhammer GmbH

Germany, West – German quarterly DM7.90

Index numbers of prices for building services and price indices for buildings.

15177 **MILCHERZEUGUNG UND-VERWENDUNG (2030422)**
W. Kohlhammer GmbH

Germany, West – German annual DM3.00

Figures for milk production.

15178 **MINERALISCHE ROHSTOFFE**
Bundesminister fur Wirtschaft

Germany, West – German 1987 48pp free

Booklet summarizing the mineral situation including details of major suppliers to Germany.

15179 **MINERALOLSTEUER (2140930)**
W. Kohlhammer GmbH

Germany, West – German annual DM4.50

Statistics on mineral oil tax.

15180 **MITTELSTANDISCHE UNTERNEHMEN (HANDBOOK OF MEDIUM SIZED COMPANIES)**
Verlag Hoppenstedt & Co.

Germany – German annual DM260

Handbook on 21,000 medium-sized German companies.

15181 **LE MODELE ECONOMIQUE ALLEMAND: MYTHES ET REALITE NOTES ET ETUDES DOCUMENTAIRES NO 4549-50**
La Documentation Francaise

Germany, West – French 1980 236pp FrF50
ISSN No. 0029 4004

15182 **MOLKEREIBERICHT**
Bunderministerium fur Ernahrung, Landwirtschaft und Forsten

Germany, West – German weekly free

Current news of the dairy industry.

15183 **MONTHLY REPORT–DEUTSCHE BUNDESBANK**
Deutsche Bundesbank

Germany, West – German/English/French/Spanish monthly c79pp free

These monthly reports have five series of statistical supplements which are published in German with English insert and deal with the following topics:
Series 1, Banking statistics by group of banks.
Series 2, Securities statistics.
Series 3, Balance of payment statistics.
Series 4, Seasonally adjusted economic data.
Series 5, Currencies of the world (appears quarterly).

15184 **NACHRICHTEN FUR AUSSENHANDEL***
Bundesstelle fur Aussenhandelsinformation

Germany, West – German 5 times weekly DM72.50 annual

Up-to-date news on the world economy of specific interest to exporters in Germany.

15185 **DIE NICHT NOTIERTEN DEUTSCHEN AKTIENGESELLSCHAFTEN**
Verlag Hoppenstedt & Co.

Germany – German annual DM725

Unquoted German joint-stock companies.

15186 **OECD ECONOMIC SURVEYS–GERMANY**
OECD

Germany, West – English annual 70pp £2.40/DM12/US$5/FrF24

A detailed analysis of recent developments in demand production, employment, prices and wages, conditions in the money and capital markets and developments in the balance of payments. It includes short-term forecasts as well as analyses of medium-term problems of specific relevance to the elaboration of the country's economic policies.

15187 **PERFORMANCE OF GERMAN PRODUCTS IN THE UK**
German Chamber of Industry and Commerce

Germany, West – English £6.00

15188 **PERMANENT IMPORT OF PRIVATE MOTOR VEHICLES INTO GREAT BRITAIN**
German Chamber of Industry and Commerce

Germany, West – English £5.00

15189 **PERSONENVERKEHR DER STRASSENVERKEHRSUNTERNEHMEN (2080320)**
W. Kohlhammer GmbH

Germany, West – German quarterly DM4.80 annual DM14.30

Statistics on passenger transport by road carriers.

15190 **PREISE**
W. Kohlhammer GmbH

Germany, West – German annual 6-10pp

Prices.

15191 **PREISE UND PREISINDIZES FUR DIE EIN-UND AUSFUHR (2170800)**
W. Kohlhammer GmbH

Germany, West – German monthly DM6.40 annual DM15.90

Prices and price indices for imports and exports.

15192 **PREISE UND PREISINDIZES FUR DIE LAND-UND FORSTWIRTSCHAFT (2170100)**
W. Kohlhammer GmbH

Germany, West – German monthly DM4.80 annual DM9.00

Prices and price indices for agriculture and forestry.

15193 **PREISE UND PREISINDIZES FUR DIE LEBENSHALTUNG (2170700)**
W. Kohlhammer GmbH

Germany, West – German monthly DM9.60 annual DM20.60

Consumer prices and consumer price indices.

15194 **PREISE UND PREISINDIZES FUR GEWERBLICHE PRODUKTE (ERZEUGERPREISE) (2170100)**
W. Kohlhammer GmbH

Germany, West – German monthly DM6.40 annual DM12.70

Prices and price indices for industrial products–producers' prices.

15195 **PREISE UND PREISINDIZES FUR VERKEHRSLEISTUNGEN (2170900)**
W. Kohlhammer GmbH

Germany, West – German annual DM7.50

Transport prices.

15196 **PRESSEINFORMATIONEN**
Bundesanstalt fur Arbeit

Germany, West – German 60-80 per year 14pp free

Labour market.

15197 **PROBLEM AREAS IN BRITISH EXPORTS TO GERMANY**
German Chamber of Industry and Commerce

Germany, West – English £5.00

15198 **PRODUCT LIABILITY IN THE FEDERAL REPUBLIC OF GERMANY**
German Chamber of Industry and Commerce

Germany, West – English £12.00

15199 **PRODUKTION IM PRODUZIERENDEN GEWERBE DES IN- UND AUSLANDES (2040310)**
W. Kohlhammer GmbH

Germany, West – German quarterly DM20.60 annual DM19.50

Statistics on the output of the production, mining and manufacturing industries, and employment and turnover in mining and manufacturing industries.

15200 **PRODUKTION IM PRODUZIERENDEN GEWERBE NACH WIRTSCHAFTSZWEIGEN UND ERZEUGNISGRUPPEN**
W. Kohlhammer GmbH

Germany, West – German annual DM16.50
ISBN/ISSN No. 2040320

Output of production industries by branches of economic activity and groups of products.

15201 **QUELLEN FUR STATISTISCHE MARKTDATEN**
Verlag Weltarchiv GmbH

Germany, West – German 1985 140pp DM39.00

Guide to sources of statistical market data for the FRG.

15202 **REALSTEUERVERGLEICH GEWERBESTEUER (2141010)**
W. Kohlhammer GmbH

Germany, West – German annual DM10.50

Comparison of taxation on real estate, commercial tax and payroll tax: statistics on commercial tax.

15203 **REBFLACHEN**
W. Kohlhammer GmbH

Germany, West – German annual DM6.00
ISSN No. 2030315

Vine acreage.

15204 **RECHNUNGSERGEBNISSE DER KOMMUNALEN HAUSHALTE (2140330)**
W. Kohlhammer GmbH

Germany, West – German annual DM22.50

Accounting results of the government budget.

15205 **RECHNUNGSERGEBNISSE DES OFFENTLICHEN GESAMTHAUSHALTS (2140310)**
W. Kohlhammer GmbH

Germany, West – German annual DM19.50

Accounting results of the public overall budget.

15206 **REFUND OF GERMAN VALUE ADDED TAX (UST) TO BRITISH FIRMS (1987)**
German Chamber of Industry and Commerce

Germany, West – English £12

Up-to-date information designed to assist businessmen.

15207 **RENTENBESTANDE IN DEN RENTENVERSICHERUNGEN DER ARBEITER UND ANGESTELLTEN IN DER BUNDESREPUBLIK DEUTSCHLAND***
Bundesminister fur Arbeit und Sozialordnung

Germany, West – German annual DM8.00

Financial details of employees' pension and insurance funds.

15208 **DER RENTENFUHRER**
Verlag Hoppenstedt & Co.

Germany – German continuously updated 2,700pp DM380 updates DM80 per month

Fixed interest securities.

15209 **RESERVATION OF OWNERSHIP IN THE FEDERAL REPUBLIC OF GERMANY**
German Chamber of Industry and Commerce

Germany, West – English £10.00

Practical information for the businessman.

15210 **RETAILING IN THE FEDERAL REPUBLIC OF GERMANY, INCLUDING TOP 300 FOOD RETAILERS**
German Chamber of Industry and Commerce

Germany, West – English £57.50

15211 **RHEINISCH-WESTFALISCHE BORSE ZU DUSSELDORF**
Rheinisch-Westfalische Borse zu Dusseldorf

Germany, West – German/English/French annual 55pp

The stock exchange's activities, the foreign exchange market, a list of official stock exchange bodies and a directory of members.

15212 **RWI-KONJUNKTURBERICHTE**
Duncker & Humblot GmbH

Germany, West – German twice a year 1950 DM100 p.a. approx.
ISSN No. 0931-8801

Economic trends in the western world and in West Germany in particular.

15213 **RWI–MITTEILUNGEN ZEITSCHRIFT FUR WIRTSCHAFTSFORSCHUNG**
Duncker & Humblot GmbH

Germany, West – German quarterly 1950 DM200 p.a. approx
ISSN No, 0035-4465

Public sector economics.

15214 **SALING AKTIENFUHRER**
Verlag Hoppenstedt & Co.

Germany, West – German annual c1,000pp DM138.00

Official handbook giving financial and other details on all transactions of companies on the German stock exchange.

15215 **SCHAUMWEINSTEUER (2140950)**
W. Kohlhammer GmbH

Germany, West – German quarterly DM1.60

Statistics on taxes on sparkling wine.

15216 **SCHLACHTUNGEN UND FLEISCHGEWINNUNG**
W. Kohlhammer GmbH

Germany, West – German quarterly DM4.80
ISSN No. 2030421

Slaughterings and meat production.

15217 **SEESCHIFFAHRT (2080500)**
W. Kohlhammer GmbH

Germany, West – German monthly DM4.80 annual DM19.50

Statistics on seaborne shipping.

15218 **SEIBT–INDUSTRIEKATALOG/ SEIBT–EXPORT DIRECTORY OF GERMAN INDUSTRIES**
Verlag Hoppenstedt & Co.

Germany – German/English/French/ Spanish annual DM110

Suppliers' directory and buyers' guide for purchasing, includes supplies of DIN products.

15219 **SOZIALOKONOMISCHE VERHALTNISSE (2030215)**
W. Kohlhammer GmbH

Germany, West – German biennial DM16.50

Socio-economic conditions on agricultural holdings.

15220 **SOZIALVERSICHERUNG-SPFLICHTIG BESCHAFLIGTE ARBEITNEHMER**
W. Kohlhammer GmbH

Germany, West – German quarterly/annual DM4.80/DM13.50
ISSN No. 2010420

Persons engaged subject to social insurance contributions.

15221 **STAHL–UND LEICHTMETALLBAU, SCHNIENENFAHRZEUGBAU**
IFO–Institut fur Wirtschaftsforschung

Germany, West – German irregular 352pp DM89

Steel and light metal-working industries, rail vehicle manufacture.

15222 **STAND UND ENTWICKLUNG DER ERWERBSTATIGKEIT–ERGEBNISSE DER EG–ARBEITSKRAFTESTICHPROBE**
W. Kohlhammer GmbH

Germany, West – German annual DM14.70

Results of the labour force sample survey of the EC.

15223 **STAND DER REBEN UND WEINMOSTERNTE, WEINERZEUGUNG UND-BESTAND (2030351)**
W. Kohlhammer GmbH

Germany, West – German irregular, about 9 reports annually DM2.30

Figures for the state of growth of vines, the yield of wine must, the production and stocks of wine.

15224 **STANDORTWAHL DER INDUSTRIE BETRIEBE IN DER BUNDESREPUBLIK DEUTSCHLAND–VERLAGERTE, NEUERRICHTETE UND STILLGELEGTE INDUSTRIE BETRIEBE***
Bundesminister fur Arbeit und Sozialordnung

Germany, West – German biennial
DM15.00

Statistics on the selection of place of operation of industrial enterprises.

15225 **STARTING A BUSINESS IN GERMANY**
German Chamber of Industry and Commerce

Germany, West – English £10.00

Practical information of interest to foreign businessmen.

15226 **STATISTISCHER BERICHT UBER DIE MILCH–UND MOLKEREIWIRTSCHAFT IM BUNDESGEBEIT**
Bundesministerium fur Ernahrung, Landwirtschaft und Forsten

Germany, West–German annual on request

Statistical report on the dairy industry in Germany.

15227 **STATISTISCHER MONATSBERICHT**
Bundesministerium fur Ernahrung, Landwirtschaft und Forsten

Germany, West – German monthly
DM18.00 each copy

Statistical monthly report on agriculture.

15228 **STATISTISCHER WOCHENDIENST (1010300)**
W. Kohlhammer GmbH

Germany, West – German weekly DM2.20

Results of short-term statistics currently available.

15229 **STATISTISCHES HANDBUCH FUR DEN MASCHINENBAU**
Verband Deutscher Maschinen und Anlagenbau eV

Germany, West – German annual 290pp
ISBN No. 3 8163 0158 4

Production, employment and trade of the German mechanical engineering industry, including a section on the international scene.

15230 **STATISTISCHES JAHRBUCH FUR DIE BUNDESREPUBLIK DEUTSCHLAND (1010100)**
W. Kohlhammer GmbH

Germany, West – German annual
DM109.00

Statistical yearbook for the Federal Republic of Germany. A comprehensive reference book containing the most important data from all fields of official statistics in the FRG. Appendix 1 comprises selected figures for the German Democratic Republic. Appendix 2 International tables.

15231 **STATISTISCHES JAHRBUCH UBER ERNAHRUNG, LANDWIRTSCHAFT UND FORSTEN**
Bundesministerium fur Ernahrung, Landwirtschaft und Forsten

Germany, West – German annual on request

Statistical yearbook of agriculture.

15232 **STEUERHAUSHALT (2140400)**
W. Kohlhammer GmbH

Germany, West – German quarterly
DM4.80 annual DM4.50

Tax budget.

15233 **STRASSEN, BRUCKEN, PARKEINRICHTUNGEN (2080310)**
W. Kohlhammer GmbH

Germany, West – German irregular
DM14.60

Statistics on roads, bridges and parking facilities.

15234 **STRUKTUR DER MOLKEREIWIRTSCHAFT**
Bundesministerium fur Ernahrung, Landwirtschaft und Forsten

Germany, West – German every 3 years on request

Report on the economy and structure of the German dairy industry.

15235 **STRUKTUR DER MUHLENWIRTSCHAFT**
Bundesministerium fur Ernahrung, Lanwirtschaft und Forsten

Germany, West – German annual 63pp
free
ISSN No. 0178 2378

The milling industry. Includes regional data.

15236 **TABAKGEWERBE (2140912)**
W. Kohlhammer GmbH

Germany, West – German annual DM300

Statistics on the tobacco industry.

15237 **TABLES AND METHODOLOGICAL NOTES ON THE CAPITAL FINANCE ACCOUNT 1960-1982 SPECIAL SERIES NO.4**
Deutsche Bundesbank

Germany, West – German/English 1983
30pp

15238 **TARIFGEHALTER**
W. Kohlhammer GmbH

Germany, West – German semi-annual
DM14.30
ISSN No. 2160420

Agreed salaries.

15239 **TARIFLOHNE**
W. Kohlhammer GmbH

Germany, West – German semi-annual
DM20.60
ISSN No. 2160410

Agreed wages.

15240 **TATSACHEN UND ZAHLEN AUS DER KRAFTKVERKEHRWIRT-SCHAFT**
Verband der Automobilindustrie eV

Germany, West – German annual 450pp
ISSN No. 0083 548X

Motor vehicle industry.

15241 **TAX & INVESTMENT PROFILE**
Touche Ross International, USA

Germany, West – English free

Survey covering investment, trade, labour, business practices, financial system. Frequently updated.

15242 **DER TECHNOLOGIETRANSFER IN DER BUNDESREPUBLIK DEUTSCHLAND**
IFO–Institut fur Wirtschaftsforschung

Germany, West – German irregular 252pp
DM96

Technology transfer.

15243 **TEXTILINDUSTRIE**
IFO–Institut fur Wirtschaftsforschung

Germany, West – German irregular 228pp
DM68

Textile industry.

15244 **TRADE ENQUIRIES FROM GERMANY**
German Chamber of Industry and Commerce

Germany, West – English bi-monthly free

Bi-monthly bulletin of trade opportunities.

15245 **TRANSFERT DE TECHNOLOGIE: LA STRATEGIE ALLEMANDE NOTES ET ETUDES DOCUMENTAIRES NO 4705-06**
La Documentation Francaise

Germany, West – French 1983 88pp FrF50
ISBN No. 0029 4004

Covers technology transfer in West Germany.

15246 **UK SUBSIDIARIES OF GERMAN INDUSTRIAL COMPANIES: INVESTMENT INTENTIONS--PRODUCTIVITY–RETURN ON INVESTMENT–EMPLOYEES–LABOUR RELATIONS**
German Chamber of Industry and Commerce

Germany, West – English £18.00

15247 **UMSATZSTEUER (2140800)**
W. Kohlhammer GmbH

Germany, West – German biennial DM16.50

Statistics on turnover.

15248 **UMWELT IN ZAHLEN**
W. Kohlhammer GmbH

Germany, West – German annual 6-10pp

The environment in figures.

15249 **VAT ON EXHIBITIONS AND TRADE FAIR SERVICES IN WEST GERMANY**
German Chamber of Industry and Commerce

Germany, West – English £5.00

15250 **VALUE ADDED TAX IN WEST GERMANY**
German Chamber of Industry and Commerce

Germany, West – English £5.00

15251 **VERBANDE, BEHORDEN, ORGANISATIONEN DER WIRTSCHAFT**
Verlag Hoppenstedt & Co.

Germany, West – German annual 1,520pp DM141

Information on over 1300 institutions in economic and business life.

15252 **VERKEHRSWIRTSCHAFTLICHE ZAHLEN**
Bundesverband des Deutschen Guterfernverkehrs (BDF) eV

Germany, West – German annual 70pp ISSN No. 0083 5021

Long-distance goods traffic.

15253 **VERMOGENSTEUER (2140740)**
W. Kohlhammer GmbH

Germany, West – German triennial DM11.60

Figures on property tax and standard values.

15254 **VEROFFENTLICHUNGEN DER DG BANK DEUTSCHE GENOSSENSCHAFTSBANK**
Deutsche Genossenschaftsbank (DG BANK)

Germany, West – German every 1-2 years 1966 170pp DM40

Cooperatives.

15255 **VERSICHERUNGS–JAHRBUCH**
Verlag Hoppenstedt & Co.

Germany, West – German annual c850pp DM460.00

Directory of German insurance firms giving details of branches, type of service provided and financial organization.

15256 **VIEHBESTAND UND TIERISCHE ERZEUGUNG (2039100)**
W. Kohlhammer GmbH

Germany, West – German annual DM9.00

Figures for livestock production.

15257 **VIERTELJÄHRLICHE KASSENERGEBNISSE DER ÖFFENTLICHEN HAUSHALTE (2140200)**
W. Kohlhammer GmbH

Germany, West – German quarterly DM8.00

Quarterly figures for public finance and accounting results.

15258 **WACHSTUM UND ERNTE–FELDFRÜCHTE, GEMÜSE, OBST, TRAUBEN (2030321)**
W. Kohlhammer GmbH

Germany, West – German irregular, about 4 reports annually DM3.20

Figures for the growth and yield of agricultural field crops, grassland and vegetables.

15259 **WARENEINKAUF, LAGERBESTAND UND ROHERTRAG IM GROSSHANDEL, EINZELHANDEL (2060120)**
W. Kohlhammer GmbH

Germany, West – German annual DM1.20

Purchases of goods, stocks and gross proceeds in the wholesale trade: statistics for the retail trade.

15260 **WARENVERKEHR MIT BERLIN (WEST)(2060500)**
W. Kohlhammer GmbH

Germany, West – German monthly DM3.20 annual DM2.20

Trade with West Berlin.

15261 **WAS DIE D-MARK IN AUSLAND WERT IST**
W. Kohlhammer GmbH

Germany, West – German annual 6-10pp

The value of the D-Mark abroad.

15262 **WEINERZEUGUNG**
W. Kohlhammer GmbH

Germany, West – German annual DM4.50

Wine production.

15263 **WIRTSCHAFT UND BORSE**
Verlag Hoppenstedt & Co.

Germany, West – German annual c120pp DM40.50

Overview of the previous year's trading on the stock exchange.

15264 **WIRTSCHAFT UND STATISTIK (1010200)**
W. Kohlhammer GmbH

Germany, West – German monthly DM165.00 annually

Articles on economics and analysis of current statistics. There are occasional articles in English.

15265 **WIRTSCHAFTSKONJUNKTUR. MONATSBERICHTE DES IFO–INSTITUTS FUR WIRTSCHAFTSFORSCHUNG**
Duncker & Humblot GmbH

Germany, West – German monthly 1949 50pp DM195
ISSN No. 0043-6283

Results of an ongoing survey into industrial trends. Includes an analysis of economic trends and graphic representation of statistical data.

15266 **WOCHENBERICHT**
Duncker & Humblot GmbH

Germany, West – German weekly 1934 10-16pp DM110 p.a.
ISSN No. 0012-1304

Economic developments and trends in both east and west Germany and the western world.

15267 **WSI–MITTEILUNGEN**
Wirtschafts und Sozialwissenschaftliches Institut des Deutschen Gewerkschaftsbundes GmbH

Germany, West – German monthly 56pp DM63 p.a.

Analyses and forecasts of economic development, personal income/investment, public expenditure, social policy etc.

15268 **YOUR BUSINESS WITH GERMANY–PRACTICAL HINTS FOR BRITISH EXPORTS; CONFERENCE PAPERS; A SUMMARY**
German Chamber of Industry and Commerce

Germany, West – English £18.00

15269 **ZAHLENKOMPASS (1040100)**
W. Kohlhammer GmbH

Germany, West – German/English/French/Spanish 48pp annual DM3.00

Pocket book-sized summary of comparative data over the preceding few years.

15270 ZUSAMMENFASSENDE UBERSICHTEN FUR DEN AUSSENHANDEL (2070100)
W. Kohlhammer GmbH

Germany, West – German monthly DM9.50
annual DM16.50

Summary surveys of foreign trade.

GERMAN DEMOCRATIC REPUBLIC

16001 **ABECOR COUNTRY REPORT – GERMAN DEMOCRATIC REPUBLIC**
Abecor

Germany, East – English 1987 2pp free

Brief economic report.

16002 **COUNTRY PROFILES – GERMANY, EAST**
Economist Publications Ltd

Germany, East – English annual 40pp £25 UK, subscription varies in rest of world

Resumé of politics, economy and industry including statistical summaries.

16003 **COUNTRY REPORTS – GERMANY, EAST**
Economist Publications Ltd

Germany, East – English quarterly 25pp £58 UK, subscription varies in rest of world

Economic policies and development plans, trends in production and demand, monetary and fiscal conditions, wages and prices, merchandise, trade, invisibles, capital flows, exchange rates and foreign debt plus a forecast of the economic prospects.

16004 **EAST GERMANY: A COUNTRY STUDY**
US Government Printing Office American University Foreign Area Studies

Germany, East – English 1982 350pp

Describes and analyses economic, national security, political and social systems and institutions.

16005 **GDR–FACTS AND FIGURES**
Panorama DDR

Germany,East – English and 21 other languages annual 63pp

Politics, economy, industry, agriculture, foreign trade, housing, incomes and consumption, health, education, sport and leisure.

16006 **GDR REVIEW**
Verlag Zeit im Bild/available from Collets Holdings Ltd

Germany, East – German/Danish/English/Finnish/French/Italian/Swedish monthly 64pp £2.50 p.a.

A variety of articles with facts and figures about the country and its policy, economy, science and education.

16007 **THE GERMAN DEMOCRATIC REPUBLIC**
Panorama DDR

Germany, East – German irregular 306pp

History and foreign policy, economy, social policy, education, culture, health services, leisure and sport.

16008 **HINTS TO EXPORTERS**
Department of Trade and Industry

Germany, East – English annual

Practical guide for businessmen giving general information, useful addresses, methods of doing business and relevant regulations.

16009 **HORIZONT**
Collets Holdings Ltd

Germany, East – German weekly

Politics and economics.

16010 **NACHRICHTEN AUS DER AGRAR- UND ERNAHRUNGWIRTSCHAFT DER DDR***
Bundesministerium fur Ernahrung, Landwirtschaft und Forsten, FRG

Germany, East – German monthly free

Current news on the agriculture of the German Democratic Republic.

16011 **NACHRICHTEN AUS DER FORST- UND HOLZWIRTSCHAFT DER DDR***
Bundesministerium fur Ernahrung, Landwirtschaft und Forsten, FRG

Germany, East – German quarterly free

Current news of the situation in the forestry industry.

16012 **PRISMA**
Verlag Zeit im Bild/available from Collets Holdings Ltd

Germany, East – English/German/French quarterly 128pp £1.50 p.a.

Topical political events and major aspects of the GDR's domestic and foreign policy.

16013 **STATISTICAL POCKET BOOK OF THE GERMAN DEMOCRATIC REPUBLIC**
Staatsverlag der Deutschen Demokratischen Republik

Germany, East – English annual 159pp

Statistics on the economy, industry, trade, finance and social trends.

16014 **STATISTISCHE JAHRBUCH**
Staatsverlag der Deutschen Demokratischen Republik

Germany, East – German annual 600pp

Detailed statistics on all aspects of social, political and economic life.

16015 **STATISTISCHES TASCHENBUCH DER DEUTSCHEN DEMOKRATISCHEN REPUBLIK**
Staatsverlag der Deutschen Demokratischen Republik

Germany, East – German/English annual c180pp

Statistics on all aspects of the economy.

16016 **WARENVERKEHR MIT DER DEUTSCHEN DEMOKRATISCHEN REPUBLIK UND BERLIN (OST) REISENVERKEHR (2060600)**
W. Kohlhammer GmbH. FRG

Germany, East – German monthly DM9.60 annual DM12.70

Trade between the Federal German Republic and the DDR and East Berlin.

16017 **WOCHENBERICHT**
Duncker & Humblot, GmbH

Germany – German weekly 1934 10-16pp DM110 p.a.
ISSN No. 0012-1304

Economic developments and trends in both East and West Germany and the western world.

GIBRALTAR

17001 ABECOR COUNTRY REPORT – GIBRALTAR
Abecor

Gibraltar – English irregular 2pp free

Brief economic report.

17002 ABSTRACT OF STATISTICS
Economic Planning and Statistics Office

Gibraltar – English annual 1972 80pp £2.00

Statistics on population, housing, education, health, public safety, civil administration, employment, income and expenditure, trade, tourism, public finance, banking, transport and communication, public activities, meteorological data.

GREECE

18001 **AGRA EUROPE SPECIAL REPORT NO. 21–GREEK AGRICULTURE SINCE ACCESSION. SITUATION AND OUTLOOK**
AGRA Europe (London) Ltd

Greece – English 1984

A survey of the Greek agricultural situation including a statistical annexe.

18002 **AGRICULTURAL STATISTICS OF GREECE**
National Statistical Service of Greece

Greece – Greek/English annual US$4

18003 **ANNUAL INDUSTRIAL SURVEY**
National Statistical Service of Greece

Greece – Greek/English annual US$12

18004 **ANNUAL REPORT – NATIONAL BANK OF GREECE**
National Bank of Greece

Greece – Greek/English annual c80pp free

Annual report including survey of the economy.

18005 **ANNUAL REPORT–AGRICULTURAL BANK OF GREECE**
Agricultural Bank of Greece

Greece – Greek annual 65pp free

As well as reviewing the Bank's activities the report includes a survey of main developments in the Greek economy and developments in the agricultural economy in particular, such as crop and fishery production, forestry, cottage industry and handicrafts.

18006 **ANNUAL STATISTICAL SURVEY ON MINES, QUARRIES AND SALTERNS**
National Statistical Service of Greece

Greece – Greek/English annual US$2.50

18007 **BUILDING ACTIVITY STATISTICS**
National Statistical Service of Greece

Greece – Greek annual 1977 100pp US$4
ISSN No. 0256-7970

18008 **BULLETIN DE STATISTIQUE DU COMMERCE EXTERIEUR**
National Statistical Service of Greece

Greece – Greek/French quarterly US$10

Statistical bulletin of foreign trade.

18009 **COMMERCE EXTERIEUR DE LA GRECE**
National Statistical Service of Greece

Greece – Greek/French annual 2 vols. US$15 per volume

Statistics on foreign trade.

18010 **CONCISE STATISTICAL YEARBOOK OF GREECE**
National Statistical Service of Greece

Greece – Greek/English annual US$5

18011 **COUNTRY PROFILES**
Economist Publications Ltd

Greece – English annual 40pp £25 UK, subscription varies in rest of world.

Resumé of politics, economy and industry including statistical summaries.

18012 **COUNTRY PROFILE–GREECE**
British Overseas Trade Board

Greece – English irregular 62pp

Beginning with a socio-political survey of Greece and its membership of the EEC, the report covers trade conditions, doing business, export conditions, investment, living and working in Greece and a list of useful addresses.

18013 **COUNTRY REPORTS**
Economist Publications Ltd

Greece – English quarterly 25pp £58 UK, subscription varies in rest of world.

Economic policies and development plans, trends in production and demand, monetary and fiscal conditions, wages and prices, merchandise, trade, invisibles, capital flows, exchange rates and foreign debt plus a forecast of the economic prospects.

18014 **DOING BUSINESS IN GREECE**
Price Waterhouse

Greece – English occasional 121pp

Includes sections on investment climate, exchange controls, regulating agencies, investment incentives, banking and finance, exporting to Greece, types of business, labour relations, accounting and taxation. The guide is aimed at those doing business in Greece.

18015 **ECONOMIC BULLETIN***
Commercial Bank of Greece

Greece – English quarterly c37pp free

Report on the economy.

18016 **ECONOMIC SURVEYS–GREECE**
Australia & New Zealand Banking Group
International Economic Dept, ANZ Bank

Greece – English 6pp free

Brief economic reports with selected statistics.

18017 **EXPRESS***
Hellenews

Greece – Greek/English daily

Daily newspaper concentrating on economic and financial matters.

18018 **FOREIGN ECONOMIC TRENDS AND THEIR IMPLICATIONS FOR THE UNITED STATES-GREECE**
US Department of Commerce

Greece – English annual 11pp US$1

Includes data on key economic indicators followed by a survey of the economy including a forecast for the long-term economic outlook with particular reference to US-Greek trade.

18019 **"LA GRECE, DIXIEME MEMBRE DES COMMUNAUTES EUROPEENNES" NOTES ET ETUDES DOCUMENTAIRES NO 4593-94**
La Documentation Francaise
Jean Catiapis

Greece – French 1980 168pp FrF50
ISSN No. 0029-4004

Survey of Greece.

18020 **GREECE – THE FIVE YEAR ECONOMIC AND SOCIAL DEVELOPMENT PLAN 1983-87–SUMMARY**
Centre for Planning and Economic Research

Greece – English 75pp

Summarizes Greece's five-year plan and is divided into sectoral development and regional development.

18021 **GREECE – MARKET REPORT ON CONSUMER GOODS**
Department of Trade and Industry

Greece – English occasional 21pp

Surveys the consumer sector including retail distribution, how to approach the market and a series of statistical tables on such areas as imports and exports of consumer goods, consumer price indices and structure of private domestic consumption.

18022 **GREECE – MARKET REPORT ON FOODSTUFFS**
British Overseas Trade Board

Greece – English 1985 60pp

Surveys the agricultural situation in Greece and includes details on how to do business in the agricultural sector in Greece. Also contains a series of annexes covering such areas as leading supermarkets, food and drink legislation, imports and exports of agricultural produce, food manufacturers and relevant trade journals.

18023 **THE GREEK ECONOMY IN FIGURES***
Electra Press Publications

Greece – Greek/English annual c250pp

Statistical data presented in the following sections: demographics, national accounts, productive capacity, production, money, credit, public finance, prices, balance of payments, foreign trade.

18024 **HINTS TO EXPORTERS**
Department of Trade and Industry

Greece – English annual

Practical guide for businessmen giving general information, useful addresses, methods of doing business and relevant regulations.

18025 **LABOUR FORCE SURVEY**
National Statistical Service of Greece

Greece – Greek annual 1981 90pp US$5
ISSN No. 0256-3576

18026 **LANDERBERICHT GRIECHENLAND**
Federal Statistical Office of Germany

Greece – German irregular DM7.90

Statistical survey of Greece including such areas as demography, geography, education, employment, agriculture, production, overseas trade, transport, tourism, finance, wages and prices and national accounts.

18027 **MONTHLY STATISTICAL BULLETIN**
Bank of Greece

Greece – Greek/English monthly 110pp

Statistics on money, public finance, balance of payments.

18028 **MONTHLY STATISTICAL BULLETIN**
National Statistical Service of Greece

Greece – Greek/English monthly US$3 per copy

18029 **MOUVEMENT NATUREL DE LA POPULATION DE LA GRECE**
National Statistical Service of Greece

Greece – French/Greek annual 222pp Dr300 US$10

Demographic statistics of Greece.

18030 **NOTES ON FOREIGN TRADE***
Commercial Bank of Greece

Greece – English monthly 4pp free

Brief notes on economic matters especially foreign trade.

18031 **OECD ECONOMIC SURVEYS – GREECE**
OECD

Greece – English annual 70pp £2.40/ DM12/US$5/FrF24

A detailed analysis of recent developments in demand, production, employment, prices and wages, conditions in the money and capital markets and developments in the balance of payments. It includes short-term forecasts as well as analyses of medium-term problems of specific relevance to the elaboration of the country's economic policies.

18032 **PUBLIC FINANCE STATISTICS**
National Statistical Service of Greece

Greece – Greek/English irregular 150pp Dr100 US$4

Data on direct and indirect taxation of the state and public legal entities, revenue and expenditure, income tax, property tax, import duties, consumption and transactions taxes, expenditure, investment and public credit.

18033 **REPORT – BANK OF GREECE**
Bank of Greece

Greece – English annual 150pp free

The economy, finance and prices.

18034 **RESULTS OF SEA FISHERY SURVEY BY MOTOR VESSELS**
National Statistical Service of Greece

Greece – Greek/English annual US$3

18035 **SHIPPING STATISTICS**
National Statistical Service of Greece

Greece – Greek/English annual US$7

18036 **SOCIAL WELFARE AND HEALTH STATISTICS**
National Statistical Service of Greece

Greece – Greek/English annual US$7

18037 **STATISTICAL BULLETIN ***
Thessaloniki Port Authority

Greece – English annual c45pp

Brief description of the port and statistical tables on shipping traffic.

18038 **STATISTICAL BULLETIN OF PUBLIC FINANCE**
National Statistical Service of Greece

Greece – Greek/English quarterly US$16 p.a.

18039 **STATISTICAL YEARBOOK OF GREECE**
National Statistical Service of Greece

Greece – Greek/English annual US$20.00

18040 **STATISTICAL YEARBOOK OF PUBLIC FINANCE**
National Statistical Service of Greece

Greece – Greek/English annual US$4

18041 **STATISTICS OF THE DECLARED INCOME OF LEGAL ENTITIES AND ITS TAXATION**
National Statistical Service of Greece

Greece – Greek annual US$4

18042 **STATISTICS OF THE DECLARED INCOME OF PHYSICAL PERSONS AND ITS TAXATION**
National Statistical Service of Greece

Greece – Greek annual US$4

18043 **TOURISM AND ECONOMY***
Hellenews

Greece – Greek monthly

Journal of the tourist catering trade.

18044 **TOURISM STATISTICS**
National Statistical Service of Greece

Greece – Greek/English irregular 134pp Dr300 US$10

Data on such areas as arrivals of tourists by charter and by yachts, hotel capacity, use of hotel units by tourists, overseas earnings from tourism and use of spas.

18045 **TRADE WITH GREECE**
Athens Chamber of Commerce and Industry

Greece – English/Greek/French/German 3 times a year 40pp

Brief reports on current developments in Greek trade and industry.

18046 **TRANSPORT AND COMMUNICATIONS STATISTICS**
National Statistical Service of Greece

Greece – Greek annual US$5

18047 **VITAL STATISTICS OF GREECE**
National Statistical Service of Greece

Greece – Greek/French annual 1956 230pp US$10
ISSN No. 0077-6114

HUNGARY

19001 ABECOR COUNTRY REPORT – HUNGARY
Abecor

Hungary – English 1987 2pp free

Brief economic report.

19002 ABSTRACTS OF HUNGARIAN ECONOMIC LITERATURE
World Market Research

Hungary – English bi–monthly

19003 ACTA OECONOMICA
Institute of Economics Hungarian Academy of Sciences Budapest

Hungary – English/Russian bi–monthly

19004 THE AGRICULTURE OF FRANCE AND HUNGARY 1980–1982
Statistical Publishing House

Hungary – Hungarian Ft76

Review of agriculture in France and Hungary.

19005 AGRICULTURAL POWER MACHINES AND MACHINERY
Statistical Publishing House

Hungary – Hungarian annual 1984 116pp Ft70
ISSN No 0236–5154

Collection of statistical data.

19006 BUSINESS PARTNER HUNGARY
Collets Holdings Ltd

Hungary – English/German/Hungarian quarterly US$28

Changes and recent developments in the Hungarian economy, new legislation and regulations and practical information for businessmen.

19007 COUNTRY PROFILE – HUNGARY
Department of Trade and Industry

Hungary – English irregular free

Information on the economic and financial situation in Hungary and on the business climate opportunities for British exporters. Includes a directory of useful addresses.

19008 COUNTRY REPORTS – HUNGARY
Economist Publications Ltd

Hungary – English quarterly 25pp £58 UK, subscription varies in rest of world

Economic policies and development plans trends in production and demand, monetary and fiscal conditions, wages and prices, merchandise, trade, invisibles, capital flows, exchange rates and foreign debt plus a forecast of the economic prospects.

19009 DATA ON THE 1983 WORLD PROGRAMME OF INDUSTRY STATISTICS – HUNGARY
Statistical Publishing House

Hungary – Hungarian Ft 169

19010 DATA ON THE SOCIO–ECONOMIC DEVELOPMENT IN THE 6th FIVE–YEAR PLAN PERIOD
Statistical Publishing House

Hungary – Hungarian

19011 DEMOGRAPHY
Statistical Publishing House

Hungary – Hungarian quarterly 1958 180pp Ft269 per year

Journal publishing statistical data on the population.

19012 ECONOMIC BULLETIN OF THE NATIONAL BANK OF HUNGARY
National Bank of Hungary

Hungary – English/Russian biennial

Review of business and the economy.

19013 ECONOMY OF AGRICULTURAL ENTERPRISES
Statistical Publishing House

Hungary – Hungarian annual 1984 264pp Ft153
ISSN No 0230–6492

Collection of statistical data.

19014 EMPLOYMENT RATE AND INCOME PROPORTIONS
Statistical Publishing House

Hungary – Hungarian annual 140pp Ft84
ISSN No 0133–543X

Collection of statistical data.

19015 HANDBOOK OF THE HUNGARIAN CHAMBER OF COMMERCE
Hungarian Chamber of Commerce

Hungary – English/French/German

A manual of the Hungarian Chamber of Commerce.

19016 HETI VILAGGAZDASAG (WORLD MARKET WEEKLY)
Hungarian Chamber of Commerce

Hungary – Hungarian weekly

A weekly journal covering economic events in Hungary.

19017 HINTS TO EXPORTERS
Department of Trade and Industry

Hungary – English annual

Practical guide for businessmen giving general information, useful addresses, methods of doing business and relevant regulations.

19018 HUNGARIAN AGRICULTURAL REVIEW
Agroinform

Hungary – English with Hungarian headings quarterly 30pp

Technical and scientific and economic reports on agricultural developments, including abstracts of relevant publications and current research programmes.

19019 HUNGARIAN BUSINESS HERALD
Collets Holdings Ltd

Hungary – English/German quarterly Ft21

News and information relevant to the economy.

19020 THE HUNGARIAN ECONOMY
Figyelo (Observer)

Hungary – English quarterly

Review of business and the economy.

19021 HUNGARIAN FOREIGN TRADE
Collets Holdings Ltd

Hungary – English quarterly

19022 HUNGARIAN FOREIGN TRADE*
Hungarian Chamber of Commerce

Hungary – English/French/German/ Russian quarterly US$12.50

News on products and technical developments.

19023 **HUNGAROPRESS ECONOMIC INFORMATION**
Hungarian Chamber of Commerce

Hungary – English/French/Russian/ German/Spanish/Italian/Arabic fortnightly

News and information relevant to the economy.

19024 **HUNGARY**
Pannonia Press

Hungary – English/French/Spanish/ German/Russian annual 252pp

General information on politics, the economy and social and cultural life. There are a few basic statistics but the text mostly consists of descriptive narrative.

19025 **HUNGARY: A MARKET FOR PRODUCTS FROM DEVELOPING COUNTRIES**
International Trade Centre UNCTAD/GATT

Hungary – English/French/Spanish irregular 130pp US$30

Foreign trade patterns, trade with developing countries, Hungary's foreign trade system, techniques for approaching the Hungarian market, practical information for foreign businesses and summary comments and data on the market for agricultural produce, fertilizers, perfumery and allied products, rubber, hide, skins, leather and products, textile, clothing, radio and television receivers.

19026 **HUNGARY IN FIGURES**
Hungarian Chamber of Commerce

Hungary – English/German/French/ Russian/Spanish annual

A folder of statistical data covering all aspects of Hungarian economy and society.

19027 **INCOME AND CONSUMPTION OF THE POPULATION**
Statistical Publishing House

Hungary – Hungarian annual Ft59

19028 **INCOME DISTRIBUTION IN THE NATIONAL ECONOMY**
Statistical Publishing House

Hungary – Hungarian irregular

19029 **INFORMATION – ELECTRONICS**
Statistical Publishing House

Hungary – Hungarian bimonthly 1966 60pp Ft300p.a.

Journal publishing statistical information on the electronics industry.

19030 **IPARGAZDASAG (INDUSTRIAL ECONOMY)**
Collets Holdings Ltd

Hungary – Hungarian monthly £17.75

19031 **IPARI FORMA**
Hungarian Chamber of Commerce

Hungary – Hungarian bi–monthly

Journal of the industrial design industry.

19032 **KOZGAZDASAGI SZEMLE (ECONOMIC REVIEW)**
Collets Holdings Ltd

Hungary – Hungarian monthly £19.00

19033 **KULGAZDASAG (FOREIGN TRADE)**
Collets Holdings Ltd

Hungary – Hungarian monthly

19034 **KULKERESKEDELMI ERTESITO**
Collets Holdings Ltd

Hungary – Hungarian weekly £11.50

19035 **LANDERBERICHT UNGARN**
Federal Statistical Office of Germany

Hungary – German irregular DM7.90

Statistcial survey of Hungary including such areas as demography, geography, education, employment, agriculture, production, overseas trade, transport, tourism, finance, wages and prices and national accounts.

19036 **MAIN PROCESSES ON NATIONAL ECONOMY**
Statistical Publishing House

Hungary – Hungarian annual 1984 136pp Ft81
ISSN No 0139–1488

Statistical data collection, macroeconomic information, analyses.

19037 **MAGYAR IMPORTS***
Hungarian Chamber of Commerce

Hungary – Hungarian monthly US$9.50

Information for Hungarian businessmen about opportunities for foreign co–operation and joint ventures.

19038 **MARKETING–PIACKUTATAS***
Hungarian Institute for Market Research

Hungary – Hungarian frequent US$12.50, annual

Official reports on marketing and market research.

19039 **MONTHLY BULLETIN OF STATISTICS**
Statistical Publishing House

Hungary – Hungarian monthly 1957 Ft480 p.a.

19040 **NEW HUNGARIAN EXPORTER**
Collets Holdings Ltd

Hungary – English monthly 30pp £10.50

Trade and economic news.

19041 **NOUVELLES ETUDES HUNGROISES**
Corvina Publishers

Hungary – French annual

19042 **POCKET BOOK OF AGRICULTURAL STATISTICS**
Statistical Publishing House

Hungary – Hungarian annual 1959 Ft45

19043 **POCKET BOOK OF INDUSTRY**
Statistical Publishing House

Hungary – Hungarian annual 164pp Ft26 p.a.

A statistical compendium on Hungarian industry.

19044 **POCKET BOOK OF INVESTMENTS, BUILDING INDUSTRY AND HOME-BUILDING**
Statistical Publishing House

Hungary – Hungarian annual 168pp Ft27

A statistical publication covering the building, construction and housing industry.

19045 **POCKET BOOK ON POPULATION AND SOCIAL STATISTICS**
Statistical Publishing House

Hungary – Hungarian annual 1983 312pp Ft64
ISSN No 0230–9170

Collection of statistical data.

19046 **PROPAGANDA – REKLAM**
Hungarian Chamber of Commerce

Hungary – Hungarian bi–monthly

Journal of the advertising and publicity industries with advertisements for foreign clients.

19047 **QUARTERLY REVIEW – NATIONAL BANK OF HUNGARY**
National Bank of Hungary

Hungary – English quarterly 44pp

Contains a survey of developments in the Hungarian economy followed by a statistical annexe containing such data as output, sales, prices, wages, retail trade, turnover, consumer price indices, foreign trade, balance of payments, foreign debt, exchange rates.

19048 **REGIONAL STATISTICAL YEARBOOK**
Statistical Publishing House

Hungary – Hungarian annual 244pp Ft142

Regional statistical data.

19049 **REGIONAL STATISTICS**
Statistical Publishing House

Hungary – Hungarian bi–monthly 90pp Ft198

Journal of regional statistics.

19050 **SCIENTIFIC RESEARCH AND DEVELOPMENT**
Statistical Publishing House

Hungary – Hungarian annual 204pp Ft120
ISSN No 0230–7359

Collection of statistical data.

19051 **A KORNYEZET ALLAPOTA ES VEDELME/STATE AND PROTECTION OF THE ENVIRONMENT**
Kozponti Statisztikai Hivatal

Hungary – Hungarian 330pp Ft500

Population, housing, transport, soil, water resources and use, forests, national parks, climate, noise pollution, household and industrial waste and spending on environmental protection.

19052 **STATISTICAL POCKET BOOK OF AGRICULTURE**
Statistical Publishing House

Hungary – Hungarian annual 300pp Ft45

Principle results of Hungarian agriculture .

19053 **STATISTICAL POCKET BOOK OF BUDAPEST**
Statistical Publishing House

Hungary – Hungarian annual 276pp Ft42

Statistical data collection.

19054 **STATISTICAL POCKET BOOK OF HUNGARY**
Hungarian Central Statistical Office

Hungary – English/Russian annual 216pp

Statistics on population, employment, income, housing, social welfare, public helath, education, trade, industry, agriculture, transport etc.

19055 **STATISTICAL REVIEW**
Statistical Publishing House

Hungary – Hungarian monthly 1923 100pp Ft396p.a.

Statistical journal.

19056 **STATISTICAL YEARBOOK**
Statistical Publishing House

Hungary – Hungarian/English/Russian annual 1872 400pp Ft260

Collection of statistical data.

19057 **STATISTICAL YEARBOOK OF BUDAPEST**
Statistical Publishing House

Hungary – Hungarian annual 328pp Ft189

Collection of statistical data.

19058 **STATISTICAL YEARBOOK OF FOREIGN TRADE**
Statistical Publishing House

Hungary – Hungarian annual 452pp Ft260

Statistical data covering overseas trade.

19059 **VOCATIONAL TRAINING AT COURSES**
Statistical Publishing House

Hungary – Hungarian annual 1984 240pp Ft140
ISSN No 0231–2948

Collection of statistical data.

19060 **YEARBOOK OF AGRICULTURAL STATISTICS**
Statistical Publishing House

Hungary – Hungarian annual 1981 240pp Ft140
ISSN No 0230–4066

Collection of statistical data.

19061 **YEARBOOK OF COMPUTER TECHNIQUES**
Statistical Publishing House

Hungary – Hungarian biennial 1978 136pp Ft59

A statistical publication on the computing sector.

19062 **YEARBOOK OF CONSTRUCTION STATISTICS**
Statistical Publishing House

Hungary – Hungarian annual 1982 324pp Ft187
ISSN No 0231–1720

Collection of statistical data.

19063 **YEARBOOK OF DEMOGRAPHY**
Statistical Publishing House

Hungary – Hungarian annual c420pp Ft250

A demographic statistical publication.

19064 **YEARBOOK OF HOUSING STATISTICS**
Statistical Publishing House

Hungary – Hungarian annual 1983 240pp Ft140
ISSN No 0236–9524

Collection of statistical data.

19065 **YEARBOOK OF INDUSTRIAL STATISTICS**
Statistical Publishing House

Hungary – Hungarian annual 412pp Ft237

Industrial statistics compendium.

19066 **YEARBOOK OF INTERNAL TRADE**
Statistical Publishing House

Hungary – Hungarian annual 256pp Ft156

A statistical publication of internal trade.

19067 **YEARBOOK OF INVESTMENT STATISTICS**
Statistical Publishing House

Hungary – Hungarian annual 1981 132pp Ft79
ISSN No 0231–1712

Collection of statistical data.

19068 **YEARBOOK OF POSTAL SERVICES AND TELECOMMUNICATIONS**
Statistical Publishing House

Hungary – Hungarian annual 40pp Ft22

Statistical data on the postal and telecommunications industry.

19069 **YEARBOOKS OF THE COUNTIES**
Statistical Publishing House

Hungary – Hungarian annual 19 vols 350pp per vol Ft190 per vol

Baranya	468pp	101Ft
Bacs–Kiskun	434pp	94Ft
Bekes	434pp	94Ft
Borsod–Abauj–Zemplen	508pp	109Ft
Csongrad	428pp	92Ft
Fejer	418pp	91Ft
Gyor–Sopron	448pp	96Ft
Hajdu–Bihar	454pp	98Ft
Heves	416pp	91Ft
Komarom	404pp	87Ft
Nograd	440pp	93Ft
Pest	492pp	106Ft
Somogy	434pp	94Ft
Szabpics–Szatmar	434pp	94Ft
Szolnok	418pp	91Ft
Tolna	414pp	90Ft
Vas	428pp	92Ft
Veszprem	432pp	94Ft
Zala	456pp	97Ft

19070 **YEARBOOK OF REGIONAL STATISTICS**
Statistical Publishing House

Hungary – Hungarian annual Ft142

19071 **YEARBOOK OF TOURISM**
Statistical Publishing House

Hungary – Hungarian annual 1981 284pp Ft165
ISSN No 0230–44–14

Collection of statistical data.

19072 **YEARBOOK OF TRANSPORT**
Statistical Publishing House

Hungary – Hungarian annual 1986 208pp Ft122
ISSN No 0237–8280

Collection of statistical data.

ICELAND

20001 **ABECOR COUNTRY REPORT – ICELAND**
Abecor

Iceland – English 1980 2pp free

Brief economic report.

20002 **ANNUAL REPORT – CENTRAL BANK OF ICELAND**
Central Bank of Iceland

Iceland – English annual c80pp free

English version of the annual report including a review of the economy.

20003 **ANNUAL REPORT: FISHERIES LOAN FUND OF ICELAND**
Utvegsbanki Islands

Iceland – English annual

20004 **ANNUAL REPORT – LANDSBANKI ISLANDS***
Landsbanki Islands

Iceland – Icelandic/English summary annual c50pp free

Annual report and accounts of the Icelandic National Bank.

20005 **ANNUAL REPORT: UTVEGSBANKI ISLANDS**
Utvegsbanki Islands

Iceland – English annual free

English version of the annual report and accounts of the Fisheries Bank.

20006 **A BRIEF ON THE ICELANDIC ECONOMY**
National Economic Institute of Iceland

Iceland – English

20007 **COUNTRY PROFILES**
Economist Publications Ltd

Iceland – English annual 40pp £25 UK, subscription varies in rest of world

Resumé of politics, economy and industry including statistical summaries.

20008 **COUNTRY REPORTS**
Economist Publications Ltd

Iceland – English quarterly 25pp £58 UK, subscription varies in rest of world

Economic policies and development plans, trends in production and demand, monetary and fiscal conditions, wages and prices, merchandise trade, invisibles, capital flows, exchange rates and foreign debt plus a forecast of the economic prospects.

20009 **ECONOMIC OUTLOOK***
Landsbanki Islands

Iceland – English 4/5 times a year c8pp free

General economic report.

20010 **ECONOMIC STATISTICS**
Central Bank of Iceland

Iceland – English quarterly c30pp free

Brief statistical data.

20011 **FJARMALA TIDINDI (ECONOMIC REVIEW)**
Central Bank of Iceland

Iceland – Icelandic quarterly

20012 **HAGTIDINDI**
Hagstofa Islands (Statistical Bureau of Iceland)

Iceland – Icelandic monthly c350pp IKr1,200.00

Monthly statistical bulletin with data on the fish catch, foreign trade, cost of living, production, employment.

20013 **HINTS TO EXPORTERS**
Department of Trade and Industry

Iceland – English annual

Practical guide for businessmen giving general information, useful addresses, methods of doing business and relevant regulations.

20014 **ICELAND**
Central Bank of Iceland

Iceland – English 1986 c520pp US$50

General handbook covering the following topics: history, population, government, foreign relations, economic policy, finance, industry, energy, culture, sport and social life.

20015 **ICELAND – YEARBOOK OF TRADE AND INDUSTRY**
Iceland Review

Iceland – English annual 1981 100–120pp US$12 surface mail US$15 air mail ISSN No 2053–8075

Feature articles and statistics on all main aspects of trade, industry and commerce in Iceland. Coverage on fisheries, power intensive industries, major industrial products, exports, and import/export as well as communications and tourism.

20016 **ICELAND REVIEW**
Iceland Review

Iceland – English quarterly 1963 80–95pp US$25 ISSN No 0019–1094

Feature articles on Iceland's present life, culture, society, history, industry, physical nature presented in attractive design with full colour photographs throughout each issue.

20017 **LANDERBERICHT ISLAND**
Federal Statistical Office of Germany

Iceland – German irregular DM7.90

Statistical survey of Iceland including such areas as demography, geography, education, employment, agriculture, production, overseas trade, transport, tourism, finance, wages and prices and national accounts.

20018 **MANNFJOLDASKYRSLUR ARIN 1961–70 (POPULATION AND VITAL STATISTICS 1961–70)**
Hagstofa Islands (Statistical Bureau of Iceland)

Iceland – Icelandic with English headings every 5 or 10 years 1911–15 200pp IKr1,000.00

Population by geographic and demographic distribution, vital statistics, migration, life tables, population projections.

20019 **NATIONAL ECONOMIC PROGRAMME, 1987**
National Economic Institute of Iceland

Iceland – English annual 36pp

Ouput and expenditure, economic goals and policies, prospects.

20020 NEWS FROM ICELAND
Iceland Review

Iceland – English monthly 1974 32–40pp US$19.95 surface mail US$21.95 airmail Europe US$24.95 airmail outside Europe ISSN No 0253-8083

General news, current events, politics, economy, trade, industry (emphasis fishing), communications, culture, tourism, people etc.

20021 SVEITARSJODAREIKNINGAR
Hagstofa Islands (Statistical Bureau of Iceland)

Iceland – Icelandic with English headings 1979–1986 (1988)

Statistics on local finance giving patterns of income and expenditure.

20022 TOLFRAEDIHANDBOK 1984 (STATISTICAL ABSTRACT OF ICELAND 1984)
Hagstofa Islands (Statistical Bureau of Iceland)

Iceland – Icelandic with English headings irregular 1967 270pp IKr1,200.00

Geography and climate; population; labour market; agriculture; fishing and fish processing; manufacturing; housing and construction; energy; internal and external trade; transport and communications; wages, prices, income, consumption; credit and monetary conditions; national accounts; public finance; health and social affairs; justice; education and cultural activities; elections.

20023 VERSLUNARSKYRSLUR
Hagstofa Islands (Statistical Bureau of Iceland)

Iceland – Icelandic with English headings annual c260pp IKr1,000.00

Exports and imports classified by value, country of origin of destination, and commodity.

REPUBLIC OF IRELAND

21001 **ACCOUNTANCY IRELAND**
Institute of Chartered Accountants in Ireland

Irish Republic – English bi–monthly

Finance, banking, accounting etc.

21002 **ANNUAL REPORT – ALLIED IRISH BANKS LTD.**
Allied Irish Bank

Irish Republic – English annual c40pp free

21003 **ANNUAL REPORT – BORD FAILTE**
Bord Failte – Irish Tourist Board

Irish Republic – English annual 500pp free

Annual report including brief statistics on tourism in Ireland.

21004 **ANNUAL REPORT**
Central Bank of Ireland

Irish Republic – English annual 1944 free

21005 **ANNUAL REPORT – CONFEDERATION OF IRISH INDUSTRY***
Confederation of Irish Industry

Irish Republic – English annual free

There are also seperate annual reports for the following sectors: Apparel Industries Federation, Building Materials Federation, Engineering Industries Federation, Food, Drink and Tobacco Federation, Irish Textiles Federation, Plastics Industries Association.

21006 **ANNUAL REPORT**
Industrial Development Authority of Ireland

Irish Republic – English annual

21007 **ANNUAL REPORT OF THE MINISTER FOR AGRICULTURE**
Stationery Office

Irish Republic – English annual I£4.40

21008 **ANNUAL REPORT OF THE REVENUE COMMISSIONERS. YEAR ENDED 31 DECEMBER (C6/68)**
Stationery Office

Irish Republic – English annual I£6.65

21009 **CII NEWSLETTER***
Confederation of Irish Industry

Irish Republic – English weekly 50p each issue

Information on all aspects of industry.

21010 **CII/ESRI BUSINESS FORECAST***
Confederation of Irish Industry

Irish Republic – English monthly £25.00 annually

Results of a monthly survey of business including details of production, employment, orders, sales and prices.

21011 **1977 CENSUS OF DISTRIBUTION (U78)**
Stationery Office

Irish Republic – English

This census covered all permanent establishments engaged in retail and wholesale trade. The following reports have been published:
Vol I Summary for Retail and Wholesale Trade (1982) I£1.35
Vol II Detailed results for Retail Establishments (1983) I£2.25
Vol III Detailed Results for Wholesale Establishments (1983) I£1.12

21012 **CENSUS OF INDUSTRIAL PRODUCTION (U112/4)**
Stationery Office

Irish Republic – English 1983 I£5.20

Industrial production.

21013 **CENSUS OF POPULATION 1981 (U40)**
Stationery Office

Irish Republic – English 12 Vols

Vol 1. Population of district electoral divisions towns and larger units of area I£3.00
Vol 2. Age and marital status classified by areas I£4.95
Vol 3. Household composition and family units I£2.20
Vol 4. Principal economic status and industries I£3.45
Vol 5. Religion I£2.00
Vol 6. Irish language I£2.00
Vol 7. Occupations I£8.90
Vol 8. Housing I£8.55
Vol 9. Part I – Usual residence and migration Part II – Birthplaces I£5.20
Vol 10. Part I – Education
Part II – Scientific and technological qualifications I£6.30
Vols 11 & 12 To be published.

21014 **CENSUS OF POPULATION 1986**
Stationery Office

Irish Republic – English 3 Vols

Preliminary Population Figures I£0.35
Preliminary Report I£1.85
Local Population Reports (Series) I£3.00 each

21015 **CENTRAL BANK STATISTICAL SUPPLEMENT**
Central Bank of Ireland

Irish Republic – English 8 times a year 1944 free

Updates key monetary and financial data included in the quarterly bulletin.

21016 **COMPANIES ANNUAL REPORT BY THE DEPARTMENT OF INDUSTRY AND COMMERCE (I.10/63)**
Stationery Office

Irish Republic – English annual 75pp

21017 **CONSTRUCTION INDUSTRY STATISTICS**
National Institute for Physical Planning and Construction Research

Irish Republic – English annual I£6.00

21018 **CONSUMER PRICE INDEX**
Central Statistics Office (CSO)

Irish Republic – English quarterly

21019 **COUNTRY PROFILES – IRELAND**
Economist Publications Ltd

Irish Republic – English annual 40pp £25 UK subscription varies in rest of world.

Resumé of politics, economy and industry including statistical summaries.

21020 **COUNTRY REPORTS – IRELAND**
Economist Publications Ltd

Irish Republic – English quarterly 25pp £58 UK subscription varies for rest of world

Economic policies and development plans, trends in production and demand, monetary and fiscal conditions, wages and prices, merchandise, trade, invisibles, capital flows, exchange rates and foreign debt plus a forecast of the economic prospects.

21021 CUSTOMS AND EXCISE TARIFF OF IRELAND
Stationery Office

Irish Republic – English 1987 I£60.00

21022 DEPARTMENT OF THE ENVIRONMENT REPORT 1985 (K24/55)
Stationery Office

Irish Republic – English 1987 I£4.25

21023 THE DETERMINANTS OF IRISH IMPORTS 1987
Economic and Social Research Institute
J Fitzgerald

Irish Republic – English I£8.50

21024 EEC POLICY ON COMPETITION A GUIDE FOR IRISH BUSINESS (185) 1986
Stationery Office

Irish Republic – English I£2.20

21025 ECONOMIC BACKGROUND TO THE BUDGET 1987 (F 125/11)
Stationery Office

Irish Republic – English annual I£1.10

21026 ECONOMIC REVIEW AND OUTLOOK (F 75/20)
Stationery Office

Irish Republic – English annual I£2.95

21027 ECONOMIC SERIES
Stationery Office

Irish Republic – English monthly I£3.00

Issued monthly and designed to update the quarterly Statistical Bulletin.

21028 ECONOMIC TRENDS*
Confederation of Irish Industry

Irish Republic – English monthly 50p each issue

Brief commentary on trends in the economy including graphs.

21029 ENERGY IN IRELAND
Department of Energy

Irish Republic – English quarterly

21030 EXTERNAL TRADE – PROVISIONAL FIGURES
Central Statistics Office

Irish Republic – English monthly

21031 FARM MANAGEMENT SURVEY
Agriculture Institute Headquarters

Irish Republic – English annual

21032 FINANCE ACCOUNTS FOR THE FINANCIAL YEAR 1ST JANUARY 1978 TO 31ST DECEMBER (F5/68)
Stationery Office

Irish Republic – English annual I£4.00

21033 FISHERIES
Central Statistics Office

Irish Republic – English annual I£3.35

A statistical account of the fisheries in the Irish Republic and a summary of the activities of the EEC as they affect the Irish fishing industry.

21034 FOLDER OF IRISH ECONOMIC STATISTICS
Central Bank of Ireland

Irish Republic – English annual

Consumer expenditure, investment, government expenditure, trade, prices, production, manpower, banking and finance.

21035 HINTS TO EXPORTERS
Department of Trade and Industry

Irish Republic – English annual

Practical guide for businessmen giving general information, useful addresses, methods of doing business and relevant regulations.

21036 INVESTING IN IRELAND
Allied Irish Bank

Irish Republic – English approximately every 2 years 10–12pp free

Brief profile on Ireland focused on new companies investing in Ireland.

21037 IRELAND IN FIGURES
Allied Irish Bank

Irish Republic – English 8pp free

Leaflet giving brief statistics on all aspects of the Irish economy.

21038 IRISH AGRICULTURE IN FIGURES
Agricultural Institute Headquarters

Irish Republic – English annual

21039 THE IRISH ENGINEERING INDUSTRY: STRATEGIC ANALYSIS AND POLICY RECOMMENDATION
Economic and Social Research Institute
E. O'Malley

Irish Republic – I£8.00

21040 IRISH HORTICULTURE IN FIGURES
Agricultural Institute Headquarters

Irish Republic – English approximately every three years

21041 IRISH JOURNAL OF AGRICULTURAL ECONOMICS AND RURAL SOCIOLOGY
Agricultural Institute Headquarters

Irish Republic – English annual 1967/68 I£2.50

21042 THE IRISH MARKET – FACTS AND FIGURES 1987
Wilson Hartnell Advertising Barry O'Neill

Irish Republic – English every 2 years 1975 32pp free

Booklet giving brief details on the demography and economy of Ireland with particular reference to marketing.

21043 IRISH REPUBLIC
UK Iron and Steel Statistics Bureau

Irish Republic – English 1986 with annual statistical summary £25.00

Report on the steel industry showing production consumption and details of imports and exports.

21044 IRISH TAX CASE LEAFLETS
Stationery Office

Irish Republic – English frequent 75p each

21045 JOURNAL OF INDUSTRIAL AND COMMERCIAL PROPERTY
Stationery Office

Irish Republic – English bi–monthly I£130.00 annually

21046 LABOUR FORCE SURVEY 1985
Stationery Office

Irish Republic – English 1986 I£2.20

Survey based on samples of 30,000–40,000 households.

21047 LABOUR INSPECTION REPORT FOR 1983/4 (V.1/18)
Stationery Office

Irish Republic – English I£2.95

21048 LANDERBERICHT IRLAND
Federal Statistical Office of Germany

Irish Republic – German irregular DM7.90

Statistical survey of Republic of Ireland including demography, geography, education, employment, agriculture, production, overseas trade, transport, tourism, finance, wages and prices and national accounts.

21049 **MEDIUM – TERM REVIEW**
Economic and Social Research Institute

Irish Republic – English annual I£15.00

Supplements the Quarterly Economic Commentary by assessing the effects of international developments and Irish economic policies on the domestic economy in recent years and by providing a longer–term perspective for years ahead.

21050 **MONTHLY INDUSTRIAL SURVEY**
Confederation of Irish Industry

Irish Republic – monthly

The survey is carried out using a statistically representative sample of manufacturing firms each month and responses weighted by net output, employment and exports.

21051 **NATIONAL ECONOMIC AND SOCIAL COUNCIL REPORTS**
National Economic and Social Council

Irish Republic – English frequent various prices

Reports on all aspects of the economy and financial policy.

21052 **NATIONAL INCOME AND EXPENDITURE 1985**
Stationery Office (U1/26)

Irish Republic – English annual I£3.35

Thorough statistical analysis of the financial transactions of the public authorities sector, and the national accounts.

21053 **OUTLINE OF IRISH FINANCIAL PROCEDURES (F.138)**
Stationery Office

Irish Republic – English 1983 I£1.12

21054 **QUARTERLY BULLETIN**
Central Bank of Ireland

Irish Republic – English (Irish articles appear occasionally) quarterly 1958 free

National economy, monetary development, international development.

21055 **QUARTERLY ECONOMIC COMMENTARY**
Economic and Social Research Institute

Irish Republic – English quarterly 1968 I£40.00p.a.

A comprehensive examination and assessment of economic affairs under the headings: international economy, domestic economy, appraisal.

21056 **REPORT INTO THE HORSE BREEDING INDUSTRY (A85) 1986**
Stationery Office

Irish Republic – English I£7.00

Horse breeding in the Irish Republic.

21057 **REPORT OF THE REGISTRAR OF BUILDING SOCIETIES FOR THE YEAR ENDED 31 DECEMBER (I.166/7)**
Stationery Office

Irish Republic – English quarterly I£2.20 annually I£1.85

21058 **REPORT ON VITAL STATISTICS**
Stationery Office

Irish Republic – English quarterly I£1.20 annual I£7.05

Summaries of births, deaths and marriages in each county and county borough including main causes of death.

21059 **RESTRICTIVE PRACTICES COMMISSION. ANNUAL REPORT FOR THE YEAR ENDED 31 DECEMBER (I.149/11)**
Stationery Office

Irish Republic – English annual I£1.50

21060 **RETAIL SALES INDEX**
Central Statistics Office

Irish Republic – English monthly

21061 **REVIEW**
Allied Irish Bank

Irish Republic – English quarterly 4pp free

General economic review.

21062 **REVIEW OF INDUSTRIAL PERFORMANCES 1986 (I189)**
Stationery Office

Irish Republic – English I£3.35

21063 **ROAD FREIGHT TRANSPORT SURVEY (U110/5) 1985**
Stationery Office

Irish Republic – English I£2.20

21064 **ROADS POLICY AND PLANNING FRAMEWORK (I132)**
Stationery Office

Irish Republic – English I£1.25

21065 **SITUATION AND OUTLOOK IN IRISH FARMING**
Agricultural Institute Headquarters

Irish Republic – English annual

21066 **SMALL SCALE MANUFACTURING INDUSTRY IN IRELAND 1985**
Economic and Social Research Institute
K.A. Kennedy and T. Healy

Irish Republic – English I£7.50

21067 **STATISTICAL ABSTRACT OF IRELAND (U74/48)**
Stationery Office

Irish Republic – English annual I£12.50

Statistics on area, meteorology, demography, agriculture, industrial production, trade both foreign and domestic, education, social welfare, justice, defence, transport, finance and prices.

21068 **STATISTICAL BULLETIN QUARTERLY**
Stationery Office

Irish Republic – English quarterly I£5.00

Statistics on balance of payments, agriculture, tourism, wages, transport, industrial production, construction.

21069 **STATISTICAL INFORMATION RELEVANT TO THE HEALTH SERVICES 1985 (Z23/8)**
Stationery Office

Irish Republic – English I£4.25

21070 **STATISTICAL RELEASES**
Central Statistics Office

Irish Republic – English

Releases are issued frequently giving current statistics as soon as they are available on the following topics:

agricultural output	annual
crops and livestock enumeration	annual
distribution of cattle and pigs by size of herd	biennial
pigs received at bacon factories	monthly
advertising agencies	annual
hire-purchase and credit sales	annual
index numbers of retail sales	monthly
industrial production index	monthly
earnings and hours in construction	quarterly
employment in building and construction	monthly
industrial analysis of live register	monthly
area of residence analysis of live register	quarterly
occupational analysis of live register	quarterly
particulars of industrial disputes	irregular
consumer price index	quarterly
agricultural output price index numbers	monthly
agricultural input price index numbers	monthly
wholesale price index	monthly
estimated numbers and expenditure of visitors to Ireland and Irish visitors abroad	annual
animals exported by sea and air	monthly
motor registration	monthly
motor vehicles registered and licensed for the first time monthly,	annual
omnibus road services	monthly
port traffic	annual

21071 **SUMMARY OF PUBLIC EXPENDITURE PROGRAMMES 1985 (F169/4)**
Stationery Office

Irish Republic – English I£4.10

21072 **TECHNOLOGY IRELAND**
Institute for Industrial Research and Standards

Irish Republic – English eleven times a year 1969 £15p.a.

Information on all major industrial areas including new products, licensing and EEC news.

21073 TOURISM POLICY WHITE PAPER (I183) 1985
Stationery Office

Irish Republic – English I£2.20

21074 TRADE STATISTICS OF IRELAND
Stationery Office

Irish Republic – English monthly I£3.00

Details of imports and exports, classified by commodity and country. Information on prices, values, volumes and classification of value of trade by main economic areas, countries, commodities and origin.

21075 TRANSPORT POLICY GREEN PAPER 1985 (T32)
Stationery Office

Irish Republic – English I£2.00

21076 TUARASCAIL AR STAIDREAMH BEATHA (ANNUAL REPORT ON VITAL STATISTICS)
Stationery Office

Irish Republic – Irish annual I£7.05

Includes statistics on births, deaths and marriages and analyses and compares demographics.

ITALY

22001 **ABECOR COUNTRY REPORT – ITALY**
Abecor

Italy – English 1980 2pp free

Brief economic report.

22002 **ANNUARIO DI CONTABILITA NAZIONALE**
Istituto Centrale di Statistica

Italy – Italian annual 430pp L17,000

Detailed statistics on national accounts.

22003 **ANNUARIO DI STATISTICA AGRARIA**
Istituto Centrale di Statistica

Italy – Italian annual 300pp L14,000
ISSN No. 0075 1669

Data on all aspects of agriculture including comparative statistics with recent years.

22004 **ANNUARIO GENERALE ITALIANO**
Guida Monaci Spa

Italy – Italian with English/French/German summaries annual L240.000

Volume 1 lists international agencies, ministries, government institutions, banks and industrial and commercial enterprises classified by activity. Volume 2 is who's who in Italian activities. Volume 3 is an index for category entries and localities.

22005 **ANNUARIO STATISTICO ITALIANO**
Istituto Centrale di Statistica

Italy – Italian annual 700pp L32,000
ISSN No. 0066 4545

Statistical yearbook covering climate and geography; population; social security and health; education; justice; agriculture; industry; construction; transport and communications; external trade; internal trade; finance, both public and private; prices; labour and wages; consumption; balance of payments; international relations.

22006 **BI–ANNUAL REPORT ON THE ITALIAN ECONOMIC SITUATION**
Istituto Nazionale per lo Studio della Congiuntura

Italy – English biannual 30pp L15,000
ISSN No 0392–6761

An analysis of the current Italian economic situation as well as a forecast of the next 12–18 months development.

22007 **BOLLETTINO ECONOMICO**
Banca d'Italia

Italy – Italian 1983 125pp

The economic situation in Italy, balance of payments, public finance, financial and money markets.

22008 **BOLLETINO MENSILE DI STATISTICA**
Istituto Centrale di Statistica

Italy – Italian monthly c200pp L95,000
ISSN 0021 3136

Up–to–date statistics on all aspects of social, financial and economic life including comparative statistics with other countries.

22009 **BOLLETTINO STATISTICO**
Banca d'Italia

Italy – Italian quarterly 1946 350pp

Credit, financial markets, balance of payments, public finance.

22010 **COMMERCIO ESTERO**
Istituto Centrale di Statistica

Italy – Italian monthly 12pp L88,000

Brief details of imports and exports by country and product.

22011 **COMPENDIO STATISTICO ITALIANO**
Istituto Centrale di Statistica

Italy – Italian annual c600pp L14,000
ISSN 0069 7958

Summarized version of statistics covering all aspects of political, economic, social and cultural life.

22012 **CONGIUNTURA ITALIANA – RASSEGNA MENSILE**
Istituto Nazionale per lo Studio della Congiuntura

Italy – Italian monthly 80pp L9,000 per issue
ISSN No 0010–5759

National accounts, production, trade, prices, financial and money markets, public finance, labour.

22013 **I CONSUMI DELLE FAMIGLIE**
Istituto Centrale di Statistica

Italy – Italian annual L17,000

Statistics on domestic consumption.

22014 **I CONTI DEGLI ITALIANI**
Istituto Centrale di Statistica

Italy – Italian annual 101pp L10,000
ISSN No. 0390 6574

Statistics on national accounts.

22015 **CONTI ECONOMICI TRIMESTRALI**
Istituto Centrale di Statistica

Italy – Italian quarterly 20pp L10,000

Economic and statistical indicators.

22016 **COUNTRY PROFILES**
Economist Publications Ltd

Italy – English annual 40pp £25 UK subscription varies in rest of world

Resumé of politics, economy and industry including statistical summaries.

22017 **COUNTRY REPORTS**
Economist Publications Ltd

Italy – English quarterly 25pp £58 UK subscription varies in rest of world

Economic policies and development plans, trends in production and demand, monetary and fiscal conditions, wages and prices, merchandise, trade, invisibles, capital flows, exchange rates and foreign debt plus a forecast of the economic prospects.

22018 **DATI CUMULATIVI DI 1603 SOCIETA ITALIANE**
Mediobanca

Italy – Italian annual 250pp

Aggregate financial data on Italian companies and industrial sectors, including production and sales.

22019 **ECONOMIC SURVEYS – ITALY**
Australia and New Zealand Banking Group

Italy – English 6pp free

Brief economic report with selected statistics.

22020 ELECTRICITY SUPPLY IN ITALY
Electricity Council

Italy – English irregular 16pp

The structure of the industry, generating resources, transmissions, distribution and tariffs.

22021 HINTS TO EXPORTERS
Department of Trade and Industry

Italy – English annual

Practical guide for businessmen giving general information, useful addresses, methods of doing business and relevant regulations.

22022 INDICATORI MENSILI
Istituto Centrale di Statistica

Italy – Italian monthly c16pp L27,000
ISSN No. 0390 6620

Monthly statistical indicators on population, productivity, foreign trade, prices and salaries.

22023 ITALIAN BUSINESS TRENDS
Europrospects Ltd

Italy – English monthly 46pp £94
ISSN No 0268–1226

The national scene, financial markets and main industrial sectors.

22024 ITALIAN ECONOMIC REVIEW*
Associazione fra le Societa Italiane per Azioni

Italy – Italian/English bi–monthly 6pp

Official journal of the association of joint stock companies.

22025 ITALIAN ECONOMIC SURVEY*
Associazione fra le Societa Italiane per Azioni

Italy – English bi–monthly c12pp

General economic survey including abridged statistical tables on the cost of living.

22026 ITALIAN ECONOMY
Banca Commerciale Italiana – Economic Research Dept

Italy – English monthly October 1977 30pp free

Italian economy.

22027 ITALY
W. Kohlhammer GmbH, FRG

Italy – German 1987 DM8.60

Summary economic report.

22028 ITALY
UK Iron and Steel Statistics Bureau

Italy – English 1986 with annual statistical summary £25

Report on the steel industry showing production, consumption and details of imports and exports.

22029 ITALY: A COUNTRY PROFILE
Department of Trade and Industry

Italy – English 1983 70pp
ISSN No 0264 6048

General information about the country in addition to information on trade and opportunities and export conditions.

22030 KOMPASS REGISTER
Kompass Publishers, UK

Italy – Italian/English/French/German/Spanish annual £130

Comprehensive business directory giving information on over 27,000 companies listed geographically and cross–referenced to a directory of products and services.

22031 LIST OF ITALIAN STOCKS*
Banca Commerciale Italiana

Italy – English monthly c36pp free

Brief review of the stock market and data on movement of stocks, prices, dividends. There are also notes on current developments in major industrial companies.

22032 IL MONDO DEL LATTE
Associazione Italiana Lattiero–Casearia

Italy – Italian monthly c70pp L30,000

Technical journal of the dairy industry.

22033 MONETARY TRENDS
Banca Commerciale Italiana – Economic Research Department

Italy – English 2–3 numbers a year 1975 20pp free

Italian economy.

22034 IL MONDO DEL LATTE
Associazione Italiana Lattiero–Casearia

Italy – Italian monthly c70pp L30,000

Technical journal of the dairy industry.

22035 NOTIZIARIO COMMERCIALE QUINDICINALE DI COMMERCIO ESTERO / BIMONTHLY FOREIGN TRADE BULLETIN.

International - Italian bimonthly November 1985 25pp

Italian and foreign legislation, foreign trade regulations; economic and political issues; tenders; supply and demand of goods, agents etc.

22036 NOTIZIARIO ISTAT
Istituto Centrale di Statistica

Italy – Italian Series 1 L22,000; Series 2 L66,000; Series 3 L22,000; Series 4 L13,000

Provisional results of statistical surveys published in 4 series: demographic and social statistics; production statistics; statistics on employment, salaries and prices; and miscellaneous.

22037 NOTIZIARIO STATISTICO
Associazione Nazionale Fra Industrie

Italy – Italian monthly 90pp L250,000

Statistical bulletin on the Italian motor industry, giving details of production and exports. Also covers other major motor manufacturing countries.

22038 OECD ECONOMIC SURVEYS – ITALY
Organisation for Economic Cooperation and Development (OECD)

Italy – English annual 70pp £2.40/DM12/US$5/FrF24

A detailed analysis of recent developments in demand, production, employment, prices and wages, conditions in the money and capital markets and developments in the balance of payments. It includes short–term forecasts as well as analyses of medium–term problems of specific relevance to the elaboration of the country's economic policies.

22039 PROBLEMI DI STATISTICHE E DI PREVISIONI DEMOGRAFICHE PERLE PICCOLE AREE/ STATISTICS AND POPULATION FORECASTS: PROBLEMS FOR SMALL AREAS
Istituto di Ricerche sulla Popolazione

Italy – Partially Italian/English/French irregular 1984 102pp

Problematic issues in small areas: population estimation and forecasting.

22040 LE PROSPETTIVE DELL'INDUSTRIA ITALIANA
Centro Studi Con Findustria

Italy – Italian annual 150pp L24,000

Detailed survey of Italian industry. Each sector covers employment, production, investment and exports. Includes short – term forecasts.

22041 QUADERNI DELLA RASSEGNA DI TURISMO SPETTACOLO E SPORT
Ministero del Turismo e dello Spettacolo

Italy – Italian annual 1971 288pp free

Statistics on tourism and entertainment in Italy.

22042 **QUARTERLY REVIEW**
Banca Nazionale del Lavoro

Italy – Italian/English quarterly c550pp

In–depth articles on all aspects of the economy.

22043 **RAPPORTO ASSINFORM SULLA SITUAZIONE DELL'INFORMATICA IN ITALIA**
Associazione Costruttori Macchine Attleezature per Ufficio e per il Trattamento delle Informazioni

Italy – Italian annual 120pp

Statistics on computer and industrial automation sectors in Italy.

22044 **RAPPORTO ANNUALE**
Borsa Valori di Milano

Italy – Italian with English summary annual c100pp free

Annual report of the stock exchange including a brief review of the economy.

22045 **RAPPORTO MESE (LA BORSA VALORI) MONTHLY REPORT**
Borsa Valori di Milano

Italy – Italian/English monthly 8pp free

Report of the Milan stock exchange including every month brief up–to–date profiles of some major companies.

22046 **RAPPORTO SULLA INDUSTRIA COTONIERA ITALIANA**
Associazione Cotoniera Italiana

Italy – Italian annual 60pp

Report on the Italian cotton industry covering trade, labour and finance.

22047 **RASSEGNA ECONOMICA**
Banco di Napoli

Italy – Italian bi–monthly c300pp

In–depth technical articles on all aspects of the economy including a specific section dealing with Southern Italy.

22048 **RELAZIONE DELLA PRESIDENZA**
Associazione Italiana Lattiero–Casearia

Italy – Italian annual c60pp

Report of the president of the association of dairy industries including statistics for production and trade classified by geographical area.

22049 **REVIEW OF ECONOMIC CONDITIONS IN ITALY**
Banco di Roma

Italy – Italian/English quarterly c200pp

In–depth articles on the economy in particular financial matters.

22050 **RILEVAZIONE DELLE FORZE DI LAVORO**
Istituto Centrale di Statistica

Italy – Italian frequent reports

Statistics on the labour force.

22051 **STATISTICA ANNUALE DEL COMMERCIO CON L'ESTERO**
Istituto Centrale di Statistica

Italy – Italian annual 7 vols

Detailed statistics of foreign trade classified by product and country of origin or destination.

22052 **STATISTICA DEGLI INCIDENTI STRADALI**
Istituto Centrale di Statistica

Italy – Italian annual c220pp L11,500
ISSN No. 0075 188X

Statistics on road accidents covering damage to both persons and vehicles.

22053 **STATISTICHE DELL'ATTIVITA EDILIZIA E DELLE OPERE PUBBLICHE 1987**
Istituto Centrale di Statistica

Italy – Italian irregular 200pp L11,500
ISSN No 0075 1804

Statistics on construction industry and public works.

22054 **STATISTICHE DEI BILANCI DELLE AMMINISTRAZIONI REGIONALI PROVINCIALI E COMUNALI**
Istituto Centrale di Statistica

Italy – Italian annual c340pp L14,000
ISSN No. 0075 1820

Statistics on regional accounts and financial systems.

22055 **STATISTICHE DELLA CACCIA, PESCA AND CO–OPERAZIONE**
Istituto Centrale di Statistica

Italy – Italian annual 1988 117pp L8,400
ISSN No 0390 6426

Statistcs on hunting, fishing and agricultural co–operatives.

22056 **STATISTICA DEL COMMERCIO CON L'ESTERO**
Istituto Centrale di Statistica

Italy – Italian quarterly L88,000
ISSN No. 0535 9821

Statistical bulletin on foreign trade classified by product group and by country of origin or destination.

22057 **STATISTICHE DEL COMMERCIO INTERNO**
Istituto Centrale di Statistica

Italy – Italian annual c230pp L15,800
ISSN 0075–1732

Statistics on internal trade.

22058 **STATISTICHE DEL LAVORO**
Istituto Centrale di Statistica

Italy – Italian annual 160pp L12,000

Labour statistics including wages, family consumption, industrial action, and hours of work.

22059 **STATISTICHE DEMOGRAFICHE**
Istituto Centrale di Statistica

Italy – Italian annual 250pp L11,500
ISSN No. 0075 1685

Annual statistics on demography covering the following topics; internal mobility: births, deaths and marriages. The data is compared with that of previous years.

22060 **STATISTICHE FORESTALI**
Istituto Centrale di Statistica

Italy – Italian annual c140pp L12,600
ISSN No. 0075 1707

Statistics on the forestry industry including data for preceding years, climate, production, utilization and external trade.

22061 **STATISTICHE INDUSTRIALI**
Istituto Centrale di Statistica

Italy – Italian annual c315pp L15,000
ISSN No. 0075 1723

Statistics on industry, covering production, consumption, plant and machinery, prices and wages, foreign trade. The data is retrospective and there is comparative international data.

22062 **SUPPLEMENTO AL BOLLETTINO STATISTICO**
Banca d'Italia

Italy – Italian irregular 1948

Credit, financial markets, balance of payments and other similar topics.

22063 **TAVOLE STATISTICHE**
Unioni Industriali Pastei Italiani

Italy – Italian annual

Data on production and export of pasta, import and export of grains and prices.

22064 **TAX AND INVESTMENT PROFILE**
Touche Ross International, USA

Italy – English free

Survey covering investment, trade, labour, business practices, financial system. Frequently updated.

22065 **YOUNG PEOPLE AND THE LABOUR MARKET IN ITALY**
Istituto di Ricerche sulla Popolazione

Italy – English irregular 15pp

Accession of young people to the labour force in Italy.

LIECHTENSTEIN

23001 11 AUFSTREBENDE GEMEINDEN–ELEVEN PROGRESSIVE COMMUNITIES
Liechtensteinische Fremdenverkehrszentrale

Liechtenstein – German/English/French/Spanish/Dutch/Italian/Portuguese every 2 years 1977 15pp free

Description of individual parishes, including history.

23002 AUSLANDERSTATISTIK
Amt fur Volkwirtschaft

Liechtenstein – German 3 issues per year140pp

Statistics on foreigners in Liechtenstein.

23003 BANKENSTATISTIK
Amt fur Volkwirtschaft

Liechtenstein – German annual

Banking.

23004 BAUSTATISTIK
Amt fur Volkwirtschaft

Liechtenstein – German annual

Building.

23005 COMPANIES AND TAXES IN LIECHTENSTEIN 1988
Liechtenstein Verlag AG

Liechtenstein – French/German/English 1982 100pp SF39
ISBN No. 3-85789-823-9

23006 THE ECONOMY OF THE PRINCIPALITY OF LIECHTENSTEIN
Press & Information Office of the Liechtenstein Government

Liechtenstein – German/English/French last issue 1982 free

Brief review of the economy.

23007 ENERGIESTATISTIK
Amt fur Volkwirtschaft

Liechtenstein – German annual

Energy.

23008 FERIENHANDBUCH FUR DAS FURSTENTUM LIECHTENSTEIN 1987 TOURISM HANDBOOK/GUIDE OF THE PRINCIPALITY OF LIECHTENSTEIN 1987

Liechtenstein – German/English/French/Italian/Spanish annual January 1983 60pp free

Tourism in the Principality of Liechtenstein.

23009 FREMDENVERKEHRSSTATISTIK
Amt fur Volkwirtschaft

Liechtenstein – German twice a year 25pp

Statistics on tourism in Liechtenstein.

23010 GESELLSCHAFTSFORMEN UND STEUERBELASTUNG IM FURSTENTUM LIECHTENSTEIN
Verwaltungs-und Privatbank AG
B. Guggi

Liechtenstein – German irregular 72pp SF5.00

Overview of legislation and taxation of companies.

23011 HINTS TO EXPORTERS
Department of Trade and Industry

Liechtenstein, Switzerland – English annual

23012 JAHRESBERICHT/ANNUAL REPORT VERWALTUNGS-UND PRIVATBANK AG

Liechtenstein – German annual 30pp

Annual report of the bank's activities.

23013 KONJUNKTURTEST
Amt fur Volkwirtschaft

Liechtenstein – German quarterly

Business trends in Liechtenstein.

23014 LANDERBERICHT LIECHTENSTEIN
Federal Statistical Office of Germany

Liechtenstein – German irregular DM7.90

Statistical survey of Liechtenstein including such areas as demography, geography, education, employment, agriculture, production, overseas trade, transport, tourism, finance, wages and prices and national accounts.

23015 LIECHTENSTEIN IN FIGURES
Verwaltungs-und Privatbank AG

Liechtenstein – English 9pp free

Leaflet giving abbreviated figures on population, occupations, agriculture and forestry, industry, exports, energy use, services, tourism, communications, banking, finance, social security, education, automobile traffic.

23016 LIECHTENSTEIN WIRTSCHAFTSFRAGEN
Verwaltungs-und Privatbank AG

Liechtenstein – German irregular 20pp

Several booklets are issued in the series each year covering specific economic and financial topics.

23017 LIECHTENSTEIN IN ZAHLEN
Amt fur Volkwirtschaft

Liechtenstein – German annual

Liechtenstein in figures.

23018 LIECHTENSTEINISCHE GESELLSCHAFTSFORMEN
Verwaltungs-und Privatbank AG

Liechtenstein – German loose leaf SF40.00

A binder with a survey of the most important provisions on forms of companies in Liechtenstein.

23019 MOTORFAHRZEUGBESTAND
Amt fur Volkwirtschaft

Liechtenstein – German annual

Motor vehicles.

23020 THE PRINCIPALITY OF LIECHTENSTEIN–A DOCUMENTARY HANDBOOK
Press & Information Office of the Liechtenstein Government

Liechtenstein – German/English/French last English edition 1981, German/French 1982 free

General guide covering all aspects of life including taxation, banking, national income, population, industry, trade, forestry, tourism and electricity supply.

23021 **STATISTISCHES JAHRBUCH**
Amt fur Volkwirtschaft

Liechtenstein – German annual 1977
370pp

Statistical abstract covering social and economic conditions in Liechtenstein.

23022 **STATISTIK DER INDUSTRIELLEN BETRIEBE**
Amt fur Volkwirtschaft

Liechtenstein – German annual

Industrial concerns.

23023 **WOHNBEVOLKERUNGS-STATISTIK**
Amt fur Volkwirtschaft

Liechtenstein – German annual

Resident population.

23024 **ZIVILSTANDSSTATISTIK**
Amt fur Volkwirtschaft

Liechtenstein – German annual

Births, marriages and deaths.

LUXEMBOURG

24001 ANNUAIRE DES SOCIETES ANONYMES*
Banque Internationale a Luxembourg

Luxembourg – French annual free

Yearbook of joint-stock companies.

24002 ANNUAIRE STATISTIQUE
Service Central de la Statistique et des Etudes Economiques

Luxembourg – French annual c500pp LF1000.00

Annual statistical report in two parts. The first part contains detailed statistics on the economy, population and social welfare of the country. The second part contains comparative international data.

24003 BELGIUM/LUXEMBOURG
UK Iron and Steel Statistics Bureau

Luxembourg – English 1986 with annual statistical summary £25

Report on the steel industry showing production, consumption and details of imports and exports.

24004 BULLETIN DU STATEC
Ministere de l'Economie

Luxembourg – French eight issues per year 1963 LF680 p.a.

Results of and commentaries on statistical surveys and studies into economic problems and other topics of general interest.

24005 BULLETIN TRIMESTRIEL (QUARTERLY BULLETIN)
Institut Monetaire Luxembourgeois

International – French quarterly 1977 40-80pp LF150 per issue.

Domestic and international financial and statistical analysis.

24006 CAHIERS ECONOMIQUES
Ministere de l'Economie

Luxembourg – French irregular various prices

Comprises four series on the economy, national accounts, industry and other topics of general interest.

24007 COMMERCE EXTERIEUR DU LUXEMBOURG
Service Central de la Statistique et des Etudes Economiques

Luxembourg – French annual LF100.00

Statistics on foreign trade.

24008 COMPTES NATIONAUX
Service Central de la Statistique et des Etudes Economiques

Luxembourg – French 1988 LF480.00

Details on the national accounts, theories and policy, including retrospective data.

24009 COTE OFFICIEL DE LA BOURSE DE LUXEMBOURG
Societe de la Bourse de Luxembourg

Luxembourg – French daily, weekly and monthly

Bulletin of the stock exchange giving stock and share prices and price movements.

24010 COUNTRY PROFILES
Economist Publications Ltd

Belgium, Luxembourg – English annual 40pp £25 UK, subscription varies in rest of world

Resumé of politics, economy and industry including statistical summaries.

24011 COUNTRY REPORTS
Economist Publications Ltd

Belgium, Luxembourg – English quarterly 25pp £58 UK, subscription varies in rest of world

Economic policies and development plans, trends in production and demand, monetary and fiscal conditions, wages and prices, merchandise trade, invisibles, capital flows, exchange rates and foreign debt plus a forecast of the economic prospects.

24012 ECONOMIE LUXEMBOURGEOISE EN 1984 ET 1985
Service Central de la Statistique et des Etudes Economiques

Luxembourg – French 1987 373pp LF480.00

Overall review of the economy over two years with statistical tables and a bibliography.

24013 ETUDES (STUDIES)
Institut Monetaire Luxembourgeois

International – French [illegible]
LF150 per issue

Monetary, economic and legal studies concerning Luxembourg and the work of the IML.

24014 EUROBOND TRADING *
Banque Internationmale a Luxembourg

Luxembourg – English monthly free

24015 GRAND DUCHY OF LUXEMBOURG IN FIGURES 1986
Ministere de l'Economie

Luxembourg – English/French/German/Dutch annual 1967 17pp free

Leaflet giving abbreviated figures on territory, climate, population, employment, national accounts, agriculture, industry, services, trade, prices, wages and education.

24016 HINTS TO EXPORTERS
Department of Trade and Industry

Belgium, Luxembourg – English annual

Practical guide for businessmen giving general information, useful addresses, methods of doing business and relevant regulations.

24017 INDICATEURS RAPIDES MENSUELS
Service Central de la Statistique et des Etudes Economiques

Luxembourg – French monthly LF480.00 annually

Economic indicators published in loose-leaf form in 12 categories covering all aspects of the economy.

24018 INDICES MENSUELS DE L'ACTIVITE (INDUSTRIE ET CONSTRUCTION) 1980-1986
Service Central de la Statistique et des Etudes Economiques

Luxembourg – French 1987 70pp LF150.00

Monthly indices of industry.

24019 **INDUSTRIE LUXEMBOURGEOISE 1966-1983**
Service Central de la Statistique et des Etudes Economiques

Luxembourg – French 1987 c580pp LF480.00

In-depth study of industry.

24020 **KOMPASS REGISTER**
Kompass Publishers, UK

Luxembourg – English/French/German/ Spanish/Italian annual £80.00

Comprehensive business directory giving information on over 15,000 companies listed geographically and cross-referenced to a directory of products and services.

24021 **DE KONSUMENT**
Union Luxembourgeoise des Consommateurs

Luxembourg – French/German 10 issues a year BF500

Articles on consumer topics, with some figures and tables.

24022 **'LA LUXEMBOURG SITUATION POLITIQUE, ECONOMIQUE ET SOCIALE' NOTES ET ETUDES DOCUMENTAIRES NO. 4651-52**
La Documentation Francaise

Luxembourg – French 1982 144pp FrF50 ISBN/ISSN No. 0029-4004

The political, economic and social situation in Luxembourg.

24023 **LUXEMBOURG STOCK EXCHANGE**
Societe de la Bourse de Luxembourg

Luxembourg English/French 1987 26pp

Introduction to the Luxembourg Stock Exchange.

24024 **THE LUXEMBOURG STOCK EXCHANGE–ANNUAL REPORT**
Societé de la Bourse de Luxembourg

Luxembourg – English annual 22pp

Report with tables on share movements, bonds, new issues.

24025 **THE LUXEMBOURG STOCK EXCHANGE–FACTS AND FIGURES**
Societé de la Bourse de Luxembourg

Luxembourg – English/French biannual 8pp

24026 **MEMORIAL. RECUEIL ADMINISTRATIF ET ECONOMIQUE**
Ministere d'Etat

Luxembourg – French frequent

Official government communications on economic and administrative matters.

24027 **NOTES TRIMESTRIELLES DE CONJONCTURE**
Ministere de l'Economie

Luxembourg – French quarterly 1970 LF420 p.a.

Survey of the main aspects of the economic climate, both in Luxembourg and internationally.

24028 **OECD ECONOMIC SURVEYS–BELGIUM-LUXEMBOURG**
Organisation for Economic Cooperation and Development (OECD)

Belgium, Luxembourg – English annual 70pp £2.40/DM12/US$5/FrF24

A detailed analysis of recent developments in demand production, employment, prices and wages, conditions in the money and capital markets and developments in the balance of payments. It includes short-term forecasts as well as analyses of medium-term problems of specific relevance to the elaboration of the country's economic policies.

24029 **POPULATION LUXEMBOURGEOISE**
Service Central de la Statistique et des Etudes Economiques

Luxembourg – French 1988 LF480.00

In-depth study of the population.

24030 **RAPPORT ANNUEL ET BILANS DE LA BIL***
Banque Internationale a Luxembourg

Luxembourg – French with condensed English version annual free

Annual report and accounts.

24031 **RECUEIL DE STATISTIQUES PAR COMMUNE**
Service Central de la Statistique et des Etudes Economiques

Luxembourg – French 1984 140pp LF650.00

Statistics on climate, population, economy and politics, classified by commune.

24032 **LA SITUATION ECONOMIQUE EN GRAND-DUCHE**
Ministere de l'Economie

Luxembourg – French quarterly LF420

Economic review.

24033 **STATISTIQUES DU COMMERCE EXTERIEUR DE L'UNION ECONOMIQUE BELGO-LUXEMBOURGEOISE**
Institut National de Statistique

Belgium, Luxembourg – French monthly/ annual BF660 BF6170

Foreign trade.

24034 **TAX & INVESTMENT PROFILE**
Touche Ross International, USA

Luxembourg – English free

Survey covering investment, trade, labour, business practices, financial system. Frequently updated.

MALTA

25001 **ANNUAL ABSTRACT OF STATISTICS**
Central Office of Statistics

Malta – English annual 270pp Lm1.75

Summary of principal statistics of a demographic, social and economic nature.

25002 **ANNUAL REPORT (CENTRAL BANK OF MALTA)**
Central Bank of Malta

Malta – English annual free

Details of the financial and banking sector.

25003 **BUDGET ESTIMATES**
Ministry of Finance and Customs (available from the Government printer)

Malta – English annual 250pp 75c

Detailed estimate of government income and expenditure.

25004 **THE BUDGET SPEECH**
Minister of Finance and Customs (available from the Government printer)

Malta – Maltese annual 120pp Lm1

25005 **CENSUS 1985 3 vols**
Central Office of Statistics

Malta –1986

25006 **CENSUS OF AGRICULTURE**
Central Office of Statistics

Malta – English biannual 75pp 65c

Statistics on output and employment in agricultural and fisheries sectors.

25007 **CENSUS OF INDUSTRIAL PRODUCTION: REPORT AND SUMMARY TABLES**
Central Office of Statistics

Malta – English annual report Lm2 summary 60c

Detailed analysis of Maltese industry.

25008 **COMMERCIAL COURIER***
Chamber of Commerce

Malta – English every 3 weeks

Current commercial news.

25009 **COUNTRY PROFILES**
Economist Publications Ltd

Tunisia,Malta – English annual 40pp £25 UK subscription varies in rest of world

Resumé of politics, economy and industry including statistical summaries.

25010 **COUNTRY REPORTS**
Economist Publications Ltd

Tunisia, Malta – English quarterly 25pp £58 UK subscription varies in rest of world

Economic policies and development plans, trends in production and demand, monetary and fiscal conditions, wages and prices, merchandise trade, invisibles, capital flows, exchange rates and foreign debt plus a forecast of the economic prospects.

25011 **DEMOGRAPHIC REVIEW OF THE MALTESE ISLANDS**
Central Office of Statistics

Malta – English annual 70pp Lm1

25012 **ECONOMIC SURVEY**
Department of Information

Malta – English annual 50pp 50c

Review of the economy and statistical data covering the first nine months of the year.

25013 **ECONOMIC TRENDS**
Central Office of Statistics

Malta – English monthly 4pp free

Statistical economic indicators.

25014 **THE EXPORTER***
Ministry of Trade

Malta – English monthly c12pp

News on developments in exports and trade.

25015 **HINTS TO EXPORTERS**
Department of Trade and Industry

Malta – English annual

Practical guide for businessmen giving general information, useful addresses, methods of doing business and relevant regulations.

25016 **INDUSTRY TODAY**
Federation of Industries

Malta – English quarterly 10/12 20pp Lm0.25

25017 **INDUSTRY TRENDS SURVEY**
Federation of Industries

Malta – English every six months March 1983 36pp Lm1.50

25018 **LANDERBERICHT MALTA**
Federal Statistical Office of Germany

Malta – German irregular DM7.90

Statistical survey of Malta including demography, geography, education, employment, agriculture, production, overseas trade, transport, tourism, finance, wages and prices and national accounts.

25019 **MALTA FINANCIAL REPORT**
Department of Information

Malta – English annual 200pp 50c

Report on the accounts and finances of the Government of Malta.

25020 **MALTA HANDBOOK**
Department of Information

Malta – English annual 170pp Lm1

General information on Malta.

25021 **MANUFACTURERS AND EXPORTERS**
Ministry of Trade

Malta – English with French/German/Italian headings annual c150pp

Directory of over 400 companies cross-referenced to a list of products giving location, key personnel, languages used, bank, products, date of establishment, number of employees. There is also a directory of Maltese trade representatives abroad.

25022 **NATIONAL ACCOUNTS OF THE MALTESE ISLANDS**
Central Office of Statistics

Malta – English annual 45pp Lm1

Statistical review of Malta's national income, balance of payments, private and public consumption and capital expenditure and input-output data for the last ten-year period.

25023 QUARTERLY DIGEST OF STATISTICS
Central Office of Statistics

Malta – English quarterly 70pp 75c

Statistical data on the major sectors of the Maltese economy.

25024 QUARTERLY REVIEW
Central Bank of Malta

Malta – English quarterly c60pp free

Review of international and Maltese monetary and financial developments.

25025 SHIPPING AND AVIATION STATISTICS
Central Office of Statistics

Malta – English annual 130pp Lm1

Covers shipping, aviation, passenger movements and tourism.

25026 TRADE DIRECTORY
Chamber of Commerce

Malta – English annual c450pp Lm2

Details of the members and activities of the chamber with a review of the economy including statistics on foreign trade.

25027 TRADE STATISTICS
Central Office of Statistics

Malta – English three times a year 500pp Lm2

Statistical analysis of Malta's foreign trade by product and country of origin.

25028 THE YEAR BOOK: MALTA
De La Salle Brothers Publications

Malta – English annual c400pp

General guide giving information on politics, society and economy, including a bibliography.

THE NETHERLANDS

26001 **ABN ECONOMIC REVIEW**
Algemene Bank Nederland Nv

Netherlands – English bi-monthly c28pp free

Review of current economic developments, statistical analysis and key economic indicators.

26002 **ABECOR COUNTRY REPORT – NETHERLANDS**
Abecor

Netherlands – English 1986 2pp free

Brief economic report.

26003 **AGRICULTURAL DATA**
Netherlands Central Bureau of Statistics

Netherlands – Dutch with English summary annual DF27.25

26004 **AMRO STOCK MARKET NEWS**
Amro Bank

Netherlands – English irregular 4pp free

The Amsterdam Stock Exchange, market topics, investments, companies quoted.

26005 **ANNUAL REPORT—ABN BANK**
Algemene Bank Nederland Nv

Netherlands – English annual c100pp free

Annual report including survey of the Dutch money market.

26006 **ANNUAL REPORT—DE NEDERLANSCHE BANK**
De Nederlansche Bank

Netherlands – Dutch/English annual c220pp DF26-46

Macro-economic policy analysis and statements on the monetary policy conducted by the Bank (with statistical appendix).

26007 **APPENDIX TO THE MONTHLY BULLETIN OF PRICE STATISTICS**
Netherlands Central Bureau of Statistics

Netherlands – Dutch/English summary monthly

26008 **BANKENBOEJE**
Nederlands Instituut voor het Bank-en Effectenbedrijt

Netherlands – Dutch annual DF22.50

26009 **BRITAIN IN THE NETHERLANDS**
Netherlands British Chamber of Commerce

Netherlands – English £15.00 every 5 years

Directory of UK subsidiaries in the Netherlands.

26010 **CENSUS OF AGRICULTURE 1985: TYPES OF HOLDING BY STANDARD FARM UNITS 1968 AND 1975 (J3)**
Netherlands Central Bureau of Statistics

Netherlands – Dutch with English summary 1985 DF35.00

26011 **CENTRAAL ECONOMISCH PLAN (CENTRAL ECONOMIC PLAN)**
Centraal Planbureau

Netherlands – Dutch annual

A review of economic development of the past year and updated forecasts for the current year.

26012 **CIVIL AVIATION STATISTICS (N50)**
Netherlands Central Bureau of Statistics

Netherlands – Dutch with English summary annual DF21.50

26013 **COUNTRY PROFILES**
Economist Publications Ltd

Netherlands – English annual 40pp £25 UK subscription varies in rest of world

Resumé of politics, economy and industry including statistical summaries.

26014 **COUNTRY REPORTS**
Economist Publications Ltd

Netherlands – English quarterly 25pp £58UK subscription varies in rest of world

Economic policies and development plans, trends in production and demand, monetary and fiscal conditions, wages and prices, merchandise trade, invisibles, capital flows, exchange rates and foreign debt plus a forecast of the economic prospects.

26015 **DNB STATISTICAL CAHIERS SERIES**
De Nederlansche Bank

Netherlands – Dutch 1986

Series covers national accounts and financial institutions.

26016 **DAIRY STATISTICS (J15)**
Netherlands Central Bureau of Statistics

Netherlands – Dutch with English summary annual

26017 **DUTCH COMPANIES AND THEIR UK AGENTS/DISTRIBUTORS**
Netherlands British Chamber of Commerce

Netherlands – English £6.00

Food section only (every 2 years).

26018 **DUTCH COMPANIES AND THEIR UK ASSOCIATES**
Netherlands British Chamber of Commerce

Netherlands – English £15.00 every 2 years.

26019 **GENERAL ENVIRONMENTAL STATISTICS (C14)**
Netherlands Central Bureau of Statistics

Netherlands – Dutch with English summary annual DF41.00

26020 **HINTS TO EXPORTERS**
Department of Trade and Industry

Netherlands – English annual

Practical guide for businessmen giving general information, useful addresses, methods of doing business and relevant regulations.

26021 **HOLLAND EXPORTS**
Verlag Hoppenstedt & Co.

Netherlands – English/Spanish/French/German

4 volumes covering industrial products, consumer goods/non food, consumer goods/food, commercial gardening and farming.

26022 **HORTICULTURAL DATA**
Netherlands Central Bureau of Statistics

Netherlands – Dutch with English summary annual DF22.50

26023 **INDUSTRIAL ACCIDENTS STATISTICS (C10)**
Netherlands Central Bureau of Statistics

Netherlands – Dutch with English summary annual DF13.00

26024 **INDUSTRIAL PRODUCTS**
Netherlands British Chamber of Commerce

Netherlands – English annual £15.00

Lists the following products available for export: finished products, semi-finished articles, raw materials.

26025 **INDUSTRY TEST (K 4)**
Netherlands Central Bureau of Statistics

Netherlands – Dutch with English summary monthly with annual supplement DF52.50

26026 **INFORMATION CONTACTS IN THE NETHERLANDS**
Netherlands British Chamber of Commerce

Netherlands – English £15.00 every 10 years

Lists over 300 organizations.

26027 **KOMPASS REGISTER**
Kompass Publishers, UK

Netherlands – English/French/German/Spanish/Italian annual £120.00

Comprehensive business directory giving information on over 18,000 companies listed geographically and cross-referenced to a directory of products and services.

26028 **LANBOUWOHFERS (AGRICULTURAL FIGURES)**
Landbouw-Economisch Instituut

Netherlands – Dutch (English explanations available) annual 1948 250pp DF27.50

Over 300 tables with data on type and size of holdings, production, income, trade, prices, costs etc. in agricultural production.

26029 **MAJOR COMPANIES IN THE NETHERLANDS**
Netherlands British Chamber of Commerce

Netherlands – English £10.00 every 2 years

Details of 200 companies.

26030 **MONETARY MONOGRAPHS**
De Nederlansche Bank

Netherlands – Dutch/English 1984

Series covers financial and economic policy, money supply.

26031 **MONTHLY BULLETIN (AZ 2)**
Netherlands Central Bureau of Statistics

Netherlands – Dutch with English summary monthly DF93.50

26032 **MONTHLY BULLETIN OF AGRICULTURAL STATISTICS (J 1)**
Netherlands Central Bureau of Statistics

Netherlands – Dutch with English summary monthly DF75.00

26033 **MONTHLY BULLETIN OF CONSTRUCTION STATISTICS (K 3)**
Netherlands Central Bureau of Statistics

Netherlands – Dutch with English summary monthly

26034 **MONTHLY BULLETIN OF DISTRIBUTION AND SERVICE TRADE STATISTICS (L 10)**
Netherlands Central Bureau of Statistics

Netherlands – Dutch with English summary monthly DF100.00

26035 **MONTHLY BULLETIN OF FINANCIAL STATISTICS (OR 1)**
Netherlands Central Bureau of Statistics

Netherlands – Dutch with English summary monthly DF108.25

26036 **MONTHLY BULLETIN OF POPULATION STATISTICS (BC 1)**
Netherlands Central Bureau of Statistics

Netherlands – Dutch with English summary monthly DF75.00

26037 **MONTHLY BULLETIN OF PRICE STATISTICS (U2)**
Netherlands Central Bureau of Statistics

Netherlands – Dutch with English summary monthly DF81.25

26038 **MONTHLY BULLETIN OF TRANSPORT STATISTICS (N1)**
Netherlands Central Bureau of Statistics

Netherlands – Dutch with English summary monthly DF100.00

26039 **MONTHLY STATISTICAL BULLETIN OF FOREIGN TRADE BY COMMODITIES (M 1)**
Netherlands Central Bureau of Statistics

Netherlands – Dutch with English summary monthly DF118.25

26040 **MONTHLY STATISTICAL BULLETIN OF FOREIGN TRADE BY COUNTRIES (M 2)**
Netherlands Central Bureau of Statistics

Netherlands – Dutch with English summary monthly DF91.70

26041 **MONTHLY STATISTICAL BULLETIN OF MANUFACTURING (K 2)**
Netherlands Central Bureau of Statistics

Netherlands – Dutch with English summary monthly DF107.00

26042 **MOTOR-CAR STATISTICS**
Netherlands Central Bureau of Statistics

Netherlands – Dutch with English summary annual DF7.00

26043 **NATIONAL ACCOUNTS (P2)**
Netherlands Central Bureau of Statistics

Netherlands – Dutch with English summary annual DF67.25

26044 **NEDERLANDS ABC**
Verlag Hoppenstedt & Co.

Netherlands – Dutch annual DM162.50

Information on manufacturers, importers and products.

26045 **NETHERLANDS**
UK Iron and Steel Statistics Bureau

Netherlands – English 1986 with annual statistical summary £25

Report on the steel industry showing production, consumption and details of imports and exports.

26046 **NETHERLANDS ECONOMIC REPORT**
Amro Bank

Netherlands – English quarterly 4pp free

A review of the Dutch economy.

26047 **THE NETHERLANDS ECONOMY**
Centraal Planbureau

Netherlands – English annual

26048 **OECD ECONOMIC SURVEYS–NETHERLANDS**
Organisation for Economic Cooperation and Development (OECD)

Netherlands – English annual 70pp £2.40/ DM12/US$5/FrF24

A detailed analysis of recent developments in demand, production, employment, prices and wages, conditions in the money and capital markets and developments in the balance of payments. It includes short-term forecasts as well as analyses of medium-term problems of specific relevance to the elaboration of the country's economic policies.

26049 **POCKET YEARBOOK (AZ4)**
Netherlands Central Bureau of Statistics

Netherlands – Dutch with English summary annual DF14.25

Concise statistical tables on all aspects of the economy and society.

26050 **POPULATION OF THE MUNICIPALITIES OF THE NETHERLANDS (B 1)**
Netherlands Central Bureau of Statistics

Netherlands – Dutch with English summary annual DF15.00

26051 **PRODUCTION STATISTICS**
Netherlands Central Bureau of Statistics

Netherlands – annual

A series of publications covering all manufacturing output.

26052 **QUARTERLY BULLETIN**
De Nederlansche Bank

Netherlands – Dutch/English quarterly 1969 c130pp DF12.50/19.50

A quarterly review of macro-economic developments and of central bank policy in the Netherlands, including statistical data.

26053 **QUESTIONNAIRE REGIONAL ECONOMIC DEVELOPMENT ROTTERDAM MUNICIPAL (ERBO-ROTTERDAM)**
Chamber of Commerce and Industry for Rotterdam and the Lower Maas

Netherlands – Dutch annual 1987 40-50pp

Economic development of the city of Rotterdam.

26054 **REVIEW OF THE NETHERLANDS ECONOMY**
Bank Mees and Hope NV

Netherlands – English bi-monthly

Balance of payments, government financing, wages, prices.

26055 **STATISTICAL BULLETIN (A2 1)**
Netherlands Central Bureau of Statistics

Netherlands – Dutch c100 issues a year DF52.50

26056 **STATISTICAL YEARBOOK OF THE NETHERLANDS**
Netherlands Central Bureau of Statistics

Netherlands – Dutch/English annual c500pp DF84.00

Statistical tables covering topography, demography, social welfare, labour, industry and manufacturing, agriculture, foreign trade, transport, finance both national and private, prices.

26057 **STATISTICS OF AGRICULTURE (J 2)**
Netherlands Central Bureau of Statistics

Netherlands – Dutch with English summary annual DF35.25

26058 **STATISTICS OF CONSUMER CREDIT (O 2)**
Netherlands Central Bureau of Statistics

Netherlands – Dutch with English summary annual DF11.50

26059 **STATISTICS OF FIXED CAPITAL FORMATION IN INDUSTRY (I 2)**
Netherlands Central Bureau of Statistics

Netherlands – Dutch with English summary annual DF14.75

26060 **STATISTICS OF INTERNATIONAL INLAND WATERWAY TRANSPORT (N35)**
Netherlands Central Bureau of Statistics

Netherlands – Dutch with English summary annual DF31.00

26061 **STATISTICS OF MORTGAGES AND MORTGAGE BANKS (05)**
Netherlands Central Bureau of Statistics

Netherlands – Dutch with English summary annual DF18.25

26062 **STATISTICS OF THE INLAND FLEET (N30)**
Netherlands Central Bureau of Statistics

Netherlands – Dutch with English summary biennial DF15.00

26063 **STATISTICS OF THE INTERNATIONAL GOODS TRAFFIC (N4)**
Netherlands Central Bureau of Statistics

Netherlands – Dutch with English summary annual DF53.10

Special section giving statistics for Rotterdam and Amsterdam.

26064 **STATISTICS OF THE INTERNATIONAL PORT TRAFFIC: ROTTERDAM AND AMSTERDAM (N 2)**
Netherlands Central Bureau of Statistics

Netherlands – Dutch with English summary annual DF38.50

26065 **STATISTICS OF TRADE UNIONS (V25)**
Netherlands Central Bureau of Statistics

Netherlands – Dutch with English summary annual DF11.50

26066 **STATISTICS OF WATER QUALITY MANAGEMENT AND CONTROL (C 18)**
Netherlands Central Bureau of Statistics

Netherlands – Dutch with English summary annual

Statistics on discharge, purification, costs and financing.

26067 **STATISTICS ON PASSENGER TRANSPORT (N 15)**
Netherlands Central Bureau of Statistics

Netherlands – Dutch with English summary annual DF16.75

26068 **STATISTICS ON RENT AND ON PRICES OF FARMLANDS (J 10)**
Netherlands Central Bureau of Statistics

Netherlands – Dutch with English summary annual DF23.50

26069 **STATISTICS OF SEABORNE SHIPPING (N36)**
Netherlands Central Bureau of Statistics

Netherlands – Dutch with English summary annual DF33.88

26070 **TAX & INVESTMENT PROFLE**
Touche Ross International, USA

Netherlands – English free

Survey covering investment, trade, labour, business practices, financial system. Frequently updated.

26071 **TOURISM STATISTICS (X3)**
Netherlands Central Bureau of Statistics

Netherlands – Dutch with English summary annual DF23.75

26072 **TUINBOUWUJFERS (HORTICULTURAL FIGURES)**
Landbouw Economisch Instituut

Netherlands – Dutch (English explanation available) annual 1968 150pp DF22.50

190 tables with data on production, holdings and many economic variables in Dutch horticulture.

26073 **YEARLY AND QUARTERLY FINANCIAL AND MONETARY TIME SERIES 1957-1983**
De Nederlansche Bank

Netherlands – Dutch 1985 287pp free

NORWAY

27001 ABECOR COUNTRY REPORT—NORWAY
Abecor

Norway – English 1981 2pp free

Brief economic report.

27002 AGRICULTURAL STATISTICS
Central Bureau of Statistics

Norway – English annual

Statistics on all aspects of agriculture.

27003 ALT OM LO (ALL ABOUT THE NORWEGIAN FEDERATION OF TRADE UNIONS)
The Norwegian Federation of Trade Unions

Norway – Norwegian 1985 300pp NKr100
ISBN No. 82-10-02717-4

History, incomes policy, unions, economic policy, industrial relations etc.

27004 ANNUAL REPORT (DEN NORSKE CREDITBANK)*
Den Norske Creditbank

Norway – Norwegian/English annual 30pp free

Annual report and accounts.

27005 ANNUAL REPORT
The Oslo Stock Exchange

Norway – Norwegian/English annual free

Statistics about the Oslo Stock Exchange and companies.

27006 ARCHITECTURAL AND OTHER TECHNICAL SERVICES CONNECTED WITH CONSTRUCTION
Central Bureau of Statistics

Norway – English annual

Information on the number of establishments, employment, value of production, costs of materials, gross fixed capital formation.

27007 BOERSKURSLISTEN
The Oslo Stock Exchange

Norway – Norwegian daily NKr1700

Trading prices index, news about the companies, members of the Oslo Stock Exchange.

27008 BUILDING STATISTICS
Central Bureau of Statistics

Norway – English annual

Statistics on building work currently in train, number of dwellings, floor space.

27009 CAR REPAIR SHOPS ETC.
Central Bureau of Statistics

Norway – English annual

Information on establishments, persons engaged, wages, value of production for the industry group, repair of vehicles, household apparatus and commodities for personal use.

27010 CAUSES OF DEATH
Central Bureau of Statistics

Norway – English annual

Causes of death classified by sex and age with multiple tables for countries.

27011 CENSUS OF HORTICULTURE
Central Bureau of Statistics

Norway – English 1985

27012 COMMERCIAL AND SAVINGS BANKS —STATEMENT OF ACCOUNT FOR THE INDIVIDUAL BANKS
Central Bureau of Statistics

Norway – English annual

27013 A CREDIT MODEL FOR NORWAY
Norges Bank

Norway – English 1978

27014 CONSTRUCTION STATISTICS
Central Bureau of Statistics

Norway – English annual

Details on all aspects of the construction industry.

27015 COUNTRY PROFILES–NORWAY
Economist Publications Ltd

Norway – English annual 40pp £25 UK subscription varies in rest of world

Resumé of politics, economy and industry including statistical summaries.

27016 COUNTRY REPORTS–NORWAY
Economist Publications Ltd

Norway – English quarterly 25pp £58 UK subscription varies in rest of world

Economic policies and development plans, trends in production and demand, monetary and fiscal conditions, wages and prices, merchandise trade, invisibles, capital flows, exchange rates and foreign debt plus a forecast of the economic prospects.

27017 DNC OIL NOW*
Den Norske Creditbank

Norway – English c20pp free

Periodical comprising articles on current developments in the Norwegian oil industry.

27018 ECONOMIC BULLETIN
Norges Bank

Norway – English quarterly c150pp free

Commentary on financial and economic matters with a large statistical section.

27019 ECONOMIC SURVEY
Central Bureau of Statistics

Norway – English annual

General survey of the economy, appears annually in no. 1A of Økonomiske Analyser (Economic Trends).

27020 ECONOMIC TRENDS (ØKONOMISKE ANALYSER)
Central Bureau of Statistics

Norway – Norwegian monthly

Report and analysis of current economic trends.

27021 ELECTRICITY STATISTICS
Central Bureau of Statistics

Norway – English annual

Statistical data covering supplies, production, employment and operations of installations for both electricity and gas.

27022 **EMBALLERING***
A/S Selvig

Norway – Norwegian 10 issues a year NKr100.00

Review of the organization and distribution structure of the packaging industry.

27023 **ENERGY STATISTICS**
Central Bureau of Statistics

Norway – English annual

Statistics covering total energy consumption, production, prices and other indices for electricity, crude petroleum, natural gas, petroleum products, coal and coke.

27024 **ENVIRONMENTAL STATISTICS NATURAL RESOURCES AND POLLUTION**
Central Bureau of Statistics

Norway – Norwegian 1983

Comment and analytic survey derived from official statistics. Annual reports are also presented.

27025 **EXTERNAL TRADE**
Central Bureau of Statistics

Norway – English annual 2 vols

Statistics on imports and exports classified by commodity and by country of origin or destination.

27026 **FINANCIAL REVIEW**
Norwegian Bankers Association

Norway – English quarterly c12pp free

Commentary on economic and financial subjects and review of developments in banking. Section on key economic indicators and banking statistics.

27027 **FISHERY STATISTICS**
Central Bureau of Statistics

Norway – English annual

Statistics on all aspects of the fishing industry.

27028 **FISHING AND REARING OF SALMON ETC**
Central Bureau of Statistics

Norway – Norwegian annual

Data on sea and river fishing and rearing.

27029 **FISKETS GANG**
Fiskeridirektoratet

Norway – Norwegian with English headings semi-monthly NKr250.00

Reports on current developments in the fishing industry including statistics on catches, exports, analysed by type of fish.

27030 **FORESTRY STATISTICS**
Central Bureau of Statistics

Norway – English annual

Statistics on all aspects of the forestry sector.

27031 **GROWTH POLICIES IN A NORDIC PERSPECTIVE 1987**
Institute of Industrial Economics

Norway, Sweden, Finland, Denmark – English 1984
ISBN No. 91 7204 276-1

Economic policies and outlook.

27032 **TAX & INVESTMENT PROFILE**
Touche Ross International, USA

Norway – English free

Booklet providing information on financial system and legislation including taxation and currency regulations which is frequently updated.

27033 **TAX STATISTICS**
Central Bureau of Statistics

Norway – English annual

Assessed property and income tax liabilities.

27034 **TELEVERKET STATISTIKK (NORWEGIAN TELECOMMUNICATIONS STATISTICS)**
Norwegian Telecommunications Administration

Norway – Norwegian with separately published English summary annual

27035 **TRANSPORT AND COMMUNICATION STATISTICS**
Central Bureau of Statistics

Norway – English annual

Statistics on railways, trams, roads, registration of automobiles, driving licences, aircraft, accidents, postal services, telecommunications and broadcasting.

27036 **WAGE STATISTICS**
Central Bureau of Statistics

Norway – Norwegian annual

Monthly earnings for the following occupation groups: agriculture and horticulture, mining and manufacturing, wholesale and retail trade, banks, insurance firms, sea transport, local government, hotels and restaurants. A summary is given in a separate volume.

27037 **WEEKLY BULLETIN OF STATISTICS**
Central Bureau of Statistics

Norway – Norwegian weekly NKr300

Summary of current data.

27038 **WHOLESALE AND RETAIL TRADE STATISTICS**
Central Bureau of Statistics

Norway – English annual

27039 **YELLOW PAGES**
S. M. Bryde

Norway – Norwegian annual 1,600pp free
ISSN No. 82 7030 119 1

27040 **HINTS TO EXPORTERS**
Department of Trade and Industry

Norway – English annual

Practical guide for businessmen giving general information, useful addresses, methods of doing business and relevant regulations.

27041 **HOLIDAY SURVEY 1982**
Central Bureau of Statistics

Norway – English

Survey on duration, place, form of activity and type of accommodation on holidays. Other reports are issued at irregular intervals.

27042 **HUNTING STATISTICS**
Central Bureau of Statistics

Norway – English annual

Statistics on number of shooters, game felled, yield of small game, and damage compensation.

27043 **INCOME STATISTICS**
Central Bureau of Statistics

Norway – Norwegian triennial

Statistics on personal and household incomes.

27044 **LABOUR MARKET STATISTICS**
Central Bureau of Statistics

Norway – English annual

Current data on the labour market.

27045 **LANDERBERICHT NORWEGEN**
Federal Statistical Office of Germany

Norway – German irregular DM7.90

Statistical survey of Norway including demography, geography, education, employment, agriculture, production, overseas trade, transport, tourism, finance, wages and prices and national accounts.

27046 **LEVEL OF LIVING SURVEY**
Central Bureau of Statistics

Norway – Norwegian 1983

Survey of persons aged 16-79 giving occupation, working conditions, household conditions.

27047 **MANUFACTURING STATISTICS**
Central Bureau of Statistics

Norway – English annual 2 vols

Figures on production, labour, wages, costs.

27048 **MARKETING PLAN**
Oslo Tourist Board

Norway – Norwegian annual 76pp

Statistics on tourist trade, plans, projects.

27049 **MONENTER SKIPSFART OG OFFSHORE**
Norges Rederiforbund

Norway – Norwegian monthly

Shipping industry and offshore activities.

27050 **MONTHLY BULLETIN OF EXTERNAL TRADE**
Central Bureau of Statistics

Norway – Norwegian monthly NKr160.00

Detailed monthly data on imports and exports.

27051 **MONTHLY BULLETIN OF STATISTICS**
Central Bureau of Statistics

Norway – Norwegian monthly NKr200.00

Current monthly and quarterly statistics on all aspects of the economy, articles on current economic trends.

27052 **MONTHLY SURVEY***
Den Norske Creditbank

Norway – English monthly 8pp free

Statistical survey of trade, industry and finance.

27053 **MONTHLY SURVEY OF THE NORWEGIAN STOCK MARKET***
Den Norske Creditbank

Norway – English monthly c12pp free

Current trading figures and graphs.

27054 **NATIONAL ACCOUNTS**
Central Bureau of Statistics

Norway – English annual

Data on domestic product, consumption, expenditure, private and public finance.

27055 **NORDISK FORSAKRINGSTIDSKRIFT**
Svenska Forsakringsforeningen

Norway, Finland, Sweden, Denmark – Scandinavian/English/German quarterly 1921 90pp SKr40 p.a.
ISBN/ISSN No. 0348-6516

Private and public insurance.

27056 **NORGES BANK–ANNUAL REPORT AND ACCOUNTS**
Norges Bank

Norway – English annual c150pp free

27057 **NORWAY**
National Westminster Bank

Norway – English irregular 4pp free

Brief economic report.

27058 **NORWAY**
UK Iron and Steel Statistics Bureau

Norway – English 1986 with annual statistical summary £25

Report on the steel industry showing production, consumption and details of imports and exports.

27059 **NORWEGIAN DIRECTORY OF COMMERCE**
S. M. Bryde

Norway – annual NKr 300
ISBN/ISSN No. 82 7030 118 3

27060 **NORWEGIAN MONETARY AND CREDIT SYSTEM**
Norges Bank/Leif Eide and Knut Holli

Norway – Norwegian/English 1980 55pp

Detailed review of the financial system with many statistical tables.

27061 **NORWEGIAN SHIPPING NEWS***
A/S Selvig

Norway – English 19 issues a year with 4 statistical supplements NKr150.00

27062 **OECD ECONOMIC SURVEYS–NORWAY**
Organisation for Economic Cooperation and Development (OECD)

Norway – English annual 70pp £2.40/ DM12/US$5/FrF24

A detailed analysis of recent developments in demand, production, employment, prices and wages, conditions in the money and capital markets and developments in the balance of payments. It includes short-term forecasts as well as analyses of medium-term problems of specific relevance to the elaboration of the country's economic policies.

27063 **OFFSHORE ENGINEER***
A/S Selvig

Norway – Norwegian/English monthly NKr200.00 £20.00

27064 **OIL AND GAS ACTIVITY**
Central Bureau of Statistics

Norway – English quarterly

Data on exploration, finds, production, employment, wages, accidents, taxes and other financial conditions.

27065 **OKONOMISK REVY**
Norwegian Bankers Association

Norway – Norwegian monthly NKr250.00

Economic review.

27066 **PETROLEUM ACTIVITIES IN NORWAY**
Bergen Bank

Norway – English 1981 free

Thorough guide to oil industry and current activities.

27067 **POPULATION STATISTICS VOL I**
Central Bureau of Statistics

Norway – English annual

Demographic statistics presented by municipality.

27068 **POPULATION STATISTICS VOL II**
Central Bureau of Statistics

Norway – English annual

Population classified by age, sex and marital status.

27069 **POPULATION STATISTICS VOL III**
Central Bureau of Statistics

Norway – English annual

Data on both external and internal migration classified by age, sex, marital status and other demographic characteristics.

27070 **POPULATION PROJECTIONS 1985-2050**
Central Bureau of Statistics

Norway – English

Population projections by sex and age classified by municipality.

27071 **PRIVATE MOTORING**
Central Bureau of Statistics

Norway – Norwegian 1980

Data on use of cars, mileage, number of persons carried and characteristics of owners.

27072 **PROPERTY STATISTICS 1982**
Central Bureau of Statistics

Norway – Norwegian 1982

Data on property and owners classified by type of property and income.

27073 **PUBLIC SECTOR FINANCES 1972-1985**
Central Bureau of Statistics

Norway – Norwegian

Data on the finances of the treasury, central government accounts, social security, local government, state enterprises.

27074 ROAD GOODS TRANSPORT 1986
Central Bureau of Statistics

Norway – Norwegian every 5 years

Data on length of transport, capacity, classified by ownership, size and fuel consumption.

27075 ROAD TRAFFIC ACCIDENTS
Central Bureau of Statistics

Norway English annual

Road traffic accidents classified by type of accident, time, place and damage to either vehicles or persons.

27076 ROUNDWOOD CUT FOR SALE AND INDUSTRIAL PRODUCTION
Central Bureau of Statistics

Norway – English annual

Statistics on roundwood cut for sale and industrial use, classified by species of tree, buyer and municipality.

27077 SERVICES
Central Bureau of Statistics

Norway – English annual

Figures from business services, machinery and equipment rental and leasing; also sanitary and similar services, laundries etc.

27078 SCHEDULED ROAD TRANSPORT
Central Bureau of Statistics

Norway – English annual

Data on concessionary bus and lorry lines, equipment, staff and traffic classified by county.

27079 SKIPSVERKSTEDER BATBYGGERIERSKIPSMOTORER*
A/S Selvig

Norway – Norwegian/English annual
NKr70.00 US$14.00

Report on shipyards, boatbuilders and marine engines.

27080 SOCIAL STATISTICS
Central Bureau of Statistics

Norway – English annual

Data on child welfare, social care, home help services, services for elderly and handicapped people.

27081 STATISTICAL YEARBOOK OF NORWAY
Central Bureau of Statistics

Norway – English annual

Main statistics on all aspects of social, political, environmental and economic life.

27082 STATISTICS OF ACCOUNTS MINING AND MANUFACTURING
Central Bureau of Statistics

Norway – English annual

Data on profit and loss accounts, expenditure investment and assets.

27083 STATISTICS ON ACCOUNTS WHOLESALE TRADE
Central Bureau of Statistics

Norway – English annual

Data on profit and loss, expenditure, investment and assets.

27084 STRUCTURAL DATA FROM THE MUNICIPAL ACCOUNTS
Central Bureau of Statistics

Norway – English annual

Budget expenditure, revenues and balance sheets by municipality.

POLAND

28001 ABECOR COUNTRY REPORT – POLAND
Abecor

Poland – English 1981 2pp free

Brief economic report.

28002 BIULETYN STATYSTYCZNY
Glowny Urzad Statystyczny

Poland – Polish with English/Russian table of contents monthly 83pp Zl21.150

Current statistical data including imports and exports, prices and wages, production and consumption.

28003 BUDNOWNICTIVO OKETAV (SHIPPING)
Collets Holdings Ltd

Poland – Polish monthly £51.00

28004 CONCISE STATISTICAL YEARBOOK OF POLAND*
Glowny Urzad Statystyczny

Poland – Polish/English annual c260pp

Pocket book giving concise statistical data on the country's socio-economic development during the preceding year.

28005 CONTEMPORARY POLAND *
Polska Agencja Interpress

Poland – English/French/Spanish/German/Russian semi-monthly c40pp US$13.00

Brief news on current events.

28006 COUNTRY PROFILES
Economist Publications Ltd

Poland – English annual 40pp £25 UK subscription varies in rest of world

Resumé of politics, economy and industry including statistical summaries.

28007 COUNTRY REPORTS
Economist Publications Ltd

Poland – English quarterly 25pp £58 UK subscription varies in rest of world

Economic policies and development plans, trends in production and demand, monetary and fiscal conditions, wages and prices, merchandise trade, invisibles, capital flows, exchange rates and foreign debt plus a forecast of the economic prospects.

28008 FOREIGN ECONOMIC TRENDS AND THEIR IMPLICATIONS FOR THE UNITED STATES – POLAND
US Department of Commerce

Poland – English annual 10pp US$1.00

Data on key economic indicators followed by a survey of the economy including a forecast for the long-term economic outlook with particular reference to US-Polish trade.

28009 A FOREIGN INVESTOR'S GUIDE TO THE LAW OF 23 APRIL 1986 ON COMPANIES WITH FOREIGN CAPITAL PARTICIPATION
Polish Chamber of Foreign Trade – Information and Legal Aid Centre

Poland – English 1986 27pp

28010 GOSPODARKA MORSKA: PRZEGLAD STATYSTYCZNY
Instytut Morski

Poland – Polish with a list of tables in English annual 1960 250pp

Statistical review of the maritime economy covering Polish and international seaborne trade, ports, shipping, shipbuilding, shiprepairing, fisheries, protection of environment, costs and revenues, forecasts.

28011 GOSPODARKA PLANOWA
Collets Holdings Ltd

Poland – Polish monthly £48.00

28012 HANDEL ZAGRANICZNY
Polish Chamber of Foreign Trade

Poland – Polish monthly 1956 32-48pp US$56
ISSN No. 0017-7245

Information on Polish foreign trade and international economic and financial relations.

28013 HINTS TO EXPORTERS
Department of Trade and Industry

Poland – English annual

Practical guide for businessmen giving general information, useful addresses, methods of doing business and relevant regulations.

28014 INFORMATION BULLETIN
Narodowy Bank Polski

Poland – English annual 65pp
ISSN No. 0239 3395

Covers the economy, overseas trade and the financial sector.

28015 INFORMATION FOR BUSINESSMEN TRADING WITH POLAND
Polish Chamber of Foreign Trade

Poland – English 1985 287pp

General information, lists of export/import organizations, classified by product, regulations and services.

28016 LANDERBERICHT POLEN
Federal Statistical Office of Germany

Poland – German irregular DM7.90

Statistical survey of Poland including demography, geography, education, employment, agriculture, production, overseas trade, transport, tourism, finance, wages and prices and national accounts.

28017 MORZE (MARITIME)
Collets Holdings Ltd

Poland – Polish monthly £11.00

28018 POLAND STATISTICAL DATA*
Glowny Urzad Statystyczny

Poland – Polish/English/French/German/Russian annual c70pp

Abridged version of 'Concise Statistical Yearbook'.

28019 POLAND–STATISTICAL DATA
Glowny Urzad Statystyczny (Central Statistical Office)

Poland – English/French irregular 90pp

Statistical data on Poland covering geography, politics, population, employment, national income, incomes and cost of living, investment, industry, construction, agriculture, trade, transport, education, health, tourism and housing.

28020 POLAND TOURISM*
Polska Agencja Interpress

Poland – English/French/German monthly

Up-to-date review of the industry.

28021 **POLISH ECONOMIC NEWS/REVUE DE L'ECONOMIE POLNAIS/ POLNISCHER WIRTSCHAFTSANZEIGER**
AGPOL–Polexportpress

Poland – English/French/German/Russian fortnightly 1970 4pp US$2 one issue US$43 per edition

Latest news concerning Polish foreign trade, recently signed contracts and negotiations.

28022 **POLISH ENGINEERING/ ENGINEERING POLONAIS/ POLNISCHES ENGINEERING**
AGPOL–Polexportpress

Poland – English/French/German/Russian bi-monthly 1970 44pp US$1.80 per issue US$10 p.a.
ISSN No. 0209-0260 English, 0209-0287 French, 0209-0279 German

Production, industry and exports.

28023 **POLISH FOREIGN TRADE**
Collets Holdings Ltd

Poland – English/French/Spanish/German/ Russian monthly/quarterly 1949 40pp £6.00

Articles on Polish international trade, industries, new products, new items.

28024 **POLISH MARITIME NEWS**
Collets Holdings Ltd

Poland – English monthly £13.50

28025 **POLISH TRADE MAGAZINE (MAGAZINE COMMERCIAL POLONAIS)**
AGPOL–Polexportpress

Poland – English/German/French quarterly 1982 44pp US$1.80 each US$7.20 p.a.
ISSN No. 0239 989X/0239-9903/0239-9873

Polish foreign trade covering consumer goods, services and cooperation.

28026 **PRACE INSTYTUTU KRAJOWYCH WLOKIEN NATURALNYCH**
Institute of Natural Fibres

Poland – Polish irregular 1945 200pp Zl1000 per issue

Research articles in the field of natural fibres.

28027 **PRZEDSIEBIORSTWO I RYNEK**
Instytut Rynku Wewnetrznego I Konsumpcji (Institute of Home Market and Consumption)

Poland – Polish quarterly 1983 120pp Zl250 each

Economics, economic reform, marketing and markets.

28028 **PRZEGLAD ZACHODNIOPOMORSKI (West-Pomeranian Review)**
University of Szczecin

Poland – Polish quarterly 1957 220pp
ISSN No. 0552-4245

Economic and social problems concerning the region of the Odra and Nysa river.

28029 **ROCZNIK STATYSTYCZNY**
Glowny Urzad Statystyczny

Poland – Polish annual c550pp

Detailed statistics on all aspects of life in Poland.

28030 **ROCZNIK STATYSTYCZNY HANDLU ZAGRANICZNEGO**
Glowny Urzad Statystyczny

Poland – Polish/Russian/English text in Polish annual 340pp Zl21,300

Statistics on the external trade of Poland including imports and exports by product group/country and import and exports country/product group.

28031 **ROCZNIK STATYSTYCZNY PRZERNYSLU**
Glowny Urzad Statystyczny

Poland – Polish annual 340pp Zl21,330

Yearbook of industrial statistics.

28032 **RYNKI ZAGRANICZNE**
Polish Chamber of Foreign Trade

Poland – Polish three times a week 7.4.1957 8pp Zl77
ISSN No. 35039

Information on foreign trade and the world economy.

28033 **TECKNIKA I GOSPODARKA MORSKA (SHIPPING SUMMARIES)**
Collets Holdings Ltd

Poland – English monthly £63.00

28034 **ZESZYTY NAUKOWE UNIWERSYTETU SZCZECINSKIEGO**
University of Szczecin

Poland – Polish irregular 1985 150-200pp

Economic problems of transport, industries and enterprises.

PORTUGAL

29001 **THE 1000 LARGEST COMPANIES OF PORTUGAL**
Oporto Chamber of Commerce and Industry–Oporto Commercial Association

Portugal – Portuguese/English annual 1985 200pp free

Economic data about the largest Portuguese companies.

29002 **ABECOR COUNTRY REPORT – PORTUGAL**
Abecor

Portugal – English 1981 2pp free

Brief economic report.

29003 **AGRA EUROPE SPECIAL REPORT NO.29–PORTUGUESE AGRICULTURE AFTER ACCESSION**
Agra Europe (London) Ltd

Portugal – English occasional 63pp £48

Surveys agriculture in Portugal, the accession arrangements for Portugal to the EC, the effect of accession on each agricultural sector, and the Portuguese food industry.

29004 **ANNUAL REPORT–EFTA INDUSTRIAL DEVELOPMENT FUND FOR PORTUGAL**
European Free Trade Association (EFTA)

Portugal – Portuguese/English annual since 1979 free
ISSN. No. 1011-3657 (Portuguese) 1011-3711 (English)

29005 **ANUARIO ESTATISTICO**
Instituto Nacional de Estatistica

Portugal – Portuguese/French annual Esc1500

Statistics on climate, labour, demography, education, social security, culture and recreation, living conditions, salaries and prices, finance both public and private, tourism, trade both foreign and domestic, mining and manufacturing, energy, construction, transport and communications.

29006 **BALANCOS DE APROVISIONAMENTO**
Instituto Nacional de Estatistica

Portugal – Portuguese irregular 1987 Esc100
ISBN/ISSN No. 0870-4420

Provisional information about agriculture.

29007 **BOLETIM ANIMEE**
Associacao Nacional dos Industriais de Material Electrico e Electronico (ANIMEE)

Portugal – Portuguese monthly 1976 (June) 52/56pp free
ISSN No. 0870-2829

General information about the enterprises of the sector, economics, technology, statistics, legislation etc.

29008 **BOLETIM MENSAL DAS ESTATISTICAS DO COMERCIO EXTERNO**
Instituto Nacional de Estatistica

Portugal – Portuguese/French Esc5000 p.a.

Monthly statistical bulletin on foreign trade.

29009 **BOLETIM MENSAL DE ESTATISTICA**
Instituto Nacional de Estatistica

Portugal – Portuguese/French monthly Esc7500 p.a.

Monthly statistical bulletin covering all aspects of economic, social and political life.

29010 **BOLETIM TRIMESTRAL***
Banco Nacional Ultramarino

Portugal – Portuguese quarterly c140pp

Economic review with emphasis on finance.

29011 **BOLETIM TRIMESTRAL/ QUARTERLY BULLETIN (BANCO DE PORTUGAL)**
Banco de Portugal

Portugal – Portuguese/English quarterly 160pp

Statistics on money, finance, exchange rates, output and employment.

29012 **BUSINESS AND ECONOMIC NEWS***
Septibel

Portugal – English quarterly c25pp Esc400 US$12.00

Brief commercial news

29013 **COMERCIO EXTERNO PORTUGUES**
Instituto do Comercio Externo de Portugal

Portugal – Portuguese annual 107pp

Detailed statistical survey of Portuguese trade by country and within each country by product.

29014 **COMERCIO EXTERNO PORTUGUES**
Instituto do Comercio Externo de Portugal

Portugal – Portuguese quarterly 18pp

Detailed statistical survey of Portuguese trade by country and by product.

29015 **CONTAS NACIONAIS**
Instituto Nacional de Estatistica

Portugal – Portuguese annual Esc320
ISSN No. 0870-2659

Data on national accounts.

29016 **COUNTRY PROFILE–PORTUGAL**
British Overseas Trade Board

Portugal – English occasional 68pp

An overview of the social, political and economic situation in Portugal with sections on UK trade, Portuguese trade, new opportunities for trade. The second half concentrates on doing business with Portugal, export conditions, marketing methods, investment, living and working in Portugal, travel and a list of useful addresses.

29017 **COUNTRY PROFILES**
Economist Publications Ltd

Portugal – English annual 40pp £25 UK subscription varies in rest of world.

Resumé of politics, economy and industry including statistical summaries.

29018 **COUNTRY REPORTS**
Economist Publications Ltd

Portugal – English quarterly 25pp £58 UK subscription varies in rest of world

Economic policies and development plans, trends in production and demand, monetary and fiscal conditions, wages and prices, merchandise trade, invisibles, capital flows, exchange rates and foreign debt plus a forecast of the economic prospects.

29019 DOING BUSINESS IN PORTUGAL
Price Waterhouse

Portugal – English occasional 40pp

Data on exchange controls and foreign investment, regulating agencies, investment incentives, banking, exporting to Portugal, types of business, labour relations and the tax system.

29020 EFTA INDUSTRIAL DEVELOPMENT FUND FOR PORTUGAL
European Free Trade Association (EFTA)

Portugal – Portuguese/English irregular free

Leaflet giving summarized information on the Fund and including some statistical data.

29021 ESTATISTICAS AGRICOLAS
Instituto Nacional de Estatistica

Portugal – Portuguese/French annual 160pp Esc962

Statistics on all aspects of agriculture including production, consumption, distribution, salaries and prices.

29022 ESTATISTICAS DO COMERCIO EXTERNO
Instituto Nacional de Estatistica

Portugal – Portuguese/French annual Esc1760

Statistics on foreign trade.

29023 ESTATISTICAS DA CONSTRUCAO E DA HABITACHO
Instituto Nacional de Estatistica

Portugal – Portuguese/French annual 112pp Esc675

Statistics on construction and housing.

29024 ESTATISTICAS DAS CONTRIBICOES E IMPOSTOS
Instituto Nacional de Estatistica

Portugal – Portuguese/French annual 175pp Esc825

Statistics on taxation.

29025 ESTATISTICA DEMOGRAFICAS
Instituto Nacional de Estatistica

Portugal – Portuguese annual 235pp Esc1100

Demographic statistics including details of births, deaths and marriages and population mobility.

29026 ESTATISTICAS DA ENERGIA
Instituto Nacional de Estatistica

Portugal – Portuguese/French annual 78pp Esc480

Statistics on the production, consumption, distribution and national balances of energy.

29027 ESTATISTICAS DAS FINANCAS PUBLICAS
Instituto Nacional de Estatistica

Portugal – Portuguese annual 203pp Esc1280

Statistics on government finance both national, regional and local.

29028 ESTATISTICAS INDUSTRIAS
Instituto Nacional de Estatistica

Portugal – Portuguese annual 2 vols vol.1 Esc480 vol.2 Esc3450

Statistics on industry. Vol.1 covers mining, electricity, gas and water. Vol.2 covers manufacturing industries.

29029 ESTATISTICAS MONETARIAS E FINANCEIRAS
Instituto Nacional de Estatistica

Portugal – Portuguese annual Esc880

Statistics on commerce, finance and monetary trends.

29030 ESTATISTICAS DA PESCA
Instituto Nacional de Estatistica

Portugal – Portuguese annual Esc320

Statistics on fishing covering yield, consumption, prices, financial structure including data on related industries.

29031 ESTATISTICAS DE PROTECCAO SOCIAL, ASSOCIACOES SINDICAIS E PATRONAIS
Instituto Nacional de Estatistica

Portugal – Portuguese annual Esc680

Social security statistics.

29032 ESTATISTICAS DOS SALARIOS
Instituto Nacional de Estatistica

Portugal – Portuguese annual 1980 Esc675
ISSN No. 0870-4325

Statistics on wages.

29033 ESTATISTICAS DOS SALARIOS
Instituto Nacional de Estatistica

Portugal – Portuguese irregular 1987 Esc50
ISSN No. 0870-4414

Data on employment, wages and hours of work.

29034 ESTATISTICAS DAS SOCIEDADES
Instituto Nacional de Estatistica

Portugal – Portuguese irregular 85pp Esc480

Statistics on companies both public and private classified by region and activity including details of those operating in the Azores and Madeira.

29035 ESTATISTICAS DOS TRANSPORTES E COMUNICACOES
Instituto Nacional de Estatistica

Portugal – Portuguese/French annual 180pp Esc 1200

Statistics on land, sea and air transport, both domestic and external and other communications.

29036 ESTATISTICAS DO TURISMO
Instituto Nacional de Estatistica

Portugal – Portuguese/English annual 260pp Esc1360

Tourism statistics.

29037 FOREIGN ECONOMIC TRENDS AND THEIR IMPLICATIONS FOR THE UNITED STATES–PORTUGAL
US Department of Commerce

Portugal – English annual 11pp US$1.00

Data on key economic indicators followed by a survey of the economy including a forecast for the long-term economic outlook with particular reference to US–Portuguese trade.

29038 HINTS TO EXPORTERS
Department of Trade and Industry

Portugal, Madeira and Azores – English annual

Practical guide for businessmen giving general information, useful addresses, methods of doing business and relevant regulations.

29039 INDICADORES ECONOMICOS/ ECONOMIC INDICATORS
Banco de Portugal

Portugal – Portuguese/English annual 20pp

Data for the past 6 years on areas such as production, national accounts, foreign trade.

29040 INDICE DE PRECOS NO CONSUMIDOR
Instituto Nacional de Estatistica

Portugal – Portuguese monthly Esc1800

Detailed statistics and analysis of consumer price indices.

29041 INDICES DE PRODUCAO INDUSTRIAL
Instituto Nacional de Estatistica

Portugal – Portuguese monthly 10pp Esc45

Indices of industrial production.

29042 **INQUERITO AO EMPREGO**
Instituto Nacional de Estatistica

Portugal–Portuguese quarterly Esc2000

Labour survey giving data on employment and working population by age, occupation etc.

29043 **INQUERITO AO EMPREGO: INFORMACAO ANTECIPADA**
Instituto Nacional de Estatistica

Portugal – Portuguese quarterly 1983 Esc300

Advance data on employment, unemployment and working population by occupation.

29044 **INQUERITO MENSAL DE CONJUNTURA A INDUSTRIA TRANSFORMADORA**
Instituto Nacional de Estatistica

Portugal – Portuguese monthly 1987 Esc1800
ISSN No 0870 - 4392

Data on processing industries, production of consumer goods, intermediate goods and investment goods.

29045 **INQUIRITO MENSAL DE CONJUNTURA A INDUSTRIA TRANSFORMADORA**
Instituto Nacional de Estatistica

Portugal – Portuguese bi-annual 1987 100pp Esc1200 in Portugal Esc1500 overseas

Contains a section on statistical methodology followed by a survey of Portuguese industrial production for the half year. The bulk of the journal is made up of monthly data of industrial production, consumption and investment.

29046 **INQUIRITO MENSAL DE CONJUNTURA INDUSTRIA TRANSFORMADORA**
Instituto Nacional de Estatistica

Portugal – Portuguese monthly 6pp Esc30

Main industrial indicators in graphic and tabular form.

29047 **INQUERITO AO TRANSPORTE RODOVIARIO DE MERCADORIAS 1983**
Instituto Nacional de Estatistica

Portugal – Portuguese irregular Esc1000
ISSN No 0870-2586

Data on the road haulage industry.

29048 **INQUERITO TRIMESTRAL DE CONJUNCTURA AO COMERCIO**
Instituto Nacional de Estatistica

Portugal – Portuguese quarterly 1974 Esc1000
ISSN No. 0377-2373

Data on wholesale and retail trade.

29049 **INQUIRITO TRIMESTRAL DE CONJUNTURA AO COMERCIO**
Instituto Nacional de Estatistica

Portugal – Portuguese quarterly 48pp Esc600

29050 **LANDERBERICHT PORTUGAL**
Federal Statistical Office of Germany

Portugal – German irregular DM7.90

Statistical survey of Portugal including demography, geography, education, employment, agriculture, production, overseas trade, transport, tourism, finance, wages and prices and national accounts.

29051 **MONTHLY BULLETIN–BOLSA DE VALORES DE LISBOA**
Bolsa de Valores de Lisboa

Portugal – Portuguese monthly Esc30

Monthly bulletin of the Lisbon Stock exchange.

29052 **NEWSLETTER OF THE PORTUGUESE INDUSTRIAL ASSOCIATION***
Associacao Industrial Portuguesa

Portugal – English frequent c8pp free

Brief news of current economic developments.

29053 **OECD ECONOMIC SURVEYS–PORTUGAL**
Organisation for Economic Cooperation and Development (OECD)

Portugal – English annual 70pp £2.40/ DM12/US$5/FrF24

A detailed analysis of recent developments in demand production, employment, prices and wages, conditions in the money and capital markets and developments in the balance of payments. It includes short-term forecasts as well as analyses of medium-term problems of specific relevance to the elaboration of the country's economic policies.

29054 **O TURISMO EM**
Direccao Geral do Turismo

Portugal – Portuguese annual 1970 300pp Esc500

Statistics on tourism in Portugal covering hotels, camping, restaurants etc.

29055 **O TURISMO ESTRANGEIRO EM PORTUGAL**
Direccao Geral do Turismo

Portugal – Portuguese annual 190pp Esc500

Statistics on tourism in Portugal giving data on country of origin of tourists, regions visited etc.

29056 **PORTUGAL**
Instituto Nacional de Estatistica

Portugal – Portuguese/English annual 1969 Esc140
ISSN No. 0777-2470

A statistical summary.

29057 **PORTUGAL CONTINENTO: INQUIRITO DO EMPREGO**
Instituto Nacional de Estatistica

Portugal – Portuguese quarterly 72pp Esc300

Statistical data on employment and unemployment.

29058 **THE PORTUGUESE ECONOMY***
Banca Totta e Acores, UK

Portugal – English bi-monthly c4pp free

Newsletter published by the London branch of the bank with sections on the economy, industry, prices, wages, employment, money and banking, trade.

29059 **RECENSEAMENTO DAS EMPRESAS DO SECTOR DOS TRANSPORTES 1982**
Instituto Nacional de Estatistica

Portugal – Portuguese irregular Esc1500
ISSN No. 0870-4317

Census of companies in the transport sector.

29060 **RECENSEAMENTO INDUSTRIAL**
Instituto Nacional de Estatistica

Portugal – Portuguese Esc250/280

Results of the 1984 census of industrial establishments giving information on numbers, value added, turnover, investment, expenditure, energy consumption, wages analysed by size of enterprise, region and type of activity.

29061 **RECENSEAMENTO DA POPULACAO E DA HABITACAO**
Instituto Nacional de Estatistica

Portugal – Portuguese various volumes Esc200-600
ISSN No. 0377-2454

Results of the 1981 census.

29062 **RELATORIO–BOLSA DE VALORES DE LISBOA**
Bolsa de Valores de Lisboa

Portugal – Portuguese/English annual 170pp Esc2500

Annual report of the Lisbon Stock Exchange containing detailed statistics of stock market transactions.

29063 **REPORT OF THE BOARD OF DIRECTORS (BANCO DE PORTUGAL)**
Banco de Portugal

Portugal – Portuguese/English annual c250pp free

Annual report including a detailed economic and financial survey with statistics on output, wages, employment, prices, foreign trade, balance of payments.

29064 **SINTESE MENSAL DA CONJUNTURA**
Banco de Portugal

Portugal – Portuguese monthly 60pp

Statistics on production, balance of payments and financial markets.

29065 **SITUACACO ECONOMICA NACIONAL**
Instituto de Analise da Conjunctura e Estudos de Planeconento

Portugal – Portuguese quarterly 120pp

Articles on various aspects of the Portuguese economy of industrial production, energy consumption, investment, consumption, wages and salaries etc. Plus a statistical annexe containing basic economic data.

29066 **STATISTICAL INFORMATION ON THE SECURITIES MARKET**
Bolsa de Valores de Lisboa

Portugal – Portuguese monthly Esc750

ROMANIA

30001 **ABECOR COUNTRY REPORT – ROMANIA**
Abecor

Romania – English 1981 2pp free

Brief economic report.

30002 **ANNUAL REPORT ANGLO-ROMANIAN BANK**
Anglo-Romanian Bank Limited

Romania – English annual 1974 12pp free

Anglo-Romanian Bank activity and results.

30003 **ANUARUL STATISTIC AL REPUBLICII SOCIALISTE ROMANIA**
Directia Centrala de Statistica

Romania – Romanian annual 400pp

Statistics on population, geography, economic indicators, labour force, industry, agriculture, investment, building, transport, domestic and foreign trade, budget, education, culture, health, services with comparative international data.

30004 **COUNTRY PROFILES–ROMANIA, BULGARIA, ALBANIA**
Economist Publications Ltd

Romania, Bulgaria, Albania – English annual 40pp £25 UK subscription varies in rest of world

Resumé of politics, economy and industry including statistical summaries.

30005 **COUNTRY REPORTS–ROMANIA, BULGARIA, ALBANIA**
Economist Publications Ltd

Romania, Bulgaria, Albania – English quarterly 25pp £58 UK subscription varies in rest of world

Economic policies and development plans, trends in production and demand, monetary and fiscal conditions, wages and prices, merchandise trade, invisibles, capital flows, exchange rates and foreign debt plus a forecast of the economic prospects.

30006 **ECONOMIC AND COMMERCIAL GUIDE TO ROMANIA**
Chamber of Commerce and Industry

Romania – French/English/German/Spanish 1988

General survey of the economic and commercial conditions in Romania.

30007 **FOREIGN ECONOMIC TRENDS AND THEIR IMPLICATIONS FOR THE UNITED STATES–ROMANIA**
US Department of Commerce

Romania – English irregular 12pp US$1.00

Data on key economic indicators followed by a survey of the economy including a forecast for the long-term economic outlook with particular reference to prospects for the Romanian trade.

30008 **FORESTA**
Chamber of Commerce and Industry

Romania – English/French/Russian/German/Spanish quarterly

Wood, furniture and building materials of wood.

30009 **HINTS TO EXPORTERS**
Department of Trade and Industry

Romania – English annual

Practical guide for businessmen giving general information, useful addresses, methods of doing business and relevant regulations.

30010 **LANDERBERICHT RUMANIEN**
Statistisches Bundesamt

Romania – German irregular 85pp DM7.90

Statistical survey of Romania covering demography, education, employment, agriculture, manufacturing, overseas trade, transport, tourism, finance, wages and prices, national accounts, balance of payments and economic planning. Time series data is included for about 10 years.

30011 **ROMANIA: A GEOGRAPHICAL OUTLINE**
Scientific & Encyclopaedic Publishing House

Romania – English irregular 200pp

Besides giving information on the geography of Romania also includes data on the economy, transport, trade and tourism.

30012 **ROMANIA AT A GLANCE**
Chamber of Commerce and Industry

Romania – French/English/German/Spanish 1987

[illegible] economic and business information of use to the foreign businessman.

30013 **ROMANIA: ESSENTIAL INFORMATION**
Scientific & Encyclopaedic Publishing House

Romania – English irregular 41pp

A booklet giving basic information on the country including population, history and the economy.

30014 **ROMANIA YEAR BOOK**
Scientific & Encyclopaedic Publishing House

Romania – English 1977 251pp free

Chronology of the year's events including survey of the economy with retrospective comparative statistics to 1950.

30015 **ROMANIAN CHEMISTRY**
Chamber of Commerce and Industry

Romania – English/French/Russian/German/Spanish quarterly

All aspects of the Romanian chemical industry.

30016 **ROMANIAN ENGINEERING**
Chamber of Commerce and Industry

Romania – English/French/Russian/German/Spanish quarterly

Information on the Romanian mechanical, electrical and electronic engineering industries.

30017 **ROMANIAN FOREIGN TRADE**
Chamber of Commerce and Industry

Romania – English quarterly 50pp

Trade news including legislation and regulations relevant to foreign trade.

30018 **SCIENTIFIC ANNALS OF THE 'AL I CUZA' UNIVERSITY OF IASI SECTION III C ECONOMIC SCIENCES**
Universitatea 'Al i Cuza' Iasi

Romania – Romanian with summaries in foreign languages annual 1955 104pp Lei35

Economic thought, macroeconomics, perfection of the economic financial mechanism, microeconomics, notes and commentary, book reviews.

30019 TRADING WITH ROMANIA
Department of Trade and Industry

Romania – English irregular 16pp free

How to do business with Romania including organization of industry and foreign trade, manufacturing under licence, joint companies, counter trade, how to approach the market, visits, price quotations and terms of payment, commercial debts, advertising, exhibitions and trade fairs, lectures, trade missions, patents and trade marks. Includes a detailed survey of UK-Romanian trade.

30020 YOUR COMMERCIAL PARTNER IN ROMANIA
Chamber of Commerce and Industry

Romania – French/English/German/Spanish 1988

A directory of all foreign trade enterprises.

SOVIET UNION

31001 **ABECOR COUNTRY REPORT – USSR**
Abecor

USSR – English 1987 2pp free

Brief economic report.

31002 **ANNUAL REPORT – INTERNATIONAL INVESTMENT BANK**
International Investment Bank

USSR – English annual 1971 16pp

31003 **ANNUAL REPORT – MOSCOW NARODNY BANK***
Moscow Narodny Bank

USSR – English annual c14pp

31004 **AZERBAIDJANSKOE NEFTIANOE HOZIAISTVO**
V/o Mezhdunarodnya Kniga

USSR – Russian/Azerbaijani monthly Rub25.80

The Azerbaijan oil industry.

31005 **COUNTRY PROFILES – USSR**
Economist Publications Ltd

USSR – English annual 40pp £25 UK subscription varies in rest of world

Resumé of politics, economy and industry including statistical summaries.

31006 **COUNTRY REPORTS–USSR**
Economist Publications Ltd

USSR – English quarterly 25pp £58 UK subscription varies in rest of world

Economic policies and development plans, trends in production and demand, monetary and fiscal conditions, wages and prices, merchandise trade, invisibles, capital flows, exchange rates and foreign debt plus a forecast of the economic prospects.

31007 **DENJGI I KREDIT**
V/o Mezhdunarodnya kniga

USSR – Russian monthly Rub24.60

Covers finance and credit.

31008 **ECOTAS–THE ECONOMIC AND COMMERCIAL BULLETIN OF THE SOVIET NEWS AGENCY TASS**
Pergamon Press plc

USSR – English/French/Italian/German weekly DM1020 per year

A selection of news items covering economic development in the USSR, new contracts with foreign countries, foreign economic relations of socialist countries and new technological developments.

31009 **EKONOMIKA I ORGANIZACIA PROMYSHLENNOGO PROIZVODSTVA**
V/o Mezhdunarodnya Kniga

USSR – Russian monthly Rub50.40

The economics and organization of industrial production.

31010 **EKONOMIKA SELJSKOHOZIAISTVENNYH I PERERABATYVAIUSCIH PREDPRIIATIJ**
V/o Mezhdunarodnya Kniga

USSR – Russian monthly Rub 28.80

The economics of agricultural and agriproduct processing enterprises.

31011 **ECONOMIKA SOVETSKOI UKRAINY**
V/o Mezhdunarodnya Kniga

USSR – Russian monthly Rub19.30

The economy of Soviet Ukraine.

31012 **EKONOMIKA STROITELJSTVA**
V/o Mezhdunarodnya Kniga

USSR – Russian monthly Rub28.80

Construction economics.

31013 **ELEKTRICHESKIE STANTCII**
Available from V/o Mezhdunarodnya Kniga

USSR – Russian monthly Rub49.20

'Power plants'–technical journal covering the practical aspects of power stations. Major topics are: the economy, design and planning of power production, relevant technology and comparative reviews of the efficiency of extant power plants.

31014 **ELEKTRICHESTVO**
available from V/o Mezhdunarodnya Kniga

USSR – Russian monthly Rub49.20

'Electricity'–journal of the electrical industry covering new research, technological developments.

31015 **ENERGIA: EKONOMIKA, TEHNIKA, EKOLOGIA**
V/o Mezhdunarodnya Kniga

USSR – Russian monthly Rub24.00

Economic, technological and ecological aspects of energy.

31016 **FINANSY SSSR**
V/o Mezhdunarodnya Kniga

USSR – Russian monthly Rub25.80

Finances of the USSR.

31017 **FOREIGN ECONOMIC TRENDS AND THEIR IMPLICATIONS FOR THE US**
US Department of Commerce

USSR – English annual 15pp US$1.00

31018 **FOREIGN TRADE**
V/o Mezhdunarodnya Kniga

USSR – English/Russian/French/German/Spanish/Hungarian monthly 40pp £27.50

The official journal of the USSR Ministry of Foreign Trade, covering trade and political relations with other countries as well as international trade.

31019 **FOREIGN TRADE OF THE USSR***
Ministry of Foreign Trade available from Central Statistical Department

USSR – Russian annual c600pp

31020 **GAZOVAIA PROMYSHLENNOSTJ**
V/o Mezhdunarodnya Kniga

USSR – Russian monthly Rub31.20

The gas industry.

31021 **HIMIAI TEHNOLOGIA TOPLIV I MASEL**
Available from V/o Mezhdunarodnya Kniga

USSR – Russian monthly Rub31.80

'Chemistry and Technology of Fuels and Oils' –economics and technology of the oil-refining and petro-chemical industries.

31022 **HIMICHESKAIA PROMYSHLENNOSTJ**
V/o Mezhdunarodnya Kniga

USSR – Russian monthly Rub49.20

The chemical industry.

31023 **HIMICHESKIE VOLOKNA**
Available from V/o Mezhdunarodnya Kniga

USSR – Russian bi-monthly Rub 25.80

'Chemical Fibres'–technology and economics of the production of chemical fibres and their applications.

31024 **HINTS TO EXPORTERS**
Department of Trade and Industry

USSR – English annual

Practical guide for businessmen giving general information, useful addresses, methods of doing business and relevant regulations.

31025 **HOW TO DO BUSINESS WITH THE RUSSIANS**
Quorum Books

USSR – English 1987 311pp £40.00

A handbook and guide for western business people. Part 1–trading with the Soviet Union, how it operates. Part 2–the structure of Soviet foreign trade operations and orders of a business transaction. Statistical appendices containing basic economic data of production, trade, demography.

31026 **INFORMATION MOSCOW**
Information Moscow

USSR – English every 6 months 268pp £6

Directory of useful addresses including government departments, foreign trade organizations, restaurants, hotels and shops, services, travel organizations, diplomatic and consular representatives, foreign business representatives in Moscow and throughout the USSR.

31027 **THE JOURNAL OF THE BRITISH SOVIET CHAMBER OF COMMERCE**
British Soviet Chamber of Commerce

USSR – English irregular 44pp

Articles concerning USSR/UK trade relations in general and individual contracts.

31028 **KOJEVENNO OBUVNAIA PROMYSHLENNOSTJ**
V/o Mezhunarodnya Kniga

USSR – Russian monthly Rub24.60

The tanning and footwear industry.

31029 **KOMMERCHESKIJ VESTNIK**
Available from V/o Mezhdunarodnya Kniga

USSR – Russian bi-monthly Rub34.80

'Bulletin of Commerce'–official journal of the Ministry of Trade providing information on the consumer goods market, supply-and-demand, marketing with particular emphasis on advertising.

31030 **LANDERBERICHT SOWJETUNION**
Federal Statistical Office of Germany

USSR – German irregular DM7.90

Statistical survey of USSR including demography, geography, education, employment, agriculture, production, overseas trade, transport, tourism, finance, wages and prices and national accounts.

31031 **LESNAIA PROMYSHLENNOSTJ**
Available from V/o Mezhdunarodnya Kniga

USSR – Russian Rub28.80

'Timber industry'–reports on the scientific, technical and economic aspects of the following branches of the timber industry: logging, timber rafting, sawing, primary timber processing, construction of timber complexes and forest roads.

31032 **METALLURG**
Available from V/o Mezhdunarodnya Kniga

USSR – Russian monthly Rub19.30

'Metallurgist'–covers both foreign and Soviet achievements in iron and steel production.

31033 **MOLOCHNAIA I MIASNAIA A PROMYSHLENNOSTJ**
Available from V/o Mezhdunarodnya Kniga

USSR – Russian bi-monthly Rub12.00

'Dairy and Meat Products Industry'–the problems of the dairy and meat products industry, economics, equipment and mechanization of dairy production.

31034 **NARODNOE HOZIAISTVO BELORUSSII**
V/o Mezhdunarodnya Kniga

USSR – Russian monthly Rub 24.00

The national economy of Belorussia.

31035 **NARODNOE HOZIAISTVO KAZAHSTANA**
V/o Mezhdunarodnya Kniga

USSR – Russian monthly Rub 17.40

The national economy of Kazakhstan.

31036 **NEFTIANAIA I GAZOVAIA PROMYSHLENNOSTJ**
V/o Mezhdunarodnya Kniga

USSR – Russian quarterly Rub11.60

The oil and gas industry.

31037 **NOVYE TOVARY**
Available from V/o Mezhdunarodnya Kniga

USSR – Russian monthly Rub30.60

'New goods'–official journal of the Ministry of Trade which gives details of new products.

31038 **PISCEVAIA PROMYSHLENNOSTJ**
V/o Mezhdunarodnya Kniga

USSR – Russian monthly/quarterly Rub24.00 (monthly) Rub13.80 (quarterly)

The food industry.

31039 **PROSPECTS FOR SOVIET AGRICULTURAL PRODUCTION AND TRADE**
Organisation for Economic Cooperation and Development (OECD)

USSR – English/French 1983 118pp

Report with special reference to meat and grain. An outlook on agricultural developments to 1990.

31040 **A REPORT ON AGRICULTURE AND THE 1990 TARGETS FOR AGRICULTURAL PRODUCTION IN THE USSR**
British Agricultural Export Council

USSR – English 1985 55pp £25

Agriculture, crop production, livestock production, agricultural equipment and inputs.

31041 **RYBNOYE HOZIAISTVO**
Available from V/o Mezhdunarodnya Kniga

USSR – Russian monthly Rub28.80

'Fish Industry'–covers fish stocks, operations of fishing fleets, technological equipment, fish processing, organization of production.

31042 **SCIENCE AND TECHNOLOGY IN THE USSR**
Longman Group

USSR – English irregular 1987 400pp £63
ISSN No. 0582 900530

Information on organizations and research and development programmes in the USSR. Part 1 describes the background to Soviet science and technology and Part 2 consists of surveys of major fields such as energy, computers, biotechnology and transport giving details of research programmes and organizations.

31043 **SHVEINAIA PROMYSHLENNOSTJ**
Available from V/o Mezhdunarodnya Kniga

USSR – Russian bi-monthly Rub 14.40

'Clothing industry'–economics and technological developments in the industry, labour and production organizations.

31044 **SOVETSKAIA TORGOVLIA**
Available from V/o Mezhdunarodnya Kniga

USSR–Russian Rub28.80

'Soviet Trade' – report on domestic trade networks, marketing and personnel training for distribution.

31045 **SOVIET EXPORT**
V/o Vneshtorgreklama

USSR – Englsh/Russian/Czech/Finnish/French/German/Hungarian/Polish/Spanish bi-monthly 1957 60pp
ISSN No. 0201 4505

General articles on foreign trade, companies, industries.

31046 **SOVIET GROSS NATIONAL PRODUCT IN CURRENT PRICES, 1960-1980**
Central Intelligence Agency

USSR – English 1983 24pp

Detailed coverage of Soviet GNP by end use, type of income, sector and growth rate.

31047 **SOVIET NEWS***
Soviet Embassy, UK

USSR – English weekly c8pp

Brief news giving information on world events relative to the USSR.

31048 **SOVIET STATISTICS ON CAPITAL FORMATION**
Central Intelligence Agency

USSR – English 1982 16pp

Compilation of statistics on fixed capital assets and capital investment.

31049 **SOVIET WEEKLY***
Soviet Weekly

USSR – English weekly 16pp £6.50

Newspaper giving information on Soviet industry, economy and international relations.

31050 **STALJ**
Available from V/o Mezhdunarodnya Kniga

USSR – Russian monthly Rub33

'Steel'– all aspects of the steel industry including comparative international developments.

31051 **STANKI I INSTRUMENTY**
Available from V/o Mezhdunarodnya Kniga

USSR – Russian monthly Rub26.40

'Machines and Tools'–reports on research and technological developments.

31052 **STATISTICS RELATING TO TRADE BETWEEN THE UNITED KINGDOM AND THE USSR**
British Soviet Chamber of Commerce

USSR – English annual 20pp

Detailed statistics of products exported from the UK to the USSR and imported into the UK from the USSR.

31053 **SUDOSTROIENIE**
Available from V/o Mezhdunarodnya Kniga

USSR – Russian monthly Rub39.00

Technical journal of the ship-building industry covering ship design, ship equipment, automatic devices, electronic equipment, navigation instruments, general review of the structure, economics and organization of the industry.

31054 **TEKSTILJNAIA PROMYSHLENNOSTJ**
Available from V/o Mezhdunarodnya Kniga

USSR – Russian monthly Rub31.80

'Textile Industry'–developments in all branches of the textile and knitting industries: production, variety and quality of output, raw materials, techniques, manufactured goods, dyeing and finishing.

31055 **TORFIANAIA PROMYSHLENNOSTJ**
Available from V/o Mezhdunarodnya Kniga

USSR – Russian monthly Rub23.40

'Peat Industry'–reports on new trends, the use of peat in power engineering, agriculture and construction.

31056 **TORGOVLIA ZA RUBEJOM**
V/o Mezhdunarodnya Kniga

USSR – Russian monthly

Foreign trade.

31057 **TRAKTORY I SELJSKOHOZIAISTVENNYE MASHINY**
Available from V/o Mezhdunarodnya Kniga

USSR – Russian monthly Rub 25.30

'Tractors and Farm Machines'–theory, design and testing of new machinery with general information on the technology, economics and production of the industry.

31058 **UGOLJ**
Available from V/o Mezhdunarodnya Kniga

USSR – Russian monthly Rub36

'Coal'–technical equipment in the coal industry, research, practical application of scientific discoveries, the economics and organization of production and labour.

31059 **USSR FACTS AND FIGURES ANNUAL**
Academic International Press

USSR – English annual

Statistical survey of the USSR covering governmnt, foreign affairs, demography, armed forces, the economy, energy industry, agriculture, foreign trade and aid, science, transport, health and welfare, regional statistics.

31060 **USSR IN FIGURES***
Central Statistical Department

USSR – Russian/English annual c220pp

Pocket-sized book containing statistical information on the economic and social development of the USSR. The topics covered are: population and territory; summary indicators; science and technology; industry; agriculture; transport and communications; capital construction; labour; welfare and incomes; services; education and culture. Some of the data is comparative with other socialist countries.

31061 **USSR TRADE MISSION REPORT**
Birmingham Chamber of Commerce, UK

USSR – English annual 12pp £3.50

31062 **VNESHNIAIA TORGOVLIA SSSR: PRILOJENIEK JURNALU 'VNESHNIAIA TORGOVLIA (GODOVOI STATISTICHESKIJ OBZOR)**
V/o Mezhdunarodnya Kniga

USSR – Russian annual Rub9.50

Annual statistical survey of foreign trade of the USSR which forms a supplement to the journal 'Foreign Trade'.

SPAIN

32001 **ABECOR COUNTRY REPORT – SPAIN**
Abecor

Spain – English 1987 2pp free

Brief economic report.

32002 **ACTIVIDADES DE LA BANCA PRIVADA**
Instituto Nacional de Estadistica

Spain – Spanish annual PTA450

Activity in the private banking sector.

32003 **AGRICULTURA**
Ministerio de Agricultura, Pesca y Alimentacion

Spain – Spanish monthly PTA2500

Information on the Spanish agricultural sector in the context of the domestic, European and international markets.

32004 **AGRICULTURA Y SOCIEDAD**
Ministerio de Agricultura, Pesca y Alimentacion

Spain – Spanish quarterly c300pp PTA3000

Journal containing articles on all aspects of agriculture.

32005 **AGRO EUROPA–AGRO EUROPE**
Informativos Agrarios SA

Spain – Spanish weekly 1986 PTA50,000 (plus VAT)

Cattle, food and agriculture both in Spain and the European Community.

32006 **ALIMENTEC**
Editorial Alimentec SA

Spain – Spanish monthly 1983 PTA4,000
ISSN No. 0212-6400

Aimed at retailers. The publication covers the food sector.

32007 **ANUARIO ESTADISTICA DE ESPANA EDICION MANUAL**
Instituto Nacional de Estadistica

Spain – Spanish annual PTA1750

Pocket version of the statistical handbook.

32008 **ANNUAL REPORT ASOCIATION ESPANOLA DE BANCA PRIVADA**

Spain – Spanish annual 1979 80pp free

Covers legal, labour, economic, tax and international matters, banking in general.

32009 **ANUARIO DE ESTADISTICA AGRARIA**
Ministerio de Agricultura, Pesca y Alimentacion

Spain – Spanish annual c630pp PTA2,700

Annual agricultural statistics including comparative statistics with previous years and other countries. Data covers land distribution, agricultural production, forestry, livestock, prices, finance and trade.

32010 **ANUARIO DE ESTUDIOS COOPERATIVOS**
Universidad de Deusto

Spain – Spanish annual 1985 280pp PTA850
ISSN No. 84-7485-063-0

The cooperative phenomenon and its roots in the Basque society.

32011 **ANUARIO ESTADISTICO DE ESPANA–EDICION EXTENSA**
Instituto Nacional de Estadistica

Spain – Spanish annual c930pp PTA2,500

Comprehensive statistical yearbook.

32012 **ANUARIO DE ESTADISTICAS DE TURISMO**
Ministerio de Transportes, Turismo y Communicaciones

Spain – Spanish annual 490pp

Data on all aspects of tourism with retrospective information covering a ten-year time span.

32013 **ANUARIO HORTOFRUTICOLA ESPANOL–SPANISH HORTICULTURAL AND FRUIT GROWING YEARBOOK**
Sucro SA

Spain – Spanish annual 1967 PTA5,000

Spanish exports and European imports of fruit and horticultural products. It also includes a directory of Spanish exporters and European importers.

32014 **ARAL**
Tecnipublicaciones SA

Spain – Spanish weekly 1967 PTA13,500

Food and drink trade including imports, prices and suppliers.

32015 **BALANZA DE PAGOS DE ESPANA***
Ministerio de Comercio

Spanish – Spanish annual PTA350

Official report on the balance of payments including comparative data for preceding years.

32016 **BOLETIN ECONOMICO**
Banco de Espana

Spain – Spanish monthly PTA25,000

Economics.

32017 **BOLETIN ECONOMICO DE INFORMACION COMERCIAL ESPANOLA**
Ministerio de Economia y Hacienda

Spain – Spanish weekly PTA7,500

32018 **BOLETIN ESTADISTICO**
Banco de Espana

Spain – Spanish monthly PTA25,000

Gives general statistics.

32019 **BOLETIN DE ESTADISTICA Y SUPLEMENTO**
Instituto Nacional de Estadistica

Spain – Spanish monthly c200pp PTA625 per issue

Monthly statistical bulletin.

32020 **BOLETIN INFORMATIVO***
Banco Central

Spain – Spanish/English monthly c35pp

Economic bulletin with key economic indicators.

32021 **BOLETIN INFORMATIVO ANUARIO ESTADISTICA GENERAL**
Ministerio del Interior, Direccion General de Trafico

Spain – Spanish annual

Statistics on car ownership and registration, accidents and licensing.

32022 **BOLETIN DE INFORMACION ECONOMICA**
Banco Exterior de Espana

Spain – Spanish monthly free

Monthly economic report with regular supplements covering the economies of other countries.

32023 **BOLETIN TRIMESTRAL DE COYUNTURA**
Instituto Nacional de Estadistica

Spain – Spanish quarterly PTA3,748-4,404

32024 **CENSO AGRARIO 6 VOLS 1982**
Instituto Nacional de Estadistica

Spain – Spanish

32025 **CENSO DE LA POBLACION 4 VOLS PLUS NOMENCLATOR 1981**
Instituto Nacional de Estadistica

Spain – Spanish

32026 **EL COMERCIO HISPANO–BRITANICO**
Spanish Chamber of Commerce, UK

Spain – Spanish/English monthly c30pp

News on Anglo-Spanish trade.

32027 **CONTABILIDAD NACIONAL DE ESPANA**
Instituto Nacional de Estadistica

Spain – Spanish annual PTA1545

Statistics on national accounts.

32028 **COUNTRY PROFILES**
Economist Publications Ltd

Spain – English annual 40pp £25 UK subscription varies in rest of world

Resumé of politics, economy and industry including statistical summaries.

32029 **COUNTRY REPORTS**
Economist Publications Ltd

Spain – English quarterly 25pp £58 UK subscription varies in rest of world

Economic policies and development plans, trends in production and demand, monetary and fiscal conditions, wages and prices, merchandise trade, invisibles, capital flows, exchange rates and foreign debt plus a forecast of the economic prospects.

32030 **ECONOMIC REPORT (ON THE OCCASION OF THE SPANISH BANKING ASSOCIATION ANNUAL GENERAL MEETING)**
Asociacion Espanola de Banca Privada

Spain – Spanish annual 1978 130pp free

Spanish economy, matters related to banking, economic perspectives.

32031 **ECONOMIC SURVEY–SPAIN**
Australia and New Zealand Banking Group

Spain – English 6pp free

Brief economic report with selected statistics.

32032 **L'ECONOMIE ESPAGNOLE. PERSPECTIVES ET ENJEU EUROPEEN NOTES ET ETUDES DOCUMENTAIRES NO 4643-44**
La Documentation Francaise

Spain – French 1981 176pp FrF50
ISBN No. 0029-4004

Reviews the Spanish economy.

32033 **EL ECONOMISTA***
El Economista

Spain – Spanish weekly PTA3,436

Economic and financial journal.

32034 **ENCUESTA INDUSTRIAL**
Instituto Nacional de Estadistica

Spain – Spanish annual 365pp PTA2,251

Industrial production by sector, area of industrial activity and region. Each issue covers four years.

32035 **L'ESPAGNE ET LE PORTUGAL DANS LA CEE. INTERROGATIONS ET ENJUEX. NOTES ET ETUDES DOCUMENTAIRES NO 4819**
La Documentation Francaise

Spain and Portugal – French 1986 FrF50
ISBN No. 0029-4004

Looks at the position of Spain and Portugal in the European Community.

32036 **ESTADISTICA DEL COMERCIO EXTERIOR DE ESPANA VOL 1 & 2 (SPANISH FOREIGN TRADE STATISTICS)**
Direccion General de Advanas

Spain – Spanish annual 1,000pp per volume PTA2,000 (2 volumes)

Spanish imports and exports by country and commodity.

32037 **ESTADISTICA DE MOVIMIENTO VIAJEROS EN ESTABLECIMIENTOS TURISTICOS**
Instituto Nacional de Estadistica

Spain – Spanish annual PTA1096

Tourism.

32038 **ESTADISTICA DE SOCIEDADES MERCANTILES**
Instituto Nacional de Estadistica

Spain – Spanish annual PTA625

Statistics on trade and commerce.

32039 **EXTEBANK MONTHLY ECONOMIC REPORT**
Banco Exterieur de Espana

Spain–English monthly free

Monthly economic report which is a shortened version of the Spanish 'Boletin de Informacion Economica'.

32040 **FLORICULTURA Y HORTICULTURA–HORTICULTURE, FRUIT AND FLOWER GROWING**
Editorial Hegeo SA

Spain – Spanish monthly 1984 PTA2,000
ISSN No. 0212-7660

All subjects appertaining to horticulture, fruit and flower growing.

32041 **HINTS TO EXPORTERS**
Department of Trade and Industry

Spain – English annual

Practical guide for businessmen giving general information, useful addresses, methods of doing business and relevant regulations.

32042 **INDICADORES DE COYUNTURA**
Instituto Nacional de Estadistica

Spain – Spanish monthly PTA5,060

32043 **INDICADORES ESTADISTICOS REGIONALES**
Instituto Nacional de Estadistica

Spain – Spanish annual PTA781

Regional statistics.

32044 **INDICE DE PRECIOS DE CONSUMO RESUMEN ANUAL**
Instituto Nacional de Estadistica

Spain – Spanish annual PTA1,595

Consumer price index.

32045 **INDICES DE PRECIOS INDUSTRIALES**
Instituto Nacional de Estadistica

Spain – Spanish PTA450

Industrial price indices.

32046 **INFORMACION AGROPECUARIA**
Consorcio para el Fomento de la Riqueza Ganadera

Spain – Spanish weekly 1975 free

Weekly prices for agricultural products on national markets; news articles relating to provincial, regional and national agricultural sectors.

32047 **INFORMACION COMERCIAL ESPANOLA**
Ministerio de Economia y Hacienda

Spain – Spanish weekly c140pp PTA17,550

Commercial news.

32048 **INFORMACION SIDERURGICA**
Union de Empresas Siderurgicas (UNESID)

Spain – Spanish quarterly 87pp PTA7,000

Journal on the steel industry both nationally and internationally. Includes a statistical section on trade and data on prices.

32049 **INFORME ANUAL**
Banco de Espana

Spain – Spanish annual free

This annual review of the Spanish economy is distributed free to subscribers to the 'Boletin Estadistico'.

32050 **KOMPASS REGISTER**
Kompass Publishers Ltd, UK

Spain – Spanish/English/French/German/Italian annual £105.00

Comprehensive business directory giving information on companies listed geographically and cross-referenced to a directory of products and services.

32051 **LANDERBERICHT SPANIEN**
Federal Statistical Office of Germany

Spain – German irregular DM7.90

Statistical survey of Spain including demography, geography, education, employment, agriculture, production, overseas trade, transport, tourism, finance, wages and prices and national accounts.

32052 **MEMBERS HANDBOOK**
British Chamber of Commerce in Spain

Spain – English/Spanish annual 1987 140pp £30.00

Review of Anglo-Spanish trade and details of activities of members of the Chamber.

32053 **MEMORIA**
Ministerio de Obras Publicas y Urbanismo

Spain – Spanish with English introduction and headings annual 240pp

Port statistics.

32054 **MEMORIA ESTADISTICA (STATISTICAL REPORT)**
Direccion General de Seguros

Spain – Spanish annual or biannual 500pp

Statistics on the insurance sector.

32055 **MONETARY EVOLUTION REPORT**
Asociacion Espanola de Banca Privada

Spain – Spanish 1st quarter 1980 54pp free

Monetary aggregates, external position, balance of payments, exchange rate, relative prices and inflation, state finances, monetary basis, evolution of credit interest rates, funding of private sector.

32056 **MOVIMIENTO DE VIAJEROS EN ESTABLECIMIENTOS TURISTICOS**
Instituto Nacional de Estadistica

Spain – Spanish annual 150pp

Tourist statistics.

32057 **NUMEROS INDICES DE LA PRODUCCION INDUSTRIAL**
Instituto Nacional de Estadistica

Spain – Spanish quarterly PTA450

Index numbers of industrial production.

32058 **OECD ECONOMIC SURVEYS–SPAIN**
Organisation for Economic Cooperation and Development (OECD)

Spain – English annual 70pp £2.40/DM12/US$5/FrF24

A detailed analysis of recent developments in demand production, employment, prices and wages, conditions in the money and capital markets and developments in the balance of payments. It includes short-term forecasts as well as analyses of medium-term problems of specific relevance to the elaboration of the country's economic policies.

32059 **PRESTAMOS HIPOTECARIOS**
Instituto Nacional de Estadistica

Spain – Spanish annual PTA475

Mortgage statistics.

32060 **RESUMEN ESTADISTICO DE EXPORTACION**
Ministerio de Economia y Hacienda

Spain – Spanish monthly 225pp PTA13,000 p.a.

Exports.

32061 **RESUMEN ESTADISTICO DE IMPORTACION**
Ministerio de Economia y Hacienda

Spain – Spanish monthly 225pp PTA13,000 p.a.

Imports.

32062 **REVISTA GONDOLA**
Editorial de Medios Tecnicos de Expresion SA

Spain – Spanish monthly 1980 PTA7,000

The food sector, including market studies of individual products.

32063 **SALARIOS MEDIAS ANUALES**
Instituto Nacional de Estadistica

Spain – Spanish annual PTA450

Wages and salaries.

32064 **SPAIN AND PORTUGAL**
UK Iron and Steel Statistics Bureau

Spain and Portugal – English 1986 with annual statistical summary £25

Report on the steel industry showing production, consumption and details of imports and exports.

32065 **TAX & INVESTMENT PROFILE**
Touche Ross International, USA

Spain–English free

Survey covering investment, trade, labour, business practices, financial system. Frequently updated.

SWEDEN

33001 ABECOR COUNTRY REPORT – SWEDEN
Abecor

Sweden – English 1988 2pp free

Brief economic report.

33002 AFFARSVARLDEN*
Affarsvarlden

Sweden – Swedish weekly SKr390.00

Business and financial journal.

33003 AIRPORT STATISTICS
The Swedish Civil Aviation Administration

Sweden – Swedish monthly 1973 100pp SKr160

Landings, passengers, freight and mail at Swedish airports with scheduled services.

33004 ALKOHOLSTATISTIK
National Board of Health and Welfare

Sweden – Swedish annual 50pp

Sales of and expenditure on alcoholic beverages, production, trade and alcohol-related offences.

33005 ALLMAN FORSAKRING
Rikftorsakringsverket

Sweden – Swedish annual

National Insurance.

33006 ALLMAN MANADSSTATISTIK
Statistika Centralbyran

Sweden – Swedish monthly SKr350 p.a.

Main data from Swedish short-term statistics (normally monthly and quarterly, in many cases indexed) on: labour market, population, construction/building industry, export industry, agriculture, fishery, prices, monetary and credit systems, official finance, traffic accidents, crime, communications etc.

33007 ANNUAL REPORT SVENSKA HANDELSBANKEN*
Svenska Handelsbanken

Sweden – Swedish/English annual free

33008 ANNUAL REPORT SVERIGES RIKSBANK
Sveriges Riksbank

Sweden – English/Swedish annual 50-60pp
ISSN No. 0347-5042

33009 ANNUAL REPORT SWEDBANK
Swedbank-Sparbankernas Bank

Sweden – Swedish/English annual free

Financial statement and data of Swedbank.

33010 ARBETSMARKNADSSTATISTIK ÅRSBROK 198-
Statistika Centralbyran

Sweden – Swedish annual SKr95.00

Labour market statistics.

33011 ARSREDOVISNING
Postverket

Sweden – Swedish/English annual 50pp free

The Swedish Post Office Annual Report.

33012 ATTARSBANKERNA
Bankinspektionen

Sweden – Swedish annual

Commercial banks.

33013 BANKAKTIEBOLAGEN, FONDKOMMISSIONARERNA FONDBÖRSEN & VPC
Statistika Centralbyran

Sweden – Swedish annual SKr50.00

Limited banking companies, the stock exchange and brokers.

33014 BEFOLKNINGS ANDRINGAR, DEL 1 FÖRSAMLINGAR, KOMMUNER OCH A-REGIONER
Statistika Centralbyran

Sweden – Swedish 1981 SKr90.00

Population changes. Part 1, parishes, municipalities and A-regions.

33015 BEFOLKNINGS ANDRINGAR DEL 2 FLYTTNING MELLAN KOMMUNER
Statistika Centralbyran

Sweden – Swedish 1981 SKr120

Population changes. Part 2, moving between municipalities.

33016 BEFOLKNINGS ANDRINGAR DEL 3 HELA RIKET OCH LÅNEN M.M.
Statistika Centralbyran

Sweden – Swedish SKr120

Population changes. The whole country and the counties etc.

33017 BETALNING, VALUTA OCH FINANSIERING VID EXPORT AFFÅRER
Sveriges Exportråd/Anders Grath available from Naringslivets Forlag

Sweden – Swedish 1986 214pp SKr195

Payment, currency and financing in the export business. The book shows how to formulate terms of payment, what the consequences are of the choice of currency and how to find a suitable financing method.

33018 BODSTADS–OCH BYGGNADSSTATISTIK ARSBOK
Statistika Centralbyran

Sweden – Swedish annual

Yearbook of housing and building statistics.

33019 BOSTADKREDITER OCH AVREGLERINGAR 2, ed 1987
Svenska Bankforeningen

Sweden – Swedish irregular 1984 22pp single copies free
ISSN No. 91 7064 045 9

House financing credits and regulations.

33020 BRANSLEN LEVERANSER OCH FORBRUKNING AV BRANSEN OCH SMORJMEDEL
Statistika Centralbyran

Sweden – Swedish quarterly SKr120

Data on deliveries and consumption of fuels and lubricants.

33021 COUNTRY PROFILES–SWEDEN
Economist Publications Ltd

Sweden – English annual 40pp £25 UK subscription varies in rest of world

Resumé of politics, economy and industry including statistical summaries.

33022 **COUNTRY REPORTS–SWEDEN**
Economist Publications Ltd

Sweden – English quarterly 25pp £58 UK subscription varies in rest of world

Economic policies and development plans, trends in production and demand, monetary and fiscal conditions, wages and prices, merchandise trade, invisibles, capital flows, exchange rates and foreign debt plus a forecast of the economic prospects.

33023 **DAIRY INDUSTRY IN SWEDEN**
Svenska Mejeriernas Riksforening

Sweden – English 19pp

Report from the dairy industry association.

33024 **DAIRY INGENUITY**
Swedish Dairies Association

Sweden – English biennial 1980 20pp free

Presentation of the dairy industry in Sweden.

33025 **EKONOMISKA MEDDELAND**
Svenska Bankforeningen

Sweden – Swedish weekly SKr480

Economic bulletin.

33026 **ENERGY**
Statistika Centralbyran

Sweden – Swedish monthly/quarterly/ annually SKr800

Monthly, quarterly and annual reports on energy.

33027 **ENSKILDA FORSAKRINGSTORETAG**
Forsakringsinspektionen (Swedish Private Insurance Supervisory Scheme)

Sweden – Swedish annual SKr150

Private insurance companies–published and sold by the insurance inspectorate.

33028 **EXPORTKREDITGUIDE**
Svenska Bankforeningen

Sweden – Swedish 1985 SKr25

Guide to the export credit system.

33029 **FACT SHEETS ON SWEDEN***
The Swedish Institute

Sweden – English 2pp free

Fact sheets issued at regular intervals on a variety of topics.
Among subjects covered in 1980:
The Economic Situation of Swedish Households
The Swedish Economy
The Swedish Metalworking Industry
The Swedish Motor Industry
The Swedish Shipbuilding Industry
Electrical Engineering and Electronics in Sweden
The Swedish Steel Industry
The Swedish Shipping Industry
Sweden's Chemical Industry
Agriculture in Sweden
Forestry and Forest Industry in Sweden
Taxes in Sweden
Energy Supply in Sweden
The Swedish Mining Industry
Consumer Cooperatives in Sweden
The Swedish Construction Industry
Swedish Trade Policy
The Swedish System of Investment Funds
Sweden's Foreign Trade
The Distributive Trade in Sweden
Transport Policy and Traffic Trends in Sweden
Fisheries in Sweden
Swedish Consumer Policy
Labour Relations in Sweden
Swedish Labour Market Policy
The Swedish Press and other Media
Environment Protection in Sweden
Immigrants in Sweden
The Swedish Book Market
The Swedish Population

33030 **FAKTA OM SVERIGES EKONOMI**
Swedish Employers' Federation

Sweden – Swedish annual 62pp SKr40
ISSN No. 0280-3364

Approximately 50 diagrams with comments on the Swedish economy.

33031 **FASTIGHETSTAXERING–SERIES P–PRICES AND CONSUMPTION**
Statistika Centralbyran

Sweden – Swedish

Statistical reports on real estate.

33032 **FOLKMANGD 31 DEC – PART 3**
Statistika Centralbyran

Sweden – Swedish annual SKr120

Report on the population at 31 December by sex, age, civil status and community.

33033 **FÖRETAGEN, EKONOMISK REDOVISNING**
Statistika Centralbyran

Sweden – Swedish annual SKr90

Economic report on companies.

33034 **DEN FRAMTIDA BEFOLKNINGEN PROGNOS FORAREN 1986-2025**
Statistika Centralbyran

Sweden – Swedish

Population projections 1986-2025.

33035 **GROWTH POLICIES IN A NORDIC PERSPECTIVE 1987**
Institute of Industrial Economics

Norway, Sweden, Finland – English 1984
ISBN No. 91 7204 276-1

Economic policies and outlook.

33036 **HINTS TO EXPORTERS**
Department of Trade and Industry

Sweden – English annual

Practical guide for businessmen giving general information, useful addresses, methods of doing business and relevant regulations.

33037 **HUSHÅLLENS UTGIFTER**
Statistika Centralbyran

Sweden – Swedish 1985 SKr90

The household budget survey, part 1, basic data on private consumption of various goods and services collected from different groups of households.

33038 **INDUSTRI. DEL 1: FORDELADE ENLIGT SVENSK STANDARD FOR NORINGSGRENSINDELNING**
Statistika Centralbyran

Sweden – Swedish SKr120

Manufacturing data grouped according to the Swedish Standard Industrial Classification of all economic activities.

33039 **INDUSTRI. DEL 2: PRODUKTION AV VARER OCH T JANSTER FORDELADE ENLIGT CCC–NONENKLAUREN OCH ENLIGT SITC REV. 2**
Statistika Centralbyran

Sweden – Swedish SKr150

Production of commodities and services grouped according to the SITC, Revision 2.

33040 **INDUSTRIARET***
Sveriges Industriförbund

Sweden – Swedish annual approx 40pp free

Annual report from the Federation of Swedish Industries covering the administrative sector and the personnel sector.

33041 **INSURANCE SCHEMES ON THE SWEDISH LABOUR MARKET: STATUTORY SCHEMES: SCHEMES UNDER COLLECTIVE AGREEMENTS: INSURANCE SCHEMES FOR THE SELF-EMPLOYED**
Svenska Arbetsgivareföreningen

Sweden – English annual 7pp free

Report by the Swedish Employers' Confederation.

33042 **JORDBRUKSEKONOMISKA MEDDELANDEN**
Jordbruksnämnden available from Liber Forlag

Sweden – Swedish monthly c40pp

'The Journal of Agricultural Economics'–articles, summaries and notices on Swedish and foreign agricultural economics, with production, price and market statistics.

33043 **JORDBRUKSSTATISTIK ÅRSBOK**
Statistika Centralbyran

Sweden–Swedish annual SKr150

Annual agricultural statistics.

33044 **JOURNAL OF CRITICAL STATISTICS**
Statistika Centralbyran

Sweden – Swedish quarterly SKr250

Statistical magazine on methods and policy.

33045 **KOMMUNERNASFINANSER**
Statistika Centralbyran

Sweden – Swedish annual SKr90

Local council finances.

33046 **KOMPASS REGISTER**
Kompass Publishers Ltd, UK

Sweden – English/French/Spanish/German/Italian annual £100

Comprehensive business directory giving information on companies listed geographically and cross-referenced to a directory of products and services.

33047 **KONSUMENT PRISER OCH INDEXBERÄKNINGAR**
Statistika Centralbyran

Sweden – Swedish annual SKr50

Consumer price index. Up-to-date information on the index can be obtained from answerphone 08 783 4468 in Stockholm or 08 783 4762 in Stockholm.

33048 **KREDIT–OCH VALUTAÖVERSIKT***
Riksbanken available from Liber Forlag

Sweden – Swedish quarterly SKr70.00

'Credit and Currency Review'. Information about the Bank of Sweden's credit and currency policies and the market development.

33049 **KREDITMARKNADEN**
Svenska Bankforeningen (Swedish Bankers Association)

Sweden – Swedish annual 4pp

Statistical leaflet on credit market in Sweden.

33050 **LANDERBERICHT SCHWEDEN**
Federal Statistical Office of Germany

Sweden – German irregular DM7.90

Statistical survey of Sweden including demography, geography, education, employment, agriculture, production, overseas trade, transport, tourism, finance, wages and prices and national accounts.

33051 **LONER E SYSSELSATHING INOM AFFENTLIG SEKTOR PART 1 STATSANSTALLA PART 2 KOMMUNAL PERSONAL**
Statistika Centralbyran

Sweden – Swedish annual

Wage rates of civil servants (Part 1) and local authority personnel (Part 2).

33052 **LONER OCH SYSSELSATTNING INOM PRIVAT SEKTOR**
Statistika Centralbyran

Sweden – Swedish annual 200pp

Level and trends of wages and salaries, labour costs, hours of work and occupations of employees.

33053 **LUFTFARTSVERKET**
Luftfartsverket available from Statistika Centralbyran

Sweden – Swedish annual SKr22.00

Statistics on the national civil aviation administration.

33054 **LUFTFARTSVERKET**
The Swedish Civil Aviation Administration

Sweden – Swedish/English annual 1961 70pp SKr30
ISBN/ISSN No. 0348-2251

A statistical description in tables and diagrams of the Swedish CAA's activity and other air traffic activity.

33055 **NATURRESURSER OCH MILJO**
Statistika Centralbyran

Sweden – Swedish SKr180 p.a.

Statistical reports on natural resources and the environment.

33056 **NEW FACTORIES**
Swedish Employers' Federation

Sweden – English SKr40

Report on factories and types of production systems which emerged during the 1970s.

33057 **NON-SCHEDULED PASSENGER STATISTICS**
The Swedish Civil Aviation Administration

Sweden – Swedish/summary in English twice a year 1970 17pp SKr75

Number of passengers carried on non-scheduled flights from Swedish airports to foreign destinations.

33058 **NON-WAGE LABOUR COSTS IN SWEDEN**
Swedish Employers' Federation

Sweden – English annual 18pp free

33059 **NORDISK FORSAKRINGSTIDSKRIFT**
Svenska Forsakringsforeningen

Norway, Finland, Sweden, Denmark – Scandinavian/English/German quarterly 1921 90pp SKr40 p.a.
ISSN No. 0348-6516

Private and public insurance.

33060 **PAY–A MANAGEMENT TOOL**
Swedish Employers' Federation

Sweden – English 1986 16pp free
ISBN No. 91 7152 381 2

33061 **PAY REFORM IN SWEDEN**
Swedish Employers' Federation

Sweden – English irregular 1977 84pp SKr27
ISSN No. 91 7152 083 X

Report on new payment systems.

33062 **PAYMENT BY RESULTS–13 CASE STUDIES FROM SWEDEN**
Swedish Employers' Federation

Sweden – English 1987 110pp SKr110
ISBN No. 91 7152 430 4

A description of how 13 firms have shaped their own wage systems.

33063 **PRAKTISK PRISSÅTTNING PÅ HEMMA MARKNAD OCH EXPORT**
Sveriges Exportråd/Lage Roswall

Sweden – Swedish 1986 170pp SKr120

Price determination in a practical way for the domestic and export markets.

33064 **QUARTERLY REVIEW SVERIGES RIKSBANK**
Sveriges Riksbank

Sweden – English/Swedish quarterly 1979 80-90pp
ISSN No. 0348-6583

33065 **OVARTILEN (NEWSLTTER OF THE SWEDISH STATISTICAL ASSOCIATION)**
Svenska Statistikersamfundet (Swedish Statistical Association)

Sweden – Swedish 4 issues per year January 1986 16pp
ISSN No. 0283-3654

Statistics.

33066 **THE RAILWAYS OF SWEDEN**
State Railways

Sweden – Swedish annual 1953 33pp SKr25
ISSN No. 00 81-9964

Swedish railways.

33067 **REGIONALT FÖRDELADE LEVERANSER AV DRIUMEDEL OCH ELDNINGSOLJOR**
Statistika Centralbyran

Sweden – Swedish

Deliveries of petroleum products by municipality.

33068 **SAF STADGAR**
Svenska Arbetsgivareföreningen

Sweden – Swedish/English/French/German 36pp

Constitution of Swedish Employers' Federation.

33069 **SAFS KALENDER**
Svenska Arbetsgivareföreningen

Sweden – Swedish annual SKr100

Swedish Employers' Federation board, delegates, general annual meeting, administration, confederation and the organizations where SAF is represented.

33070 **SAFs, LOs, TCOs, OCH SAVO/SRs UPPBYGGNAD**
Svenska Arbetsgivareföreningen

Sweden – Swedish annual free

The structure and organization of: The Swedish Employers' Confederation (SAF), The Trade Union Congress (LO), The Swedisn Central Organisation of Salaried Employees (TCO), The Swedish Confederation of Professional Associations (SACO).

33071 **SAF's VERKSAMHETSBERÄTTELSE**
Svenska Arbetsgivareföreningen

Sweden – Swedish annual free

The annual report from the Swedish Employers' Confederation covering SAF's administrative work, wage negotiations, co-operation with other organizations.

33072 **SCB-INDIKATORER**
Statistika Centralbyran

Sweden – Swedish monthly SKr170

Swedish statistical indicators.

33073 **SJÖFART**
Statistika Centralbyran

Sweden – Swedish annual SKr90

Statistics on shipping.

33074 **SKEPPNINGSHANDBOKEN**
Sveriges Exportråd

Sweden – Swedish 610pp SKr590

The Shipping Handbook, trade, customs and consulate invoices, B/Ls, Certificates of Origin, legalization fees, import restrictions, customs regulations, marking and packing regulations samples, export licences, export bans.

33075 **SKOGSSTATISTIK ÅRSBOK**
Skogsstyrelsen

Sweden – Swedish annual SKr100

Forestry statistics.

33076 **SPARBANKERNA**
Statistika Centralbyran

Sweden – Swedish annual SKr50

Statistics on savings banks.

33077 **STATISTICAL YEARBOOK**
Sveriges Riksbank

Sweden–Swedish/English annual 180pp

33078 **STATISTICAL YEARBOOK (SWEDISH POST OFFICE)**
Postverket, General Directorate of Posts

Sweden – Swedish/English/French annual 80-100pp SKr30
ISBN/ISSN No. 0347-660X

Statistical information on postal items, staff, cash transactions, organisation and financial situation.

33079 **STATISTISK ÅRSBOK FÖR SVERIGE**
Statistika Centralbyran

Sweden – Swedish annual SKr230

Comprehensive statistics on economic, social, political and cultural conditions in Sweden. International summaries. Extensive list of sources, a list of official statistical publications issued by statistics Sweden and by other authorities, plus an extensive subject index.

33080 **STATISTISKA MEDDELANDEN BYGGINDEX: KOSTNADSINDEX MED KONJUNKTURESIKBT**
Statistika Centralbyran

Sweden – Swedish monthly

Factor price index and contral work index.

33081 **STATISTISKA MEDDELANDEN SERIE AM ARBETSMARKNAD SERIE AM**
Statistika Centralbyran

Sweden – Swedish SKr1,200

Various booklets in the series 'Wages & Employment' covering wages and salaries in all sectors of industry, commerce and civil service.

33082 **STATISTISKA MEDDELANDEN SERIE AM SYSSELSATTNING OCH LONESUMMOR FOR ANSTEMAN INOM INDUSTRIE**
Statistika Centralbyran

Sweden – Swedish quarterly SKr120

Statistics on employment and wages for white-collar workers in industry.

33083 **STATISTISKA MEDDELANDEN SERIE AM–ARBETS KOSTNADSINDEX FOR INDUSTRIARBETARE**
Statistika Centralbyran

Sweden – Swedish quarterly SKr120

Labour cost index for industrial workers.

33084 **STATISTISKA MEDDELANDEN SERIE AM ARBETSKRAFTSUNDERSOKNINGAR (AKU)**
Statistika Centralbyran

Sweden – Swedish monthly/quarterly and annual SKr240, 120 and 70

Monthly, quarterly and annual manpower surveys from November of one year to October the next.

33085 **STATISTISKA MEDDELANDEN SERIE SYSSELSÄTTNING OCH LÖNESUMMOR SYSSELSÄTTNING OCH LÖNESUMMOR FÖR ANSTÄLLDA INOM VARUHANDELN**
Statistika Centralbyran

Sweden – Swedish quarterly SKr120

Employment and wages for employees in the retail industry.

33086 **STATISTISKA MEDDELANDEN SERIE AM SYSSELSÄTTNING OCH LÖNESUMMOR FOR ARBETARE INOM BYGGNADSVERKSAMHET**
Statistika Centralbyran

Sweden – Swedish quarterly SKr120

Employment and wages for workers in the construction industry.

33087 **STATISTISKA MEDDELANDEN SERIE AM SYSSELSÄTTNING OCH LÖNESUMMOR SYSSELSÄTTNING OCH LÖNER FOR ARBETARE INOM INDUSTRI**
Statistika Centralbyran

Sweden – Swedish monthly SKr240

Employment and wages for industrial workers.

33088 **STATISTISKA MEDDELANDEN SERIE SYSSELÄTTNING OCH LÖNESUMMOR FÖR PERSONAL I OFFENTLIG TJANST**
Statistika Centralbyran

Sweden – Swedish quarterly SKr120

Employment and wages for personnel in the public sector.

33089 **STATISTISKA MEDDELANDEN SERIE BO LÅNEOBJEKTSTATISTIK**
Statistika Centralbyran

Sweden – Swedish

Booklets published in the BO Series of Statistical Reports covering borrowing requirements, mortgages etc. for various types of houses.

33090 **STATISTISKA MEDDELANDEN SERIE F**
Statistika Centralbyran

Sweden – Swedish 1981 SKr300

Reports on all aspects of company economics covering construction companies, foreign assets and liabilities, taxed income, industrial companies, investments in all company sectors, available funds in larger industrial and commercial companies.

33091 **STATISTISKA MEDDELANDEN SERIE H**
Statistika Centralbyran

Sweden – Swedish SKr950

Reports published in the 'H' Series of Statistical reports on foreign trade

33092 **STATISTISKA MEDDELANDEN SERIE 1B**
Statistika Centralbyran

Sweden – Swedish SKr750 for the whole series.

Statistical data for industry (manufacturing).

32393 **STATISTISKA MEDDELANDEN SERIE J**
Statistika Centralbyran

Sweden – Swedish SKr240

Series of statistical data in booklet form for fishing covering size and composition of fishing fleet, catches at sea and professional fishermen's incomes and outgoings.

33094 **STATISTISKA MEDDELANDEN SERIE J OCH SKUGSBRUK**
Statistika Centralbyran

Sweden – Swedish SKr900

Statistical data in booklet form covering agriculture and forestry; harvest estimates, size and monetary value, breeding statistics for pigs, agricultural economics, normal harvest statistics per county, changes in agriculture, future prospects, damage estimates etc.

33095 **STATISTISKA MEDDELANDEN SERIES K: KREDITMARKNAD**
Statistika Centralbyran

Sweden – Swedish SKr600

Statistical reports on the credit market, banking and insurance.

33096 **STATISTISKA MEDDELANDEN SERIE N: NATIONAL RAKENSKAPER**
Statistika Centralbyran

Sweden – Swedish SKr320

Statistical reports on national accounts.

33097 **STATISTISKA MEDDELANDEN SERIE O: KOMMUNALSKATERNA**
Statistika Centralbyran

Sweden – Swedish monthly 30pp

Preliminary data on local taxes.

33098 **STATISTISKA MEDDELANDEN SERIE 0: OFTENTLIGA FINANSER**
Statistika Centralbyran

Sweden – Swedish SKr160

Public finances.

33099 **STATISTISKA MEDDELANDEN SERIE P: FAKTORPRISINDEX FOR BOSTADER**
Statistika Centralbyran

Sweden – Swedish quarterly SKr120

Indices of construction cost for housing.

33100 **STATISTISKA MEDDELANDEN SERIE P: FASTIGHETSTATISTIK JARD–OCH SKOGSBRUK**
Statistika Centralbyran

Sweden – Swedish annual

Prices of real estate, agriculture and forestry.

33101 **STATISTISKA MEDDELANDEN SERIE P: FASTIGHETS PRIS STATISTIK**
Statistika Centralbyran

Sweden – Swedish annual

Property price index.

33102 **STATISTISKA MEDDELANDEN SERIE P: HUSHÅLLENS INKÖPSPLANER, HIP**
Statistika Centralbyran

Sweden – Swedish

Household purchase plans.

33103 **STATISTISKA MEDDELANDEN SERIE P: KONSUMENT PRIS INDEX**
Statistika Centralbyran

Sweden – Swedish monthly

Consumer price index.

33104 **STATISTISKA MEDDELANDEN SERIE P: KONSUMENTPRISINDEX LEVNADSKOSTNADSINDEX , NETTOPRISINDEX, PENSIONSPRISTALET BASBE LUPPET**
Statistika Centralbyran

Sweden – Swedish

Consumer price index; living cost index; net price index; pension price value; percentages for changes in certain maintenance allowances.

33105 **STATISTISKA MEDDELANDEN SERIE P NETTOPRISINDEX KONSUMENTPRISINDEX**
Statistika Centralbyran

Sweden – Swedish monthly SKr260

Consumer price index.

33106 **STATISTISKA MEDDELANDEN SERIE P: PRISINDEX I PRODUCENT–IMPORTED**
Statistika Centralbyran

Sweden – Swedish monthly SKr200 p.a.

Price indices in producer and import stages.

33107 **STATISTISKA MEDDELANDEN SERIE T: TRANSPORT O KOMMUNIKATION**
Statistika Centralbyran

Sweden – Swedish SKr[illegible] whole series

Statistical data on transport and communication.

33108 **STATLIGA MYNDIGHETER 1986**
Statkontoret

Sweden – Swedish irregular 376pp SKr175
ISSN No. 91-7220-025-1

Description of the organization, functions and structure of government departments and agencies.

33109 **SVENSKA KREDITMARKNADEN**
Svenska Bankforeningen

Sweden – Swedish/English biannual SKr20

The Swedish credit market.

33110 **SVENSK FORSAKRINGSARBOK**
Svenska Forsakringsforeningen

Sweden – Swedish annual 1916 380pp SKr120
ISSN No. 0081-9794

Private and public insurance, facts and figures, in Sweden.

33111 **SVENSK OBLIGATIONSBOK**
Svenska Bankforeningen (Swedish Bankers Association)

Sweden – Swedish annual 150pp SKr420

Swedish bonds.

33112 **SVERIGES JARNVAGAR 198-**
Statens Jarnvagar

Sweden – Swedish annual SKr25

Statistics on railways.

33113 **SVERIGES RIKSBANK STATISTIK ARSBOK**
Sveriges Riksbank

Sweden – Swedish with English table headings annual 170pp

Banks and other financial institutions, government finance, bonds, the credit market, money supply, interest rates, balance of payments.

33114 **SWEDEN**
National Westminster Bank

Sweden – English irregular 4pp free

Brief economic report.

33115 **SWEDEN**
UK Iron and Steel Statistics Bureau

Sweden – English 1986 with annual statistical summary £25

Report on the steel industry showing production, consumption and details of imports and exports.

33116 **SWEDEN BUSINESS REPORT***
Affärsvälden

Sweden – English 21 issues a year c8pp SKr360

Regular bulletin on trade and the economy with reports on industrial sectors together with brief news items on trade deals, company performances, industrial sectors.

33117 **THE SWEDISH-BRITISH TRADE DIRECTORY**
Swedish Chamber of Commerce

Sweden – English annual 315pp £15 approximately–free to members

Reference book on Swedish-British trade, with articles, general information on both countries, and a complete list of member companies.

33118 **THE SWEDISH BUDGET**
available from The Swedish Institute

Sweden – English annual c150pp SKr17

Official budget report.

33119 **THE SWEDISH CREDIT MARKET**
Svenska Bankforeningen (Swedish Bankers Association)

Sweden – English/Swedish biennial 36pp SKr20
ISBN No. 91 7064 0475

Credit market.

33120 **THE SWEDISH ECONOMY**
National Institute of Economic Research Stockholm

Sweden – English annual 170pp

Trade, production, labour market, household finances, investments, credit market, business and public sectors.

33121 **THE SWEDISH LABOUR MARKET**
National Labour Market Board

Sweden – English/Swedish annual SKr25

Annual report of the Swedish labour market administration.

33122 **TAX & INVESTMENT PROFILE**
Touche Ross International, USA

Sweden – English free

Booklet providing information on financial system and legislation including taxation and currency regulations. Frequently updated.

33123 **TELEVERKET**
Televerket

Swedish – English/French annual

Telecommunications statistics resumé in French and English.

33124 **TRADE PROFILES: DEVELOPING COUNTRIES**
Sveriges Exportrad

Sweden – English 1987 61pp SKr325

Sweden's trade with 58 developing countries 1982-1986.

33125 **TRADE PROFILES: INDUSTRIAL COUNTRIES**
Sveriges Exportrad

Sweden – English 1987 39pp SKr225

Sweden's trade with 36 industrialized countries including Eastern Europe 1982-86.

33126 **UNDERSTODSFORENINGAR 1985**
Forsakringsinspektionen (Swedish Private Insurance Supervisory Scheme)

Sweden – SKr70

Friendly societies.

33127 **UTRIKESHANDEL:ARSSTATISTIK**
Statistika Centralbyran

Sweden – Swedish annual 200pp

Import and export data in volume and value for the current and previous year.

33128 **UTRIKESHANDEL: KVARTALSSTATISTIK**
Statistika Centralbyran

Sweden – Swedish quarterly 100pp

Import and export data (in 2 separate volumes) in value and volume for the quarter year to date.

33129 **UTRIKESHANDEL: MANADSSTATISTIK**
Statistika Centralbyran

Sweden – Swedish monthly 70pp

Import and export data for the year to date.

33130 **VIEWPOINT***
Federation of Swedish Industries

Sweden – English monthly 4pp free

Brief details of current developments in the economy.

33131 **WHY WAGE DIFFERENTIALS?**
Swedish Employers' Federation

Sweden – English 1986 121pp SKr120
ISBN/ISSN No. 91 7152 397 9

A systematic analysis of the possible effects on the economy in the wage dispersion on the private sector of the labour market in Sweden.

SWITZERLAND

34001 ABECOR COUNTRY REPORT – SWITZERLAND
Abecor

Switzerland – English 1987 2pp free

Brief economic report.

34002 ANNUAIRE SUISSE DE L'ECONOMIE FORESTIERE ET DE L'INDUSTRIE DU BOIS/JAHRBUCH DER SCHWEIZERISCHES WALD UND HOZWIRTSCHAFT
Office Federal de la Statistique

Switzerland – French/German annual 120pp SF25.00

Yearbook of the forestry and forest products industry.

34003 ANNUAL REPORT – CREDIT SUISSE
Credit Suisse

Switzerland – English/French/German annual 65pp free

A brief survey of the Swiss economic position followed by details of the Bank's accounts.

34004 ANNUAL REPORT (SCHWEIZERISCHE NATIONAL BANK)
Schweizerische Nationalbank

Switzerland – German/French annual free

34005 ANNUAL REPORT
Swiss Bank Corporation

Switzerland – German/French/English annual c70pp free

Annual report of bank's activities with a review of the Swiss economy in relation to world economy.

34006 ANNUAL REPORT
Union Bank of Switzerland

Switzerland – German/French/English annual free

34007 LA BALANCE TOURISTIQUE DE LA SUISSE/DIE FREMDENVERKEHRSBILANG DER SCHWEIZ
Office Federal de la Statistique

Switzerland – French/German annual 22pp SF6.00

Receipts and expenditure since 1975, including overnight stays and income by type of establishment.

34008 LES BANQUES SUISSE EN 19..
Schweizerische Nationalbank

Switzerland – French/German annual SF20.00

Banking statistics.

34009 BASLER BORSE/BASLE STOCK EXCHANGE
Basler Borsenkammer

Switzerland – German/English/French annual 70pp free

Includes the organizational structure of the stock exchange, the annual report, a statistical survey of the exchange and a directory of members.

34010 BRITISH SWISS BULLETIN
British-Swiss Chamber of Commerce in Switzerland

Switzerland – English 10 per year 8pp free to members only

Trade opportunities, commercial news on British and Swiss trade, exhibitions, new products, Chamber notices and news from members.

34011 BULLETIN
Credit Suisse

Switzerland – German/French monthly English/Italian quarterly c40pp

General economic information with emphasis on financial matters.

34012 CHARGE FISCALE EN SUISSE/ STEVERBELASTUNG IN DER SCHWEIZ
Administration Federale des Contributions Division Statistique de Documentation

Switzerland – German/French annual 100pp SF20

Taxes on income, profits, capital and wealth with statistical tables by canton.

34013 DIE CHEMISCHE INDUSTRIE DER SCHWEIZ UND IHRE NEBEN-PRODUKTE
Verlag fur Wirtschaftsliteratur GmbH

Switzerland – German/French/English irregular 480pp SF80

A directory of the chemical industry including an index of companies, products and trade marks.

34014 COMPANY STUDIES
Union Bank of Switzerland

Switzerland – German/French/English monthly free

34015 COMPTES NATIONAUX DE LA SUISSE/DIE NATIONALE BUCHHALTUNG DER SCHWEIZ

Switzerland – German/French annual 115pp SF21.00

Complete results, detailed commentary and supplementary data on Swiss national accounts.

34016 THE CORPORATION IN SWITZERLAND: FORMATION, TAXATION AND FINANCING OF JOINT STOCK COMPANIES AND LIMITED LIABILITY COMPANIES
Swiss Bank Corporation

Switzerland – English 1979 30pp free

Description of the organization and legislation relevant to joint stock companies.

34017 COUNTRY PROFILE – SWITZERLAND
British Overseas Trade Board

Switzerland – English annual 70pp

Includes general economic and social background to Switzerland with detailed surveys of the leading market sectors and sections on how to do business including marketing in Switzerland.

34018 COUNTRY PROFILES – SWITZERLAND
Economist Publications Ltd

Switzerland – English annual 40pp £25 UK subscription varies in rest of world

Resumé of politics, economy and industry including statistical summaries.

34019 COUNTRY REPORTS–SWITZERLAND
Economist Publications Ltd

Switzerland – English quarterly 25pp £58 UK subscription varies in rest of world.

Economic policies and development plans, trends in production and demand, monetary and fiscal conditions, wages and prices, merchandise trade, invisibles, capital flows, exchange rates and foreign debt plus a forecast of the economic prospects.

34020 **DEVISENHANDEL UND GELD-MARKTGESCHAFTE**
Swiss Bank Corporation

Switzerland – German/English/French/Italian/Spanish 1980

Foreign exchange and money market operations.

34021 **ECONOMIC & FINANCIAL PROSPECTS**
Swiss Bank Corporation

Switzerland – English 6 per year 20pp free

Review articles on the Swiss and world economies. A statistical survey including domestic and international financial markets and key macroeconomic data such as labour costs, prices, employment, stocks.

34022 **ECONOMIC SURVEY OF SWITZERLAND**
Union Bank of Switzerland

Switzerland – German/French/English annual 80pp free

An overview of the Swiss economy including outlook with detailed analysis of various industrial, trade and professional sectors.

34023 **GELD, WAHRUNG UND KONJUNKTUR, QUARTALSHEFT/ MONNAIE ET CONJUNCTURE**
Schweizerische Nationalbank

Switzerland – German/French quarterly 1983 70pp SF25

A selection of articles covering finance, monetary conditions and the economic situation in Switzerland and overseas.

34024 **GENEVA STOCK EXCHANGE**
Bourse de Geneve

Switzerland – English annual 1986 215pp SF49.00

History of the Geneva Stock Exchange and the Geneva Stock Exchange today including a statistical survey of the money markets.

34025 **DIE GIESSEREI UND METALLINDUSTRIE DER SCHWEIZ**
Verlag fur Wirtschaftsliteratur GmbH

Switzerland – German/French irregular 220pp SF40

Directory of the metallurgical industry giving details of manufacturers and importers of ferrous and non-ferrous metals and products.

34026 **GRUNDUNG, BESTEUERUNG UND FINANZIERUNG VON AKTIENGESELLSCHAFTEN UND GESELLSCHAFTEN MIT BESCHRANKTER HAFTUNG IN DER SCHWEIZ**
Swiss Bank Corporation

Switzerland – German/French/English 1979

Report on Swiss corporations: the formation, taxation and financing of joint-stock and limited liability companies.

34027 **HANDBUCH DER SCHWEIZERISCHEN TEXTILBEKLEIDUNGS UND LEDERWIRTSCHAFT**
Verlag fur Wirtschaftsliteratur GmbH

Switzerland – German/French 4 yearly 214pp SF70.00

Directory of the textile, clothing and leather industries giving details of manufacturers and trade organizations.

34028 **HINTS TO EXPORTERS**
Department of Trade and Industry

Switzerland – English annual

Practical guide for businessmen giving general information, useful addresses, methods of doing business and relevant regulations.

34029 **INVESTMENT NEWSLETTER**
Union Bank of Switzerland

Switzerland – German/French/English monthly free

34030 **JAHRESBERICHT– SCHWEIZERISCHE AUSSENHANDELSSTATISTIK/ COMMENTAIRES ANNUELS–STATISTIQUE DU COMMERCE EXTERIEUR DE LA SUISSE**
Direction Generale des Douanes

Switzerland – German/French annual (2 parts) 380pp SF46.00

Annual report of Swiss foreign trade. Part I by origin and destination, Part II by branches of the economy.

34031 **JAHRESBERICHT– SCHWEIZERISCHES BANKVEREIN**
Swiss Bank Corporation

Switzerland – German/French/English/Italian/Spanish annual free

Annual report.

34032 **KLEINES HANDBUCH DER SCHWEIZER AKTIEN**
Swiss Bank Corporation

Switzerland – German/French/English 1979 free

Handbook of selected Swiss shares.

34033 **KOMPASS REGISTER**
Kompass Publishers Ltd, UK

Switzerland–English/French/German/Spanish/Italian annual £100

Comprehensive business directory giving information on companies listed geographically and cross-referenced to a directory of products and services.

34034 **DIE KUNSTOFF INDUSTRIE DER SCHWEIZ**
Verlag fur Wirtschaftsliteratur GmbH

Switzerland – German/French annual 384pp SF85.00

A directory of the plastics industry including an index of firms and products.

34035 **LAGEBEURTEILUNG DER BAUWIRTSCHAFT**
St Galler Zentrum fur Zukunftsforschung

Switzerland – German annual 1973 90pp SF200.00

Forecast for the construction industry.

34036 **LANDERBERICHT SCHWEIZ**
Federal Statistical Office of Germany

Switzerland – German irregular DM7.90

Statistical survey of Switzerland including demography, geography, education, employment, agriculture, production, overseas trade, transport, tourism, finance, wages and prices and national accounts.

34037 **DIE LEBENSMITTEL UND GETRANKE–INDUSTRIE DER SCHWEIZ**
Verlag fur Wirtschaftsliteratur GmbH

Switzerland – German/French 400pp SF85

Directory of the food and beverages industry giving information on over 5,000 firms, distribution and trade associations.

34038 **MARCHES ETRANGERS**
Swiss Office for Trade Promotion

Switzerland – French/German monthly SF90 in Switzerland, SF100 abroad

Information on foreign markets designed for Swiss businessmen.

34039 **MITTEILUNGEN DES ST GALLER ZENTRUMS FUR ZUKUNFTSFORSCHUNG**
St Galler Zentrum fur Zukunftsforschung

Switzerland – German quarterly 1978 30pp SF250.00 p.a.

Information on the developments in the economy.

34040 **MONTHLY BULLETIN**
British-Swiss Chamber of Commerce in Switzerland

Switzerland – English monthly

34041 **MONTHLY BULLETIN**
Schweizerische Nationalbank

Switzerland – German/French monthly SF30.00

34042 **OECD ECONOMIC SURVEYS–SWITZERLAND**
Organisation for Economic Cooperation and Development (OECD)

Switzerland – English annual 70pp £2.40/ DM12/US$5/FrF24

A detailed analysis of recent developments in demand production, employment, prices and wages, conditions in the money and capital markets and developments in the balance of payments. It includes short-term forecasts as well as analyses of medium-term problems of specific relevance to the elaboration of the country's economic policies.

34043 **PRODUCTS AND SERVICES OF SWITZERLAND (SWISS EXPORT DIRECTORY)**
Swiss Office for Trade Promotion (OSEC)

Switzerland – English/German/French/ Spanish 1,400pp SF30.00 abroad

Publication supplying information on 10,000 export products (capital and consumer goods, semi-manufactured products) and services offered by 8,500 export firms. 15th edition.

34044 **RECENSEMENT FEDERAL DES ENTREPRISES/EIDGENOSSISCHE BETRIEBSZAHLUNG**
Office Federal de la Statistique

Switzerland – French/German decennial 5 parts various per part SF145 in total

Federal census of companies.

34045 **RECENSEMENT FEDERAL DES ENTREPRISES AGRICOLES/ EIDGENOSSISCHE BETRIEBSZAHLUNG**
Office Federal de la Statistique

Switzerland – French/German decennial 7 parts various per part SF148 in total

Federal census of agriculture including agriculture, forestry and fisheries.

34046 **REPORT AND ACCOUNTS**
British-Swiss Chamber of Commerce in Switzerland

Switzerland – English annual c12pp

34047 **LES RESULTATS COMPTABLES DES ENTREPRISES SUISSES/ BUCHHALTUNGSERGEBRISSE SCHWEIZERISCHER UNTERNEHMUNG**
Office Federal de la Statistique

Switzerland – French/German annual 62pp SF13.00

Financial accounts of Swiss companies. Also gives data on gross value added per person and has annexes surveying macroeconomic data.

34048 **DIE SCHWEIZ**
Swiss Bank Corporation

Switzerland – German/English/French/ Italian/Spanish/Japanese 1979 free

General account of the country.

34049 **SCHWEIZER EINKAUFSFUHRER FUR BEKLEIDUNG UND SCHUHE**
Verlag fur Wirtschaftsliteratur GmbH

Switzerland – German/French/English annual 1976 200pp SF18
ISBN No. 3-909214-04

A directory of the Swiss clothing and shoe industry including an index of companies, products, trade marks and exhibitions.

34050 **DER SEKTORALE STRUKTURWANDEL IN DER SCHWEIZ**
St Galler Zentrum fur Zukunftsforschung

Switzerland – German 1983 120pp SF18.00
ISBN No. 3725301913

Structural change in the Swiss economy.

34051 **SOCIETE ANONYMES EN SUISSE/ AKTIENGESELLSCHAFTEN IN DER SCHWEIZ**
Office Federal de la Statistique

Switzerland – French/German annual 1902 50pp SF11.00

Number of companies by economic class, by size of company and by Canton.

34052 **STATISTIQUE ANNUELLE–DU COMMERCE EXTERIEUR DE LA SUISSE/JAHRESSTATISTIK–DES AUSSENHANDELS DER SCHWEIZ**
Direction Generale des Douanes

Switzerland – French/German annual (3 volumes) 1,280pp SF165.00

Annual statistics of Swiss imports and exports by quantity and value, by commodities and by countries.

34053 **STATISTIQUE MENSUELLE DU COMMERCE EXTERIEUR DE LA SUISSE/MONATSSTATISTIK - DER AUSSENHANDELS DER SCHWEIZ**
Direction Generale des Douanes

Switzerland – French/German monthly 250pp SF185.00

Monthly statistics of Swiss imports and exports by quantity and value by commodities and by countries.

34054 **STATISTICHE ERHEBUNGEN UND SCHAZUNGEN***
Schweizerische Bauernsekretariat

Switzerland – German/French annual c200pp

Statistics on agriculture and food.

34055 **STATISTISCHES JAHRBUCH DER SCHWEIZ–ANNUAIRE STATISTIQUE DE LA SUISSE**
Bundesamt fur Statistik

Switzerland – German/French annual c600pp

Statistics on population, agriculture, industry, trade both foreign and domestic, transport, finance, tourism, prices, household expenditure, national accounts, labour, company structures, culture, education, development, health, sport, justice, politics.

34056 **SWISS REVIEW OF POLITICAL ECONOMY AND STATISTICS**
Schweizerische Gesellschaft fur Statistik und Volkswirtschaft (SGSV)

Switzerland – French/German/English quarterly 1864 650pp Inland SF80, overseas SF90

34057 **SWISS STOCK GUIDE**
Union Bank of Switzerland

Switzerland – German/French/English annual free

34058 **THE SWISS WATCHMAKING INDUSTRY**
Union Bank of Switzerland

Switzerland – German/French/English/ Italian 1986 61pp free

History of Swiss watchmaking. Structure of the industry, foreign trade, trends on the global watch market.

34059 **SWITZERLAND**
National Westminster Bank

Switzerland – English irregular 4pp free

Brief economic report.

34060 **SWITZERLAND**
UK Iron and Steel Statistics Bureau

Switzerland – English 1986 with annual statistical summary £25

Report on the steel industry showing production, consumption and details of imports and exports.

34061 **SWITZERLAND IN FIGURES**
Union Bank of Switzerland

Switzerland – German/French/English annual 1p free

Factsheet providing statistical overview of Switzerland in tabular and graphic form.

34062 **SWITZERLAND'S LARGEST COMPANIES**
Union Bank of Switzerland

Switzerland – English/French annual free

34063 **SWITZERLAND YOUR PARTNER**
Swiss Office for Trade Promotion (OSEC)

Switzerland – English/French/Spanish every 3 years 1979 100pp free

Collection of 10 brochures devoted to the following Swiss investment goods: telecommunications, agriculture and food processing, transportation and communications, public health, building and construction, energy generation and distribution, hotel-keeping and tourism, environment, conservation, industrial production, education and training.

34064 **TAX & INVESTMENT PROFILE**
Touche Ross International, USA

Switzerland – English free

Survey covering investment, trade, labour, business practices, financial system. Frequently updated.

34065 **TELECOMMUNICATIONS INDUSTRY IN SWITZERLAND**
Union Bank of Switzerland

Switzerland – English/German/French/Italian 1986 12pp free

34066 **TEXTILES SUISSES**
Swiss Office for Trade Promotion

Switzerland – French/German/English quarterly SF66 in Switzerland SF76 abroad

Journal of the fabric trade especially clothing fabrics.

34067 **TEXTILES SUISSES–INTERIEUR**
Swiss Office for Trade Promotion

Switzerland – French/German/English/Italian semi-annual SF33 in Switzerland SF38 abroad

Journal dealing with home textiles.

34068 **TOURISME EN SUISSE/ TOURISMOS IN DER SCHWEIZ**
Office Federal de la Statistique

Switzerland – French/German annual 1933 (previously known as Le Mouvement Hotelier en Suisse) 122pp SF25

Annual and retrospective data on the Swiss tourism industry.

34069 **TOURISME EN SUISSE–SEMESTRE D'ETE/ TOURISMUS IN DER SCHWEIZ–SOMMERHALBJAHR**
Office Federal de la Statistique

Switzerland – French/German annual 40pp SF6

Swiss tourist industry in summer.

34070 **TOURISME EN SUISSE–SEMESTRE D'HIVER/ TOURISMOS IN DER SCHWEIZ–WINTERHALBJAHR**
Office Federal de la Statistique

Switzerland – French/German annual 30pp SF6.00

The Swiss tourist industry in winter.

34071 **TRANSPORTS, TRAFFIC ROUTIER/ALLG VERKEHR, STRASSENVERKEHR**
Office Federal de la Statistique

Switzerland – French/German annual 6 parts various per part, SF128 complete

Includes accidents, registration of vehicles by canton, sales of new vehicles, imports and exports.

34072 **UBS BUSINESS FACTS AND FIGURES**
Union Bank of Switzerland

Switzerland – German/French/English/Italian/Spanish 10 issues a year c20pp free

Brief review of commerce, trade and the economy.

34073 **LA VIE ECONOMIQUE/DIE VOLKSWIRTSCHAFT**
Schweizerisches Handelsamtsblatt

Switzerland – French/German monthly 1930

The Swiss economy and social statistics including text, charts and economic statistics.

34074 **VORPORT/JAHRESBERICHT**
Schweizerischer Handels und Industrie-verein

Switzerland – German/French annual 200pp

A review of the economic situation and economic policy, including monetary policy, business outlook, financial policy, energy, transport policy, agriculture, labour market, social insurance, media policy and environment. Also includes a statistical survey.

34075 **THE WORLD BANK GROUP AND SWITZERLAND**
The Union Bank of Switzerland

Switzerland – English/German 1987 79pp free

IBRD, IDA, IFC–organization, tasks, financing and relations of these organizations with Switzerland.

34076 **DIE ZURCHER BORSE JAHRESBERICHT**
Effektenborsenverein

Switzerland – German annual 80pp free

Surveys the organization and development of the Zurich stock exchange and includes detailed statistical tables of stock prices and movements.

TURKEY

35001 **AGRICULTURAL STRUCTURE AND PRODUCTION**
State Institute of Statistics

Turkey – Turkish/English annual

35002 **ANNUAL FOREIGN TRADE STATISTICS**
State Institute of Statistics

Turkey – Turkish/English annual

Imports and exports classified by commodities and countries of origin and destination.

35003 **ANNUAL MANUFACTURING INDUSTRY STATISTICS**
State Institute of Statistics

Turkey – Turkish/English annual

35004 **ANNUAL REPORT**
Central Bank of the Republic of Turkey

Turkey – English annual

Analysis of economic developments in the world at large and in Turkey considers the Turkish economy in the context of world economy.

35005 **ANNUAL STATISTICS OF TRADE AND SERVICE**
State Institute of Statistics

Turkey – Turkish/English

35006 **BIRTH STATISTICS (IN PROVINCES WHERE HEALTH SERVICES ARE SOCIALIZED)**
State Institute of Statistics

Turkey – Turkish irregular

35007 **BUDGETS (MUNICIPALITIES, SPECIAL ADMINISTRATION, VILLAGES)**
State Institute of Statistics

Turkey – Turkish/English annual

35008 **BULLETIN OF ACCOMMODATION STATISTICS**
Ministry of Culture and Tourism Research and Statistics

Turkey – Turkish/English annual 1976 69pp

Arrivals and nights spent of foreigners and citizens in registered accommodation establishments (by type of establishments, months, nationality, regions and provinces), average length of stay.

35009 **BULLETIN OF CONSTRUCTION STATISTICS**
State Institute of Statistics

Turkey – Turkish/English annual

35010 **BULLETIN OF TOURISM STATISTICS**
Ministry of Culture and Tourism Publication of Directorate of Socio-Ekonomic Research and Statistics

Turkey – Turkish/English 1972 85pp

Frontier arrivals and departures (foreigners, citizens and tourists) by months, means of transport, nationality, by means of provinces of entry, tourism receipts and expenditures.

35011 **CALISMA ISTATISTIKLERI VE ISGUCU MALIYETI**
Turkish Confederation of Employer Associations

Turkey – Turkish annual 1975 16pp

Employment, trades unions, labour costs etc.

35012 **CENSUS OF INDUSTRY AND BUSINESS ESTABLISHMENTS**
State Institute of Statistics

Turkey – Turkish/English

Part I large-scale manufacturing industries; part II small-scale manufacturing industries; part III wholesale and retail trade; part IV service; part V hotel-restaurant and cafes; part VI other establishments. (Preliminary and second stage results.)

35013 **CENSUS OF POPULATION BY ADMINISTRATIVE DIVISION**
State Institute of Statistics

Turkey – Turkish/English 5 years

35014 **CENSUS OF POPULATION SOCIAL AND ECONOMIC CHARACTERISTICS 1980**
State Institute of Statistics

Turkey – Turkish/English 5 years

35015 **CONSTRUCTION STATISTICS (CONSTRUCTION PERMITS AND OCCUPANCY PERMITS)**
State Institute of Statistics

Turkey – Turkish/English annual

35016 **COUNTRY PROFILES–TURKEY**
Economist Publications Ltd

Turkey – English annual 40pp £25 UK subscription varies in rest of world

Resumé of politics, economy and industry including statistical summaries.

35017 **COUNTRY REPORTS–TURKEY**
Economist Publications Ltd

Turkey – English quarterly 25pp £58 UK subscription varies in rest of world

Economic policies and development plans, trends in production and demand, monetary and fiscal conditions, wages and prices, merchandise trade, invisibles, capital flows, exchange rates and foreign debt plus a forecast of the economic prospects.

35018 **ECONOMIC REPORT**
Istanbul Chamber of Commerce

Turkey – English 2 per annum

World/Turkish economy.

35019 **THE ECONOMY**
Turkish Cypriot Chamber of Commerce

Turkey – Turkish weekly 1978 8pp

Economics.

35020 **FISHERY STATISTICS**
State Institute of Statistics

Turkey – Turkish/English annual

35021 **FOREIGN TRADE STATISTICS**
State Institute of Statistics

Turkey – Turkish/English annual

35022 **GIUNA GIBERKEN TURK EKONOMISI (TURKISH ECONOMY AT THE BEGINNING OF...)**
Turkish Industrialists' and Businessmens' Association (TUSIAD)

Turkey – Turkish annual 1974 150pp

Economic conjecture within Turkey.

35023 **GÖRÜS**
Turkish Industrialists' and Businessmen's Association (TUSIAD)

Turkey – Turkish monthly 1973 32pp

Monthly review of economic topics.

35024 **HINTS TO EXPORTERS**
Department of Trade and Industry

Turkey – English annual

Practical guide for businessmen giving general information, useful addresses, methods of doing business and relevant regulations.

35025 **HOUSEHOLD LABOUR FORCE SURVEY RESULTS**
State Institute of Statistics

Turkey – English/Turkish

35026 **INTERNAL TRADE STATISTICS: COMMERCIAL COMPANIES AND CONSUMER COOPERATIVES**
State Institute of Statistics

Turkey – Turkish/English annual

35027 **I.S.E. MONTHLY BULLETIN**
Istanbul Stock Exchange
I.S.E. Statistics and Valuation Department

Turkey – Turkish/English monthly Turkish 1986 – English 1986 Turkish 6pp English 4pp TL0.60

Monthly price movements of stocks for the first and some of the second market companies, indexes, monthly trading volume, general information about first market companies.

35028 **I.S.E. SIX MONTHLY BULLETIN**
Istanbul Stock Exchange

Turkey – Turkish/English twice a year 1987 6pp TL0.60

Six-monthly price movements of stocks for the first and some of the trading second market companies, indexes, six-monthly trading volume, general information about the first market companies, charts.

35029 **I.S.E. WEEKLY BULLETIN**
Istanbul Stock Exchange

Turkey – Turkish weekly 1986 6pp TL0.60

Weekly price movements of stocks for the first and some of the second market companies, indexes, weekly trading volumes, information summary about 40 first market companies.

35030 **I.S.E. YEARBOOK OF COMPANIES**
Istanbul Stock Exchange
I.S.E.

Turkey – Turkish annual 1988 88pp US$10

Detailed information of 40 companies in the first market, balance and income sheets, financial ratios, graphics.

35031 **'ISVEREN' ('THE EMPLOYER')**
Turkish Confederation of Employer Associations

Turkey – Turkish monthly October 1962 32pp
ISSN No. 2250

Labour, economic, social and industrial relations.

35032 **JOURNAL OF ECONOMICS AND ADMINISTRATIVE SCIENCES**
Faculty of Economics and Administrative Sciences
Abdullah Oger

Turkey – Turkish/English twice a year spring 1984 250pp TL500

Analysis of various socio-economic problems of Turkey, especially at regional level.

35033 **LANDERBERICHT TURKEI**
Federal Statistical Office of Germany

Turkey – German irregular DM7.90

Statistical survey of Turkey including demography, geography, education, employment, agriculture, production, overseas trade, transport, tourism, finance, wages and prices and national accounts.

35034 **MANUFACTURING INDUSTRY, QUARTERLY EMPLOYMENT, PRODUCTION AND EXPECTATION (PROVISIONAL RESULTS)**
State Institute of Statistics

Turkey – Turkish/English quarterly

35035 **MANUFACTURING INDUSTRY PRODUCTION INDEXES (QUARTERLY)**
State Institute of Statistics

Turkey – Turkish/English quarterly

35036 **MINING STATISTICS**
State Institute of Statistics

Turkey – English/Turkish annual

35037 **MONTHLY BULLETIN OF CONSTRUCTION STATISTICS**
State Institute of Statistics

Turkey – Turkish/English monthly

35038 **MONTHLY BULLETIN OF STATISTICS**
State Institute of Statistics

Turkey – Turkish monthly

35039 **MONTHLY ECONOMIC INDICATORS**
State Institute of Statistics

Turkey – English/Turkish monthly

Economic outlook of Turkey to public and private users who may be interested in keeping track of short-term economic changes.

35040 **MONTHLY PRICE INDEXES**
State Institute of Statistics

Turkey – Turkish/English

35041 **OECD ECONOMIC SURVEYS–TURKEY**
Organisation for Economic Cooperation and Development (OECD)

Turkey – English annual 70 pp £2.40/ DM12/US$5/FrF24

A detailed analysis of recent developments in demand production, employment, prices and wages, conditions in the money and capital markets and developments in the balance of payments. It includes short-term forecasts as well as analyses of medium-term problems of specific relevance to the elaboration of the country's economic policies.

35042 **OPPORTUNITIES FOR INVESTORS (TOURISM)**
Ministry of Culture and Tourism
Tourism General Directorate

Turkey – English 39+6pp documents for tourism investors

General views of tourism sector, foreign investment companies, foreign management companies, role of government in the tourism sector, tourism investment projects, planning studies, investment procedures, letter of undertaking, clean letter of credit, state-owned land allocation for tourist investments, tourism encouragement, law encouragement, conditions and incentives.

35043 **PRICES RECEIVED BY FARMERS**
State Institute of Statistics

Turkey – Turkish/English annual

35044 **RETAIL PRICE STATISTICS**
State Institute of Statistics

Turkey – Turkish/English annual

35045 **REVIEW OF ECONOMIC CONDITIONS**
Turkiye is Bankasi AS

Turkey – English quarterly

35046 **STATISTICAL POCKET BOOK OF TURKEY**
State Institute of Statistics

Turkey – Turkish/English

35047 **STATISTICAL YEARBOOK OF TURKEY**
State Institute of Statistics

Turkey – Turkish/English annual

35048 STATISTICS OF VESSELS COASTWISE AND INTERNATIONAL SEA TRANSPORTATION
State Institute of Statistics

Turkey – Turkish/English

35049 SUMMARY OF AGRICULTURAL STATISTICS
State Institute of Statistics

Turkey – Turkish/English annual

35050 SUMMARY TABLES OF FOREIGN TRADE STATISTICS
State Institute of Statistics

Turkey – Turkish monthly

35051 TISK INFORMATION
Turkish Confederation of Employer Associations

Turkey – English quarterly April 1987 4pp

Labour, economic, social and industrial relations.

35052 TOURISM STATISTICS
State Institute of Statistics

Turkey – Turkish/English annual

35053 TRANSPORTATION AND ROAD TRAFFIC ACCIDENT STATISTICS
State Institute of Statistics

Turkey – Turkish/English 2 years

35054 TURKEY
National Westminster Bank

Turkey – English irregular 4pp free

Brief economic report.

35055 TURKEY MAIN ECONOMIC INDICATORS
State Planning Organisation

Turkey – English monthly

35056 THE TURKISH ECONOMY
Turkish Industrialists' and Businessmen's Association (TUSIAD)

Turkey – English annual 1976 220pp

The social and economic aspects of the development in Turkey and statistical series.

35057 WHOLESALE PRICE STATISTICS: REGISTERED COMMODITIES IN COMMODITY EXCHANGES
State Institute of Statistics

Turkey – Turkish/English annual

35058 WHOLESALE AND CONSUMER PRICE INDEXES MONTHLY BULLETIN
State Institute of Statistics

Turkey – Turkish/English monthly

UNITED KINGDOM

36001 **50 CENTRES–A GUIDE TO OFFICE AND INDUSTRIAL RENTAL TRENDS IN ENGLAND AND WALES**
Jones Lang Wootton

UK – English 2 a year

36002 **ADAS–ANNUAL REPORT**
HMSO

UK – English annual £8.00

Annual report of the Agricultural Development and Advisory Service covering agriculture, agricultural science, land, land drainage, veterinary science.

36003 **A-Z OF UK BRAND LEADERS**
Euromonitor

UK – English £28.00

500 companies in the UK which have brand leadership in a significant sector of the UK consumer market.

36004 **A-Z OF UK RETAILING**
Euromonitor

UK – English £35.00

Classification of retail outlets, sales and turnovers of retail outlets, top 50 retailing groups with financial breakdown, summary of main sources.

36005 **ABSTRACT OF STATISTICS FOR INDEX OF RETAIL PRICES, AVERAGE EARNINGS, SOCIAL SECURITY BENEFITS AND CONTRIBUTIONS**
HMSO

UK – English annual £15.00

36006 **ADVERTISING FORECAST**
Advertising Association

UK – English quarterly £345.00

Reference source for the advertising industry covering 19 media categories, 21 product categories and 350 individual product groups.

36007 **ADVERTISING STATISTICS YEARBOOK**
Advertising Association

UK – English annual 150pp £25.00

Statistics on expenditure and other relevant matters with an index of media rates and cover prices.

36008 **AEROSOL REVIEW**
Morgan-Grampian Book Publishing Co. Ltd

UK – English annual £18.00

36009 **AGRICULTURAL LABOUR IN ENGLAND AND WALES–EARNINGS, HOURS AND NUMBERS OF PERSONS**
HMSO

UK – English annual £3.50

36010 **AGRICULTURAL MARKETING INFORMATION DIRECTORY**
Institute of Marketing

UK – English 1984 £5.00

36011 **AGRICULTURAL STATISTICS: UNITED KINGDOM**
HMSO

UK – English annual £10.20

36012 **AGRICULTURE IN SCOTLAND**
HMSO

UK – English annual £6.40

36013 **ANNUAL ABSTRACT OF STATISTICS**
HMSO

UK – English annual £18.50

36014 **ANNUAL REPORT (ACAS)**
Advisory, Conciliation and Arbitration Service

UK – English annual free

Report of the official government body for industrial arbitration.

36015 **ANNUAL REPORT—ADVERTISING ASSOCIATION**
Advertising Association

UK – English annual free

36016 **ANNUAL REPORT, AGRICULTURAL AND FOOD RESEARCH COUNCIL**
HMSO

UK – English annual £6.00

36017 **ANNUAL REPORT OF THE BUILDING SOCIETIES COMMISSION**
HMSO

UK – English annual 1986-1987 £6.10

36018 **ANNUAL REPORT: COAL RESEARCH ESTABLISHMENT**
British Coal

UK – English annual free

36019 **ANNUAL REPORT–FORESTRY COMMISSION**
HMSO

UK – English annual £8.50

36020 **ANNUAL REPORT—FURNITURE INDUSTRY RESEARCH ASSOCIATION**
Furniture Industry Research Association

UK – English annual c30pp free

Annual report containing summary of the previous year's research and publications.

36021 **ANNUAL REPORT—IPA**
Institute of Practitioners in Advertising

UK – English annual free

36022 **ANNUAL REPORT–NEDO**
National Economic Development Council

UK – English annual

36023 **ANNUAL REPORT—NATIONAL INSTITUTE OF ECONOMIC AND SOCIAL RESEARCH**
National Institute of Economic and Social Research

UK – English annual c30pp free

Report on the Institute's activities during the preceding year, including details of publications and current research projects.

36024 ANNUAL REVIEW OF AGRICULTURE
HMSO

UK – English annual £7.40

36025 APPROPRIATION ACCOUNTS
HMSO

UK – English annual (12 volumes) Each volume individually priced

A comparison between the actual expenditure of governmental departments during the previous financial year and the provision in the Supply Estimates for that year.

36026 BSA BULLETIN
Building Societies Association

UK – English quarterly £5.00 per copy

Commentary on building societies and the housing markets in the preceding quarter, regular tables on trends in building society activity and in the housing market and special articles on underlying trends.

36027 BSRIA STATISTICS BULLETIN
Building Services Research and Information Association

UK – English quarterly £85 UK £90 Europe free to members

Statistics, market reviews and forecasts for the building services industry.

36028 BANK OF ENGLAND QUARTERLY BULLETIN
Bank of England

UK – English quarterly £27.00 UK £33-£50 overseas depending on air mail zone

Review and developments in principal sectors of the economy and detailed statistics on the banking system, exchange rates, interest rates and balance of payments.

36029 BANK OF ENGLAND—REPORT AND ACCOUNTS
Bank of England

UK – English annual free

Account of the operations of the Bank in all financial and monetary matters.

36030 THE BANKER
Financial Times Business Information

UK – English monthly £57.00 UK £85.00 Europe £105 rest of the world

Specialist publication designed for the international banking community.

36031 BASIC HORTICULTURAL STATISTICS FOR THE UK
HMSO

UK – English annual free

36032 BENEFITS
Reward Group

UK – English annual £50.00

Trends and details of benefits and conditions of service.

36033 BRITISH AID STATISTICS
HMSO

UK – English annual £6.00

Statistics of UK economic aid to developing countries.

36034 BRITISH BANKING DIRECTORY
Financial Times Business Information

UK – English 398pp 1986

Directory of deposit banks, British merchant banks, London discount houses, merchant banking subsidiaries of foreign banks, joint-ventures, and London branches of international banks. The information includes details of financial status, overseas connections and representation and leading personnel.

36035 BRITISH BUSINESS
HMSO

UK – English weekly £75.00 Europe £98.00 overseas

Articles on general topics of economic and commercial interest.

36036 BRITISH EXPORTS
Kompass Publishers

UK – English with headings in French, German and Spanish annual 3 vols £75.00

36037 BRITISH TOURISM SURVEY
British Tourist Authority

UK – English annual £9.75

36038 BUSINESS CARS SURVEY 1985
British Institute of Management

UK – English 56pp £31.25
ISBN No. 0 946 559147

An evaluation of business car management, covering purchasing, finance and allocation to depreciation, replacement and disposal. Also includes tax treatment of company cars.

36039 BUSINESS MONITORS: ANNUAL CENSUS OF PRODUCTION REPORTS
HMSO

UK – English £5.95 each issue

Series of individual industry reports which tabulate the results of the latest annual census of production covering turnover, net output, costs, employment.

Energy and water supply industries
PA 111 Coal extraction and manufactures of solid fuels
PA 120 Coke ovens
PA 130 Extraction of mineral oil and natural gas
PA 140 Mineral oil processing
PA 161 Production and distribution electricity
PA 162 Public gas supply
PA 170 Water supply industry

Extraction of minerals and ores other than fuels: manufacture of metals and mineral products and chemicals
PA 210 Extraction and preparation of metalliferous ores
PA 221 Iron and steel industry
PA 222 Steel tubes
PA 223 Drawing, cold rolling and cold forming of steel
PA 224 Non-ferrous metals industry
PA 231 Extraction of stone, clay, sand and gravel
PA 239 Extraction of miscellaneous minerals (including salt)
PA 241 Structural clay products
PA 242 Cement, lime and plaster
PA 243 Building products of concrete, cement or plaster
PA 244 Asbestos goods
PA 245 Working of stone and other non-metallic minerals
PA 246 Abrasive products
PA 247 Glass and glassware
PA 248 Refractory and ceramic goods
PA 251 Basic industrial chemicals
PA 255 Paints, varnishes and printing ink
PA 256 Specialised chemical products mainly for industrial and agricultural purposes
PA 257 Pharmaceutical products
PA 258 Soap and toilet preparations
PA 259 Specialised chemical products mainly for household and office use
PA 260 Production of manmade fibres

Metal goods, engineering and vehicle industries
PA 311 Foundries
PA 312 Forging, pressing and stamping
PA 313 Bolts, nuts, washers, rivets, springs, non-precision chains, metal treatment
PA 314 Metal doors, windows, etc.
PA 316 Hand tools and finished metal goods
PA 320 Industrial plant and steelwork
PA 321 Agricultural machinery and tractors
PA 322 Metal-working machine tools and engineers' tools
PA 323 Textile machinery
PA 324 Machinery for the food, chemical and related industries; process engineering contractors
PA 325 Mining machinery, constructional and mechanical handling equipment
PA 326 Mechanical power transmission equipment
PA 327 Machinery for the printing, paper, wood, leather, rubber, glass and related industries, laundry and dry cleaning machinery
PA 328 Miscellaneous machinery and mechanical equipment
PA 329 Ordnance, small arms and ammunition
PA 330 Manufacture of office machinery and data-processing equipment
PA 341 Insulated wires and cables
PA 342 Basic electrical equipment
PA 343 Electrical equipment for industrial use, and batteries and accumulators
PA 344 Telecommunication equipment, electrical measuring equipment, electronic capital goods and passive electronic components
PA 345 Miscellaneous electronic equipment
PA 346 Domestic-type electric appliances

PA 347 Electric lamps and other electrical lighting equipment
PA 351 Motor vehicles and their engines
PA 352 Motor vehicle bodies, trailers and caravans
PA 353 Motor vehicle parts
PA 361 Shipbuilding and repairing
PA 362 Railway and tramway vehicles
PA 363 Cycles and motor cycles
PA 364 Aerospace equipment manufacturing and repairing
PA 365 Miscellaneous vehicles
PA 371 Measuring, checking and precision instruments and apparatus
PA 372 Medical and surgical equipment and orthopaedic appliances
PA 373 Optical precision instruments and photographic equipment
PA 374 Clocks, watches and other timing devices

Other manufacturing industries
PA 411 Organic oils and fats
PA 412 Processing of bacon, meat and poultry
PA 413 Preparation of milk and milk products
PA 414 Processing of fruit and vegetables
PA 415 Fish processing
PA 416 Grain milling
PA 419 Bread, biscuits and flour confectionery
PA 420 Sugar and sugar by-products
PA 421 Ice-cream, cocoa, chocolate and sugar confectionery
PA 422 Animal feeding stuffs
PA 423 Starch and miscellaneous foods
PA 424 Spirit distilling and compounding
PA 426 Wines, cider and perry
PA 427 Brewing and malting
PA 428 Soft drinks
PA 429 Tobacco industry
PA 431 Woollen and worsted industry
PA 432 Cotton and silk industries
PA 433 Throwing, texturing, etc. of continuous filament yarn
PA 434 Spinning and weaving of flax, hemp and ramie
PA 435 Jute and polypropylene yarns and fabrics
PA 436 Hosiery and other knitted goods
PA 437 Textile finishing
PA 438 Carpets and other textile floor coverings
PA 439 Miscellaneous textiles
PA 441 Leather (tanning and dressing) and fellmongery
PA 442 Leather goods
PA 451 Footwear
PA 453 Clothing, hats and gloves
PA 455 Household textiles and other made-up textiles
PA 456 Fur
PA 461 Sawmilling, planing, etc. of wood
PA 462 Manufacture of semi-finished wood products and further processing and treatment of wood
PA 463 Builders' carpentry and joinery
PA 464 Wooden containers
PA 465 Miscellaneous wooden articles
PA 466 Articles of cork and plaiting materials, brushes and brooms
PA 467 Wooden and upholstered furniture and shop and office fittings
PA 471 Pulp, paper and board
PA 472 Conversion of paper and board
PA 475 Printing and publishing
PA 481 Rubber products (including retreading and specialist repairing of tyres)
PA 483 Processing of plastics
PA 491 Jewellery and coins
PA 492 Musical instruments
PA 493 Photographic and cinematographic processing laboratories
PA 494 Toys and sports goods
PA 495 Miscellaneous manufacturing industries

Construction
PA 500 Construction

36040 BUSINESS MONITORS–MISCELLANEOUS HMSO

UK – English monthly, quarterly, annual, occasional

Monthly
MM 1 Motor vehicle registrations
MM 17 Price index numbers for current cost accounting (monthly supplement)
MM 19 Aerospace and electronics cost indices (1980 = 100)

Quarterly
MQ 5 Insurance companies' and private pension funds' investments
MQ 6 Overseas travel and tourism
MQ 7 Acquisitions and mergers of industrial and commercial companies
MQ 10 Overseas trade analysed in terms of industries
MQ 12 Import penetration and export sales ratios for manufacturing industry

Annual
MA 3 Company finance
MA 3/MO4 (Monitor package) Company finance and top company finance
MA 4 Overseas transactions
MA 6 Overseas travel and tourism
MA 8 Nationality of vessels in UK sea-borne trade
MA 16 Insurance business statistics

Occasional
MO 4 Census of overseas assets 1984
MO 14 Survey of scientific research and development carried out within the UK (1985)
MO 18 Price index numbers for current cost accounting, summary volume 1974-1982

36041 BUSINESS MONITORS–PRODUCTION SERIES HMSO

UK – English monthly, quarterly, annual, occasional monthly £19.50 per title p.a. quarterly £11.95 per title p.a.

A series of reports giving latest output estimates for individual industries and indices of production for recent periods.

Quarterly Production Monitors

Energy Industries

PQ1113 Coal mining
PQ1300 Extraction of mineral oil and natural gas
PQ1610 Electricity
PQ1620 Gas

Extraction of minerals and ores other than fuels: manufacture of metals and mineral products and chemicals
PQ2234 Steel wire and steel wire products
PQ2245 Aluminium and aluminium alloys
PQ2247 Miscellaneous non-ferrous metals and their alloys
PQ2310/2450 Extraction of stone, clay, sand and gravel, working of stone and miscellaneous non-metallic minerals
PQ2330/2396 Salt and miscellaneous minerals
PQ2437 Miscellaneous building products of concrete, cement or plaster
PQ2440 Asbestos
PQ2460 Abrasives
PQ2471/2478/2479 Flat glass, glass containers and miscellaneous glass products
PQ2481 Refractory goods
PQ2489 Ceramic goods
PQ2511 Inorganic chemicals (except industrial gases)
PQ2512 Basic organic chemicals (except specialised pharmaceutical chemicals)
PQ2513 Fertilisers
PQ2514/2515 Synthetic resins, plastics materials and synthetic rubber
PQ2516 Dyestuffs and pigments
PQ2551 Paints, varnishes and painters' fillings
PQ2552 Printing ink
PQ2562/2569 Formulated adhesives, sealants and adhesive film, cloth and foil
PQ2563/2564 Chemical treatment of oils, fats and essential oils and flavouring materials
PQ2567 Miscellaneous chemical products for industrial use
PQ2568 Formulated pesticides
PQ2570 Pharmaceutical products
PQ2581 Soap and synthetic detergents
PQ2582 Perfumes, cosmetics and toilet preparations
PQ2591/2599 Photographic materials, chemicals and polishes and miscellaneous specialised products mainly for household and office use
PQ2600 Production of man-made fibres

Metal goods, engineering and vehicle industries
PQ3111 Iron castings
PQ3112 Non-ferrous metal foundries
PQ3120 Forging, pressing and stamping
PQ3137 Bolts, nuts, washers, rivets, springs and non-precision chains
PQ3138 Heat and surface treatment of metals (including sintering)
PQ3142 Metal doors, windows, etc.
PQ3163 Hand tools and implements
PQ3162 Cutlery, spoons, forks and similar tableware: razors
PQ3163/3164 Metal storage vessels (mainly non-industrial) and packaging products of metal
PQ3165 Domestic heating and cooking appliances (non-electrical)
PQ3166 Metal furniture and safes
PQ3167 Domestic utensils of metal
PQ3169 Miscellaneous finished metal products
PQ3204 Fabricated constructional steelwork
PQ3205 Boilers and process plant fabrications
PQ3211 Agricultural machinery
PQ3212 Wheeled tractors
PQ3221 Metal-working machine tools
PQ3222 Engineers' small tools
PQ3230 Textile machinery
PQ3244 Food, drink and tobacco processing machinery; packaging and bottling machin ery
PQ3245 Chemical industry machinery; furnaces and kilns; gas, water and waste treatment plant
PQ3251 Mining machinery
PQ3254 Construction and earth-moving equipment
PQ3255 Mechanical lifting and handling equipment
PQ3261/3262 Precision chains, other mechanical power transmission equipment, ball, needle and roller bearings
PQ3275 Machinery for working wood,

rubber, plastics, leather, and making paper, glass, bricks and similar materials; laundry and dry-cleaning machinery
PQ3276 Printing, bookbinding and paper goods machinery
PQ3281 Industrial (including marine) engines
PQ3283 Compressors and fluid power equipment
PQ3284 Refrigerating, space heating, ventilating and air-conditioning equipment
PQ3285 Scales, weighing machinery and portable power tools
PQ3286 Miscellaneous industrial and commercial machinery
PQ3287 Pumps
PQ3288 Industrial valves
PQ3289 Miscellaneous mechanical marine and precision engineering
PQ3290 Ordnance, small arms and ammunition
PQ3301/3302 Office machinery and electronic data-processing equipment
PQ3410 Insulated wires and cables
PQ3420 Basic electrical equipment
PQ3432 Batteries and accumulators
PQ3433 Alarms and signalling equipment
PQ3434 Electrical equipment for motor vehicles, cycles and aircraft
PQ3435 Miscellaneous electrical equipment for industrial uses
PQ3441 Telegraph and telephone equipment
PQ3442 Electrical instruments and control systems
PQ3443 Radio and electronic capital goods
PQ3444 Components other than active components, mainly for electronic equipment
PQ3452 Gramophone records and pre-recorded tapes
PQ3453 Electronic sub-assemblies and active components
PQ3454 Electronic consumer goods and miscellaneous equipment
PQ3460 Domestic electrical appliances
PQ3470 Electric lamps and lighting equipment
PQ3510/3521 Motor vehicles, engines and motor vehicle bodies
PQ3522/3523 Trailers, semi-trailers and caravans
PQ3530 Motor vehicle parts
PQ3610 Shipbuilding and repairing
PQ3620 Railway and tramway vehicles
PQ3633/3634/3650 Motor cycles, cycles and miscellaneous vehicles
PQ3640 Aerospace equipment manufacturing and repairing
PQ3710 Measuring, checking and precision instruments and apparatus
PQ3720 Medical and surgical equipment and orthopaedic appliances
PQ3731/3732 Spectacles, unmounted lenses and optical precision instruments
PQ3733 Photographic and cinematographic equipment
PQ3740 Clocks, watches and other timing devices

Other manufacturing industries
PQ4115 Margarine and compound cooking fats
PQ4116 Organic oils and fats
PQ4122 Bacon curing and meat products
PQ4123 Poultry and poultry products
PQ4126 Animal by-products
PQ4147 Fruit and vegetable products
PQ4150 Fish products
PQ4180 Starch
PQ4196 Bread and flour confectionery
PQ4197 Biscuits and crispbread
PQ4213 Ice-cream
PQ4239 Miscellaneous foods
PQ4240 Spirit distilling and compounding
PQ4261 Wines, cider and perry
PQ4283 Soft drinks
PQ4290 Tobacco
PQ4310 Woollen and worsted
PQ4321/4336 Spinning and doubling of cotton, throwing, texturing etc of continuous filament yarn
PQ4322 Weaving of cotton, silk and manmade fibres
PQ4340 Spinning and weaving of flax, hemp and ramie
PQ4350 Jute and polypropylene yarns and fabrics
PQ4363 Hosiery and other weft knitted goods
PQ4364 Warp knitted goods
PQ4370 Textile finishing
PQ4384/4385 Carpets and other textile floor coverings
PQ4395 Lace
PQ4396 Rope, twine and net
PQ4398 Narrow fabrics
PQ4399 Miscellaneous textiles
PQ4410/4420 Leather and fellmongery and leather goods
PQ4510 Footwear
PQ4531 Weatherproof outerwear
PQ4532 Men's and boys' tailored outerwear
PQ4533 Women's and girls' tailored outerwear
PQ4534 Work clothing and men's and boys' jeans
PQ4535 Men's and boys' shirts, underwear and nightwear
PQ4536 Women's and girls' light outerwear, lingerie and infants' wear
PQ4537/4538 Hats, caps, millinery and gloves
PQ4539 Miscellaneous dress industries
PQ4555 Soft furnishings
PQ4556 Canvas goods, sacks and miscellaneous made-up textiles
PQ4557 Household textiles
PQ4560 Fur goods
PQ4610 Sawmilling, planing, etc of wood
PQ4620 Semi-finished wood products; preservation and treatment of wood
PQ4630 Builders' carpentry and joinery
PQ4640/4650 Wooden containers, miscellaneous wooden articles
PQ4663/4664 Articles of cork and plaiting materials, brushes and brooms
PQ4671 Wooden and upholstered furniture
PQ4672 Shop and office fitting
PQ4710 Pulp, paper and board
PQ4721 Wallcoverings
PQ4722 Household and personal hygiene paper products
PQ4723 Stationery
PQ4724 Packaging products of paper and pulp
PQ4725/4728 Packaging products of board and miscellaneous paper and board products
PQ4751 Printing and publishing of newspapers
PQ4752 Printing and publishing of periodicals
PQ4753 Printing and publishing of books
PQ4754 Miscellaneous printing and publishing
PQ4811/4820 Rubber tyres and inner tubes, retreading and specialist repairing of rubber tyres
PQ4812 Miscellaneous rubber products
PQ4831/4833 Plastic-coated textile fabrics and plastics floor coverings
PQ4832 Plastics semi-manufactures
PQ4834 Plastics building products
PQ4835 Plastics packaging products
PQ4836 Miscellaneous plastics products
PQ4910 Jewellery and coins
PQ4920 Musical instruments
PQ4941 Toys and games
PQ4942 Sports goods
PQ4954 Miscellaneous stationers' goods
PQ4959 Miscellaneous manufacturing industries

Quarterly Monitors covering more than one industry
PQ1002 Manufacturing industries

Monthly Production Monitors
PM3510 Car and commercial vehicle production
PM4710 Pulp, paper and board

Annual Monitors covering more than one industry
PA1001 Introductory notes
PA1002 Summary tables
PA1003 Size analyses of United Kingdom businesses
PA1007 Minerals

Annual Sales Monitors
PAS1401/1402 Mineral oil refining, lubricating oils and greases
PAS2246 Copper, brass and other copper alloys
PAS2410 Structural clay products
PAS2420 Cement, lime and plaster

Occasional Monitors covering more than one industry
PO1000 Index of commodities
PO1001 Guide to short-term statistics of manufacturers' sales
PO1007 Classified list of manufacturing businesses 1984 (issued in six parts)
PO1008 Purchases inquiry 1984

36042 BUSINESS MONITORS–SERVICE AND DISTRIBUTIVE MONITORS HMSO

UK – English monthly, quarterly, annual

Monthly
SDM6 Credit business
SDM28 Retail sales

Quarterly
SDQ7 Assets and liabilities of finance houses and other consumer credit companies
SDQ9 Computer services

Annual
SDA26 Wholesaling
SDA27 Motor trades
SDA28 Catering and allied trades

Occasional
SDO25 Retailing (1984)

36043 BUSINESS RATIO REPORT ICC Information Group Ltd

UK – English annual £121/£137.00

150 annual reports each analysing up to 100 leading companies.

36044 BUSINESS SURVEYS Jordan and Sons Ltd

UK – English

Probing reviews of Britain's major industrial sectors featuring marketing and financial analyses, future predictions, performance ratings and valuable names, addresses and telephone numbers.

36045 **BUTTERWORTH'S BUDGET TAX TABLES**
Butterworth and Co. (Publishers) Ltd/L. Livens ed.

UK – English annual

Published annually the day after the Budget, this publication summarizes changes proposed in it.

36046 **BUTTERWORTH'S ORANGE TAX HANDBOOK**
Butterworth and Co. (Publishers) Ltd

UK – English annual

Text of legislation covering inheritance tax, national insurance contributions, stamp duty and value added tax.

36047 **BUTTERWORTH'S TAX TREATIES**
Butterworth and Co. (Publishers) Ltd

UK – English updated regularly 1984 £145

Up-to-date texts of all the double tax agreements between the UK and other countries.

36048 **BUTTERWORTH'S YELLOW TAX HANDBOOK**
Butterworth and Co (Publishers) Ltd

UK – English annual

Text of legislation relating to income tax, corporation tax and capital gains tax.

36049 **CBI/FT DISTRIBUTIVE TRADES SURVEY**
Confederation of British Industry (CBI)

UK – English monthly

Reported and expected wholesaling, retailing and motor trades sectors.

36050 **CSU STATISTICAL QUARTERLY**
HMSO

UK – English quarterly £20.00

Analyses movements and changes within the graduate employment market and incorporates a salary survey of current rates for new and recent graduates.

36051 **1981-1991 CENSUS NEWSLETTER**
HMSO

UK – English irregular

Information on the preparation for the census and details of relevant services, products, meetings etc., including plans for and consultations on the 1991 Census.

36052 **CENSUS 81 COUNTY REPORTS**
HMSO

UK – English

36053 **CENSUS 81–ECONOMIC ACTIVITY COUNTIES**
HMSO

UK – English £4.00

Tables covering the classification of economic position, employment states, occupation industry, social class and socio-economic groups based on a 10 per cent sample of the census returns.

36054 **CENSUS 81–ECONOMIC ACTIVITY GREAT BRITAIN**
HMSO

UK – English £17.70
ISSN No. 011690951X

Statistics on the classification of economic position, employment status, occupation, industry, social class and socio-economic groups based on a 10 per cent sample.

36055 **CENSUS 81–HOUSEHOLD AND FAMILY COMPOSITION**
HMSO

UK – English £10.00
ISSN No. 011 690595

Structure of household and families based on a 10 per cent sample.

36056 **CENSUS 81–HOUSING AND HOUSEHOLDS**
HMSO

UK – English £18.46
ISSN No. 0116909374

Statistics on housing, householders and the availability of cars.

36057 **CENSUS 81–KEY STATISTICS FOR LOCAL AUTHORITIES GREAT BRITAIN**
HMSO

UK – English £0.10
ISSN No. 011 6909803

A selection of over 100 key census statistics for every local authority administrative areas in Great Britain.

36058 **CENSUS 81–KEY STATISTICS FOR URBAN AREAS**
HMSO

UK – English £7.80 (Scotland £6.30)

A series of reports covering the South East, the Midlands, Scotland, South West and Wales, the North.

36059 **CENSUS 81–NATIONAL MIGRATION GREAT BRITAIN**
HMSO

UK – English Part 1 £11.70, Part 2 £7.40
ISBN No. part 1 011 6909447 Part 2 011 6909617

Two-part report - the statistics are based on the 100 per cent items and are for Great Britain, constituent counties and in some cases for regions of England, metropolitan counties and regional remainders.

36060 **CENSUS 81–NATONAL REPORT GREAT BRITAIN**
HMSO

UK – English Part 1 £11.70 Part 2 £6.80
ISBN No. part 1 011 6909293 Part 2 011 690934X

Two-part report - the statistics in Part 2 are based on a 10 per cent sample.

36061 **CENSUS 81–NEW TOWNS REPORT ENGLAND AND WALES**
HMSO

UK – English Part 1 £10.80 Part 2 £5.80
ISBN No. Part 1 011 6909315 Part 2 011 6909722

Statistics for the 23 New Towns in England and Wales designated since 1946.

36062 **CENSUS 81 – QUALIFIED MANPOWER**
HMSO

UK – English £14.40
ISBN No. 011 6909609

Statistics on the qualified manpower of Great Britain based on a 10 per cent sample of the 1981 census returns.

36063 **CENSUS 81–REGIONAL MIGRATION**
HMSO

UK – English

A series of regional volumes with statistics from the 1981 census for migration within one year preceding census, based on 100 per cent items.

36064 **CHARITY TRENDS**
Charities Aid Foundation

UK – English annual £17.00

36065 **CHEMICALS '86**
Chemical Industries Association Ltd

UK – English 218pp £45.00

Listing of some 10,000 chemicals with proprietary and trade names and details of manufacturers.

36066 **CIVIL SERVICE STATISTICS**
HMSO

UK – English annual

36067 **CLERICAL AND OPERATIVE REWARDS**
Reward Group

UK – English twice a year £90.00 p.a.

Analysis of basic pay and average earnings for all main clerical and operative positions. Each job analysed by company size, location and industry.

36068 **COAL IN ... LEAFLETS**
British Coal

UK – English free

A series of illustrated leaflets covering each of British Coal's administrative areas: Scotland, North East, Western, North Yorkshire, South Yorkshire, North Derbyshire, Nottinghamshire, South Midlands, Kent, South Wales.

36069 COMMERCIAL AND INDUSTRIAL FLOORSPACE STATISTICS–WALES
HMSO

UK – English annual £5.00

36070 COMPANIES
HMSO

UK – English annual £4.95

The annual report of the Companies Division, Department of Trade and Industry and the Insolvency Service so far as it relates to corporate insolvency.

36071 COMPENDIUM OF BUILDING SOCIETY STATISTICS 7TH EDITION
Building Societies Association

UK – English irregular £25.00

A complete statistical history of building societies.

36072 CONSTITUTION AND SCHEDULE OF WAGE RATES AND WORKING CONDITIONS—CHEMICAL AND ALLIED INDUSTRIES J.I.C.
Chemical Industries Association Ltd

UK – English 1986 £1.00

National agreement covering process and general workers.

36073 CONSTRUCTION FORECASTS
National Economic Development Office

UK – English annual £15.00

Housing and non-housing construction in the public and private sectors, also repair and maintenance.

36074 CONSUMPTION AND REFINERY PRODUCTION
Institute of Petroleum

UK – English annual c9pp free

Statistics covering deliveries of petroleum products, analysed by end use and refinery production.

36075 COST OF LIVING REPORTS, REGIONAL COMPARISONS
Reward Group

UK – English twice a year £90

Detailed comparison for the eleven standard government regions as well as comprehensive assessment of the national situation for eight different lifestyles. Reports comparing specific towns are prepared to order.

36076 COSTS AND PRICES
Henley Centre for Forecasting

UK – English quarterly £450

Statistics and forecasts of cost and price movement of energy, metal freight packages and property. Cost and price change in 20 industrial sectors with data on budgeting, cost control, pricing, purchasing and marketing policy.

36077 COUNCILS, COMMITTEES AND BOARDS
CBD Research Ltd

UK – English every 2 or 3 years 1984 440pp £48.00 US$100

Directory of national and regional boards including government advisory committees, public boards, consumer consultative committees and other groups. Information includes name, address, membership, names of chairmen and secretary, terms of reference and activities.

36078 COUNTRY PROFILES
Economist Publications Ltd

UK – English annual 40pp £25 UK subscription varies in rest of world

Resumé of politics, economy and industry including statistical summaries.

36079 COUNTRY REPORTS
Economist Publications Ltd

UK – English quarterly 25pp £58 UK subscription varies in rest of world

Economic policies and development plans, trends in production and demand, monetary and fiscal conditions, wages and prices, merchandise trade, invisibles, capital flows, exchange rates and foreign debt plus a forecast of the economic prospects.

36080 DELIVERIES OF YARN
Textile Statistics Bureau

UK – English monthly £3.00 each issue

Deliveries classified by spinners, doublers and main consuming industries.

36081 DIGEST OF ENERGY STATISTICS
HMSO

UK – English annual £13.50

Tables and charts of UK energy production and consumption.

36082 DIGEST OF ENVIRONMENTAL PROTECTION AND WATER STATISTICS
HMSO

UK – English annual £8.00

36083 DIGEST OF TOURIST STATISTICS (12th EDITION)
British Tourist Authority/English Tourist Board

UK – English £8.00

36084 DIGEST OF WELSH STATISTICS
HMSO

UK – English annual £5.00

36085 DIRECTORS GUIDE
Henley Centre for Forecasting

UK – English monthly £125

A digest providing a regular review of economic and social trends and forecasts up to two years ahead.

36086 DIRECTORS REWARDS
Reward Group

UK – English annual £95.00

Full analysis of directors' remuneration and benefits. Published in association with the Institute of Directors.

36087 DIRECTORY OF BRITISH ASSOCIATIONS 1988
CBD Research Ltd

UK – English every 2 to 3 years

Interests, activities and publications of trade associations, scientific and technical societies, professional institutes, learned societies, research associations, chambers of commerce and trade, agricultural societies, trade unions, cultural, sports and welfare organizations in the UK and Eire.

36088 DIRECTORY OF EXPORT BUYERS IN THE UK
Trade Research Publications

UK – English 1987 200pp

Directory of export buyers classified by product, country, foreign firm dealt with, and location.

36089 ECONOMIC OUTLOOK
Gower Publishing Company Ltd

UK – English monthly £135.00

Journal giving a four-year business forecast of the UK economy.

36090 ECONOMIC PROGRESS REPORT
HMSO

UK – English bi-monthly free

Published by the Treasury the report contains articles on economic subjects, analysing or giving background to government economic policy.

36091 ECONOMIC PROSPECTS
Co-operative Union Ltd

UK – English annual

36092 ECONOMIC REPORT ON SCOTTISH AGRICULTURE
HMSO

UK – English annual

36093 **ECONOMIC SITUATION REPORT**
Confederation of British Industry (CBI)

UK – English monthly £156 (CBI members £104)

Report giving CBI's survey data, economic indicators and quarterly short-term forecasts for the UK economy.

36094 **ECONOMIC TRENDS**
HMSO

UK – English monthly and annual supplement
£110 including annual supplement

Commentary and selection of tables and charts provide a broad background to trends in the UK economy. The annual supplement presents very long runs quarterly for all main series.

36095 **THE ECONOMIST**
The Economist Newspaper Ltd

UK – English weekly c135pp £1.30 £65 p.a.

Commentary on financial, industrial and commercial developments, analysis of political events and main economic indicators.

36096 **EMPLOYMENT AFFAIRS REPORT**
Confederation of British Industry (CBI)

UK – English bi-monthly £70 (CBI members £53)

Comprehensive analysis of the employment scene including developments in the labour market, the legal field, industrial relations, pensions and social security, health and safety.

36097 **EMPLOYMENT GAZETTE**
HMSO

UK – English monthly £35.00 p.a. single issues £3.40

Articles, tables and charts on manpower employment, unemployment, hours worked, earnings, labour costs, retail prices, stoppages and disputes.

36098 **ENERGY TRENDS**
HMSO

UK – English monthly

Monthly and quarterly tables of production and consumption of fuel, aggregated energy consumption and fuel prices together with a commentary.

36099 **EXECUTIVE PENSIONS**
Financial Times Business Information

UK – English annual 256pp £21.50 US$36, Overseas £24
ISSN No. 090201 838

Pension plans for company directors and senior employees.

36100 **EXPENSES AND BENEFITS OF DIRECTORS AND HIGHER PAID EMPLOYEES**
London Chamber of Commerce

UK – English annual 1979 157pp £14.95
ISSN No. 0 85091 052 9

Taxation.

36101 **EXPORTS**
Textile Statistics Bureau

UK – English monthly 7 reports £3.50 each report

Each series shows monthly cumulative totals from the beginning of the year. The following products are covered: man-made fibre, waste and filament yarn; cotton yarn; spun man-made fibre yarn; woven cotton piecegoods; woven man-made fibre piecegoods by type and country; woven man-made fibre piecegoods by type of finish and country; knitted man-made fibre piecegoods.

36102 **FIRA BULLETIN**
Furniture Industry Research Association

UK – English quarterly March 1988 30pp £40 UK £50 overseas

Covers all aspects of furniture.

36103 **FACTS FOR INDUSTRY**
WINvest

UK – English/German/Japanese/Korean/Chinese annual 1979 50pp free

Summary of facts on Welsh economy for companies wishing to invest in Wales. Also covers incentives, sites, transport, employment.

36104 **FACTUAL BACKGROUND**
Bristol and West Building Society

UK – English quarterly

Building societies, general data, personal savings, personal credit and housing.

36105 **FAMILY EXPENDITURE SURVEY**
HMSO

UK – English annual £15.95

Shows in great detail income and expenditures by type of household for the UK and includes some regional analyses.

36106 **FARM BUSINESS DATA**
Department of Agricultural Economics and Management, University of Reading

UK – English annual £3.00

Farm business data for Avon, Berkshire, Buckinghamshire, Gloucestershire, Hampshire, Hereford and Worcester, Isle of Wight, Oxfordshire, Warwickshire, West Midlands and Wiltshire.

36107 **FARM BUSINESS STATISTICS FOR SOUTHEAST ENGLAND**
Agricultural Economics Unit

UK – English 1987 £3.00

Statistics analysed by type of farm.

36108 **FARM INCOMES IN THE UNITED KINGDOM**
HMSO

UK – English annual £12.00

36109 **FINANCIAL AND ACCOUNTING REWARDS**
Reward Group

UK – English annual £80.00

A full report of salaries and benefits paid to accounting staff in companies and partnerships.

36110 **FINANCIAL STATEMENT AND BUDGET REPORT**
HMSO

UK – English annual £7.20

Published by the Treasury on Budget Day, it sets out the Government's economic and financial strategy and reviews the performance and prospects of the economy.

36111 **FINANCIAL STATISTICS**
HMSO

UK – English monthly and annual supplement £85.00 p.a. and annual supplement

Key financial and monetary statistics for the UK.

36112 **FINANCIAL TIMES OFFSHORE FUND YEARBOOK**
Financial Times Business Information

UK – English annual £28.00

Comprehensive coverage on over 400 funds with more than 600 different share classes.

36113 **FOOD MANUFACTURE INGREDIENT SURVEY**
Morgan-Grampian Book Publishing Co. Ltd

UK – English annual £19.00

36114 **FOOD RETAILING**
Institute of Grocery Distribution

UK – English annual £160.00

36115 **FORECASTS FOR THE UK ECONOMY**
HMSO

UK – English monthly £50 p.a.

A comparison of independent forecasts.

36116 **FRAMEWORK FORECASTS FOR THE UK***
Henley Centre for Forecasting

UK – English monthly £800.00

Monthly forecasts of incomes, business and personal spending, cost and prices, output, money and stock market factors. Short-term forecasts by the quarter and five yearly by the year.

36117 **GENERAL HOUSEHOLD SURVEY**
HMSO

UK – English annual £10.70

A continuous sample survey of householders relating to a wide range of social and socio-economic policy areas.

36118 **GENERAL TRENDS IN SHIPPING**
HMSO

UK – English annual £12.00

36119 **GERMAN AND BRITISH ECONOMY**
German Chamber of Industry and Commerce

UK – English monthly £20 DM80 (annual subscription)

Comparative economic statistics.

36120 **GILT NEWS**
James Capel

UK – English

36121 **GROWTH MARKETS**
Market Assessment Publications Ltd

UK – English quarterly £480 per publication

Two publications covering food growth markets and non-food growth markets.

36122 **HANDBOOK OF ELECTRICITY SUPPLY STATISTICS**
Electricity Council

UK – English annual

Public electricity supply in UK including price indices and earnings. Also looks at the progress of the gas industry.

36123 **HEALTH AND PERSONAL SOCIAL SERVICES STATISTICS IN ENGLAND**
HMSO

UK – English annual £8.95

36124 **HEALTH AND PERSONAL SOCIAL SERVICES STATISTICS FOR WALES**
HMSO

UK – English annual £3.00

36125 **HEALTH AND SAFETY STATISTICS**
HMSO

UK – English biennial £9.00

36126 **HILLIER PARKER RENT INDEX**
Financial Times Business Information

UK – English semi-annually c20pp £5.00 in UK/£6.00 US$9.00 overseas

Statistics on market rental levels on different types of commercial property.

36127 **HISTORICAL DIRECTORY OF TRADE UNIONS**
Gower Publishing Company Ltd/A. Marsh and V. Ryan

UK – English 1980 vol.1 256pp £27.50 1983 vol.2 400pp £27.50 1987 vol.3 560pp £39.50 vol.4 forthcoming.

Comprehensive directory of British trade unions giving for each union–name, foundation date, details of membership, policy and events.
Vol.1, non-manual
Vol.2, engineering, iron and steel, coal, mining, agriculture, chemicals
Vol.3, transport, building
Vol.4, textiles, printing, retail distribution and miscellaneous.

36128 **HOUSE PRICE INDEX REGIONAL BULLETIN**
Halifax Building Society

UK – English quarterly

36129 **HOUSEHOLD FOOD CONSUMPTION AND EXPENDITURE**
HMSO

UK – English annual £13.00

Report on food consumption, expenditure and nutrition by type of household.

36130 **HOUSING AND CONSTRUCTION STATISTICS GREAT BRITAIN 1976/86**
HMSO

UK – English annual £25.00

36131 **HOUSING AND CONSTRUCTION STATISTICS GREAT BRITAIN**
HMSO

UK – English quarterly in two parts £30.00 annual subscription

36132 **IC STOCK MARKETS LETTER**
Financial Times Business Information

UK – English weekly £80.00

Advice on equity investment and market trends.

36133 **IDS GUIDES***
Incomes Data Services Ltd

UK – English quarterly £5.00

Detailed reports on a variety of management topics. Current subjects covered include: redundancy, profit-sharing, incentive schemes, pension schemes, job evaluation, sick pay, retirement benefits.

36134 **IMPORTERS HANDBOOK**
Trade Research Publications

UK – English £8.00
ISBN No. 0 904783189

All aspects of importing - how to import, pros and cons of buying direct from abroad or through a merchant or agent, finding suppliers, import duties and quotas, payment.

36135 **IMPORTS**
Textile Statistics Bureau

UK – English monthly 6 reports £5.50 each report

Each series shows monthly cumulative totals from the beginning of the year. The following categories are covered: man-made staple fibre, waste and filament yarn; cotton yarn; spun man-made fibre yarn; woven cotton piecegoods (two tables– grey and other than grey); woven man-made fibre piecegoods by type and country; woven man-made fibre piecegoods by type of finish and country; knitted man-made fibre piecegoods; woven cotton and man-made fibre made-up articles.

36136 **IMPORTS OF MAN-MADE FIBRE: EXPORTS OF MAN-MADE CONTINUOUS FILAMENT YARN**
Textile Statistics Bureau

UK – English monthly £5.00

Category one covers the following: staple fibre, waste, continuous filament yarns and selected spun yarns, by commodity type showing major country, weight, value and average value; weight is also shown as cumulative total.

Category two covers the following yarns: creped, bulked, textured, crimped or stretch, by commodity type showing major country, weight, value and average value; weight is also shown as cumulative total.

36137 **IMPORTS (TIME SERIES)**
Textile Statistics Bureau

UK – English monthly/quarterly £5.00

Monthly total figures for the following categories: cotton yarn, spun man-made fibre yarn, woven cotton piecegoods (total and for re-export), woven cotton made-up goods (estimated square metres), woven man-made fibre piecegoods (total and seven major sub-divisions).
Quarterly figures by major supplying countries for the following categories: cotton yarn, spun man-made fibre yarn, woven cotton piecegoods for retention in the home market, woven cotton made-up goods (value), woven man-made fibre piecegoods.

36138 **INCOMES DATA REPORT***
Incomes Data Services Ltd

UK – English semi-monthly £90.00

Information on factors affecting wage and salary levels, labour market, developments in legislation and taxation.

36139 **INDUSTRIAL TRENDS SURVEY**
Confederation of British Industry (CBI)

UK – English quarterly and monthly quarterly £176 (£110 CBI members) monthly £176 (£110 CBI members) combines £270 (£186 CBI members)

Quarterly and monthly information on current and expected trends in manufacturing industry–large sample of firms directly covering more than half of UK manufacturing.

36140 **INLAND REVENUE STATISTICS**
HMSO

UK – English annual £10.95

Statistics related to all taxes administered by the Inland Revenue: income tax, corporation tax, petroleum revenue tax, inheritance tax, capital gains tax, development land tax and stamp duties.

36141 **INLAND WATERWAYS FREIGHT STATISTICS 1986**
HMSO

UK – English occasional £10.00

36142 **INPUT-OUTPUT TABLES FOR THE UK 1984**
HMSO

UK – English approximately every 5 years £19.95

Information to aid the understanding and analysis of economic interdependence of the various industrial sectors.

36143 **INSURANCE STATISTICS**
Association of British Insurers

UK – English annual

Worldwide figures provided by insurance companies having their head office in the UK and UK figures for those companies with head offices outside the UK.

36144 **INTERNATIONAL ROAD HAULAGE BY UK REGISTERED VEHICLES**
HMSO

UK – English annual £10.00

36145 **INVESTING FOR BEGINNERS**
Financial Times Business Information

UK – English irregular 151pp £9.50 Overseas £12 US$17
ISSN No. 0902121 52 2

Guide to investment for people new to the UK stockmarket based on series in the 'Investors Chronicle'.

36146 **INVESTORS CHRONICLE**
Financial Times Business Information

UK – English weekly £57.00 £66.00 Europe £82.00 rest of world

All aspects of UK investment with particular emphasis on UK quoted shares.

36147 **INVESTOR'S GUIDE TO THE STOCK MARKET**
Financial Times Business Information

UK – English 1986 182pp £9.50 UK US$12.00 overseas £17.00

Guide to the stock market which covers operating procedures and strategies for successful dealing.

36148 **IRON AND STEEL–SHIPBUILDING**
Pergamon Press plc

UK – English 1984 203pp £23.00

Review of statistics for iron and steel and shipbuilding industries.

36149 **KEY DATA**
HMSO

UK – English annual £2.95

Over 130 tables, maps and coloured charts and a wide range of social and economic data.

36150 **KEYNOTE REPORTS**
Keynote Publications Ltd

UK – English £89.00 each

Market information on industry sectors.

36151 **KOMPASS REGISTER**
Kompass Publishers, UK

UK – English/French/Spanish/German/Italian annual 1981 £145.00

Comprehensive business directory giving information on over 30,000 companies listed geographically and cross-rererenced to a directory of products and services.

36152 **KOMPASS UK REGIONAL SALES GUIDES**
Kompass Publishers, UK

UK – English annual 7 vols £32.00

Basic information on 30,000 public and private companies arranged alphabetically by town, county and region.

36153 **LABOUR MARKET QUARTERLY REPORT**
HMSO

UK – English quarterly free

36154 **LANDERBERICHT GROSBRITANNIEN UND NORDIRLAND**
Federal Statistical Office of Germany

UK – German irregular DM7.90

Statistical survey of the UK including demography, geography, education, employment, agriculture, production, overseas trade, transport, tourism, finance, wages and prices and national accounts.

36155 **LEISURE FUTURES**
Henley Centre for Forecasting

UK – English quarterly £800.00

Analysis of leisure markets with short-term forecasts by quarter and longer-term forecasts by year.

36156 **LLOYD'S BANK REVIEW**
Lloyds Bank Ltd

UK – English quarterly c60pp free

Economic review with detailed articles on the monetary situation.

36157 **LOCAL GOVERNMENT COMPARATIVE STATISTICS**
CIPFA

UK – English annual £33.00

36158 **LOCAL GOVERNMENT FINANCIAL STATISTICS, ENGLAND**
HMSO

UK – English annual £4.90

36159 **LOCAL GOVERNMENT TRENDS**
CIPFA

UK – English annual £36.00

36160 **LONDON CHAMBER MANUFACTURING TRENDS SURVEY**
London Chamber of Commerce

UK – English quarterly 1975 8pp £5 per issue

National and international trade prospects for companies in London and the south-east of England.

36161 **LONDON WEIGHTING**
Reward Group

UK – English annual £40.00

Full analysis of payments for the private sector in London and other large towns.

36162 **MGN MARKETING MANUAL OF THE UNITED KINGDOM 1982/85**
Mirror Group Newspapers (1986) Ltd

UK – English irregular £30.00

A wide selection of consumer marketing data from published sources.

36163 **MMB ANNUAL REPORT AND ACCOUNTS**
Milk Marketing Board

UK – English annual free

36164 **MACHINE TOOL STATISTICS**
Machine Tool Trade Association

UK – English annual £25.00

36165 **MAN-MADE FIBRE PRODUCTION**
Textile Statistics Bureau

UK – English monthly £3.00 per issue

Monthly figures for production and deliveries of filament yarn classified by main consuming industries; and quarterly figures for deliveries of staple fibre.

36166 **MARKET SECTOR REPORTS**
Market Assessment Publications Ltd

UK – English annual

A series of [illegible] market sector reports, each consisting of a management summary, overview of the sector, detailed examination of products covered in terms of market size and growth, production and foreign trade, segmentation, competition and brand shares, advertising and promotion, distribution, consumer profiles and five-year forecasts.

36167 **MIDLAND BANK REVIEW**
Midland Bank Ltd

UK – English quarterly c25pp free

Brief economic review.

36168 **MONEY FOR BUSINESS—A GUIDE**
Bank of England

UK – English 1985 £3.00

Information and general advice on the types and sources of finance available to small- and medium-sized firms.

36169 **MONEY FOR EXPORTS—A GUIDE**
Bank of England

UK – English 1979 free

Introduction for the UK exporter to export credit insurance and export finance. List of relevant institutions.

36170 **MONEY MANAGEMENT**
Financial Times Business Information

UK – English monthly £40.00 UK £82.00 overseas

All aspects of personal finance including insurance, pensions, mortgages, taxation and investment.

36171 **MONTHLY BULLETIN OF INDICES: PRICE ADJUSTMENT FORMULAE FOR CONSTRUCTION CONTRACTS**
HMSO

UK – English monthly £43.25 p.a.

36172 **MONTHLY BULLETIN OF STATISTICS**
Wool Industry Bureau of Statistics

UK – English monthly c24pp £36.00

Statistics on the production of woollen and worsted by month for the main regions of the UK: also machinery capacity and utilization, employment.

36173 **MONTHLY DIGEST OF STATISTICS**
HMSO

UK – English monthly and annual supplement £60.00

Collection of main series from government departments.

36174 **MONTHLY ECONOMIC SIGNAL**
James Capel

UK – English monthly

36175 **MONTHLY OIL COMMENTARY**
James Capel

UK – English monthly

Includes prices and exploration activity.

36176 **MONTHLY STATISTICAL REVIEW**
Society of Motor Manufacturers and Traders Ltd

UK – English monthly c28pp £60.00

Bulletin of statistics on production, imports, exports, and new registrations analysed by make and type of vehicle.

36177 **MONTHLY STATISTICS–FOOTWEAR INDUSTRY**
British Footwear Manufacturers Federation

UK – English monthly £30.00

This publication provides regular statistics on the British footwear industry. There are quarterly supplements.

36178 **MOTOR INDUSTRY OF GREAT BRITAIN**
Society of Motor Manufacturers and Traders Ltd

UK – English annual £45.00

Statistical survey including retrospective data, and information on production, registrations and exports.

36179 **NATIONAL INSTITUTE ECONOMIC REVIEW**
National Institute of Economic and Social Research

UK – English quarterly c100pp £12.50

Regular review with forecasts of the economy and analytic articles on selected topics. Includes international comparisons.

36180 **NATIONAL MANAGEMENT SALARY SURVEY**
British Institute of Management Remuneration Economics Ltd

UK – English annual 2 vols £190.00

Survey of several hundred organizations providing statistical tables analysed by management level, functions, location and presented against a background report on taxation, inflation and salary movement.

36181 **NATIONAL MILK RECORDS ANNUAL REPORT**
Milk Marketing Board

UK – English annual £2.50

Details of herds by breed and area classified by production and quality. Also general articles.

36182 **NATIONALISATIONS ET DENATIONALISATIONS EN GRANDE-BRETAGNE**
La Documentation Française

UK – French 1983 144pp FrF50
ISSN No. 0029 4004

36183 **NEW EARNINGS SURVEY**
HMSO

UK – English six parts per year £55.00

Earnings of employees by industry, occupation and region.

36184 **NEWS FROM ABI**
Association of British Insurers

UK – English irregular

36185 **NEWS FROM UNIT TRUST ASSOCIATION**
Unit Trust Association

UK – English monthly free

Including monthly unit trust statistics and quarterly investment statistics.

36186 **NORTHERN IRELAND ANNUAL ABSTRACT OF STATISTICS**
HMSO

UK – English annual £10.00

36187 **OECD ECONOMIC SURVEYS–UNITED KINGDOM**
Organisation for Economic Cooperation and Development (OECD)

UK – English annual 70pp £2.40/DM12/US$5/FrF24

A detailed analysis of recent developments in demand, production, employment, prices and wages, conditions in the money and capital markets and developments in the balance of payments. It includes short-term forecasts as well as analyses of medium-term problems of specific relevance to the elaboration of the country's economic policies.

36188 **OFFSHORE TAX PLANNING**
Butterworth and Co. (Publishers) Ltd

UK – English 1986 226pp £32.00
ISBN No. 0406 50210 2'

A detailed survey of the law and practice relating to offshore tax planning with practical advice on structure and location.

36189 **OIL DATA SHEETS**
Institute of Petroleum

UK – English £3.00 per set

A set of 19 sheets covering all aspects of oil production, exports, imports for UK and the world.

36190 **OUTPUT AND UTILISATION OF FARM PRODUCE IN THE UNITED KINGDOM**
HMSO

UK – English annual £6.00

36191 **OVERSEAS TRADE STATISTICS OF THE UNITED KINGDOM**
HMSO

UK – English monthly and annual volume £210.00

Detailed statistics of exports and imports cumulated throughout the year.

36192 **PATENT LAW OF EUROPE AND THE UNITED KINGDOM**
Butterworth and Co. (Publishers) Ltd, UK/A. Walton and H. Laddie

UK – English 1978 with frequent updatings

Loose-leaf work providing information on patent law in Europe as applied to the UK.

36193 **PAYMENT OF VAT UPON THE IMPORTATION OF GOODS INTO THE UNITED KINGDOM AFTER 1 NOVEMBER 1984**
German Chamber of Industry and Commerce

UK – English £10.00

36194 **PENSION FUNDS AND THEIR ADVISERS**
A.P. Information Services

UK – English annual c900pp £40.00

Articles on pension fund investment and directory of pension funds and administrative personnel.

36195 **PERSONAL PENSIONS**
Financial Times Business Information

UK – English irregular July 1987 200pp £12.50 overseas £17.50 US$24.50
ISSN No. 185334 0022

Practical guide to and assessment of 120 tailor-made pension plans for UK company directors and senior employees.

36196 **PETROLEUM REVIEW**
Institute of Petroleum

UK – English monthly

Articles on both technical and commercial aspects of the UK oil industry.

36197 **PLANNING CONSUMER MARKETS***
Henley Centre for Forecasting

UK – English quarterly £800.00

Analysis of consumer markets by television broadcasting region. Forecasts for population trends, spending and income patterns, social developments.

36198 **PLANNING FOR SOCIAL CHANGE ANNUAL**
Henley Centre for Forecasting

UK – English annual cost on application

Statistics, forecasts and analysis of changes in social attitudes and trends and their economic significance.

36199 **POPULATION ESTIMATES SCOTLAND**
HMSO

UK – English annual £1.50

36200 **POPULATION PROJECTIONS**
HMSO

UK – English annual £10.20

Series PP2 issued by Office of Population Censuses and Surveys.

36201 **POPULATION TRENDS**
HMSO

UK – English quarterly various prices

Regular series of tables on subject for which OPCS is responsible in England and Wales in addition to articles on a variety of population and medical topics.

36202 **PORT STATISTICS**
British Ports Association

UK – English annual 1980 150pp £25
ISSN No. 0263 9149

An analysis of movement of goods through all British ports by port and commodity group; distinguishes figures for container and roll-on/roll-off traffic.

36203 **PRIVATE HOUSE-BUILDING STATISTICS**
NHBC

UK – English quarterly free

36204 **PROCESS INDUSTRIES INVESTMENTS FORECASTS**
National Economic Development Office

UK – English annual £20.00

36205 **PROPERTY INDEX**
Jones Lang Wootton

UK – English annual

Data collected in four aggregate sectors–shops, offices, industrial and warehouse, agriculture.

36206 **PROPERTY INVESTMENT QUARTERLY BULLETIN**
Richard Ellis

UK – English quarterly

36207 **PUBLIC EXPENDITURE WHITE PAPER**
HMSO

UK – English annual (2 parts)

Present government's expenditure plans with corresponding figures for last five years.

36208 **QUARTERLY BULLETIN OF STATISTICS**
Furniture Industry Research Association

UK – English quarterly £20 members £50 non-members

36209 **QUARTERLY REVIEW OF UK TRADE STATISTICS**
Wool Industry Bureau of Statistics

UK – English quarterly £22.00

A quarterly analysis in the form of category by country, detailing accumulated trade figures of UK imports and exports, together with geographical analysis and historic comparisons.

36210 **QUARTERLY STATISTICAL REVIEW**
Textile Statistics Bureau

UK – English quarterly c32pp £12.00

Statistics on production and trade in woven cloth, cotton industry, man-made fibres, knitting industry, carpets and rugs, wool industry, household textiles.

36211 **QUARTERLY SURVEY OF ADVERTISING EXPENDITURE**
Advertising Association

UK – English quarterly 150pp £150.00
ISSN No. 0951 7766

Expenditure data on all main media: TV, press, radio, posters, direct mail plus product sectors.

36212 **QUARTERLY SURVEY OF SMALL BUSINESS IN BRITAIN**
Small Business Research Trust

UK – English quarterly

36213 **QUALITY OF MARKETS QUARTERLY**
The Stock Exchange

UK – English quarterly £48.00

36214 **RICS NEWS**
Royal Institution of Chartered Surveyors

UK – English quarterly

36215 **REGIONAL TRENDS**
HMSO

UK – English annual £17.50

36216 **REGISTRAR GENERAL'S ANNUAL REPORT FOR NORTHERN IRELAND**
HMSO

UK – English

36217 **REGISTRAR GENERAL'S ANNUAL REPORT SCOTLAND**
HMSO

UK – English annual

36218 **REGISTRY OF FRIENDLY SOCIETIES. REPORT OF THE CHIEF REGISTRAR**
HMSO

UK – English annual £6.50

36219 **REPORT OF THE COMMISSIONERS OF HM CUSTOMS AND EXCISE**
HMSO

UK – English annual £7.60

Statistics related to all taxes administered by Customs and Excise including the duties on tobacco, alcoholic drink, hydrocarbon oil, betting and gaming, custom duties, agricultural levies and VAT.

36220 **REPORT OF THE COMMISSIONERS OF HM INLAND REVENUE**
HMSO

UK – English annual £11.50

Statistics on all taxes adminstered by the Inland Revenue.

36221 **RESEARCH AND DEVELOPMENT**
Reward Group

UK – English annual £100.00

Full analysis of basic pay and total remuneration payments in R&D organization and departments.

36222 **REWARD**
Reward Group

UK – English twice a year £150 p.a.

Survey of management and technical staff analysing salaries for over 140 main job occupations.

36223 **SALARY, WAGE AND CONDITIONS OF SERVICE REPORTS**
Reward Group

UK – English twice a year £90.00

Payments and analysis of salaries, wages and conditions of service for geographical areas of UK.

36224 **SALES AND MARKETING REWARDS**
Reward Group

UK – English annual £95.00

A survey giving details of salaries and benefits for all marketing and sales positions. Published in association with the Institute of Marketing.

36225 **SCOTTISH ABSTRACT OF STATISTICS**
HMSO

UK – English annual

36226 **SCOTTISH DEVELOPMENT AGENCY, ANNUAL REPORT**
HMSO

UK – English annual free

36227 **SCOTTISH ECONOMIC BULLETIN**
HMSO

UK – English six-monthly £7.00

Contains an economic review, articles on the Scottish economy and regular statistics.

36228 **SCOTTISH FISHING FLEET**
HMSO

UK – English annual £6.00

36229 **SCOTTISH HEALTH STATISTICS**
HMSO

UK – English annual £8.00

36230 **SCOTTISH HOUSING STATISTICS**
HMSO

UK – English annual £10.00

36231 **SCOTTISH LOCAL GOVERNMENT FINANCIAL STATISTICS**
HMSO

UK – English annual £4.00

36232 **SCOTTISH SEA FISHERIES STATISTICAL TABLES**
HMSO

UK – English annual £6.00

36233 **SCOTTISH TRANSPORT STATISTICS**
HMSO

UK – English annual £3.00

36234 **SEA FISHERIES STATISTICAL TABLES**
HMSO

UK – English annual £10.00

36235 **SHAWS GUIDE TO FAIR RETAIL PRICES**
Shaws Price Guides Ltd

UK – English monthly £15.00p.a.

36236 **SOCIAL SECURITY STATISTICS**
HMSO

UK – English annual £14.80

36237 **SPINNING AND WASTE SPINNING: END USE DELIVERIES**
Textile Statistics Bureau

UK – English monthly £3.50 each issue

Statistical series giving production, fibre consumption, employment, hours and shifts worked in monthly series for spinning and waste spinning and quarterly figures for end use deliveries.

36238 **STATISTICAL DIGEST FOR THE FURNITURE INDUSTRY 198-**
Furniture Industry Research Association

UK – English annual c70pp £30.00 members, £85.00 non-members

Statistics on number of firms, turnover, employment, output, imports/exports, prices, market developments, credit sales.

36239 **STATISTICAL HANDBOOK**
The Brewers Society

UK – English annual c100pp £18.00

Data on production and consumption of beer, wines, spirits, cider and soft drinks. Also covers prices, excise duties, expenditure per head and structure of the industry.

36240 **STATISTICAL HANDBOOK OF UK AGRICULTURE**
Agricultural Economics Unit/A. Burrell, B. Hill and J. Medland

UK – English 1987 £8.50

Analysis of statistical material relating to agriculture.

36241 **STATISTICAL INFORMATION SERVICE (SIS)**
Chartered Institute of Public Finance and Accountancy

UK – English annual various cost

Service covers following areas in separate publications: administration of justice, archives, block grant, education, finance and general, fire, highways and transportation, housing revenue account, leisure and recreation, personal social services, planning and development, police, probation, public libraries, rating review (Scotland), trading standards, waste disposal, airports, capital expenditure and debt financing, cemeteries and crematoria, direct labour organizations, education, environmental health, homelessness, housing rents, leisure charges, leisure usage, rate collection, smallholdings, waste collection.

36242 **STATISTICAL NEWS**
HMSO

UK – English quarterly £14.00

A comprehensive account of current developments in British official statistics. Shorter notes give news of the latest developments in many fields, including international statistics.

36243 **STATISTICAL REVIEW–FOOTWEAR INDUSTRY**
British Footwear Manufacturers Federation

UK – English annual £18.00

Statistical information on the footwear industry giving data on production costs and prices, employment, imports and exports, structure of the industry and supplies classified by product.

36244 **STATISTICAL REVIEW OF NORTHERN IRELAND AGRICULTURE**
HMSO

UK – English annual £7.50

36245 **STATISTICS STATEMENT***
Trade Union Congress

UK – English annual

Details including address and statistics on TUC affiliated unions.

36246 **SUPPLY ESTIMATES**
HMSO

UK – English annual each volume individually priced

Details of estimated cash requirements of central government departments for the forthcoming financial year.

36247 **SUPPLY OF UNIVERSITY GRADUATES 1987-1989 TRENDS AND PREDICTIONS**
HMSO

UK – English £6.60

Estimates of the numbers graduating and of the numbers available for employment over the next three years.

36248 **SURVEY OF PERSONAL INCOMES**
HMSO

UK – English annual £6.95

Analyses of taxable incomes and income tax by range, source, sex and marital status.

36249 **TUC ANNUAL REPORT***
Trade Union Congress

UK – English annual

Report of the General Council and verbatim proceedings of annual conference.

36250 **TUC ECONOMIC REVIEW***
Trade Union Congress

UK – English annual

Analytic review of the economy and description of the TUC official economic policy.

36251 **TAXATION OF OVERSEAS INCOME AND GAINS**
Butterworth and Co. (Publishers) Ltd

UK – English 228pp £14.00
ISBN No. 0 406 53873 5

The principles of double taxation relief, taxation of individuals, companies, settlements and trusts and the complications of the transfer of assets abroad.

36252 **THE TAXATION OF UNDERTAKINGS IN THE UNITED KINGDOM**
German Chamber of Industry and Commerce

UK – English £20.00

26253 **LE THATCHERISM DOCTRINE ET ACTION**
La Documentation Francaise

UK – French 1984 144pp FrF50
ISSN No. 0029 4004

36254 **THOMSON MCLINTOCK: EXPATRIATE TAX MANUAL**
Butterworth and Co. (Publishers) Ltd

UK – English 1985 172pp £15.00
ISBN No. 0 406 259968

Explains the tax implications for individuals who move to or from the UK.

36255 **TIME RATES OF WAGES AND HOURS OF WORK**
HMSO

UK – English monthly update £43.00

36256 **TOP 400 UK MARKETS**
Market Assessment Publications Ltd

UK – English annually £250.00

Provides an executive summary of the top 400 markets.

36257 **TOP PAY UNIT REVIEW***
Incomes Data Services Ltd

UK – English monthly £45.00

Review of management salaries, fringe benefits, pay reviews and recruitment levels.

36258 **TRADE ASSOCIATIONS AND PROFESSIONAL BODIES OF THE UNITED KINGDOM**
Pergamon Press Ltd

UK – English 1986 600pp £30.00
ISBN No. 0 08 0333907

Alphabetical list of trade associations and professional bodies. Geographical index of towns–chambers of commerce, trade, industry, shipping, UK offices of overseas chambers of commerce.

36259 **TRADE BULLETIN UNITED KINGDOM IMPORTS AND EXPORTS OF FISH AND FISH PRODUCTS**
Sea Fish Industry Authority

UK – English monthly

36260 **TRADE COUNCILS CONFERENCE REPORT***
Trade Union Congress

UK – English annual

36261 **TRANSPORT OF GOODS BY ROAD IN GREAT BRITAIN**
HMSO

UK – English annual £8.00

36262 **TRANSPORT STATISTICS**
HMSO

UK – English quarterly/annual £5.00 quarterly £12.00 p.a.

36263 **TRANSPORT STATISTICS GREAT BRITAIN 1976-86**
HMSO

UK – English annual £18.95

36264 **TRI-MEDIA DIGEST OF BRANDS AND ADVERTISERS**
Media Expenditure Analysis Ltd

UK – English quarterly £540 p.a.

Continuous monitor of advertising activity–television, radio and press as an aid to marketing management.

36265 **UK AIRLINES: ANNUAL OPERATING, TRAFFIC AND FINANCIAL STATISTICS**
Civil Aviation Authority

UK – English annual 1983 70pp £9.50

36266 **UK AIRLINES: MONTHLY OPERATING AND TRAFFIC STATISTICS**
Civil Aviation Authority

UK – English monthly 1983 (Jan) 50pp £29.50 p.a.

36267 **UK AIRPORTS:ANNUAL STATEMENT OF MOVEMENTS, PASSENGERS AND CARGO**
Civil Aviation Authority

UK – English annual 1983 70pp £9.50

36268 **UK AIRPORTS: MONTHLY STATEMENT OF MOVEMENTS, PASSENGERS AND CARGO**
Civil Aviation Authority

UK – English monthly 1983 (Jan) 50pp £29.50 p.a.

36269 **UK BALANCE OF PAYMENTS (CSO PINK BOOK)**
HMSO

UK – English annual £8.95

Information on visible trade, invisibles, investment and other capital transactions and official financing as well as sections on specific aspects of the balance of payments.

36270 **UK CHEMICAL INDUSTRY FACTS**
Chemical Industries Association Ltd

UK – English 1986 free

36271 **UK DAIRY FACTS AND FIGURES**
Milk Marketing Board

UK – English annual £6.50

Statistics and analysis of the UK dairy industry with comparative figures for previous years.

36272 **UK ECONOMIC ASSESSMENT**
James Capel

UK – English monthly

36273 **UK IMPORT MARKET REPORTS**
Trade Research Publications

UK – English

Reports covering UK market size, characteristics, the share held by importers, and future trends, import trade statistics analysis, tariffs and quotas, product requirements, import procedures etc. Reports covering the knitwear and furniture sectors.

36274 **UK IRON AND STEEL INDUSTRY: ANNUAL STATISTICS**
UK Iron and Steel Statistics Bureau

UK – English annual 1967 64pp £40.00, £44.00 airmail

50 detailed statistical tables relating to the UK iron and steel industry with historical comparisons and detailed trade information, available about five months after the year end.

36275 **UK NATIONAL ACCOUNTS (CSO BLUE BOOK)**
HMSO

UK – English annual £11.95

Principal data source for national acounts statistics with detailed estimates of national product, income and expenditure.

36276 **UK TRADE DATA**
British Ports Association

UK – English quarterly 1987 10pp £10 issue £40 annual subscription

UK imports and exports through British ports, by port, commodity group, trading area and mode.

36277 **UNIT TRUST YEARBOOK**
Financial Times Business Information

UK – English 1987 464pp £24.00 UK, £29.00/US$40.00 overseas

Analyses over 1,000 unit trusts in depth giving information on the type of fund, minimum investment required, charges, value of the trust, investment record, principal holdings and capital growth.

36278 **UPHOLSTERY FACT BOOK**
Furniture Industry Research Association

UK – English every 3/4 years May 87 200pp £300 members, £600 non-members

Upholstery, consumer purchasing, domestic production, fabric market.

36279 **UNITED KINGDOM DAIRY FACTS AND FIGURES**
Milk Marketing Board

UK – English annual £7.50

Current developments in the production, distribution and consumption of milk and milk products in the UK.

36280 **UNITED KINGDOM MINERAL STATISTICS**
British Geological Survey

UK – English annual

Mineral production, consumption, import and export data obtained from a wide variety of published and unpublished sources.

36281 **UNITED KINGDOM REFINING INDUSTRY**
Institute of Petroleum

UK – English 1986 12pp free

Brief survey of the refining industry with details of capacity and present installations and future development.

36282 **WATERBORNE FREIGHT IN THE UK**
HMSO

UK – English annual £15.00

36283 **WEAVING STATISTICS**
Textile Statistics Bureau

UK – English monthly £3.00 each issue

Statistics on production, employment, looms active, hours worked and yarn consumed.

36284 **WEEKLY GILT EDGED DATA SHEET**
James Capel

UK – English weekly

36285 **WELSH AGRICULTURAL STATISTICS**
HMSO

UK – English annual £3.00

36286 **WELSH ECONOMIC TRENDS**
HMSO

UK – English annual and supplement £7.50 (£5.00 supplement)

36287 **WELSH LOCAL GOVERNMENT FINANCIAL STATISTICS**
HMSO

UK – English annual £4.00

36288 **WELSH TRANSPORT STATISTICS**
HMSO

UK – English annual £3.00

36289 **WOMEN AND MEN IN BRITAIN–A STATISTICAL PROFILE 1986**
HMSO

UK – English £5.70

Prepared by the Equal Opportunities Commission, the digest depicts the position of men and women in various facets of life in the mid-eighties.

YUGOSLAVIA

37001 **ABECOR COUNTRY REPORT –YUGOSLAVIA**
Abecor

Yugoslavia – English 1986 2pp free

Brief economic report.

37002 **ANKETA O POTROSNJI DOMACINSTAVA**
Federal Statistical Office (FSO)

Yugoslavia – Yugoslavian annual

Survey on household consumption.

37003 **BANKS IN YUGOSLAVIA**
Ekonomiska Politika

Yugoslavia – English annual October 1972 120pp US$20
ISSN No. 0013 3248

37004 **CENE**
Federal Statistical Office (FSO)

Yugoslavia – Yugoslavian twice a year

Statistical bulletin on prices.

37005 **CENSUS 1981**
Federal Statistical Office (FSO)

Yugoslavia – 96,000pp

37006 **COMMUNICATIONS OF THE FEDERAL STATISTICAL OFFICE**
Federal Statistical Office (FSO)

Yugoslavia – Serbo-Croatian frequent c2pp

Regular bulletins supplying data the day it has been processed on all aspects of economic and social life.

37007 **COUNTRY PROFILES**
Economist Publications Ltd

Yugoslavia – English annual 40pp £25 UK subscription varies in rest of world

Resumé of politics, economy and industry including statistical summaries.

37008 **COUNTRY REPORTS**
Economist Publications Ltd

Yugoslavia – English quarterly 25pp £58 UK subscription varies in rest of world

Economic policies and development plans, trends in production and demand, monetary and fiscal conditions, wages and prices, merchandise trade, invisibles, capital flows, exchange rates and foreign debt plus a forecast of the economic prospects.

37009 **DEMOGRAPHIC STATISTICS**
Federal Statistical Office (FSO)

Yugoslavia – Serbo-Croatian annual YD100.00

Data on the natural movement of population including births, deaths, marriages and divorces and details of composition of households cross classified by all categories. The data also refers to other socialist countries and autonomous socialist provinces.

37010 **DRUSTVENI PROIZVODNI NARODNI DOHODAK**
Federal Statistical Office (FSO)

Yugoslavia – Yugoslavian annual

Statistical bulletin on social product and national income.

37011 **ECONOMIC BALANCES OF YUGOSLAVIA**
Federal Statistical Office (FSO)

Yugoslavia – Serbo-Croatian/English/French annual c200pp YD50.00

37012 **ECONOMIC REVIEW**
Collets Holdings Ltd

Yugoslavia – English monthly

37013 **EKONOMISKA POLITIKA**
Collets Holdings Ltd

Yugoslavia – Serbo-Croatian weekly £133.40

37014 **ENERGY BALANCES OF THE SFR YUGOSLAVIA**
Federal Statistical Office (FSO)

Yugoslavia – Serbo-Croatian annual 74pp

Data on production, imports and exports of energy as well as transformation and consumption.

37015 **FINANSIJE**
Collets Holdings Ltd

Yugoslavia – Serbo-Croatian six per year £47.00

37016 **GRADEVINARSTVO**
Federal Statistical Office (FSO)

Yugoslavia – Yugoslavian

Statistical bulletin on construction.

37017 **HANDBOOK ON EFTA MARKETS FOR YUGOSLAV PRODUCTS**
European Free Trade Association (EFTA)

Yugoslavia – English 1986 free

A guide to the markets of five EFTA countries.

37018 **HINTS TO EXPORTERS**
Department of Trade and Industry

Yugoslavia – English annual

Practical guide for businessmen giving general information, useful addresses, methods of doing business and relevant regulations.

37019 **INDEX: MONTHLY REVIEW OF ECONOMIC STATISTICS OF THE SFR OF YUGOSLAVIA**
Federal Statistical Office (FSO)

Yugoslavia – Serbo-Croatian summary in English/French monthly c70pp YD520.00

Current data on economic development with retrospective data for the preceding months. Topics covered: economy, industrial production, forestry, construction, transport, internal trade, tourism and restaurants, finance both private and public.

37020 **INDUSTRIJA**
Federal Statistical Office (FSO)

Yugoslavia – Yugoslavian annual

Statistical bulletin on manufacturing, mining and quarrying.

37021 **INDUSTRIJSKE ORGANIZACIJE VDRUZENOG RADA**
Federal Statistical Office (FSO)

Yugoslavia – Yugoslavian annual

Manufacturing organizations of associated labour.

37022 INVESTICIJE
Federal Statistical Office (FSO)

Yugoslavia – Yugoslavian annual

Statistical bulletin on investment.

37023 JOURNAL OF YUGOSLAV FOREIGN TRADE
Collets Holdings Ltd

Yugoslavia – English quarterly

37024 JUGOSLOVENSKI PREGLED
Jugoslovenski Pregled

Yugoslavia – Serbo-Croatian monthly 1957 60pp US$30.00

Information on political, economic, social and cultural developments in Yugoslavia.

37025 LANDERBERICHT JUGOSLAWIEN
Federal Statistical Office of Germany

Yugoslavia – German irregular DM7.90

Statistical survey of Yugoslavia including demography, geography, education, employment, agriculture, production, overseas trade, transport, tourism, finance, wages and prices and national accounts.

37026 LICNI DOHOCI
Federal Statistical Office (FSO)

Yugoslavia – Yugoslavian annual

Statistical bulletin on personal incomes.

37027 NASE GOSPODARSTVO (OUR ECONOMY)
Univerza v Mariboru (University of Maribor)

Yugoslavia – Slovene (synopsis in Slovene and English) bi-monthly 1954 100pp per issue
US$85 p.a.
ISSN No. YU 05473101

Any topics in the field of economic and related sciences.

37028 NAUCNOISTRAZIVACKE I RAZVOJNE ORGANIZACIJNE
Federal Statistical Office (FSO)

Yugoslavia – Yugoslavian annual

Scientific, technological and research and development organizations.

37029 NEKI POKAZATELJI TEHNICKOG RAZVOJA PRIVREDE JUGOSLAVIJE
Federal Statistical Office (FSO)

Yugoslavia – Yugoslavian annual

Selected indicators of technical development of the economy of Yugoslavia.

37030 POLJOPRIVREDNE ORGANIZACIJE UDRUZENOG RADI I ZEMLJORADNICKE ZADRUGE
Federal Statistical Office (FSO)

Yugoslavia – Yugoslavian annual

Agricultural organizations.

37031 POPIS MALE PRIVREDE U INDIVIDUALNOM SEKTORU SVOJINE
Federal Statistical Office (FSO)

Yugoslavia – Yugoslavian annual

Census of small-scale economy in the private sector.

37032 POPULATION, EMPLOYMENT AND INEQUALITY: BACHUE–YUGOSLAVIA
Gower Publishing Company Ltd, UK

Yugoslavia – English 1987

Economic - demographic study published in conjunction with the ILO.

37033 PRIVREDNI PREGLED (ECONOMICS)
Collets Holdings Ltd

Yugoslavia – Serbo-Croatian daily £297

37034 PROMET POLJOPRIVREDNIH
Federal Statistical Office (FSO)

Yugoslavia – Yugoslavian annual

Statistical bulletin on sales of agricultural products.

37035 RADNICI I CIST LICNI DOHODAK PO GRUPAMA DELATNOSTI
Federal Statistical Office (FSO)

Yugoslavia – Yugoslavian annual

Statistical bulletin on workers and net personal income according to groups of economic activity.

37036 RATARSTVO, VOCARSTVO I VINOGRADARSTVO
Federal Statistical Office (FSO)

Yugoslavia – Yugoslavian annual

Statistical bulletin on crop farming, fruit growing and viticulture.

37037 RESOURCES, EXPENDITURE, AVAILABILITY OF AMENITIES IN NON-AGRICULTURAL HOUSEHOLDS
Federal Statistical Office (FSO)/ Siobodan Bosuic

Yugoslavia – Serbo-Croatian 102pp every 5 years

Analysis of various social indicators.

37038 SAOBRACAJ I VEZE
Federal Statistical Office (FSO)

Yugoslavia – Yugoslavian annual

Statistical bulletin on transport and communications.

37039 STATISTICAL CALENDAR OF YUGOSLAVIA
Federal Statistical Office (FSO)

Yugoslavia – Serbo-Croatian (both Latin and Cyrillic alphabets), Macedonian/ Slovenian/English/French/German/Russian annual YD12.00

Pocket edition of major statistical data.

37040 STATISTICAL POCKET-BOOK OF YUGOSLAVIA
Federal Statistical Office (FSO)

Yugoslavia – Yugoslavian/English /French/ Russian annual 220pp

37041 STATISTICAL YEARBOOK OF YUGOSLAVIA
Federal Statistical Office (FSO)

Yugoslavia – Serbo-Croatian/French/ Russian (English up to 1976) annual 200pp YD250.00

37042 STATISTICS OF FOREIGN TRADE OF THE SFR YUGOSLAVIA
Federal Statistical Office (FSO)

Yugoslavia – Serbo-Croatian/English annual c600pp YD200.00

Part 1 general data of trade between the socialist republics; foreign trade balance; exports and imports classified by commodity , countries of destination and origin. Part 2 more detailed analyses of exports and imports. Part 3 exports and imports analysed by country.

37043 STOCARSTVO I RABARSTVO
Federal Statistical Office (FSO)

Yugoslavia –Yugoslavian annual

Statistical bulletin on livestock, breeding and fisheries.

37044 SUMARSTVO
Federal Statistical Office (FSO)

Yugoslavia – Yugoslavian annual

Statistical bulletin on forestry.

37045 TURIZAM
Federal Statistical Office (FSO)

Yugoslavia – Yugoslavian annual

Statistical bulletin on tourism.

37046 UNUTRASNJA TRGOVINA
Federal Statistical Office (FSO)

Yugoslavia – Yugoslavian annual

Statistical bulletin on domestic trade.

37047 THE YUGOSLAV MOTOR INDUSTRY
Poslovna Zajednica Proizvodaca Motornih Vozila

Yugoslavia – Yugoslavian with English table headings annual 100pp

Statistics on production, registration and export of motor vehicles as well as on fuels and roads.

37048 YUGOSLAV SURVEY–A RECORD OF FACTS AND INFORMATION
Jugoslovenski Pregled

Yugoslavia – English quarterly 1960 160pp US$25.00

All spheres of development in Yugoslavia, systematic factual information on political, social, economic and cultural developments in Yugoslavia.

37049 YUGOSLAVIA
National Westminster Bank

Yugoslavia – English irregular 4pp free

Brief economic report.

37050 ZAPOSLENOST
Federal Statistical Office (FSO)

Yugoslavia – Yugoslavian twice a year

Statistical bulletin on employment.

Part Two
PUBLISHING BODIES

THE '8 NETORI' PUBLISHING HOUSE
Tirania
Albania

Entry: 02014

ABC–VERLAGSHAUS
Post Box 4034
Berliner Allee 8
D–6100 Darmstadt
West Germany

Entry: 15001

A.P. INFORMATION SERVICES LTD.
33 Ashbourne Avenue
London NW11 0DU
Tel: 01 458 1607

Entry: 36194

ABECOR REPORTS AVAILABLE FROM:

BARCLAYS BANK LTD
Group Economics Department
54 Lombard Street
London EC3 3AH
UK
Tel: 01 283 8989
Telex: 887591

ACADEMIA
The Czechoslovak Academy of Sciences
Vodickova 40
11229 Praha 1
Nove Mesto
Czechoslovakia

Entry: 07009

ACADEMIC INTERNATIONAL PRESS
POB 111
Gulf Breeze
FL32561
USA

Entry: 31059

ADMINISTRATIE VOOR ENERGIE
J-A de Mostraat 30
1040 Brussels
Belgium
Tel: 02 233 61 11
Telex: 13509 ENERGI

Entry: 04028

ADMINISTRATION FEDERALE DES CONTRIBUTIONS
Division Statistique de Documentation
3003 Berne
Switzerland

Entry: 34012

ADVERTISING ASSOCIATION
Abford House
15 Wilton Road
London SW1V 1NJ
Tel: 01 828 2771

Entries: 10022 36006 36015 36172

ADVISORY, CONCILIATION AND ARBITRATION SERVICE (ACAS)
11-12 St James' Square
London SW1Y 4LA

Entry: 36014

AFFARSVALDEN
Box 1234
111 82 Stockholm
Sweden

Entries: 33002 33116

AGPOL–POLEXPORTPRESS
00-950 Warszawa – PO Box 726
Poland
Tel: 26 77 10
Telex: 81 3364 AGPOL PL

Entries: 01150 28021 28022 28025

AGRA EUROPE (LONDON) LTD.
25 Frank Road
Tunbridge Wells
TN2 5JT
Tel: (0892) 33813
Telex: 95114

Entries: 01002 01241 01245 10001 12018 12052 12073 12094 12108 18001 29003

AGRA EUROPE (LONDON) LTD.
173 Rue Stevin
1040 Brussels
Belgium
Tel: 02 230 18 94 (or) 02 230 18 78
Telex: 62748 EURBUR B

Entry: 01002

AGRICULTURAL BANK OF GREECE
23 Panepistimia Str
10564 Athens
Greece
Tel: 323 0521-27
Telex: 215810

Entry: 18005

AGRICULTURAL ECONOMICS UNIT
Wye College
Ashford
Kent TN25 5AM

Entries: 36017 36240

AGRICULTURAL INSTITUTE HEADQUARTERS
19 Sandymount Avenue
Dublin 4
Tel: 688188
Telex: 30459

Entries: 21031 21038 21040 21041 21065

AGRICULTURAL RESEARCH INSTITUTE
Ministry of Agriculture & Natural Resources
Athalassa
Nicosia
Cyprus
Tel: 40-3431

Entries: 06002 06009 06031 06035 06038 06046 06051 06052

AGROINFORM
Agrarinformacios Vallalat
1012 Budapest I
Attila Vt 93
Hungary

Entry: 19018

ALGEMENE BANK NEDERLAND NV
Vijzelstraat 32
POB 669
1000 EG Amsterdam
Netherlands
Tel: (020) 29 91 11
Telex: 11417

Entries: 26001 26005

ALLIED IRISH BANK
Bankcentre
Balls Bridge
Dublin 4
Tel: 01 600311

Entries: 21002 21036 21037 21061

ALLMANNA FORLIGET
Kundtjanst
162 89 Stockholm
Sweden

AMRO BANK
Postbus 283
1000 EH Amsterdam
Netherlands

Entries: 26004 26046

AMT FUR VOLKWIRTSCHAFT
FL–9490 Vaduz
Liechtenstein

Entries: 23002 23003 23004 23007 23009 23013 23017 23019 23021 23022 23023 23024

ANGLO-ROMANIAN BANK LIMITED
42 Moorgate
London EC2R 6EL
Tel: 01 588 4150/4
Telex: 886700

Entry: 30002

ASOCIACION ESPANOLA DE BANCA PRIVADA
Velazquez
64-66 Planta 6a
28001 Madrid
Spain
Tel: 446.00.11
Telex: 45.359

Entries: 32008 32055

ASSOCIACAO INDUSTRIAL PORTUGUESA
Praca das Industrias
1399 Lisbon Codex
Portugal
Tel: 63 90 44
Telex: 12282 FIPORT P

Entry: 29052

ASSOCIACAO NACIONAL DOS INDUSTRIAIS DE MATERIAL ELECTRICO E ELECTRONICO (ANIMEE)
Av Guerra Junqueiro
No. 11-20-E
1000 Lisbon
Portugal

Entry: 29007

ASSOCIATION OF BRITISH INSURERS
Aldermary House
Queen Street
London EC4N 1TT
Tel: 01 248 4477
Telex: 937035
Fax: 01 489 1128

Entries: 36143 36184

ASSOCIATION OF EUROPEAN AIRLINES
Avenue Louise 350 bte 4
B–1050
Brussels
Tel: 322 64031 75
Telex: 22918
Fax: 648 40 17

Entry: 10029

ASSOCIATION OF FINNISH TEXTILE INDUSTRIES
Etelaranta 10
00130 Helsinki
Finland
Tel: 0 661561
Telex: 125854

Entry: 13153

ASSOCIAZIONE COSTRUTTORI MACCHINE ATTLEZATURE PER UFFICIO E PER IL TRATTAMENTO DELLE INFORMAZIONI
Via Larga 23
20122 Milano
Italy

Entry: 22043

ASSOCIAZIONE COTONIERA ITALIANA
Via Borgonuovo 11
20121 Milano
Italy
Telex: 332046 ACOTEX I

Entry: 22046

ASSOCIAZIONE FRA LE SOCIETA ITALIANE PER AZIONI
Piazza Venezia 11
Rome 00187
Italy

Entries: 22024 22025

ASSOCIAZIONE ITALIANA LATTIERO–CASEARIA
Via Pietro Verri 8
20121 Milano
Italy
Tel: 700 350 - 700 621
Telex: 325095 Aslat I

Entries: 22032 22034 22048

ASSOCIAZIONE NAZIONALE FRA INDUSTRIE AUTOMOBILISTICHE
Corso G Ferraris 61
10128 Torino
Italy
Tel: 011/57–61
Telex: 221334
Fax: 011 545986

Entry: 22037

ATHENS CHAMBER OF COMMERCE & INDUSTRY
7 Acadimias Street
Athens 135
Greece
Tel: 3618810

Entry: 18045

AUSTRALIA AND NEW ZEALAND BANKING GROUP
Minerva House
PO Box 7
Montague Close
London SE1 9DH
Tel: 01 378 2121
Telex: 01 885043/6

Entries: 22019 32031

AUTOMOBIL–IMPORTØRERNES SAMMENSLUTNING
Ryvangs Alle 68
2900 Hellerup
Denmark
Tel: 01 62 39 99

Entry: 08076

BADEN–WURTTEMBERGISCHE WERTPAPIERBORSE ZU STUTTGART
7000 Stuttgart 1
Hospitalstrasse 12
West Germany

BANCA COMMERCIALE ITALIANA
Piazza della Scala 6
20121 Milan
Italy
Tel: 88501
Telex: 310080 BCI I

Entries: 22026 22031 22033

BANCA D'ITALIA
Via Nazionale 91
00184 Roma
Italy

Entries: 22007 22009 22062

BANCA NAZIONALE DEL LAVORO
Via Vittorio Veneto 119
00187 Rome
Italy

Entry: 22042

BANCA TOTTA E ACORES
1–3 Abchurch Yard
London EC4N 7BH
Tel: 01 283 8555
Telex: 887609

Entry: 29058

BANCO CENTRAL
Alcala 49
Madrid 14
Spain

Entry: 32020

BANCO DE ESPANA
Alcala 50
28014 Madrid
Spain
Tel: 5212259

Entries: 32016 32018 32049

BANCO EXTERIOR DE ESPANA
Carrera de San Jeronimo 36
Madrid 14
Spain
Tel: 4294477
Telex: [illegible]

Entries: 32022 32039

BANCO NACIONAL ULTRAMARINO
Rua do Comercio 84
Lisbon
Portugal

Entry: 29010

BANCO DI NAPOLI
Direzione Generale
Ufficio Studi
Napoli
Italy

Entry: 22047

BANCO DE PORTUGAL
Rua do Comercio 148
1100 Lisbon
Portugal

Entries: 29011 29039 29063 29064

BANCO DI ROMA
Via delle Botteghe Oscura 96
00186 Roma
Italy
Tel: 672051

Entry: 22049

BANK OF CYPRUS LTD.
86–90 Phaneromenis Street
PO Box 1472
Nicosia
Cyprus
Tel: 02-464064
Telex: 2451 KYPRIAKIA

Entries: 06011 06029 06033

BANK OF ENGLAND
Threadneedle Street
London EC2
UK
Tel: 01 601 4444

Entries: 36028 36029 36168 36169

BANK OF FINLAND
PO Box 160
00101 Helsinki
Finland
Tel: 1831
Telex: 121224 SPFB SF

Entries: **13007** **13008** **13009** **13063** **13064** **13102** **13139**

BANK OF GREECE
Avenue el Venizelou
Athens 21
Greece

Entries: **18004** **18027** **18033**

BANK OF JAPAN
1-2-8 Uckikanda
Chiyoda-ko
Tokyo
Japan

Entry: **01094**

BANK MEES AND HOPE NV
Herengracht 548
1017 CG Amsterdam
Netherlands

Entry: **26054**

BANK VERLAG KOLN GMBH
Melatengurtel 113–115
Postfach 300149
5000 Koln 30
West Germany
Tel: 0221 5490 0
Telex: 1722 13 50
Fax: 0221 54 90 120

Entries: **15029** **15032**

BANKINSPEKTIONEN
Box 16096
S 10322 Stockholm
Sweden
Tel: 01046 8 242120

Entry: **33012**

BANQUE BRUXELLES LAMBERT
2 Rue de la Regence
B–1000 Bruxelles
Belgium
Tel: 511 64 50

Entry: **04027**

BANQUE DE FRANCE
39 rue Croix-des-Petits-Champs
Paris 1er
France
Tel: (4) 292 42 92
Telex: 220932

Entries: **01283** **14015** **14016** **14022** **14024** **14032** **14035** **14047** **14048** **14050** **14052** **14054** **14086** **14087** **14089** **14092** **14096** **14097** **14104** **14108** **14110** **14116** **14137** **14138** **14139**

BANQUE INTERNATIONALE A LUXEMBOURG
2 Boulevard Royal
L–2953 Luxembourg
Tel: 47911
Telex: 3409

Entries: **24001** **24014** **24030**

BANQUE NATIONALE DE BELGIQUE
Boulevard de Berlaimont 5
Brussels 1000
Tel: 219 46 00

Entries: **04008** **04024**

BARCLAYS BANK LTD.
54 Lombard Street
London EC3P 3AH
Tel: 01 283 8989
Telex: 887591

Entry: **01024**

BASLER BORSENKAMMER
Aeschenplatz 7
CH–4002 Basel
Switzerland
Tel: 061 230555
Telex: 962524

Entry: **34009**

BELGO–LUXEMBOURG CHAMBER OF COMMERCE IN GREAT BRITAIN
36–37 Piccadilly
London W1V 0PI
UK
Tel: 01 434 1815
Telex: 8953411 BELCOM G

Entries: **04047** **04089** **04093**

BENN BUSINESS INFORMATION SERVICES LTD.
PO Box 20
Sovereign Way
Tonbridge
Kent TN9 1RQ
Tel: 0732 362666
Telex: 94545 BBIS G
Fax: 0732 770483

Entries: **01025** **01101** **01237**

BERGEN BANK
Corporate Communications Dept.
PO Box 826
N–5001 Bergen
Norway
Tel: 475 21 10 00
Telex: 42018 BBB60
Fax: 475 21 19 20

Entry: **27066**

BIPE/INSEE AVAILABLE FROM:

INTERNATIONAL PLANNING INFORMATION (IPI)
Rugvaenget 19–21
DK 2630 Taastrup
Denmark
Tel: 45 271 20 44
Telex: 33576 IPI DK
Fax: 45 271 20 25

BIRMINGHAM CHAMBER OF COMMERCE
75 Harborne Road
Edgbaston
Birmingham B15 3DH
UK

Entry: **31061**

BASIL BLACKWELL LTD.
108, Cowley Road
Oxford OX4 1JF
UK
Tel: 0865 722146

Entry: **12105**

BOARD OF CUSTOMS
Box 512
00101 Helsinki
Finland
Tel: 0 6141
Telex: 121559 TULHS

Entries: **13065** **13066**

BOLSA DE VALORES DE LISBOA
Praca de Comerio
1110 Lisbon
Portugal
Tel: 879416/7
Telex: 44751 BVLIS P

Entries: **29051** **29062** **29066**

BORD FAILTE–IRISH TOURIST BOARD
Baggot St Bridge
Dublin 2
Irish Republic
Tel: (0001) 765871
Telex: 93755

Entry: **21003**

BORSA VALORI DI MILANO
Palazzo della Borsa
Piazza degli Affari 6
Milan
Italy
Tel: 83 34
Telex: MICOMB/I 321430

Entries: **22044** **22045**

BOURSE DE GENEVE
8 rue de la Confederation
1211 Geneva 11
Switzerland
Tel: 022 28 06 84
Telex 423559 BGGE

Entry: **34024**

THE BREWERS SOCIETY
42 Portman Square
London W1H 0BB
Tel: 01 486 4831
Telex: 261946

Entry: **36239**

BRISTOL AND WEST BUILDING SOCIETY
PO Box 27
Broad Quay
Bristol BS99 7AX
Tel: 0272 294271
Telex: 44741
Fax: 0272 211632

Entry: **36104**

BRITISH AGRICULTURAL EXPORT COUNCIL
35 Belgrave Square
London SW1X 8QN
Tel: 01 245 9819
Telex: 919669

Entry: 31040

BRITISH BANKERS ASSOCIATION
10 Lombard Street
LONDON EC3
UK

Entry: 12034

BRITISH CHAMBER OF COMMERCE IN SPAIN
Plaza de Santa Barbara 10–1º
28004 Madrid
Spain
Tel: 410 7064
Telex: 45522
Fax: 410 4605

Entry: 32052

BRITISH COAL
Hobart House
Grosvenor Place
London SW1X 7AE

Entries: 36018 36068

BRITISH EMBASSY
Thunovska 14
Prague 1
Czechoslovakia
Tel: 533347
Telex: 121011 A/B

Entry: 07015

BRITISH FOOTWEAR MANUFACTURERS FEDERATION
Royalty House
72 Dean Street
London W1V 5HB
Tel: 01 437 5573

Entries: 36177 36243

BRITISH GEOLOGICAL SURVEY
Keyworth
Nottingham NG12 5GG

Entry: 36280

BRITISH INSTITUTE OF MANAGEMENT
Management House
Cottingham Road
Corby
Northants
NN17 1TT
Tel: 0536 204223

Entries: 36038 36180

BRITISH OVERSEAS TRADE BOARD
1 Victoria Street
London SW1H 0ET
Tel: 01–215 4858
Telex: 8811074

Entries: 18012 18022 29016 34016

THE BRITISH PETROLEUM COMPANY LTD.
Public Affairs and Information Department
Britannic House
Moor Lane
London EC2Y 9BU
Tel: 01 920 6627
Telex: 888811

Entry: 01020

BRITISH PORTS ASSOCIATION
Commonwealth House
1–19 New Oxford Street
London WC1A 1DZ
Tel: 01 242 1200
Telex: 295741
Fax: 01 405 1069

Entry: 36202 36276

BRITISH SOVIET CHAMBER OF COMMERCE
2 Loundes Street
London SW1X 9ET
Tel: 01 235 2423/2424
Telex: 881 3515

Entries: 31027 31052

BRITISH–SWISS CHAMBER OF COMMERCE IN SWITZERLAND
155 Freiestrasse
CH 8032 Zurich
Switzerland
Tel: 01 533131
Telex: 816213

Entries: 34010 34040 34046

BRITISH TOURIST AUTHORITY
Thames Tower
Black's Road
London W6 9EZ
Tel: 01 846 9000
Telex: 21231
Fax: 01 563 0302

Entry: 36037

S. M. BRYDE
Sognesvelen 75
0855 Oslo 8
Norway
Tel: 02 18 36 90

Entries: 27039 27059

BUILDING SERVICES RESEARCH AND INFORMATION ASSOCIATION
Old Bracknell Lane West
Bracknell
RG12 4AH
Tel: 0344 426511
Telex: 848288
Fax: 0344 487575

Entry: 36027

BUILDING SOCIETIES ASSOCIATION
3 Savile Row
London W1X 1AF

Entries: 36026 36071

BULGARIAN CHAMBER OF COMMERCE AND INDUSTRY
11-a Stamboliiski Blvd
Sofia 1040
Bulgaria

Entries: 05002 05003 05004 05005 05006 05007 05009 05015 05016 05026 05032

BUNDESAMT FUR STATISTIK
Hallwylstrasse 15
CH 3003 Berne
Switzerland
Tel: 031 618611
Telex: 32526

Entry: 34055

BUNDESANSTALT FUR AGRARWIRTSCHAFT
Schweizertalstrasse 36
1130 Wien
Austria
Tel: 0222 8251

Entries: 01139 03065 03078

BUNDESANSTALT FUR ARBEIT
Regensburger Strasse 104
8500 Nurnberg 30
Postanschrift Postfach
8500 Nurnberg 1
West Germany

Entries: 15009 15014 15196

BUNDESKAMMER DER GEWERBLICHEN WIRTSCHAFT
Biberstrasse 10
1010 Wien
Austria
Tel: 52 96 51/25

Entry: 03003

BUNDESMINISTER FUR ARBEIT UND SOZIAL ORDNUNG
Rochusstrasse 1
5300 Bonn 1
West Germany

Entries: 15196 15207 15224

BUNDESMINISTER FUR INNERDEUTSCHE BEZIEHUNGEN
Godesberger Allee 14D
5300 Bonn 2
West Germany
Tel: 0228 3060
Telex: 22 83 656 BMB
Fax: 306 22 59

Entry: 01370

BUNDESMINISTER FUR WIRTSCHAFT
Postfach 140260
5300 Bonn 1
West Germany
Tel: 02 28 615 4169
Telex: 8 86 747

Entries: 15077 15171 15178

BUNDESMINISTERIUM FUR ERNAHRUNG, LANDWIRTSCHAFT UND FORSTEN
Press und Informationstelle
Rochusstrasse 1
D 5300
Bonn 1
West Germany
Tel: 75-1
Telex: 886844

Entries: **15007 15036 15037 15056 15093 15094 15143 15168 15182 15226 15227 15234 15235**

BUNDESMINISTERIUM FUR FINANZEN
A–1015 Wien
Postfach 2
Himmelpfortgasse 4–8
Austria
Tel: 0222 51433
Telex: 132407

Entries: **03020 03093**

BUNDESMINISTERIUM FUR WIRTSCHAFTLICHE ANGELEGENHEITEN
1010 Vienna
Stubenring 1
Austria
Tel: 0222 75 0 00
Telex: 111780

Entry: **03041**

BUNDESPRESSEDIENST
Ballhausplatz 2
A–1014 Wien
Austria
Tel: 0222 676 15/0
Telex: 1370–900

Entries: **03069 03070**

BUNDESSTELLE FUR AUSSENHANDELSINFORMATION
Postfach 108007
5000 Koln 1
West Germany
Tel: 23 30 11
Telex: 08 882 735 BFAK D

Entry: **15184**

BUNDESVERBAND DES DEUTSCHEN GUTERFERNVERKEHRS (BDF) EV
Haus des Strassenverkehrs
6000 Frankfurt/Main 93
West Germany

Entry: **15252**

BUSINESS INTERNATIONAL
12–14 Chemin Rieu
1208 Geneva
Switzerland
Tel: 022 47 53 55
Telex: 422669 BISA CH
Fax: 478 118

Entries: **01030 01031 01090 01109 01162 11002 11008**

BUTTERWORTH AND CO. (PUBLISHERS) LTD.
88 Kingsway
London WC2B 6AB
Tel: 01 405 6900

CBD RESEARCH LTD.
15 Wickham Road
Beckenham
Kent BR3 2JS
Tel: 01 650 7745

Entries: **01300 12100 31047 36045 36046 36048 36188 36192 36251 36254**

CIPFA
1 Buckingham Place
London SW1E 6HS
Tel: 01 828 7661

CMEA BULLETIN
1051 Budapest
Vigadou 6
Hungary
Tel: 187-246

CAMERA DI COMMERCIO INDUSTRIA ARTIGIANATO E AGRICOLTURA DI MILANO
via Meravigli 9/B
20123 Milano
Italy
Tel: (02) 85155214
Telex: 312482 CONCAM
Fax: 85155227

Entry: **22035**

JAMES CAPEL
James Capel House
PO Box 551
6 Bevis Marks
London EC3A 7JQ
Tel: 01 621 0011
Telex: 888866
Fax: 01 621 0496

Entries: **36120 36174 36175 36272 36284**

CENTRAAL BUREAU VOOR DE STATISTIEK
Prinses Beatrixlaan 428
Postbus 959
2270 AZ Voorburg
Netherlands
Tel: (070) 69 43 41
Telex: 32692 CBC NL

Entries: **10017 10018 10019 10023 10030 10035**

CENTRAAL PLANBUREAU
Van Stolkweg 14
2585 JR The Hague
Netherlands
Tel: 070 514151
Fax: 070 505847

Entries: **26011 26047**

CENTRAL ASSOCIATION OF THE FINNISH CLOTHING INDUSTRY
Fredrikinkatu 41C
00120 Helsinki
Finland
Tel: 0 641014

Entry: **13022**

CENTRAL BANK OF CYPRUS
PO Box 5529
Nicosia
Cyprus

Entries: **06003 06012**

CENTRAL BANK OF ICELAND
Kalkofnsvegur 1
101 Reykjavik
Iceland
Tel: 91 699600
Telex: 2020

Entries: **20002 20010 20011 20014**

CENTRAL BANK OF IRELAND
PO Box No. 559
Dame Street
Dublin 2
Tel: 01 716666
Telex: 31041
Fax: 716561

Entries: **21004 21015 21018 21029 21032 21033 21054 21057 21066**

CENTRAL BANK OF MALTA
Castille Place
Valetta
Malta

Entries: **25002 25024**

CENTRAL BANK OF THE REPUBLIC OF TURKEY
40 Boulevard des Banques
Ulus
Ankara
Turkey
Tel: 41243050
Telex: 42321

Entry: **35004**

CENTRAL BUREAU OF STATISTICS
Skipperg 15
PB 8131 DEP 0033
N–Oslo 1
Norway
Tel: 472 41 38 20

Entries: **27002 27006 27008 27009 27010 27011 27012 27014 27019 27020 27021 27022 27024 27025 27027 27028 27030 27033 27035 27036 27037 27038 27041 27042 27043 27044 27046 27047 27050 27051 27054 27064 27067 27068 27069 27071 27072 27073 27074 27075 27076 27077 27078 27079 27080 27081 27082 27083 27084**

CENTRAL CHAMBER OF COMMERCE
PO Box 1000
SF–00101 Helsinki
Finland
Tel: +358 0 650 133
Telex: 123814 CHAMB SF
Fax: +358 0 650 133

Entry: **13087**

CENTRAL INTELLIGENCE AGENCY
Washington DC 20505
USA
Tel: (703) 351 1100

Entries: 31046 31048

CENTRAL OFFICE OF STATISTICS
Auberge de Castille
Castille Place
Valetta
Malta
Tel: 24597/23223/4/4, 25231

Entries: 25001 25005 25006 25007 25011 25013 25022 25023 25025 25027

CENTRAL STATISTICAL DEPARTMENT
Foreign Relations Department
Ulitsa Kirova 39
Moscow 103450
USSR
Tel: 2074000

Entries: 31019 31060

CENTRAL STATISTICAL OFFICE
International Division
2P Volov Street
Sofia
Bulgaria
Tel: 46-01
Telex: 22001

Entries: 05018 05019 05037 05039 05040

CENTRAL STATISTICAL OFFICE OF FINLAND
Box 504
00101 Helsinki
Finland
Tel: 0 17341
Telex: 1002111 +
Fax: 0 1734279

Entries: 13005 13011 13012 13013 13015 13016 13017 13018 13019 13020 13021 13023 13024 13025 13026 13027 13030 13031 13032 13033 13034 13035 13036 13037 13038 13039 13040 13041 13042 13046 13047 13048 13049 13050 13052 13053 13054 13055 13056 13058 13059 13072 13073 13075 13076 13077 13078 13079 13080 13081 13085 13089 13090 13091 13092 13094 13095 13097 13098 13104 13105 13106 13112 13113 13114 13115 13116 13117 13119 13121 13122 13123 13126 13127 13128 13129 13130 13131 13136 13137 13138 13140 13141 13142 13143 13144 13145 13146 13147 13148 13149 13154 13160 13161 13162 13166

CENTRAL STATISTICS OFFICE
St Stephen's Green House
Earlsfort Terrace
Dublin 2
Tel: 01 767531

Entries: 21030 21033 21060 21070 31060

CENTRE D'ETUDES DE L'EMPLOI
51 Rue de la Chaussee–d'Antin
75009 Paris
France
Tel: 285 72 07

Entry: 14017

CENTRE D'ETUDES PROSPECTIVES ET D'INFORMATIONS INTERNATIONALES (CEPII)
9 Rue Georges Pitard
75015 Paris
France
Tel:1 48 42 64 64
Telex: CEPIREY 206735

Entry: 01063

CENTRE FRANCAIS DU COMMERCE EXTERIEUR
Librairie du Commerce International
10 Avenue d'Iena
Paris 16e
France
Tel: 505 30 00
Telex: LICOMIN 613 413F

Entries: 14031 14088

CENTRE FOR PLANNING AND ECONOMIC RESEARCH
22 Ippokratous Str
Athens
Greece 10680

Entry: 18020

CENTRE DE RECHERCHE ET D'INFORMATION SOCIO-POLITIQUE (CRISP)
Rue du Congres 35
1000 Bruxelles
Belgium
Tel: 218 32 26

Entry: 04035

CENTRO STUDI CON FINDUSTRIA
Viale Pasteur 6
00144 Roma
Italy

Entry: 22040

CHAMBER OF COMMERCE
Exchange Buildings
Republic Street
Valletta
Malta
Tel: 624183

Entries: 25008 25026

CHAMBER OF COMMERCE AND INDUSTRY
22 N Balcescu Blvd
Bucharest 79502
Romania
Tel: 15 47 07
Telex: 11374

Entries: 30006 30008 30012 30015 30016 30017 30020

CHAMBER OF COMMERCE AND INDUSTRY FOR ROTTERDAM AND THE LOWER MAAS
Beursplein 37
PO Box 30025
3001 DA Rotterdam
Netherlands
Tel: 01 0 4145022
Telex: 23760
Fax: 010 4145754

Entry: 26053

CHAMBER OF COMMERCE OF THE PSR OF ALBANIA
Konferenca e Perzes Street
Tirania
Albania
Tel: 29-34
Telex: 21 79

Entry: 02003

CHAMBRE DE COMMERCE DE BRUXELLES
Rue de Treves 112
1040 Bruxelles
Belgium
Tel: 02 230 75 70

Entry: 04041

LA CHAMBRE DE COMMERCE ET D'INDUSTRIE DE PARIS
27 Avenue de Friedland
75382 Paris Cedex 08
France
Tel: 561 99 00

Entries: 14085 14095

CHAMBRE SYNDICALE DES AGENTS DE CHANGE
Centre d'Information et de Documentation
4 Place de la Bourse
75080 Paris Cedex 02
France
Tel: 1 261 85 90
Telex: SYNAGEN 230844

Entries: 14004 14018 14062 14136

CHAMBRE SYNDICALE DES PRODUCTEURS DE FER-BLANC ET DE FER-NOIR
5 Rue Paul Cezanne
75008 Paris
France
Tel: 45 63 17 10

Entry: 14055

CHAMBRE SYNDICALE DE LA SIDERURGIE FRANCAISE
BP 707–08
5 bis Rue de Madrid
75367 Paris Cedex 08
France
Tel: 387 53 59
Telex: 650392 SISYNDI PARIS

Entry: 14119

CHARITIES AID FOUNDATION
48 Pembury Road
Tonbridge TN9 2JD
Tel: 0732 771332

Entry: 36064

CHARTERED INSTITUTE OF PUBLIC FINANCE AND ACCOUNTANCY
3 Robert Street
London WC2N 6BH
Tel: 01 930 3456

Entries: 36157 36159 36241

CHEMICAL INDUSTRIES ASSOCIATION LTD.
Kings Buildings
Smith Square
London SW1P 3JJ
Tel: 01 834 3399
Telex: 916672
Fax: 01 834 4469

Entries: 01026 01065 10011 10016 36065 36072 36270

CIVIL AVIATION AUTHORITY
45-59 Kingsway
London WC2B 6TE
Tel: 01 7311
Telex: 883092

Entries: 36265 36266 36267 36268

COLLETS HOLDINGS LTD
London Road
Wellingborough
Northants
NN8 2QT
Tel: 0933 224351

Entries: 02005 02010 02011 02012 02013 05008 05010 05011 05017 05020 05022 05023 05028 05029 05030 05033 05034 05035 05036 05038 05041 07003 07006 07007 07012 07016 07017 07023 07026 07027 07029 07030 07031 07033 07037 07038 07045 07047 16009 19006 19019 19021 19030 19032 19033 19034 19040 28003 28011 28017 28023 28024 28033 37012 37013 37015 37023

COMITE INTERNATIONAL DE LA RAYONE ET DES FIBRES SYNTHETIQUES
29 rue de Courcelles
75008
Paris
France
Tel: 45 63 87 10
Telex: 650 931

Entry: 01032

COMMERCIAL BANK OF GREECE
Economic Research Division
10 Sophocleous Street
Athens 122
Greece
Tel: 3210 911

Entries: 18015 18030

COMMONWEALTH SECRETARIAT
Marlborough House
Pall Mall
London SW1Y 5HY
Tel: 01 839 3411
Telex: 27678

Entries: 01100 01119 01192 01306 01328 01329

COMPANY FACTS LTD.
Box 148
00181 Helsinki
Finland
Tel: 0 64292

Entry: 13001

CONFEDERACION NACIONAL DE CAMARAS AGRARIAS
2 Agustin de Bethencourt 17
28003 – Madrid
Spain
Tel: 91 233 7600

Entry: 01001

CONFEDERATION OF BRITISH INDUSTRY (CBI)
Centre Point
New Oxford Street
London WC1
Tel: 01 379 4700

Entries: 36049 36093 36096 36139

CONFEDERATION FRANCAISE DE L'INDUSTRIE DES PAPIERS, CARTONS ET CELLULOSES (COPACEL)
154 blvd Haussmann
75008 Paris
France
Tel: (1) 45 62 70 55
Telex: 290544

Entry: 14134

CONFEDERATION OF IRISH INDUSTRY
Confederation House
Kildare Street
Dublin 2
Tel: 779801
Telex: 24711

Entries: 21005 21009 21010 21028 21050

CONFEDERATION NATIONALE DE LA CONSTRUCTION
Rue du Lombard 34–42
1000 Brussels
Tel: 02 513 65 32

Entry: 04033

CONSEIL CENTRAL DE L'ECONOMIE
Avenue de la Joyeuse Entree 17–21
1040 Bruxelles
Belgium

Entry: 04055

CONSORCIO PARA EL FOMENTO DE LA RIQUEZA GANADERA
C/Santa Catalina 15
40003 Segovia
Spain
Tel: (911) 431414

Entry: 32046

T. C. COOMBS & CO.
4–5 Bonhill Street
London EC2A 4BX
Tel: 01 588 6209
Telex: 881304
Fax: 01 588 4589

Entry: 01284

CO-OPERATIVE UNION LTD.
Economic and Research Department
Holyoake House
Hanover Street
Manchester M60 0AS

Entry: 36091

COPENHAGEN HANDELSBANK
Economics Department
Holmens Kanal 2
DK 1091 Copenhagen
Tel: 45 1 12 86 00
Telex: 12186

Entries: 08002 08022 08057

CORVINA PUBLISHERS
1051 Budapest
Vorosmarty ter 1
Hungary
Tel: 176-222
Telex: 22-4440

Entry: 19041

COTE DESFOSSES
76 Shoe Lane
London EC4A 3JB
Tel: 01 353 0186
Telex: 23862
Also: 42 Rue Notre-Dame des Victoire
Paris 2e
France

Entries: 14006 14037 14059

COUNCIL FOR MUTUAL ECONOMIC ASSISTANCE (CMEA) AVAILABLE FROM;

LAPKIADO VALLALAT
Vigado Street No. 6
Budapest
Hungary

CREDIT LYONNAIS
Direction des Etudes Economiques et Financieres
5 Avenue du Coq
Paris 75009
Tel: 42-95-76-02

Entry: **14083**

CREDIT SUISSE
Paradeplatz 8
CH 8021 Zurich
Switzerland
Tel: (01) 215 1111
Telex: 812412

Entries: **34003** **34011**

CREDITANSTALT–BANKVEREIN
Schottengasse 6
1010 Wien
[illegible]

Entries: **03018** **03021** **03048** **03053** **03072** **03094**

CYPRUS CHAMBER OF COMMERCE AND INDUSTRY
PO Box 1455
Nicosia
Cyprus
Tel: 449500
Telex: 2077 CHAMBER

Entries: **06027** **06037**

CYPRUS EMPLOYERS AND INDUSTRIALISTS FEDERATION
PO Box 1657
Nicosia
Cyprus
Tel: 445102
Telex: 4834

Entry: **06004**

CYPRUS PORTS AUTHORITY
23 Crete Str
Nicosia
Cyprus
Tel: 02-450100
Telex: 283 3CYPA
Fax: 02-365420

Entries: **06005** **06030** **06049**

CZECHOSLOVAK CHAMBER OF COMMERCE AND INDUSTRY
Argentinska 38
170 05 Prague 7
Czechoslovakia

Entries: **07014** **07018**

DAFSA
7 Rue Bergere
75009 Paris
France
Tel: 233 21 23

Entry: **14056**

DALLOZ
11 Rue Soufflot
75240 Paris Cedex 05
France

DANISH BACON AND MEAT COUNCIL
Axeltorv 3
DK 1609 Copenhagen V
Denmark
Tel: 01 11 60 50
Telex: 22975 DS DK
Fax: 01 11 68 14

Entry: **08061**

DANISH FEDERATION OF TRADE UNIONS
12 Rosenorns Alle
1970 Copenhagen V

Entry: **08016**

DANMARKS NATIONALBANK
Havnegade 5
DK–1093
Copenhagen K
Denmark
Tel: 14 14 11
Telex: 27051

Entries: **08043** **08055**

DANMARKS STATISTIK
Sejrogade 11
2100 Copenhagen Ø
Tel: 01 298222
Telex: 16236

Entries: **01172** **08003** **08004** **08005** **08006** **08007** **08011** **08017** **08018** **08024** **08027** **08030** **08031** **08032** **08033** **08034** **08036** **08037** **08038** **08039** **08040** **08041** **08042** **08047** **08052** **08053** **08054** **08058** **08060** **08062** **08064** **08066** **08067** **08073** **08074** **08075**

DANMARKS TURISTRAD
Vesterbrogade 6D
DK–1620 Copenhagen V
Denmark
Tel: 01 11 14 15

Entries: **08009** **08071**

DATAR
1 Avenue Charles Floquet
75700 Paris
France
Tel: 783 61 20
Telex: 200 970 F

Entry: **14091**

DEN DANSKE BANK
Economics Department
Holmens Kanal 12
DK–1092 Copenhagen
Denmark
Tel: 15 65 00
Telex: 97000

Entries: **08021** **08025**

DANSKE ELVAERKERS FORENING
Rosenorns Alle 9
DK–1970 Frederiksberg
Denmark
Tel: 01 39 01 11
Telex: 16147 DANEL DK
Fax: 01 39 59 58

DANSK TURISTRAD
Vesterbrogade 6D
DK–1620
Copenhagen V
Tel: 01 11 14 15

DE LA SALLE BROTHERS PUBLICATIONS
St Benild's School
Sliema
Malta

Entry: **25028**

DELEGATION A L'AMENAGEMENT DU TERRITOIRE ET A L'ACTION REGIONALE (DATAR)
1 Avenue Charles Floquet
75007 Paris
France
Tel: (1) 47 83 61 20
[illegible]

Entries: **14042** **14058** **14064** **14082** **14141** **14142**

DEPARTMENT OF CUSTOMS AND EXCISE
Ministry of Finance
Ex-Secretariat Compound
Nicosia
Cyprus

Entry: **06007**

DEPARTMENT OF ENERGY
Clare Street
Dublin 2
Tel: 01 715233

Entry: **21029**

DEPARTMENT OF INFORMATION
Auberge de Castille
Valletta
Malta
Tel: 24901

Entries: **25012** **25019** **25020**

DEPARTMENT OF STATISTICS AND RESEARCH
13 Lord Byron Avenue
Nicosia P C 162
CYPRUS
Tel: 40-3286
Telex: 3399 MINEIN CY

Entries: **06014** **06015** **06016** **06017** **06018** **06019** **06020** **06021** **06022** **06023** **06024** **06032** **06034** **06041** **06043** **06044** **06045** **06047** **06050** **06053** **06054** **06055** **06056**

DEPARTMENT OF TRADE AND INDUSTRY
1 Victoria Street
London SW1H 0ET

DEPARTMENT OF TRADE AND INDUSTRY
Export to Europe Branch
1 Victoria Street
London SW1T 0ET

DEPARTMENT OF TRADE AND INDUSTRY
Hints to Exporters Unit
Lime Grove
Eastcote, Ruislip
Middlesex
Tel: 01 866 8771

Entries: 02002 03043 04044 04050 05021 06042 07022 07044 08029 13071 14063 15118 16008 18021 18024 19007 19017 20013 21035 22021 22029 23011 24016 25015 26020 27040 28013 29038 30009 30018 31024 32041 33036 34028 35024 37108

DEUTSCHE BANK
6000 Frankfurt am Main 1
Taunusanlage 12
West Germany

Entries: 15011 15068

DEUTSCHE BUNDESBANK
Postfach 10 06 02
6000 Frankfurt 1
West Germany
Tel: (0 69) 158 351
Telex: 414431/
Fax: (0 69) 560 1071

Entries: 15183 15237

DEUTSCHE GENOSSENSCHAFTSBANK (DG BANK)
Am Platz der Republik
6000 Frankfurt am Main 1
West Germany
Tel: 069 744701

Entries: 15099 15254

DEUTSCHES WIRTSCHAFTS-WISSENSCHAFTLICHES INSTITUT FUR FREMDENVERKEHR AN DER UNIVERSITAT MUNCHEN
Hermann-Sack-Strasse 2
8000 Munchen 2
West Germany
Tel: 26 70 91

Entry: 15142

DEVELOPMENT BUSINESS
PO Box 5850
G.C.P.O.
New York
NY 10163
USA

DIAMOND HIGH COUNCIL
Hoveniersstraat 22
2018 Antwerp
Belgium
Tel: 03 222 05 11
Telex: 34889

Entry: 01114

DIRECCAO GENERAL DO TURISMO
Avenue Antonio Augusto de Aguiar 86
1004 Lisbon
Portugal
Tel: 575217

Entries: 29054 29055

DIRECCION GENERAL DE ADVANAS
Seccion de Estadistica
Guzman el Bueno 137
Madrid
Spain

Entry: 32054

DIRECCION GENERAL DE SEGUROS
Paseo de la Castellana 44
28046 Madrid
Spain
Tel: 2754800

DIRECTIA CENTRALA DE STATISTICA AVAILABLE FROM:

ROMPRESTILATELIO
Sector import/export presa
PO Box 12–201
Bucaresti
Calea Griuitei N 64-66
Romania

Entry: 30003

DIRECTION GENERALE DES DOUANES
Monbijoustrasse 40
3003 Bern
Switzerland
Tel: 031 61 6525
Telex: 33466

Entries: 33030 33052

LA DIRECTION GENERALE DES DOUANES ET DROITS INDIRECTS
18 rue Saint Honore
75056 Paris
France
Tel: 260 33 00
Telex: DOUSTAT PARIS 230061

Entries: 14005 14029 14030 14132

LA DOCUMENTATION FRANCAISE
29–31 Quai Voltaire
75340 Paris
Cedex 07
France
Tel: 40 15 70 00
Telex: DOCFRAN PARIS 204826

Entries: 01016 01018 01135 01140 01184 01246 01247 01307 02004 11014 11015 12025 12117 14036 14041 14067 14090 14098 14107 14131 14144 15072 15084 15181 15245 18019 24022 26253 32032 32035 36182

DRESDNER BANK AG
Jurgen-Ponto-Platz 1
Postfach 11 06 61
D–6000 Frankfurt/Main 11
Tel: 263-0

Entry: 01064

DUNCKER & HUMBLOT GMBH
Dietrich-Schafer-Weg 9
1000 Berlin 41
West Germany
Tel: 791 20 26

Entries: 15085 15129 15212 15213 15265 15266 16017

EAST EUROPEAN TRADE COUNCIL
25 Victoria Street
London SW1H 0EX
Tel: 01 222 7622
Telex: 298681 COMSER G

EAST–WEST
10 Boulevard Saint Lazare
1210 Brussels
Belgium
Tel: 02 218 43 49
Telex: 21108 EUROPE B

ECONOMIC PLANNING AND STATISTICS OFFICE
Cathedral Square
Gibraltar
Tel: 75515

Entry: 17002

ECONOMIC AND SOCIAL RESEARCH INSTITUTE
4 Burlington Road
Dublin 4
Eire
Tel: 0001 760115

Entries: 21023 21039 21049 21055 21066

ECONOMIST INTELLIGENCE UNIT
Spencer House
27 St James' Place
London SW1A 1HG
UK
Tel: 01 493 6711

THE ECONOMIST NEWSPAPER LTD.
25 St James' Street
SW1A 1HG
Tel: 01 930 5155
Telex: 24344

Entry: 36095

ECONOMIST PUBLICATIONS LTD.
40 Duke Street
London W1A 1DW
Tel: 01 493 6711
Telex: 266353
Fax: 01 499 9767

Entries: 01235 02006 02007 03023 03024 04036 04037 05012 05013 06025 06026 07004 07005 08013 08014 13028 13029 14038 14039 15065 15066 16002 16003 18011 18013 19008 20007 20008 21019 21020 22016 22017 24010 24011 25009 25010 26013 26014 27015 27016 28006 28007 29017 30004 30005 31005 31006 32028 32029 33021 33022 34018 34019 35016 35017 36078 36079 37007 37008

EDITORIAL ALIMENTEC KSA
C/Modesto La Fuente 16
28010 – Madrid
Spain
Tel: 91–4455550

Entry: **32006**

EDITORIAL HEGEO SA
C/Ferraz 11
28008 Madrid
Spain
Tel: (91) 241 3400

Entry: **32040**

EDITORIAL DE MEDIOS TECNICOS DE EXPRESION SA
C/Comercio
4 Escira 1a 1º A
28007 Madrid
Spain
Tel: (91) 4336700/50

Entry: **32062**

EFFEKTENBORSENVEREIN
Bleicherweg 5
Postfach
8021 Zurich
Switzerland
Tel: 01 229 21 11
Telex: 813 065
Fax: 01 211 19 38

Entry: **34076**

EL ECONOMISTA
Calle del Conde de Aranda 8
Madrid 1
Spain
Tel: 226 42 76

Entry: **32033**

EKONOMSKA POLITIKA
Trg Marksa i Engelsa
7 Beograd 11000
Yugoslavia
Tel: 335 355/11
Telex: 11 104 YU BORBA

Entry: **37003**

ELECTRA PRESS PUBLICATIONS
4 Stadion Street
Athens
Greece

Entry: **18023**

ELECTRICITY AUTHORITY OF CYPRUS
Head Office
PO Box 4506
Nicosia
Cyprus

Entry: **06036**

ELECTRICITY COUNCIL
30 Millbank
London SW1P 4RD

ELECTRICITY COUNCIL
Overseas Relations Branch
30 Millbank
London SW1P 4RD

Entries: **08026 22020 36122**

ELINKEINOELAMAN–TUTKIMUSLAITOS (ETLA)
The Research Institute of the Finnish Economy
Lonnrotinkatu 4
SF 00120 Helsinki
Finland
Tel: 90 601322
Fax: 90 601753

Entry: **13150**

RICHARD ELLIS
Berkeley Square House
London W1X 6AN
Tel: 01 629 6290

Entry: **36206**

EUROFINANCE
9 Avenue Hoche
75008 Paris
France
Tel: 766 04 00
Telex: 290393

Entries: **01048 01076 01091 01142 01278**

EUROMONITOR
87–88 Turnmill Street
London EC1M 5QU
Tel: 01 251 8024
Telex: 21120

Entries: **01154 10025 36003 36004**

EUROPA PUBLICATIONS
18 Bedford Square
London WC1B 3JN
Tel: 01 580 8236/4139

Entry: **01075**

EUROPEAN BROADCASTING UNION
PO Box 67
CH–1218 Grand-Saconnex/GE
Switzerland
Tel: 022 98 77 66
Telex: 415 700 EBU
Fax: 022 98 58 97

Entry: **01055**

EUROPEAN CENTRE FOR THE DEVELOPMENT OF VOCATIONAL TRAINING
Bundesalle 22
D1000 Berlin 15
Tel: 030 884120

Entries: **12008 12140**

EUROPEAN ECONOMIC COMMUNITY
Office des Publications Officelles
5 Rue du Commerce
BP 1003 Luxembourg
Tel: 49 00 81

Entries: **12002 12003 12004 12005 12006 12007 12010 12011 12012 12013 12014 12015 12016 12017 12019 12020 12021 12022 12023 12024 12026 12027 12028 12029 12030 12031 12032 12035 12039 12040 12041 12042 12043 12044 12045 12046 12047 12048 12049 12050 12051 12053 12054 12055 12056 12057 12058 12059 12060 12061 12062 12063 12065 12066 12067 12068 12069 12070 12071 12072 12074 12075 12076 12077 12078 12079 12080 12081 12082 12083 12084 12085 12086 12087 12088 12090 12091 12092 12093 12095 12096 12097 12098 12099 12101 12102 12103 12104 12106 12107 12109 12110 12111 12112 12113 12114 12115 12116 12118 12119 12120 12121 12122 12123 12124 12126 12127 12128 12129 12130 12131 12132 12133 12134 12135 12136 12137 12138 12139**

EUROPEAN FOUNDATION FOR THE IMPROVEMENT OF LIVING AND WORKING CONDITIONS
Loughlinstown House
Shankill
Co Dublin
Ireland
Tel: 82 68 88

Entry: **12037**

EUROPEAN FREE TRADE ASSOCIATION (EFTA)
9–11 rue de Varembe
CH–1211 Geneva 20
Switzerland
Tel: 022 34 90 00
Telex: 22660 EFTA CH

Entries: **01057 01058 01059 01060 01099 11001 11003 11004 11006 11010 11017 12009 29004 29020 37017**

EUROPEAN INFORMATION SERVICE
46 Avenue Albert Elisabeth
1040 Brussels
Belgium
Tel: 02 736 1193
Telex: EURINF 26 005

Entries: **01074 01211**

EUROPROSPECTS LTD.
38 Mount Pleasant
London WC1X 0AP
Tel: 01 278 4707
Telex: 261177
Fax: 01 278 3608

Entry: **22023**

FABRIMETAL
Federation des Enterprises de l'Industrie des Fabrications metalliques, mecaniques, electriques et de la Transformation des Matieres Plastiques
Rue des Drapiers 12
B–1050 Brussels
Tel: 02 510 23 11
Telex: 210 78

Entries: **01017** **04068** **04072**

FACHVERBAND DER ERDOLINDUSTRIE OSTERREICHS
1031 Wien
Erdbergstrasse 72
Austria

Entry: **03051**

FACHVERBAND DER TEXTILINDUSTRIE OSTERREICHS
1013 Wien
Rudosfsplatz 12
Austria
Tel: 533 37 26
Telex: 114125
Fax: 533 37 26/40

Entries: **03073** **03083**

FACULTY OF ECONOMICS AND ADMINISTRATIVE SCIENCES
Karadeniz Technical University
Trabzon
Turkey
Tel: 11344
Telex: 83110
Fax: 15781

Entry: **35032**

FEBELGRA
Federation Belge des Industries Graphiques
Rue Belliard 20, bte 16
1040 Brussels
Tel: 02 512 36 38

FEDERAL MINISTRY OF ECONOMICS
Postfach 14 0260
5300 Bonn 1
West Germany
Tel: 0228 615 1
Telex: 886 747

Entry: **15075**

FEDERAL STATISTICAL OFFICE (FSO)
Kneza Milosa 20
PO Box 203
11 001 Belgrade
Yugoslavia

Entries: **37002** **37004** **37005** **37006** **37009** **37010** **37011** **37012** **37014** **37016** **37018** **37019** **37020** **37021** **37024** **37025** **37026** **37027** **37028** **37029** **37031** **37032** **37033** **37034** **37035** **37036** **37040**

FEDERAL STATISTICAL OFFICE OF GERMANY
W. Kohlhammer GmbH
Philipp-Rev-Strasse 3
D 6500 Mainz 42
West Germany

Entries: **01177** **01256** **02009** **03056** **05027** **06048** **07028** **18026** **19035** **20017** **21048** **23014** **25018** **27045** **28016** **29050** **31030** **32051** **33050** **34036** **35033** **36154** **37015**

FEDERALNI STATISTICKY URAD
(Federal Statistical Office of Czechoslovakia)
Sokolovska 142
Prague 8
Czechoslovakia
Tel: 81 42470

Entries: **07039** **07040** **07041** **07042**

FEDERATION BELGE DES ENTREPRISES DE DISTRIBUTION
Rue Saint-Bernard 60
1050 Brussels
Tel: 02 537 30 60
Telex: 63201
Facsimile: 5394026

Entry: **04009**

FEDERATION DES ENTREPRISES DE BELGIQUE
Rue Ravenstein 4
1000 Bruxelles
Belgium
Tel: 02 511 58 80
Telex: 26756

Entry: **04026**

FEDERATION DES ENTREPRISES DE METAUX NON FERREUX
Rue Montoyer 47
1040 Bruxelles
Belgium

Entry: **04065**

FEDERATION OF FINNISH INSURANCE COMPANIES
Bulevardi 28
SF–00120 Helsinki
Finland
Tel: +358 0 19 251
Telex: 123511
Fax: +358 0 192 5255

Entry: **13082**

FEDERATION OF FINNISH METAL AND ENGINEERING INDUSTRIES
Etelaranta 10
00130 Helsinki
Finland
Tel: 0 170922
Telex: 124997 FIMET
Fax: 0 662069

Entry: **13062**

FEDERATION OF INDUSTRIES
Development House
St Anne Street
Floriana
Malta
Tel: 234428, 222074
Telex: MW1380 AGIO

Entries: **25016** **25017**

FEDERATION DES INDUSTRIES ELECTRIQUES ET ELECTRONIQUES
11 Rue Hamelin
75116 Paris

Entry: **14069**

FEDERATION DES INDUSTRIES DES EQUIPEMENT POUR VEHICULES
112–114 Avenue Ch de Gaulle
92522 Neuilly-sur-Seine
France
Tel: 637 06 36
Telex: 630 943 F

Entry: **14070**

FEDERATION DE L'INDUSTRIE DU BETON
Boulevard A. Reyers 207–209
1040 Brussels
Tel: 02 735 80 15º

Entry: **04021**

FEDERATION DE L'INDUSTRIE CIMENTIERE
Rue Cesar Franck 46
1050 Brussels
Tel: 02 649 98 50
Telex: 21431

Entry: **04010**

FEDERATION DE L'INDUSTRIE DU GAZ (FIGAZ)
Avenue Palmerston 4
1040 Brussels
Tel: 02 733 82 32

Entries: **04004** **04012** **04053** **04073**

FEDERATION DES INDUSTRIES TRANSFORMATRICES DE PAPIER ET CARTON
Chaussee de Waterloo 715
Box 25
1180 Brussels
Tel: 02 344 19 61
Telex: 23442

Entry: **04011**

FEDERATION DE L'INDUSTRIE DU VERRE
Rue Montoyer 47
1040 Bruxelles
Tel. 02 513 3020

Entry: **04076**

FEDERATION PROFESSIONELLE DES PRODUCTEURS ET DISTRIBUTEURS D'ELECTRICITE DE BELGIQUE
Avenue de Tervueren 34–BTE
38–1040 Brussels
Tel: (02) 733 96 07

Entries: **04002** **04005**

FEDERATION OF SWEDISH INDUSTRIES
Box 5501
S–11485 Stockholm
Sweden
Tel: 08 63 50 20
Telex: 19990 SWEDINDS

Entry: **33130**

FIGYELO (OBSERVER)
1355 Budapest
Alkatmany V 10
Hungary
Tel: 127–644
Telex: 22–6613

Entry: **19020**

FINANCIAL TIMES BUSINESS INFORMATION
7th Floor
50–64 Broadway
London SW1H 0DB
Tel: 01 799 2002
Telex: 927282 FINTIM G
Fax: 01 799 2259

Entries: **01160 01327 36030 36034 36099 36126 36132 36145 36146 36147 36170 36195 36277**

FINNAIR OY
Mannerheimintie 102
00250 Helsinki
Finland
Tel: 0 410411
Telex: 124404
Fax: 0 4733648

Entry: **13003**

FINNISH BANKERS' ASSOCIATION
Annankatu 32 A
00100 Helsinki
Finland
Tel: 90 6948422
Fax: 6947844

Entries: **13010 13060**

FINNISH FOREST RESEARCH INSTITUTE
Unioninkatu 40
00170 Helsinki
Finland
Tel: 0 661401

Entry: **13165**

FINNISH INSURANCE SOCIETY
Bulevardi 28
SF 00120
Helsinki
Finland
Tel: 358 019 251
Telex: 123511
Fax: 358 0 192 5255

Entry: **13151**

FINNISH ROAD ASSOCIATION
Vironkatu 6
00170 Helsinki
Finland

Entry: **13006**

FINNISH SHIPOWNERS' ASSOCIATION
Satamakatu 4
00160 Helsinki
Finland
Tel: 170 400
Telex: 12 2751

Entries: **13100 13159**

FINNISH TOURIST BOARD
PO Box 53
SF–00521 Helsinki
Finland
Tel: 90 144 511
Telex: 122690 MEK SI

Entries: **13074 13099 13155**

FISKERIDIREKTORATET
Postboks 185/186
5001 Bergen
Norway

Entry: **27029**

FOOD AND AGRICULTURE ORGANISATION (FAO)
Vialle delle Terme di Caracalla
Rome 00153
Italy
Tel: 5797
Telex: 61181 FOODAGRI

Entries: **01038 01077 01079 01081 01082 01202 01362**

FORENINGEN AF DANSKE MEDICINFABRIKKER
Landemaerket 25
1119 Kobenhaven
Denmark
Tel: 01 11 12 70

Entry: **08069**

FORLAGET BØRSEN A/S
Møntergrade 19
Postbox 2103
DK–1014 Copenhagen K
Denmark
Tel: 01 15 72 50
Telex: BORSEN DK 2290 B

Entries: **08010 08044 08051**

FORSAKRINGSINSPEKTIONEN
(Private Insurance Supervisory Service)
PO Box 7493
10392 Stockholm
Sweden

Entries: **33027 33126**

FURNITURE INDUSTRY RESEARCH ASSOCIATION
Maxwell Road
Stevenage SG1 2EW
Tel: 0438 313433
Telex: 25102 FIRA CHACOM G
Fax: 0438 727607

Entries: **36020 36102 36208 36238 36278**

GALE RESEARCH CO.
Book Tower Building
Detroit
Michigan
USA 48226
Tel: 313 961 2242
Toll Free 1 800 223 GALE

Entries: **01047 01116**

GEDIM
19 Rue du Grand-Moulin
42029 Saint-Etienne
Cedex Lyon 26603
France
Tel: 77 32 46 13

Entry: **14003**

GENERAL AGREEMENT ON TARIFFS AND TRADE
Centre William Rappard
154 rue de Lausanne
1211 Geneve 21
Switzerland
Tel: 022 31 02 31
Telex: 28M8M GATT CH
Fax: 022 31 42 06

Entries: **01155 01346**

GENERAL DIRECTORATE OF POSTS AND TELECOMMUNICATIONS
PO Box 529
00101 Helsinki
Finland
Tel: 0 1951
Telex: 124557
Fax: 0 1954397

Entry: **15110**

GERMAN CHAMBER OF INDUSTRY AND COMMERCE
12/13 Suffolk Street
St James's
London SW1Y 4HG
Tel: 01 930 7251
Telex: 919442 GERMAN G

Entries: **15053 15060 15063 15083 15087 15088 15098 15100 15101 15102 15104 15105 15106 15107 15131 15140 15166 15174 15187 15188 15197 15198 15206 15209 15210 15225 15244 15246 15249 15250 15268 36119 36193 36252**

GESAMTVERBAND DER DEUTSCHEN VERSICHERUNGSWIRTSCHAFT EV (GDV)
Ebertplatz 1
5000 Koln 1
West Germany
Tel: 0221/77 64 119
Telex: 8 885 255
Fax: 0221/77 64 153

Entries: **15070 15103**

GIROZENTRALE VIENNA
Schubertring 5
POB 255
A–1011 Vienna
Austria
Tel: (222) 7294-0
Telex: 132591

Entries: **01176 03008 03009 03015 03017 03019 03022 03031 03032 03050 03061**

GLOWNY URZAD STATYSTYCZNY
Al Niepodleglosci 208
00–608 Warsaw
Poland
Tel: 25 24 31
Telex: 814581

Entries: **28002 28004 28018 28019 28029 28030 28031**

GOVERNMENT PRINTER
Valletta
Malta

GOWER PUBLISHING COMPANY LTD
Gower House
Croft Road
Aldershot
GU11 3HR
Tel: 0252 331551
Telex: 858001
Fax: 0252 344405

Entries: 01062 36089 36127 37022

GROUPEMENT DE LA SIDERURGIE
Rue Montoyer 47
1040 Bruxelles
Belgium

Entry: 04071

GUIDA MONACI SPA
Via Vitorchiano 107
00189 Roma
Italy

Entries: 22004

HMSO PUBLICATIONS CENTRE
PO Box 276
London SW8 5DT
Tel: (Orders) 01 622 3316
Tel: (Enquiries) 01 211 5656

Entries: 36002 36005 36009 36011 36012 36013 36016 36017 36019 36024 36025 36031 36033 36035 36039 36040 36041 36042 36050 36051 36052 36053 36054 36055 36056 36057 36058 36059 36060 36061 36062 36063 36066 36069 36070 36081 36082 36084 36090 36092 36094 36097 36098 36105 36108 36110 36111 36115 36117 36118 36123 36124 36125 36129 36130 36131 36140 36141 36142 36144 36149 36153 36158 36171 36173 36183 36186 36190 36191 36199 36200 36201 36207 36215 36216 36217 36218 36219 36220 36225 36226 36227 36228 36229 36230 36231 36232 36233 36234 36236 36242 36244 36246 36247 36248 36255 36261 36262 36269 36275 36282 36285 36286 36287 36288 36289

HAGSTOFA ISLANDS (Statistical Bureau of Iceland)
Hverfisgotu 8–10
150 Reykjavik
Iceland
Tel: 354–1–26699

Entries: 20012 20018 20021 20022 20023

HALIFAX BUILDING SOCIETY
Trinity Road
Halifax HX1 2RG
Tel: 0422 65777

Entry: 36128

HELLENEWS
23-25 Lekka Street
Athens
Greece
Telex: 219746

Entries: 18017 18043

HENLEY CENTRE FOR FORECASTING
2/4 Tudor Street
Blackfriars
London EC4Y 0AA
Tel: 01 353 9961
Telex: 298817
Fax: 01 353 2899

Entries: 01093 01097 36076 36085 36116 36155 36197 36198

HONG KONG AND SHANGHAI BANKING CORPORATION
1 Queen's Road Central
Hong Kong
Tel: 5–8221111
Telex: 73201

Entry: 06013

JOHNS HOPKINS UNIVERSITY PRESS LTD
Baltimore
Maryland 21218
USA

Entry: 01354

HUNGARIAN CENTRAL STATISTICAL OFFICE
Budapest II
Keleti Karoly utca 5–7
Hungary H–1024
Tel: (010 361) 358–530

Entry: 19054

HUNGARIAN CHAMBER OF COMMERCE
Budapest
PO Box 106
Hungary H–1389
Tel: (010 361) 533–333
Telex: 22-4745

Entries: 19015 19016 19022 19023 19026 19031 19037 19046

HUNGARIAN INSTITUTE FOR MARKET RESEARCH
Szende Pal Utca 3
1051 Budapest
Hungary
Tel: 00361 184 434
Telex: 22 5064 OPKH

Entry: 19038

ICC INFORMATION GROUP LTD.
ICC House
28–42 Banner Street
London EC17 8QE
Tel: 01 253 3906

Entry: 36043

IFO–INSTITUT FUR WIRTSCHAFTSFORSCHUNG
Poschingerstrasse 5
8000 Munchen 86
West Germany
Tel: (089) 9224–0
Telex: 5 22 269
Fax: (089) 98 53 69

Entries: 01171 15035 15064 15073 15082 15126 15127 15128 15130 15139 15170 15221 15242 15243

IFPI (INTERNATIONAL FEDERATION OF PHONOGRAM AND VIDEOGRAM PRODUCERS)
54 Regent Street
London W1R 5PJ
Tel: 01 434 3521
Telex: 919044 IFPI
Fax: 01 439 9166

Entries: 01125 01126 01345

ICELAND REVIEW
Hoefdabakka 9
PO Box 93
Reykjavik
Iceland
Tel: 1–84966
Telex: 2121

Entries: 21015 21016 21020

IMSWORLD PUBLICATIONS LTD
Kingsbourne House
229/231 High Holborn
London WC1V 7DA
UK

Entries: 01127 01128 01129 01130

INCHEBA FOREIGN TRADE CORPORATION
Drienova 24
829 57 Bratislava
Czechoslovakia

Entries: 07002

INCOMES DATA SERVICES LTD.
140 Great Portland Street
London W1
UK
Tel: 01 580 0521

Entries: 36133 36138 36257

INDUSTRIAL DEVELOPMENT AUTHORITY OF IRELAND
Wilton Park House
Wilton Place
Dublin 2
Tel: 01 686633
Telex: 93431
Fax: 01 603703

Entry: 21006

INED
27 Rue du Commandeur
75014 Paris
France
Tel: 320 13 45

Entries: 14099 14100

INFORMATION MOSCOW
Ul. Naberezhnaya 18
Babovka
Moscow
USSR
Tel: 443 40 88

Entry: 31026

INFORMATIVOS AGRARIOS SA
C/Ayala 20.5ºA
28001 – Madrid
Spain
Tel: 91–276 2707/08

Entry: 32005

INSTITUT ECONOMIQUE AGRICOLE
Ministere de l'Agriculture
Boulevard de Berlaimont, 18
1000 Brussels

Entries: 04038 04042 04043 04060 04061 04066

INSTITUT FUR ANGEWANDTE WIRTSCHAFTSFORSCHUNG (IAW)
Ob dem Himmelreich 1
7400 Tubingen
West Germany
Tel: 07071 81101

INSTITUT FUR MITTELSTANDSFORSCHUNG
Maximilianstr 20
5300 Bonn 1
West Germany
Tel: 0228 729970

Entries: 15089 15138 15165

INSTITUT FUR WELTWIRTSCHAFT AN DER UNIVERSITAT KIEL
Dusternbrooker Weg 120
Postfach 43 09
2300 Kiel 1
West Germany
Tel: (0431) 8 84 – 1
Telex: 2 92 479 WELTW D

Entries: 15071 15149

INSTITUT FUR WIRTSCHAFTSFORSCHUNG
Poschingerstr 5
8000 München 86
West Germany

Entries: 01325 01326

INSTITUT MONETAIRE LUXEMBOURGEOIS
63 Avenue de la Liberte
L–2983 Luxembourg
Tel: 478 888
Telex: 2766
Fax: 492 180

Entries: 01029 01073 24005 24013

INSTITUT NATIONAL DE LA RECHERCHE AGRONOMIQUE
147 Rue de l'Universite
75341 Paris Cedex 07
Tel: 42759000
Telex: 204719

Entry: 14129

INSTITUT NATIONAL DE LA STATISTIQUE ET DES ETUDES ECONOMIQUES (INSEE)
18 Boulevard Adolphe Pinard
75675 Paris Cedex 14
France
Tel: 45 40 12 12
Telex: 204924 F INSEEGD

Entries: 14002 14013 14014 14020 14026 14028 14033 14040 14043 14044 14045 14049 14051 14071 14102 14111 14112 14113 14118 14127 14128 14135 14144 14145 14147 14149

INSTITUT NATIONAL DE STATISTIQUE
Ministere des Affaires Economiques
Rue de Louvain 44
1000 Bruxelles
Belgium
Tel: 513 96 50

Entries: 04003 04006 04007 04029 04030 04031 04032 04052 04054 04057 04058 04059 04062 04063 04064 04067 04077 04078 04079 04080 04081 04082 04083 04084 04085 04086 04087 04092 24033

INSTITUT DE RECHERCHES ECONOMIQUES
Place Moutesruieu 3 – Bte 4
1348 Louvain La Nevue
Belgium
Tel: 010 43 41 52
Telex: 010 43 29 99

Entries: 01280 04070

INSTITUTE OF CHARTERED ACCOUNTANTS IN IRELAND
Chartered Accountants House
87–89 Pembroke Road
Dublin 4
Tel: 680400
Telex: 30567
Fax: 680842

Entry: 21001

INSTITUTE OF ECONOMICS
Hungarian Academy of Sciences
Budapest V
1 Roosevelt ter. N.9
Hungary

Entries: 02008 19003

INSTITUTE OF GROCERY DISTRIBUTION
Letchmore Heath
Watford
Hertfordshire
WD2 8DQ
Tel: 09276 7141
Telex: 8811581

Entry: 36114

INSTITUTE OF INDUSTRIAL ECONOMICS
Breiviken 2
5035 Bergen–Sandviken
Norway
Tel: 05 255660
Fax: 05 255667

Entries: 08028 13068 27031 33035

INSTITUTE FOR INDUSTRIAL RESEARCH AND STANDARDS
Ballymun Road
Dublin 9
Tel: 0001 370101

Entry: 21072

INSTITUTE OF MARKETING
Moor Hall
Cookham
SL6 9QH
Tel: 06285 24922

Entry: 36010

INSTITUTE OF NATURAL FIBRES
61–195 Poznan
ul. Wojska Polskiego 71B
Poland
Tel: 22–48–15
Telex: 0413486

Entry: 28026

INSTITUTE OF PETROLEUM
61 New Cavendish Street
London W1M 8AR
Tel: 01 636 1004
Telex: 264380

Entries: 01170 01228 01350 36074 36189 36196 36281

INSTITUTE OF PRACTITIONERS IN ADVERTISING
44 Belgrave Square
London SW1X 8QS
Tel: 01 235 7020
Telex: 918352

Entry: 36021

INSTITUTE DE RECHERCHES ECONOMIQUES
Place Montesguieu 3
Bte 4 1348 Louvain La Neuve
Belgium
Tel: 010 43 4152
Telex: 010 43 29 99

INSTITUTI I STUDIMEVE EKONOMIKE
Republika Popullore Socialiste e
Shoiperise Komisioni i Planit te Shtetit
Tirane
Albania
Tel: 79 38 64 18

INSTITUTO DE ANALISE DA CONJUNCTURA E ESTUDOS DE PLANECONENTO
Avenue D Carlos 1
126–19, 1293 Lisbon Cedex
Portugal

Entry: 29065

INSTITUTO DO COMERCIO EXTERNO DE PORTUGAL
Avenida 5 de Outuvro 101
1000 Lisbon
Portugal

Entries: 29013 29014

INSTITUTO NACIONAL DE ESTADISTICA
Avenida de Generalisimo 91
Madrid 16
Spain
Tel: 279 9300
Telex: 42086 PLDESE

Entries: **32002 32007 32011 32019 32023 32024 32025 32027 32034 32037 32038 32042 32044 32045 32056 32057 32059 32063**

INSTITUTO NACIONAL DE ESTATISTICA
Avenida Antonio Jose de Almeida
1078 Lisbon
Portugal

Entries: **29005 29006 29008 29009 29015 29021 29022 29023 29024 29025 29026 29027 29028 29029 29030 29031 29032 29033 29034 29035 29036 29040 29041 29042 29043 29044 29045 29046 29047 29048 29049 29056 29057 29059 29060 29061**

INSTYTUT MORSKI
PL 80–830 Gdansk
Dlugi Targ 41
Poland
Tel: 31 18 79

Entry: **28010**

INSTYTUT RYNKU WEWNETRZNEGO I KONSUMPCJI (INSTITUTE OF HOME MARKET AND CONSUMPTION)
Pl 3 Krzyzy 16
PL – 00–950 Warszawa skr
Poczt 31
Poland
Tel: 28 14 61
Telex: 817643 IRWIK PL

Entry: **28027**

INSURANCE INFORMATION SERVICES
Danish Insurance Association
10 Amaliegade
DK–1256
Copenhagen K
Tel: 45–1–13.75.55
Telex: 2381–112208
Fax: 45–1–11.23.53

Entry: **08015**

INTERNATIONAL ASSOCIATION OF HORTICULTURAL PRODUCERS
Postbus 361
2501 BE's Gravenhage
Netherlands
Tel: 0 70 81 46 31
Telex: 31406 PGFS NL

Entry: **01013**

INTERNATIONAL ATOMIC ENERGY AGENCY
Vienna International Centre
PO Box 100
A–1400
Vienna
Austria

Entry: **01233**

INTERNATIONAL BUREAU OF FISCAL DOCUMENTATION
PO Box 20237
1000 HE Amsterdam
Netherlands
Tel: 020 26 77 26
Telex: 13217 INTAX NL

Entries: **01010 01111 01112 01113 01301 01302 11007 11011 11012 11013**

INTERNATIONAL CHAMBER OF COMMERCE UNITED KINGDOM
Centre Point
103 New Oxford Street
London WC1A 1QB
Tel: 01 240 5558
Telex: 21332

Entry: **01110**

INTERNATIONAL COCOA ORGANISATION
22 Berners Street
London W1P 3DB
Tel: 01 637 3211
Telex: 28173
Fax: 631 0114

Entries: **01012 01251**

INTERNATIONAL CONFEDERATION OF FREE TRADE UNIONS (ICFTU)
Rue Montagne aux Herbes Potageres
37–41
B-1000 Brussels
Belgium
Tel: 217 80 85
Telex: 26785
Fax: 2188415

Entries: **01061 01098 01123 01275 07013**

INTERNATIONAL ECONOMIC REVIEW
3718 Locust Walk 6297
University of Pennsylvania
Philadelphia
PA 19104
USA
Tel: (215) 898 5841

Entry: **01149**

INTERNATIONAL ENERGY AGENCY
2 Rue Andre-Pascal
75775 Paris Cedex 16
France

Entries: **01006 01007**

INTERNATIONAL FEDERATION OF AGRICULTURAL PRODUCERS
1 rue d'Hauteville
75010 Paris
France

Entries: **01124 01339**

INTERNATIONAL INVESTMENT BANK
17 Presnensky Val
Moscow 123557
USSR
Tel: 253 80 24
Telex: LIBSU 441358

Entry: **31002**

INTERNATIONAL LEAD AND ZINC STUDY GROUP
Metro House
58 St James' Street
London SW1A 1LD
England
Tel: 01 499 9373
Telex: 299819

Entries: **01168 01189 01201 01244 01311 01313 01357**

INTERNATIONAL MONETARY FUND
Washington DC
20431
USA

Entries: **01021 01053 01054 01107 01152 01153**

INTERNATIONAL OFFICE OF COCOA, CHOCOLATE AND SUGAR CONFECTIONERY
Cortenberghlaan 172/1040
Brussels
Tel: 02/735 81 70
Telex: SIA 26246b
Fax: 02/733 94 26

Entry: **01288**

INTERNATIONAL OLIVE OIL COUNCIL
Juan Bravo
10–28006 Madrid
Spain
Tel: 275 96 06/7
Telex: 48197–100C–E

Entries: **01084 01232**

INTERNATIONAL PLANNING INFORMATION (IPI)
Nordre Ringvj 201
2600 Glostrup Copenhagen
Denmark
Tel: 45 2 63 20 44
Telex: 33576 BUSK DK

INTERNATIONAL RUBBER STUDY GROUP
Brettenham House
5–6 Lancaster Place
London WC2E 7ET

Entries: **01156 01277 01348**

INTERNATIONAL SILK ASSOCIATION
20 Rue Joseph Serlin
69001
Lyon
France
Tel: 7839 18 41
Telex: 330949

Entry: **01206**

INTERNATIONAL STATISTICAL INSTITUTE
428 Prinses Beatrixlaan
PO Box 950
2270 AZ Voorburg
The Netherlands
Tel: 070 694341
Telex: 32260

Entries: **01027 01157**

INTERNATIONAL SUGAR ORGANIZATION
28 Haymarket
London SW1Y 4SP
Tel: 01 930 3666
Telex: 24143

Entries: 01289 01296

INTERNATIONAL TEA COMMITTEE LTD.
Sir John Lyon House
5 Timber Street
London EC4N 3NY
Tel: 01 248 4672
Telex: 887911

Entries: 01004 01209

INTERNATIONAL TELECOMMUNICATION UNION
Sales Section
Place des Nations
CH–1211 Geneva 20
Switzerland

Entry: 01257

INTERNATIONAL TEXTILE MANUFACTURERS FEDERATION
Am Schanojengrab 29
Postfach
CH–8039
Zurich
Tel: 01 201 7050
Telex: 56798
Fax: 01 201 71 34

Entries: 01144 01145 01049 01159

INTERNATIONAL TIN COUNCIL
1 Oxendon Street
London SW1Y 4EQ
Tel: 01 930 0451
Telex: 918939

Entries: 01011 01208 01221 01287 01305

INTERNATIONAL TRADE CENTRE UNCTAD/GATT
Palais des National
1211 Geneva 10
Switzerland

Entry: 19025

INTERNATIONAL WHEAT COUNCIL
Haymarket House
28 Haymarket
London SW1Y 4SS
Tel: 01 930 4128
Telex: 916128

Entries: 01188 01260 01281 01360

ISTA MIELKE GMBH
Postfach 900803
Laugenburg 23
D–2100 Hamburg 90
West Germany
Tel: 60 20 81
Telex: 217789

Entries: 01230 01231

ISTANBUL CHAMBER OF COMMERCE
PO 377
Gumuspala Caddesi Eminonu
Istanbul
Turkey
Tel: 2661215/272218
Telex: 22682

Entry: 35018

ISTANBUL STOCK EXCHANGE
K221M Ismail Gurkan Cad
Cagologlu 34410
Istanbul
Turkey
Tel: 5261990
Telex: 22748
Fax: 5207111

Entries: 35027 35028 35029 35030

ISTITUTO CENTRALE DI STATISTICA
Via Cesare Balbo 16
00184 Rome
Italy
Tel: 06/4673
Telex: 61338

Entries: 22002 22003 22005 22008 22010 22011 22013 22014 22015 22022 22036 22050 22051 22052 22053 22054 22055 22056 22057 22058 22059 22060 22061

ISTITUTO NAZIONALE PER LO STUDIO DELLA CONGIUNTURA (ISCO)
Via Palermo 20
00 184 Roma
Italy

Entry: 22006

ISTITUTO DI RICERCHE SULL' ECONOMIA MEDITERRANEA
Viale a Gramsci, 5
80144
Naples
Italy

Entry: 11016

ISTITUTO DI RICERCHE SULLA POPOLAZIONE
Viale Beethoven
56 – 00144 Roma
Italy
Tel: 06 5921474/5925414

Entries: 22039 22065

JONES LANG WOOTTON
22 Hanover Square
London W1A 2NB
Tel: 01 493 6040

Entries: 36001 36205

JORDAN AND SONS LTD.
Jordan House
Brunswick Place
London N1 6EE
Tel: 01 253 3030
Telex: 261010

Entry: 36044

JUGOSLOVENSKI PREGLED
Mose Pijade 8/I
PO Box 677
11000 Beograd
Yugoslavia
Tel: 333–610

Entries: 37014 37037

JUPITER–VERLAG
Robertgasse 2
1020 Wien
Austria
Tel: (0222) 24 22 94

Entries: 03042 03060

KAMER VOOR HANDEL EN NIJVERHEID VAN HET
Arrondissement Leuven
Tiense Vest 170
3000 Leuven
Tel: 016 22 26 89

Entries: 04022 04051

KAMER VOOR KOOPHANDEL EN NIJVERHEID VAN HET
Gewest Gent
Martelaarslaan 41
9000 Gent
Tel: 091 25 3307

KANSALLIS–OSAKE–PANKKI
Aleksanterinkato 42
0010 Helsinki
Finland
Tel: 0 1631
Telex: 124412
Fax: 0 651253

Entries: 13004 13086 13096

KAUPPALEHTI OY
Box 189
00101 Helsinki
Finland
Tel: 0 5078512
Telex: 125827
Fax: 0 5663507

Entries: 13061 13088

KEYNOTE PUBLICATIONS LTD.
28–42 Banner Street
London EC1Y 8QE
Tel: 01 253 3006
Telex: 23678

Entries: 36150 36151 36152

KOBENHAVNS FONDSBORS
Nikolat Plads 2
Postbox 1040
DK 1007 Kobenhaven K
Denmark
Tel: 01933366
Telex: 16496
Fax: 01–128613

Entries: 08008 08045 08046 08050

W. KOHLHAMMER GMBH
Postfach 42 11 20
Stuttgart/Mainz
D 6500 42
West Germany
Tel: (0 61 31) 5 90 94/5
Telex: 04 187 768 DGV

Entries: 01243 01297 01298 01299 01323 15004 15005 15006 15008 15010 15012 15013 15017 15018 15019 15020 15021 15022 15023 15024 15025 15026 15033 15034 15038 15039 15040 15041 15042 15043 15044 15045 15046 15047 15048 15049 15050 15051 15052 15054 15055 15057 15058 15059 15061 15062 15074 15076 15078 15079 15080 15081 15086 15090 15092 15096 15097 15116 15117 15119 15134 15135 15136 15137 15141 15146 15147 15153 15154 15155 15156 15157 15158 15159 15160 15161 15162 15163 15164 15167 15169 15172 15173 15176 15177 15179 15189 15190 15191 15192 15193 15194 15195 15199 15200 15133 15132 15152 15202 15203 15204 15205 15215 15216 15217 15219 15220 15222 15223 15228 15230 15232 15233 15236 15238 15239 15247 15248 15253 15256 15257 15258 15259 15260 15261 15262 15264 15269 15270 16016 22027

KOMPASS PUBLISHERS
Windsor Court
East Grinstead House
East Grinstead
West Sussex
RH19 1ZB
UK
Tel: 0342 26972
Telex: 95127

Entries: 04048 08035 14084 15151 22030 24020 26027 32050 33046 34033

KOZPONTI STATISZTIKAI HIVATAL
1033 Budapest III
Kaszasdu ou 2
Hungary

Entry: 19051

KREDIETBANK NV
Arenbergstraat 7
B–1000 Brussels
Tel: 02 517 41 11
Telex: 21207 KBCOMP B

Entries: 04016 04017 04034 04040 04045 04046

LANDBOUW–ECONOMISCH INSTITUUT
PO Box 29703
2502 LS Den Haag
Netherlands
Tel: 070 614161

Entries: 26028 26072

LANDSBANKI ISLANDS
PO Box 170
Reykjavik
Iceland
Tel: 27722
Telex: 2030

Entries: 20004 20009

LIBER FORLAG
Sorterargatan 23
S–16289
Wallingby
Sweden

Entries: 33042 33048

LIECHTENSTEINISCHE FREMDENVERKEHRSZENTRALE
Postfach 139
FL–9490 Vaduz
Liechtenstein
Tel: 075/2 14 43
Telex: 889488 INTO FL

Entry: 23001

LIECHTENSTEIN VERLAG AG
PO Box 133
FL–9490 Vaduz
Liechtenstein
Tel: 75/22414
Telex: 889326

Entry: 23005

LLOYDS BANK LTD.
71 Lombard Street
London EC3P 3BS
Tel: 01 626 1500

Entry: 36156

LLOYD'S REGISTER OF SHIPPING
71 Fenchurch Street
London EC3M 4BS
Tel: 01 709 9166
Telex: 888379
Fax: 01 488 4796

Entries: 01015 01178 01179 01193 01282

LONDON CHAMBER OF COMMERCE
69 Cannon Street
London EC4N 5AB
Tel: 01 248 4444
Telex: 888 941
Fax: 01 489 0391

Entry: 36160

LONGMAN GROUP
Pinnacles
Fourth Avenue
Harlow
Essex
CM19 5AA
Tel: 0279 29655
Telex: 817484
Fax: 0279 31067

Entry: 31042

HERMANN LUCHTERHAND VERLAG
Postfach 1780
Heddesdorfer Strasse 31
5450 Neuwied 1
West Germany
Tel: 02631 801 0
Telex: 867 853

Entry: 15111

MACHINE TOOL TRADE ASSOCIATION
62 Bayswater Road
London W2 3PS

Entry: 36164

MACKINTOSH PUBLICATIONS LTD.
Mackintosh House
Napier Road
Luton
LU1 1RG

Entry: 01181

MACMILLAN PUBLISHERS LTD.
4 Little Essex Street
London WC2R 3LF
Tel: 01 836 6633
Telex: 262024
Fax: 01 379 4204

MARKET ASSESSMENT PUBLICATIONS LTD.
2 Duncan Terrace
London N18BZ
Tel: 01 278 9517
Fax: 01 278 6246

Entries: 36121 36166

MAXWELL STAMP ASSOCIATES
55–63 Goswell Road
London EC1V 7PT
Tel: 01 251 0147
Telex: 28604

MEDIA EXPENDITURE ANALYSIS LTD.
63–87 Martin's Lane
London WC2N 4JT
Tel: 01 240 1903/6
Fax: 01 240 2602

Entry: 36264

MEDIOBANCA
Ufficio Studi
Via Filodrammatici 10
20121 Milano
Italy
Tel: 8829–1

Entry: 22018

METAL BULLETIN BOOKS LTD.
Park House
Park Terrace
Worcester Park
Surrey
KT4 7HY
Tel: 01 330 4311
Telex: 21383
Fax: 01 337 8943

Entries: 01035 01133 01134 01163 01166 01194 01195 01196 01197 01217 01285 01295 01310 01338 01352 11009

MIDLAND BANK LTD.
122 Old Broad Street
London EC2P 2BX
Tel: 01 606 9911

Entry: 36167

MILK MARKETING BOARD
Giggs Hill Green
Thames Ditton
Surrey
KT7 0EL
Tel: 01 398 4101
Telex: 8956671
Fax: 01 398 8485

Entries: 01056 12036 36163 36181 36279

MINES SERVICE
[illegible] Street
Nicosia
Cyprus

Entry: 06010

MINISTERE DES AFFAIRES ECONOMIQUES
Administration des Mines
3 Rue J A de Mot
B–1040
Belgium
Tel: 230 19 19

Entries: 04001 04074 04075

MINISTERE DES AFFAIRES ECONOMIQUES
Direction Generale des Etudes et de la Documentation
Rue de l'Industrie 6
1040 Bruxelles
Belgium
Tel: (02) 512 79 50

Entries: 04039 04049 04091

MINISTERE DE L'AGRICULTURE
Service Centrale des Enquetes et Etudes Statistiques
4 Avenue de Saint Maude
75570 Paris Cedex 12
Tel: 344 46 33

Entries: 14007 14009 14010 14011 14012 14019 14023 14027 14060 14061 14068 14072 14073 14074 14075 14076 14077 14078 14079 14105 14106 14120 14121 14122 14123 14124 14125 14126 14130 14140 14143

MINISTERE DES COMMUNICATIONS
Rue de La Loi 65
1040 Brussels
Tel: 010 32 237 6711

Entry: 04090

MINISTERE DE LA CULTURE AVAILABLE FROM:

DALLOZ
11 Rue Soufflot
75240 Paris Cedex 05
France

MINISTERE DE L'ECONOMIE (STATEC)
Service Central de la Statistique et des Etudes Economiques
19–21 Boulevard Royal
2449 Luxembourg

Entries: 24004 24006 24015 24027 24032

MINISTERE DE L'ECONOMIE ET MINISTERE DU BUDGET
93 Rue de Rivoli
75056 Paris
France
Tel: 260 33 00

Entries: 14094 14133

MINISTERE DE L'EMPLOI ET DU TRAVAIL
Bibliotheque
Rue Belliard 53
1040 Bruxelles
Belgium

Entry: 04069

MINISTERE D'ETAT
Service Central de Legislation
10 Boulevard FD Roosevelt
Luxembourg

Entry: 24026

MINISTERE DE L'INDUSTRIE
Service du Traitment de l'Information et des Statistiques Industrielles
85 Boulevard de Montparnasse
75270 Paris Cedex 06
France
Tel: (1) 45 56 41 08
Telex: STISI 202 624
Fax: 45 56 40 71

Entries: 14008 14021 14025 14046 14053 14065 14066 14080 14081 14114 14115

MINISTERE DES TRANSPORTS
244 Boulevard Saint-Germain
75005 Paris
France
Tel: 544 39 93

Entry: 14093

MINISTERE DU TRAVAIL ET DE LA PARTICIPATION AVAILABLE FROM:

LA DOCUMENTATION FRANCAISE
29-31 Quai Voltaire
75340 Paris Cedex 07
France
Tel: 40 15 70 00
Telex; DOCFRAN PARIS 204826

Entries: 14117 14150

MINISTERIO DE AGRICULTURA, PESCA Y ALIMENTACION
Paseo Infanto Isabel 1
28014 – Madrid
Tel: (91) 227 97 30

Entries: 01009 32003 32004 32009

MINISTERIO DE COMERCIO
Goya 73
Madrid
Spain
Tel: 275 78 15

Entry: 32015

MINISTERIO DE ECONOMIA Y HACIENDA
Almirante 21
Madrid
Spain

Entries: 32017 32047 32060 32061

MINISTERIO DE INDUSTRIA
Paseo de la Castellana 160
Madrid 16
Spain
Tel. [illegible]

MINISTERIO DEL INTERIOR
Direccion General de Trafico
Serrano 41
Madrid
Spain
Tel: 403 43 50

Entry: 32021

MINISTERIO DE OBRAS PUBLICAS Y URBANISMO
Direccion General de Puertos y Costas
Madrid 6
Spain

Entry: 32053

MINISTERIO DE TRANSPORTES, TURISMO Y COMMUNICACIONES
Madrid 3
Spain

Entry: 32012

MINISTERO DEL TURISMO E DELLO SPETTACOLO
Via della Ferratella 51
00100 Roma
Italia
Tel: 7591897
Telex: 616400 MINTUR

Entry: 22041

MINISTRY OF COMMUNICATIONS AND WORKS
Nicosia
Cyprus
Tel: 021 2161
Telex: 3678

Entries: 06006 06008

MINISTRY OF CULTURE AND TOURISM
Gazi Mustafa Kemal
Bwl. 33
Demirtepe–Ankara
Tel: 2300241

Entries: 35008 35042

MINISTRY OF ECONOMIC AFFAIRS
Rue de l'industrie 6
B–1040
Brussels
Tel: 02 511 1930

Entry: **04013**

MINISTRY OF FINANCE AND CUSTOMS
Auberge de Castille
Valetta
Malta
Tel: 25231

Entries: 25003 25004

MINISTRY OF FINANCE ECONOMICS DEPARTMENT
Box 295
SF 00171 Helsinki
Finland
Tel: 0 1601
Telex: 123241

Entries: 13043 13107

MINISTRY OF LABOUR PLANNING DEPARTMENT
00120 Helsinki
Etelaesplanadi 4
Finland
Tel: 0 18561
Fax: 0 1856427

Entry: **13093**

MINISTRY OF SOCIAL AFFAIRS AND HEALTH
PO Box 267
00171 Helsinki
Finland
Tel: 90 1601

Entries: 13069 13070 13084 13132 13133 13134 13135 13163

MINISTRY OF TRADE
Export Promotion Division
Lascaris
Valetta
Malta
Tel: 24411
Telex: MW 104 TRADMIN

Entries: 25014 25021

MINISTRY OF TRADE AND INDUSTRY
Energy Department
Aleksanterinkatu 10
00170 Helsinki
Finland
Tel: 0 1601
Telex: 125452 +
Fax: 0 1603666

Entries: 13044 13045

MIRROR GROUP NEWSPAPERS (1986) LTD.
Holborn Circus
London EC1P 1DQ

Entry: **36162**

MORGAN–GRAMPIAN (PROCESS PRESS)
30 Calderwood Street
Woolwich
London SE18 6QH
Tel: 01 855 7777
Telex: 896238
Fax: 01 854 7476

Entry: **01186**

MORGAN–GRAMPIAN BOOK PUBLISHING CO. LTD.
Morgan–Grampian House
30 Calderwood Street
London SE18 6QH
Tel: 01 855 7777
Telex: 896238

Entries: 36008 36113

MOSCOW NARODNY BANK
24 King William Street
London EC4
Tel: 01 623 2500

Entry: **31003**

NATO INFORMATION SERVICE
1110 Brussels
Belgium

Entry: **01212**

NORTH ATLANTIC TREATY ORGANISATION
Economics and Information Directorates
B1110 Brussels
Belgium
Tel: 241 00 40
Telex: 23 867

NHBC
Information Department
58 Portland Place
London W1N 4BU
Tel: 01 580 9381

Entry: **36203**

NARINGSLIVETS FORLAG
Svarsforsandelse
Kontonummer 7000
103 30 Stockholm
Sweden

NARODOWY BANK POLSKI
Swietokrzyska 11–21
00–950 Warsaw
Poland
Tel: 200 321
Telex: 813324

Entry: **28014**

NATIONAL BANK OF GREECE
86 Eolou Street
Athens 121
Greece
Tel: 321 04 11
Telex: 214933

NATIONAL BANK OF HUNGARY
1850 Budapest
Szabadsag ter 8
Hungary
Tel: 112–600
Telex: 22–5755

Entries: 19012 19047

NATIONAL BOARD OF AGRICULTURE
PO Box 250
00171 Helsinki
Finland
Tel: 0 661771
Fax: 0 175 394

Entries: 13051 13103 13164

NATIONAL BOARD OF HEALTH
PO Box 221
00531 Helsinki
Finland
Tel: 0 77231
Telex: 121774 NBH
Fax: 0 7723442

NATIONAL BOARD OF HEALTH AND WELFARE
106 30 Stockholm
Sweden

Entry: **33004**

NATIONAL BOARD OF NAVIGATION
Box 158
00141 Helsinki
Finland
Tel: 0 18081
Telex: 121471
Fax: 0 1808355

Entries: 13108 13109

NATIONAL BOARD OF PUBLIC ROADS AND WATERWAYS
Box 33
00521 Helsinki
Finland
Tel: 0 1541
Telex: 124589 TVH SF
Fax: 0 1542662

NATIONAL BOARD OF TRADE AND CONSUMER INTERESTS
Box 5
00531 Helsinki
Finland
Tel: 0 7031

Entry: **13120**

NATIONAL ECONOMIC DEVELOPMENT COUNCIL
1 Steel House
11 Tothill Street
London SW1H 9IJ
Tel: 01 222 0565

Entry: **36022**

NATIONAL ECONOMIC DEVELOPMENT OFFICE
Millbank Tower
Millbank
London SW1P 4QX
Tel: 01 211 3100

Entries: 36073 36204

NATIONAL ECONOMIC INSTITUTE OF ICELAND
Kalkofnsvegur 1
150 Reykjavik
Iceland
Tel: 91–699500
Telex: 2020

Entries: 20006 20019

NATIONAL ECONOMIC AND SOCIAL COUNCIL
Ears Court
Adelaide Road
Dublin 2
Tel: (0001) 604077

Entry: **21051**

NATIONAL INSTITUTE OF ECONOMIC RESEARCH STOCKHOLM AVAILABLE FROM:
Allmanna Forliget
Kundtjanst
162 89 Stockholm
Sweden

Entry: 33120

NATIONAL INSTITUTE OF ECONOMIC AND SOCIAL RESEARCH
2 Dean Trench Street
Smith Square
London SW1P 3HE
Tel: 01 222 7665

Entries: 36023 36179

NATIONAL INSTITUTE FOR PHYSICAL PLANNING AND CONSTRUCTION RESEARCH
St Martins House
Waterloo Road
Dublin 4
Ireland
Tel: 01 602511
Telex: 30846

Entry: 21017

NATIONAL LABOUR MARKET BOARD
Information Division
5171 99 Solna
Sweden
Tel: 08 730 60 00

Entry: 33121

NATIONAL STATISTICAL SERVICE OF GREECE
Publications and Information Division
14–16 Lycourgou Street
Athens 112
Greece
Tel: 3244 7846

Entries: 18002 18003 18006 18007 18008 18009 18010 18025 18028 18029 18032 18034 18035 18036 18038 18039 18040 18041 18042 18044 18046 18047

NATIONAL WESTMINSTER BANK
Business Development Division
National House
14 Moorgate
London EC2R 6BS
Tel: 01 726 1000

Entries: 03007 06028 12033 15109 27057 33114 34059 35054 37037

NATIONALOKONOMISCHE GESELLSCHAFT
Liechtensteinstrasse 13/11
A–1090 Wien
Austria
Tel: (0222) 317193

Entry: 03027

NEDERLANDS INSTITUUT VOOR HET BANK– EN EFFECTENBEDRIJT (NIBE)
Postbus 19460
1000 GL Amsterdam
Netherlands

Entry: 26008

DE NEDERLANDSCHE BANK
Westeinde 1
Postbus 98
1000 AB Amsterdam
Netherlands
Tel: 020 524 91 11
Telex: 11355 DNB AM NL
Fax: 020 524 34 29

Entries: 26006 26015 26030 26052 26073

NETHERLANDS BRITISH CHAMBER OF COMMERCE
307 High Holborn
London WC1V 7LS
Tel: 01 405 1358
Fax: 01 405 1689
Telex: 23211

Entries: 25018 26009 26017 26024 26026 26029

NETHERLANDS CENTRAL BUREAU OF STATISTICS
Kloosterweg 1
Heerlen
The Netherlands
Tel: 045 736666

Entries: 26003 26007 26010 26012 26016 26019 26022 26023 26025 26031 26032 26033 26034 26035 26036 26037 26038 26039 26040 26041 26042 26043 26049 26050 26051 26055 26056 26057 26058 26059 26060 26061 26062 26063 26064 26065 26066 26067 26068 26069 26071

NOMOS VERLAGSGESELLSCHAFT MBH & CO. KG
Postfach 610
7570 Baden–Baden
West Germany
Tel: (0 72 21) 21 04–0
Telex: 0781 201

Entries: 01072 01118 12038 12089 15015

NORDIC BANK LTD.
20 St Dunstan's Hill
London EC3R 8HY

Entry: 01219

NORDIC COUNCIL
Box 19506
S–104 32
Stockholm
Sweden

Entries: 01218 01369

NORGES BANK
Postboks 1179 Sentrum
0107 Oslo 1
Norway
Tel: 31 60 00
Telex: 71369 N BANK N
Fax: 41 31 05

Entries: 27013 27018 27056 27060

NORGES REDERIFORBUND
Radhusgaten 25
Postboks 1452 Vika
0116 Oslo 1
Norway
Tel: 02 41 60 80
Telex: 21561 NORED N
Fax: 02 41 50 21

Entry: 27049

DEN NORSKE CREDITBANK
Kiregt 21
Oslo 1
Tel: 472 48 10 50
Telex: 18175

Entries: 27004 27017 27052 27053

NORWEGIAN BANKERS ASSOCIATION
Postboks 1489
Dronning Maudsgt 15
Vika
0116 Oslo 1
Norway
Tel: 41 18 30
Telex: 17218

Entries: 27026 27065

THE NORWEGIAN FEDERATION OF TRADE UNIONS
Youngsgaten 11
0181 Oslo 1
Norway
Tel: 02 40 10 50
Telex: 19861 LONOR
Fax: 02 40 17 43

Entry: 27003

NORWEGIAN TELECOMMUNICATIONS ADMINISTRATION
12386 Farsta
Norway
Tel: 03 713 1000

Entry: 27034

OBER OSTERREICH VERKAUFSFORDERUND LANDES–FREMDENVERKEHRSVERBAND
Schillerstrasse 50
A 4020 Linz
Austria
Tel: (0732) 663021 – 0
Telex: 022175

Entry: 03052

OFFICE FEDERAL DE LA STATISTIQUE
3003 Berne
Hallwylstrasse 15
Switzerland
Telex: 32526

Entries: 34002 34007 34044 34045 34047 34051 34068 34069 34070 34071

OPORTO CHAMBER OF COMMERCE AND INDUSTRY–OPORTO COMMERCIAL ASSOCIATION
Rua Ferreira Borges–Palacio da Bolsa
4000 Porto

Portugal
Tel: 24497/311448
Telex: 22159 ASSCOM P

Entry: 29001

ORAC PUBLISHING HOUSE (AUSTRIAN MUSEUM FOR ECONOMIC AND SOCIAL AFFAIRS)
Vogelsanggasse 36
A–1050 Wien
Austria

Entries: 01078 01086 01087 01088 01089 01092 01096 01120 01137 01165 01174 01183 01191 01198 01199 01200 03086

ORBIS PRESS AGENCY
120 41 Prague 2
Vinohradska 46
Czechoslovakia

Entry: 07008

ORGANISATION FOR ECONOMIC COOPERATION AND DEVELOPMENT (OECD)
2 rue Andre–Pascal
75775 Paris Cedex 16
France
Tel: (1) 45248200

Entries: 01022 01023 01037 01044 01046 01051 01067 01068 01069 01070 01085 01104 01131 01182 01210 01213 01222 01223 01224 01225 01226 01227 01249 01250 01253 01254 01255 01272 01273 01279 01294 01308 01353 03068 04056 08049 13111 15186 18031 22038 24028 26048 27062 29053 31039 32058 34042 35041 36187

THE OSLO STOCK EXCHANGE
Tollbugata 2
0152 Oslo 1
Norway
Tel: 02 42 38 80
Telex: 77242
Fax: 02 41 65 90

Entries: 27005 27007

OSLO TOURIST BOARD
Radhusgaten 19
N–0158 Oslo 1
Norway
Tel: 2 42 7170
Telex: 71969

Entry: 27048

OSTERREICHISCHE LANDERBANK
A–1011 Wien
Am Hof 2
Austria
Tel: (0222) 53124–0

Entries: 03002 03077 03081

OSTERREICHISCHE NATIONALBANK
Publizistisches Buro
Postfach 61
A–1011 Wien
Austria

Entry: 03010

OSTERREICHISCHES INSTITUT FUR WIRTSCHAFTSFORSCHUNG
Postfach 91
1103 Wien
Austria
Tel: (0222) 7826010

Entry: 03064

OSTERREICHISCHES STATISTISCHES ZENTRALAMT INFORMATIONSABTEILING
Hintere Zollamtsstrasse 2b
1033 Wien, Postfach 9000
Austria
Tel: (0222) 66 28/7414, 7655, 7654

Entries: 03004 03005 03006 03011 03012 03014 03016 03025 03026 03028 03029 03030 03033 03034 03035 03036 03037 03038 03039 03040 03044 03045 03046 03047 03049 03054 03055 03057 03058 03059 03062 03063 03066 03067 03071 03074 03075 03076 03079 03080 03082 03084 03085 03087 03088 03089 03091 03092 03095 03096 03097

OXFORD UNIVERSITY PRESS
Walton Street
Oxford
Tel: 56767

Entries: 11005 12125

PANNONIA PRESS
Franklin Printing House
Budapest

Entry: 19024

PANORAMA DDR AUSSLANDSPRESSAGENTUR GMBH
Wilhelm Pieck Strasse 49
1054 Berlin

Entries: 16005 16007

PER PRESS APS
Frederik d. VI's Alle 5
2000 Frederiksberg
Denmark
Tel: 01 86 85 84

Entry: 08068

PERGAMON PRESS PLC
Headington Hill Hall
Oxford OX3 0BW
UK
Tel: 0865 64881
Telex: 83177
Fax: 0865 60285

Entries: 05025 31008 36148 36258

PLANNING BUREAU
Planning Commission
Cyprus
Tel: 40–2714

Entry: 06040

POLISH CHAMBER OF FOREIGN TRADE
PO Box 361
00 950 Warszawa
Trebacka 4
Poland
Tel: 26 02 21
Telex: 814361

Entry: 28012

POLSKA AGENCJA INTERPRESS
ul Bagatela 12
00–585 Warszawa
Poland
Tel: 282221
Telex: 81 4775 PAI PL

Entries: 28005 28020

PORTE AUTONOMIE DE MARSEILLE
23 Place de la Joliette
13217 Marseilles Cedex 1
France
Tel: 91 90 66
Telex: 440 746 PORTAUTO MARSL

Entry: 14148

POSLOVNA ZAJEDNICA PROIZVODACA MOTORNIH VOZILA
Bulevar Vojvode Misica 14
Belgrad
Yugoslavia

Entry: 37037

POSTVERKET
General Directorate of Posts
S–105 00 Stockholm
Sweden
Tel: 08 781 1000
Telex: 13356 POSTGEN S
Fax: 08 21 96 11

Entries: 33011 33078

PRESS AND INFORMATION OFFICE OF THE LIECHTENSTEIN GOVERNMENT
Government Building
FL–9490 Vaduz
Liechtenstein
Tel: 075/6 61 11
Telex: 889 290

Entries: 23006 23020

PRICE WATERHOUSE
153 East 53rd Street
New York
NY 10022
USA

Entries: **08012** **18014** **29019**

PRIVATBANKEN
Economics Department
PO Box 1000
DK–2400 Copenhagen NV
Denmark
Tel: 451 11 11 11
Telex: 27196 PRIVCO DK

Entries: **05014** **08019**

QUORUM BOOKS
c/o Westport Publications
3 Henrietta Street
London WC2E 8LT
Tel: 01 240 1003

Entry: **31025**

RAILWAY BOARD
Box 488
00101 Helsinki
Finland
Tel: 0 7071
Telex: 12301151
Fax: 0 7073500

RAPID CZECHOSLOVAK ADVERTISING AGENCY
u/ 28 Rijna 13
112 79 Praha 1
Czechoslovakia

Entries: **07010** **07011** **07021** **07024** **07025** **07034** **07035** **07036** **07043** **07046**

REUTERS LTD.
85 Fleet Street
London EC4P 4AJ
Tel: 01 250 1122
Telex: 23222
Fax: 01 353 0156

Entries: **01263** **01264** **01265** **01266** **01267** **01268** **01269** **01270**

REWARD GROUP
Reward House
Diamond Way
Stone Business Park
ST15 0SD
Tel: 0785 813566
Telex: 36274

Entries: **36032** **36067** **36075** **36086** **36109** **36161** **36222** **36223** **36224**

RHEINISCH–WESTFALISCHE BORSE ZU DUSSELDORF
Ernst–Schneider–Platz 1
4000 Dusseldorf 1
Postfach 240263
West Germany
Tel: (0211) 8621
Fax: (0211) 133287

Entry: **15211**

RIKFTORSAKRINGSVERKET (NATIONAL SOCIAL INSURANCE BOARD)
S 103 51 Stockholm
Sweden
Tel: 01046 8 7869000

Entry: **33005**

ROMPRESTILATELIO
Sector Import/Export Presa
PO Box 12 – 201
Bucaresti
Calea Griuitei N 64–66
Romania

ROYAL DANISH MINISTRY OF FOREIGN AFFAIRS
Asiatisk Plads 2
DK–1448 Copenhagen

Entry: **08023**

ROYAL INSTITUTION OF CHARTERED SURVEYORS
12 Great George Street
Parliament Square
London SW1P 3AD
Tel: 01 222 7000
[illegible]
Fax: 01 222 9430

Entry: **36214**

ST GALLER ZENTRUM FUR ZUKUNFTSFORSCHUNG
Falken Steinstrasse 27
CH 9006
St Gallen
Switzerland

SCHWEIZERISCHE BAUERNSEKRETARIAT
Laurstr 10
5200 Brugg
Switzerland
Tel: (056) 419241

Entry: **34054**

SCHWEIZERISCHE GESELLSCHAFT FUR STATISTIK UND VOLKSWIRTSCHAFT (SGSV)
Hallwylstrasse 15
CH 3033 Bern
Switzerland
Tel: 031/61 87 60

Entry: **34056**

SCHWEIZERISCHE NATIONALBANK
Postfach
8002
Zurich
Switzerland
Tel: 01 221 37 50
Telex: 812 400 SNB CH

Entries: **34004** **34008** **34023** **34041**

SCHWEIZERISCHER HANDELS UND INDUSTRIE–VEREIN
Borsenstrasse 26
8001 Zurich
Postfach 4138
Switzerland
Tel: 01 221 2707
Telex: 813294

Entry: **34074**

SCHWEIZERISCHES HANDELSAMTSBLATT
PO Box 2170
CH 3001 Berne
Switzerland
Tel: 31 612221

Entry: **34073**

SCIENTIFIC AND ENCYCLOPAEDIC PUBLISHING HOUSE
R 71341 Piata Scinteii
Bucarest 33
Tel: 17 51 68

Entries: **30011** **30013** **30014**

SEA FISH INDUSTRY AUTHORITY
Sea Fisheries House
10 Young Street
Edinburgh EH2 4JQ
Tel: 031 225 2515
Telex: 727225

Entry: **36259**

A/U ULLVIG
PO Box 9070
Vaterland
Oslo 1
Tel: 0242 58 67
Telex: 17622

Entries: **27022** **27061** **27063**

SEPTIBEL–SOCIEDAD DE ESTUDOS PARA E PRODUTIVADE NO TRABALHO
Rua Alves Torqo 2
Lisbon
Portugal

Entry: **29012**

SERVICE CENTRAL DE LA STATISTIQUE ET DES ETUDES ECONOMIQUES
BP 304
19–20 bd Royal
Luxembourg
Tel: 4794 292

Entries: **24002** **24007** **24008** **24012** **24017** **24018** **24019** **24029** **24031**

SHAWS PRICE GUIDES LTD.
PO Box 32
Abingdon
Oxfordshire
OX14 3LJ
Tel: 0235 553233

Entry: **36235**

SININEN KIRJA OY
Uudenmaankatu 16–20
00120 Helsinki
Finland
Tel: 0 1224881

Entry: **13014**

SKOGSSTYRELSEN (FORESTRY COMMISSION)
S 551
83 Jönköping
Sweden
Tel: 01046 36 169400

Entry: **33075**

SMALL BUSINESS RESEARCH TRUST
Francis House
Francis Street
London SW1P 1DE
Tel: 01 828 5327

Entry: 36212

SOCIAL INSURANCE INSTITUTION
Box 450
00101 Helsinki
Finland
Tel: 0 43411
Telex: 412358
Fax: 0 4343333

Entry: 13124

SOCIEDADE DE ESTUDOS PARA E PRODUTIVADE NO TRABALHO (SEPTIBEL)
Rua Alves Torqo 2
Lisbon
Portugal

SOCIETE DE LA BOURSE DE LUXEMBOURG
11 Avenue de la Porte Neuve
L-2227 Luxembourg
Tel: 4779 36 1

Entries: 24009 24023 24024 24025

SOCIETY OF MOTOR MANUFACTURERS AND TRADERS LTD.
Forbes House
Halkin Street
London SW1X 7DS
Tel: 01 235 7000
Telex: 21628
Fax: 01 235 7112

Entries: 36176 36178

SOFIA PRESS
1 Levski Street
Sofia K349
Bulgaria

Entry: 05031

SOVIET EMBASSY
18 Kensington Palace Gardens
London W8
Tel: 01 229 6412

Entry: 31047

SOVIET WEEKLY
3 Rosary Gardens
London SW7 4NW
Tel: 01 373 8421
Telex: 25372

Entry: 31049

SPANISH CHAMBER OF COMMERCE
5 Cavendish Square
London W1
UK
Tel: 01 637 9061

Entry: 32026

STAATSVERLAG DER DEUTSCHEN DEMOKRATISCHEN REPUBLIK
Hans Bimler Strasse 70/72
102 Berlin
DDR
Tel: 2130
Telex: 114872

Entries: 16013 16014 16015

STATE INSTITUTE OF STATISTICS
Necatibey Caddesi 114
Ankara 114
Turkey
Tel: 256330

Entries: 35001 35002 35003 35005 35006 35007 35009 35012 35013 35014 35015 35020 35021 35022 35023 35026 35034 35035 35036 35037 35038 35039 35040 35043 35044 35046 35047 35048 35049 35050 35052 35053 35055 35057 35058

STATE PLANNING ORGANISATION
D P T Yabanci Sermaye Baskanligi
Necatibey Caddesi 110
Ankara
Turkey

STATE RAILWAYS
S -10550Stockholm C
Sweden
Tel: 764025
Telex: 19410
Fax: 320 186

Entry: 33066

STATENS JARNVAGAR
Centralstationhuset
105 50 Stockholm
Sweden
Tel: 08 762 20 00

Entry: 33112

STATIONERY OFFICE
Government Publications Sale Office
Sun Alliance House
Molesworth Street
Dublin 2

Entries: 21007 21008 21011 21012 21013 21014 21016 21021 21022 21024 21025 21026 21027 21032 21044 21045 21046 21047 21052 21053 21056 21057 21058 21059 21062 21063 21064 21067 21068 21069 21071 21073 21074 21075 21076

STATISTICAL PUBLISHING HOUSE
H-1033 Budapest
Kaszasdulo U 2
Hungary
Tel: 803-311
Telex: 22-6699

Entries: 14001 19004 19005 19009 19010 19011 19013 19014 19027 19028 19029 19036 19039 19042 19043 19044 19045 19048 19049 19050 19052 19053 19055 19056 19057 19058 19059 19060 19061 19062 19063 19064 19065 19066 19067 19068 19069 19070 19071 19072

STATISTIKA CENTRALBYRAN
Karlavagan 100
Fack
S-102 50 Stockholm 27
Sweden
Tel: 08 14 05 60

Entries: 33006 33010 33013 33014 33015 33016 33018 33020 33026 33031 33032 33033 33034 33037 33038 33039 33043 33044 33045 33047 33051 33052 33053 33055 33067 33072 33073 33076 33079 33080 33081 33082 33083 33084 33085 33086 33087 33088 33089 33090 33091 33092 33093 33094 33095 33096 33097 33098 33099 33100 33101 33102 33103 33104 33105 33106 33107 33127 33128 33129

STATISTISCHES BUNDESAMT
Gustav-Stresemann-Ring 11
6200 Wiesbaden
West Germany

Entry: 30010

STATKONTORET
Box 34107
S-100 26 Stockholm
Sweden
Tel: 08 7384000

Entry: 33108

THE STOCK EXCHANGE
London EC2N 1HP
Tel: 01 588 2355

Entry: 36213

SUCRO SA
C/Hernan Cortes S
46004 - Valencia
Spain
Tel: (96) 352 5301

SUOMEN METSATEOLLISUUDEN KESKUSLIITTO
Etelaesplanadi 2
00130 Helsinki
Finland
Tel: 0 13261
Telex: 121823
Fax: 0 174479

Entry: 13101

SVENSKA ARBETSGIVAREFORENINGEN
Sodra Blasieholmshamnen 4A
Box 16120
103 23 Stockholm
Sweden
Tel: 08 14 05 00

Entries: 01175 01324 33041 33068 33069 33070 33071

SVENSKA BANKFORENINGEN (SWEDISH BANKERS ASSOCIATION)
Box 7603 (Regeringsgaten 42V)
S – 103 94 Stockholm
Sweden
Tel: (0)8–24 33 00
Telex: 10427

Entries: **21049 33019 33025 33028 33109 33111 33119**

SVENSKA FORSAKRINGSFORENINGEN
Tegeluddsvagen 100
11587 Stockholm
Sweden
Tel: 08 7837176

Entries: **08048 13110 27055 33059 33110**

SVENSKA HANDELSBANKEN
Blasieholmstorg 11
Stockholm S–10328
Sweden

Entry: **33007**

SVENSKA MEJERIERNAS RIKSFORENING
Vasagatan 16
Fack
101 10 Stockholm
Sweden
Tel: 08 23 8700

Entry: **33023**

SVENSKA STATISTIKERSAMFUNDET (SWEDISH STATISTICAL ASSOCIATION)
Department of Statistics
University of Umea
S – 91087 Umea
Sweden
Tel: 090165596

Entry: **33065**

SVERIGES EXPORTRAD
Box 5513
S–114 85
Stockholm
Sweden

Entries: **33017 33063 33074 33124 33125**

SVERIGES INDUSTRIFORBUND
Storgatan 19
Box 5501
S–11485 Stockholm
Tel: 946 08 63 5020
Telex: 29990 SWEDIND S

Entries: **01220 33040**

SVERIGES RIKSBANK
POB 16283
S–10325 Stockholm
Sweden
Tel: 08–7870000
Telex: 19150

Entries: **33008 33064 33077 33113**

SWEDBANK–SPARBANKERNAS BANK
Brunkebergsterg 8
S–10534 Stockholm
Sweden
Tel: 46–8–790–1000

Entry: **33009**

SWEDISH CHAMBER OF COMMERCE
18 Bentinck Street
London W1M 5RL
Tel: 01 486 4545
Telex: 21550
Fax: 01 935 5487

Entry: **33117**

THE SWEDISH CIVIL AVIATION ADMINISTRATION
5–60179 Norrkoping
Sweden
Tel: Int+4611192000
Telex: 64250 CIVAIR S

Entries: **33003 33054 33057**

SWEDISH DAIRIES ASSOCIATION
Bos 24
S – 10120 Stockholm
Sweden
Tel: 08 238700
Telex: 19333
Fax: 218363

Entry: **33024**

SWEDISH EMPLOYERS' FEDERATION
S – 103 30 Stockholm
Sweden
Tel: 08 762 60 00
Telex: 19 923
Fax: 08 762 62 90

Entries: **33030 33056 33058 33060 33061 33062 33131**

THE SWEDISH INSTITUTE
Box 7434
S–103 91 Stockholm
Sweden

Entries: **33029 33118**

SWISS BANK CORPORATION
1 Aeschenvorstadt
CH 4002 Basle
Switzerland
Tel: 061 202020
Telex: 62773
AND
99 Gresham Street
London EC2P 2BR
Tel: 01 606 4000
Telex: 887434 SBCO G

Entries: **34005 34016 34020 34021 34026 34031 34032 34048**

SWISS OFFICE FOR TRADE PROMOTION
Av Avant–Poste 4
PO Box 1128
CH 1011 Lausanne
Switzerland
Tel: 021 20 32 31
Telex: 455 425
Fax: 021 20 73 37

Entries: **34038 34043 34063 34066 34067**

TALOUSELAMA OY
Box 14
00131 Helsinki
Finland
Tel: 0 643411
Fax: 0 643411

Entry: **13152**

TECNIPUBLICACIONES SA
C/Fernando VI, 27
28004 – Madrid
Spain
Tel: (91) 4197889

Entry: **32014**

TEKNISK FORLAG A/S
Skelbaekgade 4
DK–1717 Copenhagen V
Denmark
Tel: 01 216801

Entry: **08072**

TELEVERKET (SWEDISH TELECOMMUNICATIONS ADMINISTRATION)
Mårbackagt 11
123 86 Farsta
Sweden
Tel: (8) 713 10 00
Telex: 14970

Entry: **33123**

TEXTILE STATISTICS BUREAU
Reedham House
31 King Street West
Manchester M3 2PF

Entries: **36080 36101 36135 36136 36137 36165 36210 36237 36283**

THESSALONIKI PORT AUTHORITY
Thessaloniki
Greece
Tel: 526221

Entry: **18037**

TOUCHE ROSS INTERNATIONAL
1633 Broadway
New York NY 10019
USA

Entries: **04088 08070 14146 15241 22064 23034 26070 27032 32065 33122 34064**

TRADE RESEARCH PUBLICATIONS
6 Beech Hill Court
Berkhamstead
Herts
HP4 2PR
Tel: 044 273951
Telex: 8950511

Entries: **36088 36134**

TRADES UNION CONGRESS
Congress House
Great Russell Street
London WC1B 3LS
Tel: 01 636 4032

Entries: **36245 36249 36250 36260**

TRANS–MEDIA/THE OCEANA GROUP AND UNIVERSITY OF WARWICK LIBRARY
Dobbs Ferry
New York
10522
USA
Tel: 914 693 5956

Entries: 01066 01185

TURKISH CONFEDERATION OF EMPLOYER ASSOCIATIONS
Mesrutiyet Cad 1/4–5
Kizlay–Ankara
Turkey

Entries: 35011 35031 35051

TURKISH CYPRIOT CHAMBER OF COMMERCE
Redretin Demirel Avenue
Lefkosa
Mersin
10–Turkey
Tel: 78760/63
Telex: 57137 KTTO TK

Entry: 35019

TURKISH INDUSTRIALISTS' AND BUSINESSMEN'S ASSOCIATION (TUSIAD)
Cumburiyet Cad Ferah apt 233/9
Herbiye
Istanbul
Turkey

Entries: 35023 35056

TURKIYE IS BANKASI A/S
Head Office
Economic Research Department
Ankara
Turkey

Entry: 35045

UK IRON AND STEEL STATISTICS BUREAU
Canterbury House
2 Sydenham Road
Croydon
CR9 2LZ
Tel: 01 686 9050
Telex: 932575
Fax: 01 680 8616

Entries: 01158 01358 01359 04019 08020 13057 14057 15108 21043 22028 24003 26045 27058 32064 33115 34060 36274

UNCTC–UNITED NATIONS CENTRE ON TRANSNATIONAL CORPORATIONS
Room DC2–0853
United Nations
New York NY10017
USA

Entries: 01033 01215

UNCTAD–UNITED NATIONS CONFERENCE ON TRADE AND DEVELOPMENT
Palais des Nations
1211 Geneva 10
Switzerland

Entries: 01039 01115 01164 01204 01234 01258 01261 01262 01274 01291 01303 01309 01312 01314 01315 01317 01318 01363

UN DEPARTMENT OF INTERNATIONAL ECONOMIC SOCIAL AFFAIRS
Palais des Nations
1211 Geneva 10
Switzerland
Tel: 34 60 11

Entry: 01169

UNITED NATIONS DEVELOPMENT PROGRAMME
Documents Division
New York
NY 10017
USA

Entries: 01050 01102 01316

UNITED NATIONS ECONOMIC COMMISSION FOR EUROPE
Palais des Nations
1211 Geneva 10
Switzerland
Tel: 34 60 11

Entries: 01008 01028 01242 01292 01293 10002 10003 10004 10005 10006 10007 10008 10009 10010 10012 10013 10015 10021 10027 10030 10037 10038

UNESCO–UNITED NATIONS EDUCATIONAL SCIENTIFIC AND CULTURAL ORGANISATION
7 Place de Fonteroy
75700 Paris
France
Tel: 577 1610

Entries: 01319 01320

UNIDO–UNITED NATIONS INDUSTRIAL DEVELOPMENT ORGANISATION
PO Box 707, A–1001
Vienna
Austria

Entries: 01083 01138

UNION BANK OF FINLAND
Box 868
00101 Helsinki
Finland
Tel: 0 1651
Telex: 127707
Fax: 0 177508

Entries: 13156 13157

UNION BANK OF SWITZERLAND
45 Bahnhofstrasse
PO Box
8021 Zurich
Tel: 01 234 11 11
Telex: 58 811/52 205

Entries: 34006 34014 34022 34029 34057 34058 34061 34062 34065 34072 34075

UNION ECONOMIQUE BENELUX
39 Rue de la Regence
1000 Brussels
Belgium
Tel: 02 513 8680
Telex: 61540 BENELU B

Entries: 01108 01276

UNION DE EMPRESAS SIDERURGICAS (UNESID)
Castello 128
28006 Madrid
Spain

Entry: 32048

UNION LUXEMBOURGEOISE DES CONSOMMATEURS
21–26 Allee Schellar
Limpertsborg
Luxembourg
Tel: 24987

Entry: 24021

UNION DES INDUSTRIES CHIMIQUES
64 Avenue Marceau
75008 Paris
France
Tel: 720 56 03

Entry: 14109

UNIONI INDUSTRIALI PASTEI ITALIANI
Via Po 102
00198 Roma RM
Italy
Telex: 611740 UNIPI I

Entry: 22063

UNIT TRUST ASSOCIATION
65 Kingsway
London WC2 6ZD
Tel: 01 831 0898
Fax: 01 831 9985

Entry: 36185

UNITED NATIONS PUBLICATIONS
Room DC2–0853
United Nations
New York
NY 10017
USA

Entries: 01003 01041 01042 01043 01052 01107 01136 01161 01203 01205 01214 01238 01239 01240 01290 01304 01342 01343 01351 01364 01365 10020 10026 10032 10033 10034 10035

UPEA–UNION PROFESSIONELLE DES ENTREPRISES D'ASSURANCES BELGES ET ETRANGERES OPERANT EN BELGIQUE
Square de Meeus 29
1040 Brussels
Tel: 02 513 68 45

Entries: 04014 04023

US DEPARTMENT OF COMMERCE
International Trade Administration
Washington DC 20230
USA

Entries: 06039 07019 28008

US DEPARTMENT OF COMMERCE
Superintendent of Documents
GPO
Washington
DC 20402
USA

Entries: 18018 29037 30007 31017

US GOVERNMENT PRINTING OFFICE
Superintendent of Documents
Washington
DC 20402
USA

Entry: 16004

UNITED NATIONS (SALES SECTION)
Palais des Nations
CH–1211 Geneva 10
Switzerland
Tel: (22) 34 60 11
Telex: 289696

UNIVERSAL FEDERATION OF TRAVEL AGENTS' ASSOCIATIONS
World HQ
Rue Detacay 1
BTE 1
1050 Brussels
Belgium
Tel: 02/5370320
Telex: 61808

Entry: 01034

UNIVERSIDAD DE DEUSTO
Apdo 1
48080 Bilbao
Spain
Tel: (94) 445 3100
Telex: 34221 UDD E

Entry: 32010

UNIVERSITATEA 'AL I CUZA' IASI
Calea 23 August 11
Iasi 6600
Romania
Tel: 40559

Entry: 30018

UNIVERSITY OF READING
Department of Agricultural Economics and Management
Reading
Berkshire
RG6 2AH
Tel: 0734 875123
Telex: 847813

UNIVERSITY OF SZCZECIN
Av. Mickiewicza 66
70–101 Szczecin
Poland
Tel: 789–21

Entries: 28028 28034

UNIVERZA V MARIBORU (UNIVERSITY OF MARIBOR)
Krekova ul 2
62000 Maribor
Yugoslavia
Tel: (062) 22281

Entry: 37017

UTVEGSBANKI ISLANDS
Austurstraeti 19
101 Reykjavik
Iceland
Tel: 354 1 17060
Telex: 2047
Fax: 354 1 623099

Entries: 20003 20005

VAKUUTUSSANOMIA OY
Bulevardi [illegible]
SF 00120 Helsinki
Finland
Tel: +358 0 19 251
Telex: 123511
Fax: +358 0 192 5255

Entries: 13067 13083 13158

VERBAND DER AUTOMOBILINDUSTRIE EV
Postfach 17 05 63
6000 Frankfurt a M 17
West Germany

Entry: 15240

VERBAND DEUTSCHER REEDER (VDR)
Esplanade 6
D 2000 Hamburg 36
West Germany
Tel: 040/35 09 7–0
Telex: 211 407
Fax: 040/35 09 7–211

Entries: 15144 15148

VERBAND DEUTSCHER MASCHINEN–UND ANLAGENBAU EV AVAILABLE FROM:

MASCHINENBAU–VERLAG GMBH
Lyoner Str 18
6000 Frankfurt/M 71
West Germany

VERLAG GLUCKAUF GMBH
Postfach 10 39 45
D–4300 Essen 1
West Germany
Tel: 02 01 1 05 1
Telex: 8 579 545 GAUF D

Entries: 01105 01167 01368 10028 15095 15150 15229

VERLAG HOPPENSTEDT & CO.
Havelstrasse 9
Postbox 40 06
D–6100 Darmstadt 1
West Germany
Tel: 06151/380–361
Telex: 4 19 258 HOPP D
Fax: 06151/380–360

Entries: 01117 01121 01173 01322 04018 04020 10014 15030 15031 15067 15069 15114 15115 15121 15122 15123 15124 15125 15175 15180 15185 15208 15214 15218 15251 15255 15263 26044

VERLAG WELTARCHIV GMBH
Neuer Jungfernstieg 21
D–2000 Hamburg 36
West Germany
Tel: 040 35 62 500

Entry: 15201

VERLAG FUR WIRTSCHAFTSLITERATUR GMBH
Birmemsdorfstrasse 421
CH–8055 Zurich
Switzerland
Tel: [illegible]

Entries: 34013 34025 34027 34034 34037 34049

VERLAG ZEIT IM BILD AVAILABLE FROM:

COLLETS HOLDINGS LTD
London Road
Wellingborough
Northants
NN8 2QT

Entries: 16006 16012

VERWALTUNGS–UND PRIVATBANK AG
Postfach 885
FL–9490
Vaduz
Liechtenstein
Tel: 075/5 66 55
Telex: 889 200
Fax: 075/2 66 97

Entries: 23010 23012 23015 23016 23018

V/O MEZHDUNARODNAYA KNIGA
Moscow 121200
USSR
Tel: 244 10 22
Telex: 7160

Entries: 31004 31007 31010 31011 31012 31013 31014 31015 31016 31018 31020 31021 31022 31023 31028 31029 31031 31032 31033 31034 31035 31036 31037 31038 31041 31043 31044 31045 31050 31051 31053 31054 31055 31056 31057 31058 31062

V/O VNESHTORGREKLAMA
Korp 2
31 UL Kahovka
113461 Moscow
USSR
Tel: 331 95 55

WIENER BORSEKAMMER
Wipplingerstrasse 34
A–1011 Wien
Austria
Tel: (0222) 53499
Telex: 3222880

Entries: 03013 03090

WILSON HARTNELL ADVERTISING
12 Leeson Park
Dublin 2
Ireland
Tel: 978822
Telex: 93900
Fax: 975163

Entry: 21042

WINVEST
Pearl House
Greyfriars Road
Cardiff CF1 3XX
Tel: (0222) 223666
Telex: 497190
Fax: (0222) 223243

Entry: 36103

WIRTSCHAFTS UND SOZIALWISSENSCHAFTLICHES INSTITUT DES DEUTSCHEN GEWERKSCHAFTSBUNDES GMBH
Hans-Bockler-Strasse 39
4000 Dusseldorf
West Germany

Entries: 15120 15267

WOOD, MACKENZIE AND CO.
Erskine House
68–73 Queen Street
Edinburgh EH2 4NS
Tel: 031 226 4141
Telex: 72555

Entry: 01229

WOOL INDUSTRY BUREAU OF STATISTICS
60 Toller Lane
Bradford BD8 9BZ
Tel: 0274 491241

Entry: 36172

WORLD BANK
1818 H Street NW
Washington DC 20433
USA
and
66 Avenue D'iena
75116 Paris
France

Entries: 01040 01103 01143 01151 01207 01248 01286 01321 01330 01331 01332 01333 01334 01335 01336 01337 01340 01341 01347

Also available from

MICROINFO LTD.
PO Box 3
Newman Lane
Alton
Hampshire
England

WORLD BUREAU OF METAL STATISTICS
27a High Street
Ware
Hertfordshire
SG12 9BA
Tel: 0920 61274
Telex: 817746

Entries: 01252 01349 01361 01367

WORLD HEALTH ORGANISATION
1211 Geneva 27
Switzerland

Entry: 01344

WORLD MARKET RESEARCH
Hungarian Academy of Sciences
1051 Budapest
Roosevelt-ter 9
Hungary
Tel: 382 344
Telex: 22 4139

Entry: 19002

WORLD REPORTS (UK) LTD.
108 Horseferry Road
London SW1P 2EF
Tel: 01 222 3836

Entries: 01095 01106 01141 01147 01148 01180

WORLD TOURISM ORGANISATION
Capitan Haya 42
28020 Madrid
Spain
Tel: 279–2804
Telex: 42188 OMT E

Entries: 01356 01366

Index 1
SOURCES LISTED ALPHABETICALLY

B

C

F

G

H

I

J

K

L

M

N

O

P

T

Y

Z

Index 2
SUBJECT INDEX

Index 2a
SOURCES LISTED BY SUBJECT AND COUNTRY

Index 2b
SOURCES LISTED BY COUNTRY AND SUBJECT

GERMANY, EAST

GIBRALTAR

GREECE

HUNGARY

SWEDEN

SWITZERLAND

TURKEY

UNITED KINGDOM

YUGOSLAVIA